TEN STEPS TO BUILDING COLLEGE READING SKILLS

FORM B

SECOND EDITION

Ten Steps to Building College Reading Skills

Form B

Second Edition

Bill Broderick

CERRITOS COLLEGE

TOWNSEND PRESS   Marlton, NJ 08053

The Other Books in the Townsend Press Reading Series:

GROUNDWORK FOR COLLEGE READING
TEN STEPS TO BUILDING COLLEGE READING SKILLS, FORM A
TEN STEPS TO IMPROVING COLLEGE READING SKILLS
TEN STEPS TO ADVANCING COLLEGE READING SKILLS
KEYS TO BETTER COLLEGE READING
IMPROVING READING COMPREHENSION SKILLS

Books in the Townsend Press Vocabulary Series:

GROUNDWORK FOR A BETTER VOCABULARY
BUILDING VOCABULARY SKILLS
IMPROVING VOCABULARY SKILLS
ADVANCING VOCABULARY SKILLS
BUILDING VOCABULARY SKILLS, SHORT VERSION
IMPROVING VOCABULARY SKILLS, SHORT VERSION
ADVANCING VOCABULARY SKILLS, SHORT VERSION

Supplements Available for Most Books:

Instructor's Edition
Instructor's Manual, Test Bank and Computer Guide
Set of Computer Disks (Apple, IBM, or Macintosh)

Copyright © 1994 by Townsend Press, Inc.
Printed in the United States of America
ISBN 0-944210-67-8

Send book orders and requests for desk copies or supplements to:

Townsend Press
1038 Industrial Drive
Berlin, NJ 08009

For even faster service, call us at our toll-free number:

1-800-772-6410

Or FAX your request to:

1-609-753-0649

ISBN 0-944210-67-8

Contents

PART III
Ten Reading Selections   367

Note: A reading selection concludes each of the ten chapters in Part I. Here are the titles, authors, and page numbers of these ten selections:

Preface to the Instructor

We all know that many of today's beginning college students do not have the reading skills needed to do effective work in their courses. A related problem, evident even in class discussions, is that they often lack the skills required to think consistently in a clear and analytic way.

The purpose of TEN STEPS TO BUILDING COLLEGE READING SKILLS, FORM B, is to develop effective reading *and* clear thinking. To do so, the book first presents a sequence of word and reading skills that are widely recognized as forming the basis for sound comprehension:

1 Using the dictionary
2 Understanding vocabulary in context
3 Understanding main ideas
4 Understanding supporting details
5 Locating main ideas in different parts of paragraphs
6 Determining implied main ideas
7 Locating major and minor details
8 Identifying transitions
9 Identifying patterns of organization
10 Making inferences

In every chapter in Part I, the key aspects of a skill are explained and illustrated in a clear and simple way. Each skill is followed by a series of practices, and three review tests end each chapter. The last review test includes a reading selection, so that students can apply the skill just learned to real-life reading materials, including newspaper and magazine articles and excerpts from books. Each selection is followed by word and comprehension questions that focus on the skill learned in the chapter and on skills from prior chapters. In addition, a *Mapping Activity* provides a visual diagram that helps students think carefully about the basic content of the selection. And two *Discussion Questions* and *Writing Assignments* provide teachers with an opportunity to engage students in a variety of reading skills and to deepen students' understandings of a selection. Taken together, the ten chapters provide students with the skills needed for a solid understanding of reading materials.

Part II is made up of six mastery tests for each of the ten skills and six combined-skills tests. These tests progress in difficulty, giving students the additional practice they may need for a thorough learning of each skill. The tests allow for easy grading and are designed to ensure that students think carefully before answering each question.

Part III consists of ten additional readings that will help improve both reading and thinking skills. Each reading is followed by a series of *Vocabulary Questions* and *Reading Comprehension Questions* that ask students to apply the skills presented in Part I and reinforced in Part II. As with the selections in Part I, a *Mapping Activity* and two *Discussion Questions* and *Writing Assignments* are provided.

Important Features of the Book

• **Focus on the basics.** The book seeks to explain in a clear, step-by-step way the essential elements of each skill. Many examples are provided to ensure that students understand each point. In general, the focus is on *teaching* the skills, not just on explaining them and not just on testing them.

• **Frequent practice and feedback.** In the belief that progress is made largely through abundant practice and careful feedback, this book includes numerous activities. Students can get immediate feedback on the practice exercises in Part I by turning to the answer key at the back. The answers to the review tests in Part I, the mastery tests in Part II, and the readings in Part III are in the *Instructor's Edition* as well as in the *Instructor's Manual and Test Bank*.

The limited answer key enables students to take an active role in their own learning. And they are likely to use the answer key in an honest and positive way if they know that they may be tested on the many activities and selections for which answers are not provided. (Answers not in the book can be easily copied from the *Instructor's Manual* and handed out at your discretion.)

• **High interest level.** Uninteresting readings and exercises work against learning. The reading selections in this book have been chosen not only for appropriateness of their reading level but also for the commanding nature of their content. They are meant to appeal to a wide range of developmental students. They also take into account the diverse backgrounds of such students. Teachers and students alike should be able to take pleasure in the selections, and this enjoyment should facilitate the learning process.

• **Ease of use.** The straightforward sequence in each chapter—from explanation to example to practice to review test—helps make the skills easy to teach. The organization of the book into three distinct parts also makes for ease of use. Within a single class, for instance, instructors can work on a particular skill in Part I, review another skill through the use of a mastery test in Part II, and provide variety by having students read one of the selections in Part III. The limited answer key at the back of the book also makes for versatility: it means that you can assign some chapters for self-teaching. Finally, the review tests in Part I as well as the mastery and combined-skills tests in Part II—each on its own tear-out page—make it a simple matter for teachers to test and evaluate student progress.

• **Integration of skills.** Students do more than learn the skills individually in Parts I and II. They also learn to apply the skills together through the reading selections that close the chapters in Part I, through the combined-skills tests in Part II, and through the readings in Part III. Students become effective readers and thinkers through a good deal of practice in applying a combination of skills.

• **Thinking activities.** Diverse kinds of thinking activities follow each reading selection included in the book. First is a mapping activity that will help students see and understand the organizational pattern of each selection. Second are two discussion questions that are designed to encourage different points of view regarding the selection. And third are two writing activities where students can further express their opinions on some aspect of the selection. There are also two additional discussion questions and writing activities for each selection in the *Instructor's Manual and Test Bank*.

The book is designed, then, to create activities that truly involve students in the processes of reading and thinking while enabling you to provide feedback. This practice and feedback on interesting, challenging material will help your students to become effective readers and thinkers.

• **Supplementary materials.** The three helpful supplements listed below are available at no charge to instructors using the text. Any or all can be obtained quickly by writing or calling Townsend Press (Pavilions at Greentree—408, Marlton, New Jersey 08053; 1-800-772-6410).

1 An *Instructor's Edition*—chances are you are holding it in your hand—is identical to the student book except that it also provides both of the following: 1) hints for teachers (see the front of the book) and 2) answers to all the practices and tests.

2 A combined *Instructor's Manual, Test Bank, and Computer Guide* consists of the following:

   a Suggestions for teaching the course, a model syllabus, readability levels, a complete answer key, and two additional discussion questions and writing activities for each reading selection.

   b Four additional mastery tests for each of the ten skills and four additional combined-skills tests—all on letter-sized sheets so they can be copied easily for use with students.

   c A computer guide that reproduces the two additional mastery tests for each skill that are on the computer disks available with the book.

3 A *set of computer disks* (in Apple, IBM, and Macintosh formats) contains two additional mastery tests for each of the ten skill chapters in the book. The disks contain a number of other user- and instructor-friendly features: brief explanations of answers, a sound option, frequent mention of the user's first name, a running score at the bottom of the screen, and a record-keeping score file.

   Since the disk tests are reproduced in the *Computer Guide*, instructors can readily decide just how to use the materials without having to work through each test on the computer. And instructors without a computer lab can copy these tests for use in class as additional mastery tests.

• **One of a sequence of books.** This is the basic text in a series that includes two other books. TEN STEPS TO BUILDING COLLEGE READING SKILLS, FORM A, is an alternate form of this book. TEN STEPS TO IMPROVING COLLEGE READING SKILLS is an intermediate text, and TEN STEPS TO ADVANCING COLLEGE READING SKILLS is an advanced text.

The two forms of the BUILDING book are suited for a first college reading course. The IMPROVING book is suited for the core developmental reading course offered at most colleges. The ADVANCING book is a slightly higher developmental text than the IMPROVING book. It can be used as the core book for a more advanced class, as a sequel to the intermediate book, or as a second-semester alternative to it.

A companion set of vocabulary books, listed on page iv, has been designed to go with the TEN STEPS books. Recommended to accompany this book is BUILDING VOCABULARY SKILLS or BUILDING VOCABULARY SKILLS, SHORT VERSION.

Together, the books and their full range of supplements form a sequence that should be ideal for any college reading program.

The Difference Between FORM A and FORM B

This book, FORM B, has almost the same explanatory text as TEN STEPS TO BUILDING COLLEGE READING SKILLS by John Langan and Bill Broderick. (That book by Langan and Broderick is now considered FORM A.)

FORM B is different from FORM A for two reasons:

1 All of the practice materials and the readings in FORM B are different;
2 FORM B strongly emphasizes multi-cultural readings.

With FORM B (which in its first edition was titled GROUNDWORK FOR COLLEGE READING II), instructors have the option of using an alternate basic reading book from one semester to the next.

A Note on FORM B and GROUNDWORK FOR COLLEGE READING

Townsend Press also publishes a fundamental reading book by Bill Broderick titled GROUNDWORK FOR COLLEGE READING. The book includes four chapters on phonics and six chapters on basic reading comprehension skills. Some practices and readings in the book overlap with materials in FORM B. Therefore, instructors using GROUNDWORK FOR COLLEGE READING in a course should *not* follow it in a succeeding course with FORM B. The recommended sequel would be FORM A.

Summary and Acknowledgments

To summarize, TEN STEPS TO BUILDING COLLEGE READING SKILLS, FORM B, provides ten reading skills to help developmental college students become independent readers and thinkers. Through an appealing collection of readings and a carefully designed series of activities and tests, students receive considerable guided practice in the skills. The result is an integrated approach to learning that will, by the end of a course, produce better readers and stronger thinkers.

Thanks to the exceptional design skills of Janet M. Goldstein, the book enjoys a remarkably clear and "user-friendly" format. I owe appreciation to Janet and to John Langan as well for proofreading and editing help. I value especially the outstanding editorial role played by Carole Mohr, who has worked closely with me for months on every page of the book. Thanks to her insights into the nature of each skill and her sensitivity to the needs of students, the text is significantly better than it would have been otherwise. Finally, I am grateful to my wife, Tari, for her inspiration, her confidence in me, and her patience.

Bill Broderick

How to Become a Better Reader and Thinker

The chances are that you are not as good a reader as you should be to do well in college. If so, it's not surprising. You live in a culture where people watch an average of *over seven hours of television every day!!!* All that passive viewing does not allow much time for reading. Reading is a skill that must be actively practiced. The simple fact is that people who do not read very often are not likely to be strong readers.

- How much television do you watch on an average day? _____

Here are two points to consider about reading. First, you must learn to be an active reader, one who understands that you can't stare at the words on a page and hope that meaning will come to you. You must work to find the meaning that is intended. This means thinking about what the words and phrases mean and thinking about the message the author is sending you.

Second, you must regard reading as a key to success. Regular reading improves vocabulary, spelling, and reading speed and comprehension. It develops the command of language so necessary for success in today's job world. In short, it is crucial for people who want to make something of themselves. People who are achievers *make* time to read, even though their responsibilities, including job and family, are often very challenging ones.

- Do you read on a regular basis (including newspapers, weekly magazines, and novels)? _____

- When are you most likely to do your reading? _____

This book will help you build a solid foundation in the most important skills you need to become a better reader. In addition, this book will help you to

1

strengthen your ability to think clearly and logically. Reading and thinking are closely related skills, and both are vital for your success in college.

To find out just how this book will help you learn these essential skills, read the next several pages and do the brief activities as well. The activities are easily completed and will give you a good sense of how the book is arranged, what it will do for you, and what is expected of you as you interact with the book.

HOW THE BOOK IS ORGANIZED

There are three parts to the book. Each part is described below.

Part I: Ten Steps to Building College Reading Skills (Pages 7–231)

To help you become a more effective reader and thinker, this book first presents a series of ten key word and reading skills. They are listed in the table of contents on page v. Turn to that page to fill in the skills missing below:

1   Dictionary Use

2   _____

3   Main Ideas

4   _____

5   Locations of Main Ideas

6   Implied Main Ideas

7   _____

8   Transitions

9   Patterns of Organization

10 _____

Each chapter is developed in the same way. First of all, clear explanations and examples help you *understand* each skill. Practices then give you the "hands-on" experience needed to *review* the skill.

• How many practices are there for the third skill, "Main Ideas" (pages 51–73)? _____

At the end of each chapter are three review tests.

• On which pages are the first two review tests for "Main Ideas"? _____

The third review test always has two parts. The first part is a review of the chapter. The second part is a reading selection that gives you the chance both to practice the skill learned in the chapter and to perfect skills you learned in previous chapters.

- How many questions are asked in Review Test 3, Part A, for the "Main Ideas" chapter (page 67)? _____

- What is the title of the reading selection on page 68? _____

_____

The tests are perforated and can be torn out and given to your instructor. Following the tests are three kinds of activities that will improve your reading and thinking skills. The first involves a mapping activity. A map is a visual diagram that will help you think about how the reading selection is organized. Next are discussion questions and writing assignments that your instructor may assign to you to strengthen your understanding of the selection and to give you a chance to voice your opinion about some aspect of the selection.

- How many *discussion questions* are there following "They Shut My Grandmother's Room Door" on page 72? _____

- How many *writing assignments* are there following "They Shut My Grandmother's Room Door" on page 73? _____

Also note that there is a "Check Your Performance" box at the end of each chapter so you can track your progress on the three tests and the mapping activity. Your scores can also be entered on the "Reading Performance Chart" at the back of the book.

- What page is this chart on? _____

Part II: Mastery Tests (Pages 233–366)

This part of the book provides a series of tests to help you master the ten skills you studied in Part I.

- Look at pages 235–354. How many mastery tests are there for each skill?

_____

As with the review tests, these tests are perforated and can be torn out and given to your instructor. And there is a scorebox at the end of each test so you can track your progress. Your score can also be entered on the "Reading Performance Chart" at the back of the book.

Part III: Ten Reading Selections (Pages 367–458)

Part III is made up of ten reading selections, followed by questions that will help you to sharpen all of the skills you learned in Part I and practiced in Part II. Turn to the table of contents on page vi and answer the following questions:

- Which two selections may help you in other classes? _____

    _____

- Which selection may be about how to live longer? _____

    _____

Each reading selection is organized in the same way. Each starts with two sections that come before the reading selection. Look, for example, at "Life Over Death," which starts on page 369. What are the headings of the two sections that come before the reading itself?

- _____

- _____

Note that the vocabulary words in "Words to Watch" are followed by the numbers of the paragraphs where the words appear. Now look again at "Life Over Death" (pages 369–376) and explain how each vocabulary word is set off in the reading:

- _____

Activities Following Each Reading Selection

After each selection, there are five kinds of activities that will improve your reading and thinking skills. Look at the activities following "Room with a New View" (pages 443–450). Note that the first activity consists of **vocabulary questions**. The second consists of (*fill in the missing words*) _____

_____. The third is a **mapping activity**. The fourth consists of (*fill in the missing words*) _____

_____. And the fifth is **writing assignments**.

- Look at the **vocabulary questions** for "Room with a New View" on pages 445–447. The first five of these questions deal with vocabulary in context. The last five of the questions deal with words taken from the (*fill in the missing words*) _____. These questions will help you improve your understanding of key words presented in the reading.

- Now look at the **reading comprehension questions** for "Classroom Notetaking" on pages 399–401. How many questions are there in all? _____. The first questions in this and all other selections involve the "Central Point and Main Idea." The next group of questions involves *(fill in the missing words)* _____. The next groups involve "Transitions" and "Patterns of Organization." Finally, the last question or questions always involve *(fill in the missing word)*

    _____.

- Look now at the activity titled **Mapping Activity**. Keep in mind that a **map** is simply a visual diagram or outline of a selection. It shows at a glance the central point of a selection and the support for that point. Completing the map will help you focus on the most important ideas in each reading. You will sharpen your ability to get to the heart of each selection and to think logically and clearly about what you read.

    How many answers must you fill in for the mapping activity that follows "Rosa: A Success Story" on page 392? _____.

- Note and write down how many **discussion questions** there are for "Knowledge Is Power" on page 423: _____. How many **writing assignments** are there? _____. There are two of each item for every reading. These questions and assignments provide a final chance for you to deepen your understanding of each selection.

HELPFUL FEATURES OF THE BOOK

1   The book centers on *what you really need to know* to become a better reader and thinker. It presents ten key comprehension skills, and it explains the most important points about each skill.

2   The book gives you *lots of practice*. We seldom learn a skill only by hearing or reading about it; we make it part of us by repeated practice. There are, then, numerous activities in the text. They are not "busy work," but carefully designed materials that should help you truly learn each skill.

    Notice that after you learn each skill in Part I, you read a selection in Review Test 3 that enables you to apply that skill. And as you move from one skill to the next, you continue to practice and reinforce the ones already learned.

3   The selections throughout the book are *lively and appealing*. Dull and unvaried readings work against learning, so subjects have been carefully chosen for their high interest level. Almost all of the selections here are excellent examples of how what we read can capture our attention. For example, read several paragraphs of "Cipher in the Snow" and then try to *stop* reading.

HOW TO USE THIS BOOK

1   A good way to proceed is to read and reread the explanations and examples in a given chapter in Part I until you feel you understand the ideas presented. Then carefully work through the practices. As you finish each one, check your answers with the "Limited Answer Key" that starts on page 459.

For your own sake, don't just copy in the answers without trying to do the practices! The only way to learn a skill is to practice it first and *then* use the answer key to give yourself feedback. Also, take whatever time is needed to figure out just why you got some answers wrong. By using the answer key to help teach yourself the skills, you will prepare yourself for the review tests at the end of each chapter as well as for the mastery tests and the reading selection tests in the book. Your instructor can supply you with answers to those tests.

If you have trouble catching on to a particular skill, stick with it. In time, you will learn each of the ten skills.

2   Read the selections with the intent of simply enjoying them. There will be time afterwards for rereading each selection and using it to develop your comprehension skills.

3   Keep track of your progress. In the "Reading Performance Chart" on the inside back cover, enter your scores for the mastery tests in Part II. In addition, fill in the "Check Your Performance" chart at the end of each reading in Part III. These scores can also be entered on the inside-back-cover chart, giving you a good view of your overall performance as you work through the book.

In summary, TEN STEPS TO BUILDING COLLEGE READING SKILLS, FORM B, has been designed to interest and benefit you as much as possible. Its format is straightforward, its explanations are clear, its readings are appealing, and its many practices will help you learn through doing. *It is a book that has been created to reward effort*, and if you provide that effort, you will make yourself a better reader and a stronger thinker. I wish you success.

Bill Broderick

Part I

TEN STEPS TO BUILDING COLLEGE READING SKILLS

1

Dictionary Use

What do you use a dictionary for? When asked this question, most people reply, "To look up a word." That answer is correct, but not complete. A dictionary can help you do all of the following:

- Spell words
- Break words into syllables
- Pronounce words
- Find the meanings of words
- Learn parts of speech and irregular forms of words
- See where words come from
- Find synonyms for words

This chapter will show you how to use a dictionary for all the above purposes.

OWNING YOUR OWN DICTIONARIES

You can benefit greatly by owning two dictionaries. The first dictionary you should own is a paperback one, so you can carry it with you to classes. Any of the following would be an excellent choice:

The American Heritage Dictionary, Paperback Edition

The Random House College Dictionary, Paperback Edition

Webster's New World Dictionary, Paperback Edition

The second dictionary you should own is a desk-sized, hardcover edition which should be kept in the room where you study. All the above dictionaries come in hardbound versions, which contain a good deal more information than the paperback editions. And while they cost more, they are valuable study aids.

Dictionaries are often updated to reflect changes in the language. New words come into use, and old words take on new meanings. Because of such changes, you should not use a dictionary which has been lying around the house for many years. Instead, invest in a new dictionary. You will soon find that its cost will be money well spent.

FINDING A WORD IN THE DICTIONARY

Using Guidewords to Find a Word More Quickly

The two words on top of each dictionary page are called guidewords. Shown below are guidewords from a page in *The American Heritage Dictionary, Paperback Edition* (referred to from this point on as the *AHD*).

473   oath | oblong

oath (ōth) *n., pl.* **oaths** (ōthz, ōths). 1. A formal promise to fulfill a pledge, often calling upon God as witness. 2. A blasphemous use of a sacred name. [< OE *āth*.]
oat·meal (ōt′mēl′) *n.* 1. Meal made from oats; ground or rolled oats. 2. A porridge made from ground or rolled oats.
O·ba·di·ah (ō′bə-dī′ə) *n.* See table at **Bible**.
ob·bli·ga·to (ōb′li-gä′tō) *n., pl.* **-tos** or **-ti** (-tē). *Mus.* An accompaniment that is an integral, indispensable part of a piece. [Ital.]
ob·du·rate (ōb′dōō-rĭt, -dyōō-) *adj.* Hardened against influence or feeling; unyielding. [< Lat. *obdurare*, to harden.] **—ob′du·ra·cy** *n.* **—ob′du·rate·ly** *adv.* **—ob′du·rate·ness** *n.*
o·be·di·ent (ō-bē′dē-ənt) *adj.* Obeying or inclined to obey. [< Lat. *oboedire*, to obey.] **—o·be′di·ence** *n.* **—o·be′di·ent·ly** *adv.*
o·bei·sance (ō-bā′səns, ō-bē′-) *n.* 1. A gesture, as a bow, expressing respect. 2. Great deference. [< OFr. *obeir*, to obey.] **—o·bei′sant** *adj.*

lows and is governed by a preposition. [< Lat. *objectus*, p.p. of *obicere*, to oppose.]
ob·jec·tion·a·ble (ab-jĕk′shə-nə-bəl) *adj.* Arousing disapproval; offensive. **—ob·jec′tion·a·bly** *adv.*
ob·jec·tive (əb-jĕk′tĭv) *adj.* 1. Of or having to do with a material object as distinguished from a mental concept, idea, or belief. 2. Having actual existence. 3. **a.** Uninfluenced by emotion or personal prejudice. **b.** Based on observable phenomena. 4. *Gram.* Denoting the case of a noun or pronoun serving as the object of a verb or preposition. 5. Serving as the goal of a course of action. *—n.* 1. Something worked toward or striven for; goal. 2. *Gram.* The objective case or a noun or pronoun in the objective case. 3. The lens in an optical system that is closest to the object. **—ob·jec′tive·ly** *adv.* **—ob·jec′tive·ness** *n.* **—ob′jec·tiv′i·ty** (ŏb′jĕk-tĭv′ĭ-tē) *n.*
object lesson *n.* A lesson taught by concrete examples.

o·bit·u·ar·y (ō-bĭch′ōō-ĕr′ē) *n., pl.* **-ies.** A death notice, usu. with a brief biography of the deceased. [Med. Lat. *obituarius*, (report) of death.] **—o·bit′u·ar′y** *adj.*
ob·ject¹ (ab-jĕkt′) *v.* 1. To present a dissenting or opposing argument. 2. To feel or express disapproval. [< Lat. *obicere*.] **—ob·jec′tion** *n.* **—ob·jec′tor** *n.*
ob·ject² (ŏb′jĭkt, -jĕkt′) *n.* 1. Something perceptible by the senses; a material thing. 2. Something intelligible or perceptible by the mind. 3. Something serving as a focus of attention or action. 4. The purpose of a specific action. 5. *Gram.* A noun that receives or is affected by the action of a verb or that fol-

o·blit·er·ate (a-blĭt′ə-rāt′) *v.* **-at·ed, -at·ing.** 1. To destroy completely. 2. To wipe out; erase. [< Lat. *obliterare*.] **—o·blit′er·a′tion** *n.* **—o·blit′er·a·tive** (-ə-rā′tĭv, -ər-ə-tĭv) *adj.* **—o·blit′er·a′tor** *n.*
o·bliv·i·on (a-blĭv′ē-ən) *n.* 1. The condition of being completely forgotten. 2. Forgetfulness. [< Lat. *oblivisci*, to forget.]
o·bliv·i·ous (a-blĭv′ē-əs) *adj.* 1. Lacking all memory of something; forgetful. 2. Unaware or unmindful. **—o·bliv′i·ous·ly** *adv.* **—o·bliv′i·ous·ness** *n.*
ob·long (ŏb′lông′, -lŏng) *adj.* 1. Having one of two perpendicular dimensions, as length or width, greater than the other; rectangular.

In the excerpt above, *oath* and *oblong* are guidewords. *Oath* is the first word that will be defined on that page, and *oblong* is the last word defined on that page. All the other words on the page fall alphabetically between the first and second guideword.

To see if you understand guidewords, circle the two words below which would appear on the page with *oath* and *oblong*:

oak   object   obsess   obedient

The word *oak* comes earlier in the alphabet than the guideword *oath*, so we know that *oak* will not appear on the page. And *obsess* comes later in the alphabet than the guideword *oblong*, so we know that *obsess* will not appear on the page. The other two words, *object* and *obedient*, do come alphabetically between *oath* and *oblong*. They are the only two words that should be circled as appearing on the page.

➤ *Practice 1*

Below are five pairs of dictionary guidewords followed by other words. Circle the two words in each series which would be found on the page with the guidewords.

1. **cheerful / chest**

   cheetah   chew   cheat   cheep   chemist

2. **gloom / go**

   glee   gnaw   goal   glorify   globe

3. **indoor / inexact**

   illegal   indirect   industry   inertia   inexcusable

4. **misery / mistaken**

   misfortune   misuse   miscount   misspell   mitten

5. **nose cone / nothingness**

   nosebleed   northwest   notable   notch   notice

Using Hints to Find a Word You Can't Spell

Do you know how to find a word in a dictionary if you are unsure of its spelling? What you should do first is to sound out the word and write it down as best you can. Then look it up based on how you think it is spelled. On the next page are some hints that will help you find the word.

Hints for Finding Words

> **Hint 1:** Below are groups of letters or letter combinations that often sound alike. If you can't find the word as you think it is spelled, try substituting a letter or group of letters from the pairs below. For example, if a word isn't spelled with a *c*, it may be spelled with a *k*; if it isn't spelled with an *f*, try *v* or *ph*.
>
> | c / k | c / s | f / v / ph | g / j | qu / kw / k | s / c / z |
> |---|---|---|---|---|---|
> | sch / sc / sk | sh / ch | shun / tion / sion | | w / wh | able / ible |
> | ai / ay | al / el / le | ancy / ency | ate / ite | au / aw | ea / ee |
> | er / or | ie / ei | ou / ow | oo / u | y / i / e | |
>
> **Hint 2:** Look at the consonants in the word. If you used single consonants, try doubling them. If you wrote double consonants, try removing one of them.
>
> **Hint 3:** Remember that vowels often sound the same. Try an *i* in place of an *a*, an *i* in place of an *e*, and so on. For example, if you can't find a word you think starts with *hi*, try looking under *hy*.

➤ Practice 2

Use your dictionary for this practice. Apply your knowledge of guidewords and the hints above to help you find the correct spelling of the following words. Write each correct spelling in the answer space.

1. revize _____
2. kiddnapp _____
3. karry _____
4. jiant _____
5. realy _____

6. skoolteecher _____
7. pleeze _____
8. comming _____
9. releif _____
10. tunnal _____

LEARNING FROM A DICTIONARY ENTRY

Each word that is defined in the dictionary is called an *entry word*. All the information listed for that word is called an *entry*. Here, for example, is an entry for the word *inspire*.

Sample Dictionary Entry

> **in•spire** (ĭn-spīr´) *v.* **-spired, -spiring. 1.** To fill with noble or reverent emotion; exalt. **2.** To stimulate to creation or action. **3.** To elicit or create in another. **4.** To inhale. [< Lat. *inspirare*.] **—in•spir´er** *n.* **—in•spir´ ing•ly** *adj.*

All or most of the following information is provided in a dictionary entry:

1 Spelling and Syllables
2 Pronunciation Symbols and Accent Marks
3 Parts of Speech
4 Irregular Forms of Words
5 Definitions and Special Labels
6 Word Origins
7 Synonyms

The rest of the chapter will look at each kind of information. The entries used are taken from the *AHD*.

1   SPELLING AND SYLLABLES

Each dictionary entry begins with the entry word, written in **boldface**. Entry words give you the correct spelling and the syllable breakdown of a word. Dots separate the word into syllables. Each syllable is a separate sound in a word. Each syllable has one vowel sound. The following entry word, *detachment*, has three vowel sounds and three syllables.

de•tach•ment (dĭ-tăch′mənt) *n.*

How many syllables are in these entry words?

ru•mor   **ex•plic•it**   **stim•u•late**   **launch**

The dots tell you that *rumor* has two syllables and that *explicit* and *stimulate* have three syllables each. *Launch*, on the other hand, has no dots and therefore only one syllable.

➤ *Practice 3*

Use your dictionary to separate the following words into syllables. Insert dots between syllables. Then write the number of syllables in each word. An example is provided.

Example: c o n•f o r•m i•t y   ___4___ syllables

1. h i c c u p   _____ syllables

2. m i n i m a l   _____ syllables

3. d i s p o s a l   _____ syllables

4. i n s e n s i t i v e   _____ syllables

5. c o m m u n i c a t i o n   _____ syllables

2 PRONUNCIATION SYMBOLS AND ACCENT MARKS

After the entry word is information in parentheses, as you see in the entry below for *colorblind.*

col•or•blind (kŭl′ər-blīnd′) *adj.* Partially or totally unable to see differences in colors.

The information in parentheses shows you how to pronounce the word. It includes two kinds of symbols: pronunciation symbols and accent marks. Following are explanations of each.

Pronunciation Symbols

Pronunciation symbols tell you how the vowels and consonants within the entry word should be pronounced. The sounds of the consonants and vowels are shown in a *Pronunciation Key* at the beginning of the dictionary. And the pronunciation symbols for selected sounds, including vowels, are shown in a shorter key at the bottom of each page or every other page of the dictionary. Here, for example, is the shorter pronunciation key found on every other page of the *AHD*:

Pronunciation Key

ă pat	ā pay	â care	ä father	ĕ pet	ē be	ĭ pit
ī tie	î pier	ŏ pot	ō toe	ô paw, for		oi noise
ŏŏ took	ōō boot	ou out	th thin	*th* this		ŭ cut
û urge	yōō abuse	zh vision	ə about, item, edible, gallop, circus			

Each symbol in the key is pronounced like the letter or letters in bold print in the short word that comes after the symbol. For instance, you can pronounce the *u* sound in *colorblind* by referring to the key. It shows you that the *u* has the sound of *u* in the short word *cut.* The key also shows you that the *i* in *colorblind* is pronounced like the *i* in the short word *tie.*

Finally, you can pronounce the ə sound in *colorblind* by referring to the key. The symbol ə, which looks like an upside-down *e*, is known as the **schwa**. It stands for certain unaccented vowels, such as the

a in *about*
e in *item*
i in *edible*
o in *gallop*
u in *circus.*

➤ *Practice 4*

A. Use the pronunciation key to answer the questions about the following ten entry words. Circle the letter of each of your answers.

1. **con•test** (kŏn′tĕst′)
   The *o* in *contest* sounds like the *o* in
   a. *pot.*
   b. *toe.*

2. **fin•ger** (fĭng′gər)
   The *i* in *finger* sounds like the *i* in
   a. *pit.*
   b. *tie.*

3. **trust** (trŭst)
   The *u* in *trust* sounds like the *u* in
   a. *cut.*
   b. *urge.*

4. **rap•id** (răp′ĭd)
   The *a* in *rapid* sounds like the *a* in
   a. *pat.*
   b. *pay.*

5. **na•tive** (nā′tĭv)
   The *a* in *native* sounds like the *a* in
   a. *pat.*
   b. *pay.*

6. **shelf** (shĕlf)
   The *e* in *shelf* sounds like the *e* in
   a. *pet.*
   b. *be.*

7. **both•er** (bŏth′ər)
   The *th* in *bother* sounds like the *th* in
   a. *thin.*
   b. *this.*

8. **un•true** (ŭn-trōō′)
   The second *u* in *untrue* sounds like the *oo* in
   a. *took.*
   b. *boot.*

9. **sun•burn** (sŭn′bûrn)
   The second *u* in *sunburn* sounds like the *u* in
   a. *cut.*
   b. *urge.*

10. **rea•son** (rē′zən)
    The *o* in *reason* sounds like
    a. the *o* in *pot.*
    b. the schwa sound in the word *gallop.*

B. Below are pronunciation symbols for five common words. Write the word for each and tell how many schwa sounds it contains. An example is provided.

Pronunciation symbols	*Word spelled*	*Number of schwas*
Example: (ĭn•strŭk′shən)	instruction	1
11. (kən·tĭn′yo͞o)	_____	_____
12. (frĕk′əl)	_____	_____
13. (prĭz′ə-nər)	_____	_____
14. (kə-mĭt′ē)	_____	_____
15. (mĭs′ə-lā′nē-əs)	_____	_____

C. Use your dictionary to find and write the pronunciation symbols for the following words. Make sure you pronounce each word. An example is provided.

Example: postage _____ pō′stĭj _____

16. brotherhood _____

17. dehydrate _____

18. fracture _____

19. overcast _____

20. temperament _____

Accent Marks

The mark ′ which comes after the first syllable in the pronunciation guide for the word *color* is called an **accent mark**. It tells you that you should put more force, or accent, on the first syllable of *color*. If you pronounce *color* correctly, you will hear yourself pronouncing the first syllable a little louder than the second syllable.

One-syllable words have no accent mark. Longer words may have more than one accent mark, since they sometimes have emphasis on more than one syllable. For example, the word *colorblind* (kŭl′ər-blīnd′) has an accent mark after the first syllable and the third syllable. When there is more than one accent mark, one will be darker to show which syllable gets the stronger accent. In *colorblind*, the first syllable has a darker accent mark, which means it receives more stress than the last syllable.

➤ *Practice 5*

Answer the questions following each of the five words below.

1. **hem•i•sphere** (hĕm′ĭ-sfîr)

   a. How many syllables are in *hemisphere*? _____

   b. Which syllable is most strongly accented? _____

2. **dis•as•sem•ble** (dĭs′ə-sĕm′bəl)

   a. How many syllables are in *disassemble*? _____

   b. Which syllable is most strongly accented? _____

3. **en•cour•age•ment** (ĕn-kûr′ĭj-mənt)

   a. How many syllables are in *encouragement*? _____

   b. Which syllable is accented? _____

4. **spec•u•la•tion** (spĕk′yə-lā′shən)

   a. How many syllables are in *speculation*? _____

   b. Which syllable is most strongly accented? _____

5. **spe•cial•ize** (spĕsh′ə-līz′)

   a. How many syllables are in *specialize*? _____

   b. Which syllable has no stress? _____

3   PARTS OF SPEECH

Following the pronunciation symbols for each entry word are one or more letters in italics. In the entry below, these letters are *n.* and then, later in the entry, *v.* These letters are abbreviations for the parts of speech of the word. The *n.* stands for "noun." The *v.* stands for "verb."

pil•low (pĭl′ō) *n.* **1.** A cloth case stuffed with something soft and used to cushion the head during sleep. **2.** A decorative cushion. —*v.* **1.** To rest (one's head) on or as if on a pillow. **2.** To serve as a pillow for. [< Lat. *pulvinus.*] —**pil′low•y** *adj.*

When a word is more than one part of speech, the dictionary gives the definitions for each part of speech separately. For *pillow*, the noun meanings are given first. When the noun meanings end, the abbreviation *v.* tells you that the verb definitions will follow.

Entries often end with words that are built upon the entry word. Then their parts of speech are also given. The above entry, for instance, ends with the word *pillowy*. The abbreviation *adj.* tells us that *pillowy* is an adjective.

The dictionary abbreviates the parts of speech to save space. Here are common abbreviations for the eight parts of speech:

n. — noun	*v.* — verb
pron. — pronoun	*conj.* — conjunction
adj. — adjective	*prep.* — preposition
adv. — adverb	*interj.* — interjection

➢ *Practice 6*

Use your dictionary to list the parts of speech for each of the following words. Each word has more than one part of speech.

Parts of speech:

1. go   _____

2. inside   _____

3. just   _____

4. plus   _____

5. quiet   _____

4 IRREGULAR FORMS OF WORDS

After the part of speech, you will find information on irregular spellings and irregular forms of the entry word. For instance, in the entry for *goose* below, look at the letters following the *n.*

goose (go͞os) *n., pl.* **geese** (gēs). **1.** A water bird related to the ducks and swans. **2.** The female of such a bird. **3.** The edible flesh of such a bird. **4.** *Informal.* A silly person. [< OE *gōs.*]

Normal spelling rules tell us that if we want to form the plural (abbreviated *pl.*) of a noun, we add the letter *s*. If we followed normal rules of spelling for *goose*, the plural would be *gooses*. But the dictionary tells us we should not follow normal spelling rules in this case. The plural of *goose* is *geese*.

The dictionary also tells us when normal grammar rules are not followed. For instance, the comparative of most adjectives is formed by adding *-er* to the end of the adjective. The word *tall* becomes *taller*, and *green* becomes *greener*. When the normal rule is not followed, the dictionary lets us know, as in the following entry:

good (go͝od) *adj.* **bet·ter** (bĕt′ər); **best** (bĕst).

We now know that the comparative of *good* is not *gooder* but *better*, and that the superlative of *good* is not *goodest*, but *best*.

➤ *Practice 7*

The entry for each word below includes an irregular spelling or grammatical form. Use your dictionary to write the correct spelling or form for each word. An example is provided.

> ***Example:*** hero   _____ heroes _____
>
> 1. hide   _____
>
> 2. old   _____
>
> 3. deny   _____
>
> 4. write   _____
>
> 5. identity   _____

5 DEFINITIONS AND SPECIAL LABELS

Following each part of speech are the meanings for a word. These meanings are listed according to part of speech. For example, *sport* has six meanings as a noun, three as a verb, and one as an adjective:

> **sport** (spôrt, spōrt) *n.* **1.** An active pastime; diversion. **2.** A specific diversion, usually involving physical exercise and having a set form and body of rules; game. **3.** Light mockery. **4.** One known for the manner of his acceptance or defeat or criticism: *a good sport.* **5.** *Informal.* One who lives a gay, extravagant life. **6.** *Genetics.* A mutation. —*v.* **1.** To play; frolic. **2.** To joke or trifle. **3.** To display or show off. —*adj.* Of, pertaining to, or appropriate for sport: *a sport shirt.* [< ME *sporten*, to amuse.] —**sport′y** *adj.*

In addition to listing definitions, a dictionary tells if a meaning is considered something other than "Standard English." (Standard English is the form most widely accepted by educated speakers and writers. An unlabeled word is considered Standard English.) The fifth noun meaning for *sport* is labeled *"Informal."*

This means when *sport* is used with that definition, it is not considered proper for formal speech and writing. Other labels you are most likely to encounter are:

- *Slang.* Not considered proper in formal conversation or writing.
- *Non-standard.* Usage considered unacceptable, either formally or informally.
- *Archaic.* A meaning that was once common, but used very little now.
- *Obsolete.* A meaning not used any longer. It is included in a dictionary because the meaning was common in the past. If you are reading the work of a famous playwright or novelist from the past, the meaning may apply.

There are also labels for definitions that apply only to a specific field. An example is the sixth definition of *sport*, which is labeled *"Genetics."* This means that the definition which follows applies only to the field of genetics.

When words have more than one meaning, their definitions are numbered. If you look up a word from a book you are reading, you will have to match one of the word's dictionary meanings with the sentence in the book. For example, which definition of *sport* fits the sentence below?

Gail *sported* a new outfit when we went to the dance last night.

The answer is the third definition of *sport* as a verb: Gail showed off a new outfit at the dance.

➤ Practice 8

Below are five words and some of their definitions from the *AHD*. A sentence using each word is also given. Read each sentence carefully, and then write in the number of the definition that best fits the sentence.

1. **tall**   **1.** Greater than average height.
   2. Boastful.
   3. Unusual in size or difficulty.

Which definition of *tall* fits the following sentence? _____

Jill realized that finding six dozen roses was a *tall* order to fill in the middle of January.

2. **sharp**   **1.** Having a thin edge or a fine point.
   2. Abrupt or sudden.
   3. Alert.

Which definition of *sharp* fits the following sentence? _____

Even after traveling all night, the football team looked *sharp* in its pre-game workouts.

3. **conceive** **1.** To become pregnant.
       2. To form an idea.

Which definition of *conceive* fits the following sentence? _____

It's hard to *conceive* of being five stories tall, but if you look out a fifth-floor window, you'll be able to imagine how some dinosaurs viewed the world.

4. **suspect** **1.** To regard as likely or probable.
       2. To distrust or doubt.
       3. To think of as guilty without proof.

Which definition of *suspect* fits the following sentence? _____

I *suspect* the exam is going to be all essay questions.

5. **pessimist** **1.** One who takes the gloomiest possible view of a situation.
        2. One who believes that this is the worst of all possible worlds.
        3. One who believes that the evil in the world outweighs the good.

Which definition of *pessimist* fits the following sentence? _____

Don is too much of a *pessimist* to study for tests; he assumes he'll do poorly no matter how hard he tries.

6 WORD ORIGINS

Most dictionaries will tell where words have come from and what their original meanings were. For instance, the entry for the word *gorgeous* says this:

gor•geous (gôr′jəs) *adj.* **1.** Dazzlingly brilliant; magnificent: *gorgeous jewels.* **2.** Strikingly attractive. [< OFr. *gorrias*, elegant.]

The information within brackets tells us that this word originated in "OFr," which, the *Abbreviations* section (in the front of the dictionary) tells us, stands for "Old French." It came from the word *gorrias*, which meant "elegant."

➤ *Practice 9*

Use your dictionary to tell what language each of the following words came from and what the word originally meant in that language.

Word	Language	Original Meaning
1. major	_____	_____
2. hurt	_____	_____
3. magazine	_____	_____
4. pajama	_____	_____
5. lunch	_____	_____

7 SYNONYMS

A **synonym** is a word with the same or almost the same meaning as that of another word. For instance, two synonyms for the word *fast* are *quick* and *speedy*.

Dictionary entries sometimes end with synonyms. Notice that the entry below for *giant* ends with many synonyms:

> **gi•ant** (jī′ənt) *n.* **1.** A legendary manlike being of enormous size and strength. **2.** One of unusually great size or importance. —*adj.* Gigantic, huge. [< Gk. *gigas.*] —**gi′ant•ess** *n.*
>
> *Syns: giant, colossal, elephantine, enormous, gargantuan, gigantic, herculean, huge, immense, jumbo, mammoth, massive, mighty, monstrous, monumental, mountainous, stupendous, titanic, tremendous, vast* **adj.**

To find the differing shades of meaning that often exist among synonyms, look up the definitions of individual words.

Still more information on synonyms and **antonyms** (words with opposite meanings) can be found in a thesaurus, which is a collection of synonyms and antonyms. A thesaurus can improve your writing, helping you find the precise word needed to express your thoughts. A thesaurus works much like a dictionary. Entry words are listed alphabetically and are followed by synonyms and perhaps an antonym or two. Here are three good thesauruses, all of which are in paperback:

> *The New American Roget's College Thesaurus in Dictionary Form*
>
> *The Random House Thesaurus*
>
> *Webster's New World Thesaurus*

➤ *Practice 10*

Each word below has synonyms listed in the dictionary. Write the synonyms for each word in the blank space.

1. calm _____

_____

2. cold_____

_____

3. deceive _____

_____

➤ *Review Test 1*

A. Below are five pairs of dictionary guidewords followed by other words. Circle the two words in each series which would be found on the page with the guidewords.

1-2. **ailment / alcoholic**

alarm   algebra   alive   aim

3-4. **clothe / coal**

closet   clumsy   coax   clutter

5-6. **indoor / inexact**

indulge   indirect   infancy   industry

7-8. **reduce / reflex**

refer   regard   reflect   recur

9-10. **snowball / soccer**

snore   snub   society   sober

B. Use your dictionary and the hints on page 12 to find the correct spelling of the following words.

11. toppic _____   14. bycicle _____

12. kwiz _____   15. wrek _____

13. sirprise _____   16. vizitor _____

C. Use the pronunciation key on page 14 to answer the following questions.

17. In **fumble** (fŭm′bəl), the *u* is pronounced like the *u* in what common word?

_____

18. In **cable** (kā′bəl), the *a* is pronounced like the *a* in what common word?

_____

19. In **reside** (rĭ-zīd′), the first *e* is pronounced like the *i* in what common word?

_____

20. In **reside** (rĭ-zīd′), the *i* is pronounced like the *i* in what common word?

_____

➤ *Review Test 2*

Use your dictionary to do all of the following.

A. Place dots between the syllables in the following words. Then write the correct pronunciation symbols, including the accent marks.

    1. p r i o r _____

    2. i n s u r e _____

    3. e n g a g e _____

    4. l e g i b l e _____

    5. s o c i a l i z e _____

B. List the parts of speech for each of the following words.

    6. glow *Parts of speech:*_____

    7. major *Parts of speech:*_____

C. Write the irregular form for the following word.

    8. factory *Irregular form:* _____

D. What dictionary definition of *lemon* fits the following sentence?

    Don't sell me that car if you know it's a lemon.

    9. *Definition that fits:* _____

    _____

E. Write five synonyms given in the dictionary for the following word.

    10. murder *Synonyms:* _____

    _____

    _____

    _____

    _____

➤ *Review Test 3*

A. To review what you've learned in this chapter, answer each of the following questions by circling the letter of the answer you think is correct.

1. Guidewords can help you
   a. pronounce a word in the dictionary.
   b. find a word in a dictionary.
   c. define a word in a dictionary.

2. You can learn to pronounce a word by using the pronunciation symbols and the
   a. part of speech.
   b. special labels.
   c. pronunciation key.

3. A bold accent mark shows
   a. which syllable has the strongest stress.
   b. which syllable has the weakest stress.
   c. that the word has only one syllable.

4. A label such as *Genetics* or *Psychology* means the definition that follows
   a. is informal.
   b. applies only to that field.
   c. no longer is used for the entry word.

5. A thesaurus lists
   a. definitions.
   b. synonyms.
   c. word origins.

B. Here is a chance to apply your understanding of dictionary use to a full-length selection. This reading is a true story about Malcolm X, a civil rights leader in the 1950s and 1960s. In this excerpt from his autobiography, Malcolm X explains how he used his time in jail to become "truly free." Read the selection, and then answer the questions that follow.

Words to Watch

Following are some of the more difficult words that appear in the reading. Each word is followed by the number of the paragraph in which it appears and its meaning there. These words are indicated in the reading by a small circle (°).

acquire (1): get
painstaking (5): very careful
ragged (5): uneven
burrowing (6): digging
succeeding (7): following

word-base (8): vocabulary

bunk (8): bed

wedge (8): a tool shaped like a triangle, used to separate two objects

---

DISCOVERING WORDS

Malcolm X with Alex Haley

It was because of my letters [which Malcolm X wrote to people outside while he was in jail] that I happened to stumble upon starting to acquire° some kind of a homemade education.   1

I became increasingly frustrated at not being able to express what I wanted to convey in letters that I wrote. . . . And every book I picked up had few sentences which didn't contain anywhere from one to nearly all the words that might as well have been in Chinese. When I skipped those words, of course, I really ended up with little idea of what the book said. . . .   2

I saw that the best thing I could do was get hold of a dictionary— to study, to learn some words. I requested a dictionary along with some tablets and pencils from the Norfolk Prison Colony school.   3

I spent two days just riffling uncertainly through the dictionary's pages. I'd never realized so many words existed! I didn't know *which* words I needed to learn. Finally, just to start some kind of action, I began copying.   4

In my slow, painstaking°, ragged° handwriting, I copied into my tablet everything printed on that first page, down to the punctuation marks. I believe it took me a day. Then, aloud, I read back to myself everything I'd written on the tablet. Over and over, aloud, to myself, I read my own handwriting.   5

I woke up the next morning, thinking about those words— immensely proud to realize that not only had I written so much at one time, but I'd written words that I never knew were in the world. Moreover, with a little effort, I also could remember what many of these words meant. I reviewed the words whose meanings I didn't remember. Funny thing, from the dictionary's first page right now, that *aardvark* springs to my mind. The dictionary had a picture of it, a long-tailed, long-eared, burrowing° African mammal, which lives off termites caught by sticking out its tongue as an anteater does for ants.   6

I was so fascinated that I went on—I copied the dictionary's next page. And the same experience came when I studied that. With every succeeding° page, I also learned of people and places and events from history. Actually, the dictionary is like a miniature encyclopedia.   7

Finally, the dictionary's A section had filled a whole tablet—and I went on into the B's. That was the way I started copying what eventually became the entire dictionary. It went a lot faster after so much practice helped me to pick up handwriting speed.

I suppose it was inevitable that as my word-base° broadened, I   8 could for the first time pick up a book and read and now begin to understand what the book was saying. Anyone who has read a great deal can imagine the new world that opened. Let me tell you something: from then until I left the prison, in every free moment I had, if I was not reading in the library, I was reading on my bunk°. You couldn't have gotten me out of books with a wedge°. Months passed without my even thinking about being imprisoned. In fact, up to then, I never had been so truly free in my life.

Dictionary Questions

Answer the questions that follow the two dictionary entries below. Both entries are for words taken from the reading. The pronunciation key on page 14 will help you answer the pronunciation questions.

stum•ble (stŭm′bəl) *v.* **1. a.** To trip and almost fall. **b.** To move unsteadily. **c.** To act or speak falteringly or clumsily. **2.** To make a mistake; blunder. **3.** To come upon accidentally. [< ME *stumblen.*] —**stum′ble** *n.* —**stum′bler** *n.*

1. *Stumble* would be found on the dictionary page with which guidewords?
   a. strong-arm / stuff
   b. suborn / suburb
   c. stuffed shirt / subconscious
   d. stew / stint

2. How many syllables are in the word *stumble*?
   a. One
   b. Two
   c. Three
   d. Four

3. The *u* in *stumble* sounds like the *u* in
   a. *cut.*
   b. *urge.*
   c. *abuse.*
   d *circus.*

4. The part of speech of *stumble* is
   a. adjective.
   b. adverb.
   c. noun.
   d. verb.

5. Which definition of *stumble* fits the sentence below from the reading?
   a. Definition 1a
   b. Definition 2
   c. Definition 3

   It was because of my letters that I happened to stumble upon starting to acquire some kind of a homemade education. (Paragraph 1)

con•vey (kən-vā′) *v.* **1.** to carry; transport. **2.** To transmit. **3.** To communicate; impart. [< Med. Lat. *conviare*, to escort.]

6. *Convey* would be found on the dictionary page with which guidewords?
   a. conversant / coolant
   b. cooler / coral
   c. contradict / converge
   d. content / contractual

7. How many syllables are in the word *convey*?
   a. One
   b. Two
   c. Three
   d. Four

8. The *o* in *convey* sounds like
   a. the *o* in *pot.*
   b. the *o* in *toe.*
   c. the *o* in *for.*
   d. the schwa sound in *gallop.*

9. The part of speech of *convey* is
   a. adjective.
   b. adverb.
   c. noun.
   d. verb.

10. Which definition of *convey* fits the sentence below?
    a. Definition 1
    b. Definition 2
    c. Definition 3

    I became increasingly frustrated at not being able to express what I wanted to convey in letters that I wrote. (Paragraph 2)

Mapping Activity

This selection is organized by time: first one thing happened; then another; after that, another; and so on. The major events are scrambled in the list below. Write them in the diagram in their correct order.

- His education gives him freedom in jail through reading.

- He is frustrated with his weak language skills.

- He builds his vocabulary and knowledge through the dictionary.

Central point: By studying the dictionary, Malcolm X finds intellectual freedom in prison.

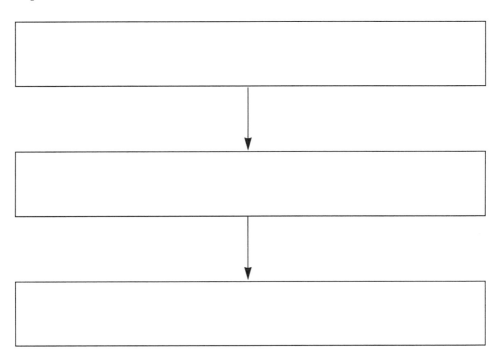

Discussion Questions

1.   At the end of the selection, Malcolm X says that even though he was still in jail, he "never had been so truly free" in his life. What did he mean by that? What is it that makes you feel free?

2.   Malcolm X says that his decision to increase his vocabulary was caused by frustration at not being able to express himself in letters to friends on the outside. What was it that made you decide to continue your education? What do you hope to do with the knowledge you are gaining?

Writing Activities

1. Write about a significant discovery in your life. Describe the time and place when the discovery occurred, and provide a detailed account of the discovery and its meaning for you.

2. Malcolm X tells us that he felt free. What does the word *freedom* mean to you? Write a paragraph on your definition of freedom, giving specific examples to show what you mean. Your first sentence will begin "Freedom is. . . ."

Check Your Performance   **DICTIONARY USE**

Activity	*Number Right*	*Points*	*Total*
Review Test 1 (20 items)	_____	x 2 =	_____
Review Test 2 (10 items)	_____	x 2 =	_____
Review Test 3, Part A (5 items)	_____	x 2 =	_____
Review Test 3, Part B (10 items)	_____	x 2 =	_____
Mapping (3 items)	_____	x 3⅓ =	_____

TOTAL SCORE = _____%

Enter your total score into the reading performance chart on the inside back cover.

2

Vocabulary in Context

Do you know the meaning of the word *queries*? How about the words *tedious* and *transmit*?

You may be having trouble thinking of the definitions of these words. However, you will be more likely to know what they mean when you see them in the following sentences:

Dan was nervous about answering Detective Miller's *queries*. Why was he asking so many questions, anyway?

Most of my history teacher's lectures were *tedious*, but the one about what really happened on Paul Revere's famous ride was very interesting.

Mosquitoes *transmit* sleeping sickness through biting.

Now, see if you can choose the meaning of each word based on the way it is used above. Circle the letter of the meaning you think is correct.

Queries are:

a. statements of fact.   b. questions.   c. charges.

Tedious means:

a. interesting.   b. long.   c. boring.

Transmit means to

a. spread.   b. enjoy.   c. cure.

To help you decide on the right meanings, you used **context clues**. These are word clues provided by the **context**, the words surrounding each word in italics. With the help of context clues, you could probably tell that *queries* means "questions," that *tedious* means "boring," and that *transmit* means to "spread."

Context clues, then, can help you figure out what new words mean. In general, using these clues will help you in three ways:

1 It will save you time, since you won't have to stop and look up every new word you read. (However, it is still important to keep a dictionary handy. Sometimes there will be no context clues.)

2 It will improve your understanding of what you read, since you will know more of the words.

3 It will improve your vocabulary because you will be learning the meanings of many new words. When you see these words more than once, they will become a part of your working vocabulary.

TYPES OF CONTEXT CLUES

Here are four common types of context clues:

1 Examples
2 Synonyms
3 Antonyms
4 General Sense of the Sentence or Passage

You will learn about each of these clues in the rest of the chapter. Examples will help you understand how each type of clue works. Practice exercises will help you to recognize and use context clues and to add new words to your vocabulary.

1   Examples

An unknown word may be followed by examples that will reveal what the word means. The examples often follow signal words such as *for example, including, for instance, such as, like,* or *e.g.* (which means "for example").

To understand how this type of clue works, read the sentences below. Examples in each serve as context clues. These examples, which are in boldfaced type, should help you figure out the meanings of the words in italics. Circle the letter of the definition of each word in italics.

1. *Assets* such as **good health, a loving family,** and **a job you enjoy** make life rewarding.

    Assets are

    a. things of value.   b. rewards on the job.   c helpful people.

2. *Conspicuous* features, including **a muscular build, good looks,** and **a height of 6′ 3″**, call attention to John F. Kennedy, Jr., wherever he goes.

Conspicuous means

    a. large.   b. noticeable.   c. famous.

3. The car had *defects* such as **a dented fender** and **torn seats**. But I didn't care. I had wanted a Corvette sports car for years, and I was going to buy it.

    Defects are

    a. faults.   b. out-of-date features.   c. foreign qualities.

Answers:

In each sentence, the examples probably helped you to figure out the meanings of the words in italics:

    1. a   The *assets* listed are "things of value."
    2. b   The *conspicuous* features mentioned are "noticeable."
    3. a   The *defects* described are "faults."

➤ *Practice 1*

In each item below, underline the examples given for the word in italics. Then circle the letter of the definition of each word in italics.

1. There is much to see at Hearst Castle. It even has an indoor swimming pool whose *dimensions* are a length of 100′, a width of 15′, and a depth of 10′.

    Dimensions are

    a. costs.   b. benefits.   c. measurements.

2. It seemed as if everyone attended the charity event. Some of the *notables* in the crowd included actor Tom Cruise, tennis star Steffi Graf, and film critics Siskel and Ebert.

    Notables means

    a. average people.   b. people worthy of notice.   c. movie stars.

3. The San Diego Zoo is famous for its wide variety of animals. It has not only such common ones as lions and tigers, but also *exotic* animals like lowland gorillas, snow leopards, and koala bears.

    Exotic means

    a. unusual.   b. dangerous.   c. ordinary.

4. *Fictitious* television investigators such as Columbo and Jessica Fletcher make detective work seem much more glamorous than it really is.

    Fictitious means

    a. true-life.   b. unknown.   c. not real.

5. Diane had *qualms* about marrying Sam after high school. First of all, she felt half-interested in going on to college. Also, she was a little worried that a sister who had married early was now divorced.

Qualms are

a fights.   b. good feelings.   c. uneasy feelings.

2 Synonyms

Synonyms are words that mean the same or almost the same as another word. For example, the words *watch, look, see,* and *observe* are synonyms—they all mean about the same thing.

Synonyms can be useful context clues. They may be purposely included by an author to help readers understand a word. In such cases, the synonyms are often set off by commas, dashes, or parentheses:

Nuptials (weddings) vary from culture to culture.

Also, they may be introduced by the words *or* and *that is*:

Carol was apprehensive, *or* fearful, of the upcoming test.

Hindsight, *that is,* understanding of events that have already occurred, can help us learn from our mistakes.

A synonym may also appear somewhere else in a sentence as a restatement of the meaning of the unknown word. The third sentence below is an example of this type of context clue.

Each sentence below uses a synonym as a context clue. Underline the synonym for each word in italics.

1. Jack was a *mediocre*, or average, student in all of his subjects.

2. It is hard to believe that my millionaire cousin was once *indigent*, so poor that he walked the streets without knowing where his next meal would come from.

3. My company has a *regulation* allowing new mothers to take three months off from work. I think there should be a rule allowing fathers the same time off.

Answers:

In each sentence, the synonym given should have helped you understand the meaning of the word in italics.

1. Someone who is *mediocre* is "average."
2. Someone who is *indigent* is "poor."
3. A *regulation* is a "rule."

➤ *Practice 2*

In each item, underline the synonym for the word in italics. Each synonym may be one or more words.

1. Danny is one of the best *patrons* of Helen's Diner. He's a steady customer, not because he likes the food there, but because he likes Helen.

2. While your *vocation* is important, most experts advise that you treat it for what it is—a job, not your entire life.

3. Dr. Jonas Salk, one of the most *eminent*, or famous, scientists in the world, came to speak at our school.

4. Your *absurd* idea that people from outer space live among us is as ridiculous as the belief that the Earth is flat.

5. The fight was so fast-paced that the referee *intervened* only twice. And both times he came between the boxers, they quickly broke apart on their own.

3 Antonyms

Antonyms are words with opposite meanings. For example, *summer* is the opposite of *winter*; *soft* is the opposite of *hard*. Antonyms are often signaled by words such as *unlike, but, however, instead of, in contrast,* or *on the other hand*. Antonyms serve as context clues by providing the opposite meaning of an unknown word.

The examples below should help you to understand how this type of clue works. Each sentence has an antonym as a context clue. Read each sentence and do two things:

(1) Underline the antonym for the word in italics.
(2) Circle the letter of the meaning of the word in italics.

1. The *adverse* weather conditions forced us to stay inside for most of our vacation. The day the weather finally turned nice, we had to leave.

   Adverse means

   a. nice.   b. bad.   c. summer.

2. I thought it was difficult to *ascend* the mountain, but I discovered that to climb down it is even worse.

   Ascend means to

   a. climb up.   b. walk around.   c. climb down.

3. After years of *defying* my parents, I decided life might be better if I tried agreeing with them once in a while.

Defying means

a. avoiding.   b. obeying.   c. opposing.

Answers:

If you looked for the antonyms of the words in italics, you will have come up with these answers:

1. b   *Adverse* weather conditions are the opposite of "nice" ones.
2. a   To *ascend* is the opposite of to "climb down."
3. c   *Defying* one's parents is the opposite of "agreeing with them."

➤ Practice 3

Antonyms provide context clues in the sentences below. Read each item, and do two things:

    (1) Underline the antonym for the word in italics. Each antonym may be one or more words.
    (2) Circle the letter of the meaning of the word in italics.

1. Your science project is much more *elaborate* than mine. In fact, mine looks downright simple compared with yours.

   Elaborate means

   a. plain.   b. large.   c. complicated.

2. Gordon would not remain an *obscure* author all his life. He knew that someday he would be famous.

   Obscure means

   a. unknown.   b. well known.   c. good.

3. The attorney introduced facts she felt were *relevant* to the case. But the judge said the facts did not apply to the case at all.

   Relevant means

   a. legal.   b. related.   c. known.

4. When you write a how-to essay, the steps must be given *in sequence*. If they are out of order, your readers will become confused.

   In sequence means

   a. all at once.   b. in an order.   c. during the summer.

5. The bank president assigned *trivial* problems to new employees. He gave the serious problems to experienced workers.

Trivial means

a. important.   b. customer.   c. unimportant.

4   General Sense of the Sentence or Passage

Often, the context of a new word contains no examples, synonyms, or antonyms. How, then, can you understand the word? You can use the general sense of the sentence or passage. Careful reading and your own experience will often give you the meaning of a word.

In each sentence below, look for general clues to the meaning of the word in italics. Then circle the letter of your choice.

1. Steve lived in Hawaii for fifteen years, so it is hard for me to *conceive of* why he decided to move to Minnesota.

Conceive of means to

a. plan.   b. believe.   c. think of.

2. Rita and Dan went to an animal shelter to adopt a puppy. Rita fell in love with a poodle, and Dan couldn't resist a collie. So they felt that there was no *alternative* but to keep both animals.

An *alternative* is a

a. choice.   b. reason.   c. confusion.

3. As a *consequence* of his bad report card, my brother could not watch TV until his teachers said he was improving.

A *consequence* is a

a. right.   b. result.   c. chance.

Answers:

Each sentence provides context clues that become clear if you read carefully.

1. c   To *conceive of* something means to "think of" something. The speaker could not think of, or imagine, why his friend Steve would move from Hawaii to Minnesota.
2. a   An *alternative* is a "choice." Rita and Dan felt they had no choice but to take both dogs home.
3. b   A *consequence* is a "result." The result of the brother's bad report card was not being able to watch TV until teachers reported that he had improved.

➤ *Practice 4*

In each item below, you must use your experience and general understanding to figure out the meaning of the word in italics. Think about the situation where the word is used, and then circle the letter of the meaning of the word.

1. Jesse was surprised when his speech *elicited* laughs from the audience; he was perfectly serious about his topic.

   Elicited means

   a. brought out.   b. hid.   c. included.

2. Elena was glad she had *ample* time to collect her thoughts for the afternoon's mid-term. Then she discovered her watch was incorrect—she was actually late for the test!

   Ample means

   a. no.   b. plenty of.   c. little.

3. My brother felt it would be *futile* to try to make the basketball team. At 5′6″, he couldn't compete with the others; they were all at least eight inches taller than he.

   Futile means

   a. helpful.   b. useless.   c. unreal.

4. The *impact* of the crash was so great that you couldn't tell the make of either car. Each was totally destroyed.

   Impact means

   a. force.   b. time.   c. place.

5. The young eagle's first flight showed what a *novice* he was at flying. He got himself all tangled up in a thornbush as he tried to land.

   A *novice* is a

   a. bird.   b. success.   c. beginner.

A Note and Study Hint

You don't always have to use context clues or the dictionary to find definitions. Textbook authors usually give formal definitions and explanations of important terms. Often one or more examples are also given, as shown with the excerpts on the next page.

Below are three short excerpts from college texts. In each case, the term to be defined is set off in **boldface** type or *italic* type, and the definition then follows. In one case, an example is also included. Which one of the three textbook excerpts includes both a definition and an example? In the margin of that excerpt, write a "DEF" beside the definition and an "EX" beside the example. You will find it helpful to mark off definitions and examples in the same way when you are reading a textbook chapter.

Excerpt from a psychology textbook:

The *case study* method is used mainly by clinical psychologists working with troubled persons. A case study is an in-depth examination of one individual. The purpose is to learn as much as possible about the person's problems. The technique is expensive and takes several sessions to complete.

Excerpt from a business textbook:

Short-range plans tend to be specific. One part of a short-range plan, **procedures**, tells employees exactly what steps to take in a given situation. A factory's procedures, for instance, may require moving raw materials from the receiving platform to the beginning of the assembly line.

Excerpt from a sociology textbook:

Some religious practices can be classified as **rituals**, or standardized sets of actions used in ceremonies or on other occasions. Rituals rely on symbols to communicate their meaning to participants.

The second textbook excerpt above includes both a definition and an example. The word being defined is *procedures*—the "part of a short-range plan" that "tells employees exactly what steps to take in a given situation." The words "for instance" signal that the author is also illustrating the new word. In this case, the author gives an example of a factory's procedures.

By using italic or boldface type, textbook authors are signaling to you that the highlighted terms are important to learn. Indeed, the first major step you should take to understand a textbook chapter is to mark off definitions and any examples in the text. Then write down those definitions and, if available, an example that makes the definition clear to you. Your focus on definitions and examples will help as you reread a chapter and work to increase your understanding of its content.

➤ *Review Test 1*

Using context clues for help, circle the letter of the best meaning for each word or phrase in italics.

1. I have found that if I *adhere to* a schedule, I accomplish more. When I don't follow a set routine, I get little done.

   Adhere to means to

   a. follow.   b. avoid.   c. buy.

2. After standing empty for fifteen years, the old mansion had *deteriorated*. The wood was decaying, the plaster was peeling, and most of the windows had broken.

   Deteriorate means to

   a. become older.   b. become worse.   c. become empty.

3. When Yoko asked Alex whether he wanted to go camping or visit her brother, he said he was *indifferent*—it didn't matter to him where they went on their vacation.

   Indifferent means

   a. not the same.   b. unable to decide.   c. having no preference.

4. Your version of the accident *distorts* the events, while mine tells it just as it happened.

   Distort means to

   a. explain.   b. misrepresent.   c. forget.

5. It was hard for Leon to *refrain* from hitting Michael. Michael had pushed him and knocked his books down.

   Refrain means to

   a. continue.   b. hold back.   c. think of.

6. Our English teacher took time in class to *commend* Maria on the outstanding work she was doing. Unfortunately, he said he could give praise to no one else in the class.

   Commend means to

   a. blame.   b. encourage.   c. praise.

7. Lucy is so *gullible* that she'll believe almost anything you make up. She believed me the other day when I told her that milk has lots of caffeine.

   Gullible means

   a. clever.   b. easy to fool.   c. willing to learn.

8. You can't *equate* winning the Super Bowl with beating me in a game of basketball. The two are just not the same.

   Equate means to

   a. treat as equal.   b. treat as normal.   c. cover up.

9. Some of my friends love mountain climbing, but I find it too *treacherous.* I prefer less dangerous activities, like floating in a swimming pool.

   Treacherous means

   a. athletic.   b. safe.   c. dangerous.

10. I have never met anyone as *obstinate* as my father. Once he makes up his mind, he won't change it for anything.

    Obstinate means

    a. stubborn.   b. agreeable.   c. serious.

➤ *Review Test 2*

Using context clues for help, write the definition for each word in italics. Choose the meanings from the words in the box below. Each word will be used once.

alone	stingy	false show
matching	witty reply	place of protection
lessen	remove	very great enthusiasm
given to		

1. Cheryl felt that the honor *bestowed on* her for work with the homeless could have been given to many others who had worked hard as well.

   Bestowed on means _____

2. Vic looked forward to being *isolated* at his mountain cabin. He had been in the crowded city too long.

   Isolated means _____

3. I had to *delete* a lot of information from my report on zoos because it was longer than my teacher wanted it to be.

   Delete means _____

4. Roland was so *miserly* that he refused to give his sons spending money. Also, to save electricity, he insisted they study by the light of one lamp.

   Miserly means_____

5. The Wildlife Animal *Refuge* is home to injured animals who have been found by concerned people.

   A *refuge* is a _____

6. Robin always comes up with quick *retorts* to people's comments, but I can never think of clever answers until it's too late.

   A *retort* is a_____

7. Experts say exercise makes the appetite *diminish*. So being on a diet provides another good reason to exercise.

   Diminish means _____

8. Antonio made a *pretense* of writing the answers to the essay test, but he was just scribbling. He hadn't studied for the test at all.

   Pretense means a _____

9. Lately there has beem a *mania* for "adult" ice creams. People don't seem able to get enough of such expensive and rich treats as Dove bars.

   Mania is a _____

10. Studies found that twins totally separated early in life often lead *parallel* lives. For instance, many study the same subjects, get similar jobs, and marry the same kind of person.

    Parallel means _____

➤ Review Test 3

A. To review what you have learned in this chapter, answer each of the following questions. Fill in the blank or circle the letter of the answer you think is correct.

1. The context of a word is
   a. its meaning.   b. its opposite.   c. the words around it.

2. One type of clue that helps readers figure out the meaning of a new word is

   the *(example, synonym, antonym)* _____ clue, which often follows signal words such as *however, but,* and *on the other hand.*

3. In the sentence below, which type of context clue is used for the word in italics?

   a. example   b. synonym   c. antonym

   Urban, or city, problems seem to be getting worse each year.

4. In the sentence below, which type of context clue is used for the word in italics?

   a. example   b. synonym   c. antonym

   > If you allow *despair* to get the upper hand, you will lose all courage, so remember to keep hope uppermost in your mind.

5. Often when textbook authors introduce a very important word, they provide you with the word's _____ to make sure you understand the word precisely.

B. Here is a chance to apply the skill of understanding vocabulary in context to a full-length selection. How much of a difference do you think reading can make in your life? Here is a story written by a woman who grew up in Brazil and read everything she could get her hands on. She tells why she reads so much and describes the impact reading has had on her life. When you finish the selection, answer the vocabulary questions that follow.

Words to Watch

Following are some words in the reading that do not have strong context support. Each word is followed by the number of the paragraph in which it appears and its meaning there. These words are indicated in the story by a small circle (°).

> *enchanted* (1): fascinating
> *devoured* (5): took in with great enthusiasm
> *intriguing* (6): interesting
> *illicit* (9): not permitted
> *sadistic* (9): cruel
> *exult* (9): rejoice
> *horizon* (12): view of the world
> *seduces* (13): attracts
> *abyss* (13): bottomless hole
> *precision* (13): exactness
> *subversive* (15): turning people against something

A LOVE AFFAIR WITH BOOKS

Bernadete Piassa

When I was young, I thought that reading was like a drug which I   1 was allowed to take only a teaspoon at a time, but which, nevertheless, had the effect of carrying me away to an enchanted° world where I experienced strange and forbidden emotions. As time went by and I took that drug again and again, I became addicted to it. I could no longer live without reading. Books became an intrinsic part of my life. They became my friends, my guides, my lovers. My most faithful lovers.

2   I didn't know I would fall in love with books when I was young and started to read. I don't even recall when I started to read and how. I just remember that my mother didn't like me to read. In spite of this, every time I had an opportunity I would sneak somewhere with a book and read one page, two pages, three, if I were lucky enough, always feeling my heart beating fast, always hoping that my mother wouldn't find me, wouldn't shout as always: "Bernadete, don't you have anything to do?" For her, books were nothing. For me, they were everything.

3   In my childhood I didn't have a big choice of books. I lived in a small town in Brazil, surrounded by swamp and farms. It was impossible to get out of town by car; there weren't roads. By train it took eight hours to reach the next village. There were airplanes, small airplanes, only twice a week. Books couldn't get to my town very easily. There wasn't a library there, either. However, I was lucky: My uncle was a pilot.

4   My uncle, who owned a big farm and also worked flying people from place to place in his small airplane, had learned to fly, in addition, with his imagination. At home, he loved to sit in his hammock on his patio and travel away in his fantasy with all kinds of books. If he happened to read a bestseller or a romance, when he was done he would give it to my mother, who also liked to read although she didn't like me to. But I would get to read the precious book anyway, even if I needed to do this in a hiding place, little by little.

5   I remember very well one series of small books. Each had a green cover with a drawing of a couple kissing on it. I think the series had been given to my mother when she was a teenager because all the pages were already yellow and almost worn-out. But although the books were old, for me they seemed alive, and for a long time I devoured° them, one by one, pretending that I was the heroine and my lover would soon come to rescue me. He didn't come, of course. And I was the one who left my town to study and live in Rio de Janeiro, taking only my clothes with me. But inside myself I was taking my passion for books that would never abandon me.

6   I had been sent to study in a boarding school, and I was soon appalled to discover that the expensive all-girls school had even fewer books than my house. In my class there was a bookshelf with maybe fifty books, and almost all of them were about the lives of saints and the miracles of Christ. I had almost given up the hope of finding something

to read when I spotted, tucked away at the very end of the shelf, a small book already covered by dust. It didn't seem to be about religion because it had a more intriguing° title, *The Old Man and the Sea*. It was written by an author that I had never heard of before: Ernest Hemingway. Curious, I started to read the book and a few minutes later was already fascinated by Santiago, the fisherman.

I loved that book so much that when I went to my aunt's house to spend the weekend, I asked her if she had any books by the man who had written it. She lent me *For Whom the Bell Tolls*, and I read it every Sunday I could get out of school, only a little bit at a time, only one teaspoon at a time. I started to wait anxiously for those Sundays. At the age of thirteen I was deeply in love with Ernest Hemingway.   7

When I finished with all his books I could find, I discovered Herman Hesse, Graham Greene, Aldous Huxley, Edgar Allan Poe. I could read them only on Sundays, so, during the week, I would dream or think about the world I had discovered in their books.   8

At that time I thought that my relationship with books was kind of odd, something that set me apart from the world. Only when I read the short story "Illicit° Happiness," by Clarice Lispector, a Brazilian author, did I discover that other people could enjoy books as much as I did. The story is about an ugly and fat girl who still manages to torture one of the beautiful girls in her town only because her father is the owner of a bookstore, and she can have all the books she wants. With sadistic° refinement, day after day she promises to give to the beautiful girl the book the girl dearly wants, but never fulfills her promise. When her mother finds out what is going on and gives the book to the beautiful girl, the girl runs through the streets hugging it and, at home, pretends to have lost it only to find it again, showing an ardor for books that made me exult°. For the first time I wasn't alone. I knew that someone else also loved books as much as I did.   9

My passion for books continued through my life, and it had to surmount another big challenge when, at the age of thirty-one, I moved to New York. Because I had almost no money, I was forced to leave all my books in Brazil. Besides, I didn't know enough English to read in this language. For some years I was condemned again to the darkness; condemned to live without books, my friends, my guides, my lovers.   10

But my love for books was so strong that I overcame even this obstacle. I learned to read in English, and was finally able to enjoy my favorite authors again.   11

Although books have always been part of my life, they still hold a mystery for me, and every time I open a new one, I ask myself which pleasures I am about to discover, which routes I am about to travel,   12 which emotions I am about to sink in. Will this new book touch me as a woman, as a foreigner, as a romantic soul, as a curious person? Which horizon° is it about to unfold to me, which string of my soul is it bound to touch, which secret is it about to unveil for me?

Sometimes, the book seduces° me not only for the story it tells, but also because of the words the author uses in it. Reading Gabriel Garcia Marquez's short story "The Handsomest Drowned Man in the World," I feel dazzled when he writes that it took "the fraction of centuries for the body to fall into the abyss°." The fraction of centuries! I read those words again and again, infatuated by them, by their precision°, by their hidden meaning. I try to keep them in my mind, even knowing that they are already part of my soul.   13

After reading so many books that touch me deeply, each one in its special way, I understand now that my mother had a point when she tried to keep me away from books in my childhood. She wanted me to stay in my little town, to marry a rich and tiresome man, to keep up with the traditions. But the books carried me away; they gave me wings to fly, to discover new places. They made me dare to live another kind of life. They made me wish for more, and when I couldn't have all I wished for, they were still there to comfort me, to show me new options.   14

Yes, my mother was right. Books are dangerous; books are subversive°. Because of them I left a predictable future for an unforeseeable one. However, if I had to choose again, I would always choose the books instead of the lackluster° life I could have had. After all, what joy would I find in my heart without my books, my most faithful lovers?   15

Vocabulary Questions

Use context clues in the reading to help you decide on the best meaning for the italicized words. Then circle the letter of your choice.

1. The word *intrinsic* in "I could no longer live without reading. Books became an intrinsic part of my life" (paragraph 1) means
    a. rare.
    b. efficient.
    c. essential.
    d. unpleasant.

2. The word *abandon* in "inside myself I was taking my passion for books that would never abandon me" (paragraph 5) means
   a. please.
   b. strengthen.
   c. leave.
   d. join.

3. The word *appalled* in "I was soon appalled to discover that the expensive all-girls school had even fewer books than my house" (paragraph 6) means
   a. shocked.
   b. unwilling.
   c. pleased.
   d. proud.

4. The word *anxiously* in "She lent me *For Whom the Bell Tolls*, and I read it every Sunday I could get out of school. . . . I started to wait anxiously for those Sundays" (paragraph 7) means
   a. fearfully.
   b. eagerly.
   c. very patiently.
   d. with much worry.

5. The word *dearly* in "day after day she promises to give to the beautiful girl the book the girl dearly wants" (paragraph 9) means
   a. foolishly.
   b. with great humor.
   c. rudely.
   d. sincerely.

6. The word *ardor* in "the girl . . . pretends to have lost it only to find it again, showing an ardor for books. . . . I knew that someone else also loved books as much as I did" (paragraph 9) means
   a. passion.
   b. doubt.
   c. kindness.
   d. improvement.

7. The word *surmount* in "My passion for books continued through my life, and it had to surmount another big challenge when . . . I moved to New York" (paragraph 10) means
   a. remain.
   b. select.
   c. overcome.
   d. search for.

8. The word *condemned* in "I didn't know enough English to read in this language. For some years I was condemned again to the darkness; condemned to live without books" (paragraph 10) means
   a. rescued.
   b. doomed.
   c. captured.
   d. attracted.

9. The word *infatuated* in "I read these words again and again, infatuated by them, by their precision, by their hidden meaning" (paragraph 13) means
   a. disturbed.
   b. protected.
   c. worried.
   d. fascinated.

10. The word *lackluster* in "She wanted me to stay in my little town, to marry a rich and tiresome man. . . . However, . . . I would always choose the books instead of the lackluster life I could have had" (paragraphs 14 and 15) means
    a. exciting.
    b. dull.
    c. famous.
    d. poor.

Mapping Activity

The selection is organized according to time, describing events in Piassa's life in the order in which they happened. The major events that happened to Piassa are scrambled below. Write them in the diagram in their correct order.

- She goes to boarding school in Rio de Janeiro.

- Piassa lives in a small town in Brazil.

- She learns to read in English.

- Piassa moves to New York.

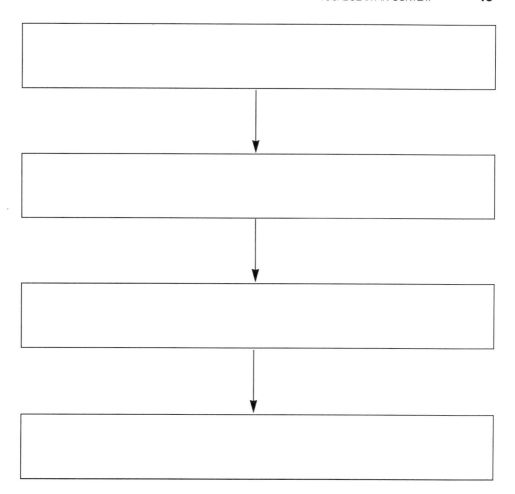

Discussion Questions

1. The author's mother discouraged her from reading. What was the attitude of the adults in your family to reading? Were you encouraged or discouraged to read?

2. What was reading like for you in school? Explain why it was a positive or a negative experience.

Writing Activities

1. Drawing upon the details you discussed in response to the above questions, write a paper that begins with one of the following sentences:

    My family encouraged me to read when I was growing up.
    My family environment discouraged me from reading when I was growing up.
    Reading in school was a positive experience for me.
    Reading in school was a negative experience for me.

    Develop your paper with detailed reasons and examples.

2. Piassa tells us how reading was an important activity in her life. Write a paper about an activity that has been very important in your life. Provide several reasons explaining why that activity has been so important.

Check Your Performance			VOCABULARY IN CONTEXT
Activity	*Number Right*	*Points*	*Total*
Review Test 1 (10 items)	_____	x 3 =	_____
Review Test 2 (10 items)	_____	x 3 =	_____
Review Test 3, Part A (5 items)	_____	x 2 =	_____
Review Test 3, Part B (10 items)	_____	x 2 =	_____
Mapping (4 items)	_____	x 2.5 =	_____
		TOTAL SCORE =	_____%

Enter your total score into the reading performance chart on the inside back cover.

3

Main Ideas

The most helpful reading skill is the ability to find an author's main idea. This chapter and chapters 5 and 6 will develop your skill in locating main ideas.

UNDERSTANDING THE MAIN IDEA

The **main idea** is a general idea. It states the central point of a paragraph. Very often, the main idea appears in a sentence called the **topic sentence**. The rest of a paragraph consists of specific ideas and details that support and explain the main idea.

Think of the main idea as an "umbrella" statement. Under the main idea, often expressed in a topic sentence, fits all the other material of the paragraph. The other material is specific ideas in the form of examples, reasons, facts, and other supporting evidence. The diagram below shows the relationship:

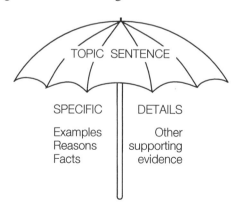

Look now at the paragraph that follows, and see if you can find its topic sentence. The topic sentence will state the main idea: a general idea that includes, or covers, all or most of the other material in the paragraph.

[1]Americans love to send greeting cards. [2]For instance, over 4 million birthday cards are sent out in this country every day. [3]During Valentine's Day last year, over 900 million cards were mailed. [4]And close to 3 billion holiday greeting cards were sent out over the Christmas season.

Which sentence states the main idea of the paragraph? In the space provided below, write in the number of the topic sentence. Then read the explanation that follows.

Topic sentence: _____

Explanation:

Sentence 1:   The idea that Americans love to send greeting cards is the most general idea in the paragraph. "Greeting cards" is broad enough to include the three specific types of cards named in the paragraph—birthday, Valentine's Day, and Christmas cards. Sentence 1 is therefore the topic sentence, the sentence that states the main idea.

Sentence 2:   The number of birthday cards sent by Americans is just one specific detail in the paragraph. Sentence 2 is not general enough to cover the details on other types of greeting cards.

Sentence 3:   The idea that Americans sent millions of Valentine's Day cards is another specific detail. It is too narrow to include the other types of greeting cards.

Sentence 4:   The number of Christmas cards sent is a final specific detail. Sentence 4 is also too narrow to include the other types of greeting cards.

In summary, the main idea of the paragraph on greeting cards is sentence 1. The other sentences support the main idea. They give specific examples of the idea that Americans love to send greeting cards. Here is the umbrella diagram again. This time it shows the relationship between the ideas in the paragraph about greeting cards.

AMERICANS LOVE TO
SEND GREETING CARDS

4 million for birthdays every day
900 million on Valentine's Day
3 billion over Christmas

Remember, then, that the main idea is a general idea that includes most or all of the other information in a paragraph. The general idea is often stated in one sentence called the topic sentence. The other information is made up of specific details that support or explain the main idea.

GENERAL VERSUS SPECIFIC IDEAS

You have learned that the main idea in a paragraph is a *general idea*. In contrast, the supporting information in a paragraph is made up of *specific* ideas. To improve your skill at finding main ideas, then, it will be helpful for you to practice separating general from specific ideas.

We often separate general and specific ideas in our lives. For example, you may do so in choosing your school classes. You may think, "I need credits in science. Should I take biology or chemistry?" In this case, *science* is the general idea, and *biology* and *chemistry* are the specific ideas. A general idea (science) includes specific ideas (biology and chemistry).

Or you may go home from school or work and think, "I'll get some fish for dinner." You may consider flounder, salmon, and tuna. In this example, *fish* is the general idea; *flounder, salmon* and *tuna* are the specific ideas.

In other words, **general ideas** are broad, and **specific ideas** are narrower. *Countries* is a broad term that includes *Brazil*, which is more narrow. *Rodent* is a broad term that includes specific terms such as *mouse* and *rat*, which are more narrow.

The practice that follows will give you experience in recognizing general and specific ideas.

➤ *Practice 1*

A. Each group of words below consists of one general idea and four specific ideas. The general idea includes all the specific ideas. Underline the general idea in each group. Before beginning, look at the two examples and explanations:

Example   anger   love   fear   <u>emotion</u>   envy

(*Emotion* is the general idea; *anger, love, fear,* and *envy* are specific kinds of emotions.)

Example   booth   table   <u>diner</u>   cash register   menus

(*Diner* is the general idea; specific parts of the diner include a booth, table, cash register, and the menus.)

  1. parrot   kitten   goldfish   hamster   pet

  2. square   circle   triangle   shape   diamond

  3. up   down   sideways   direction   north

4. soda	beer	orange juice	beverage	water
5. tires	meter	seats	taxi	doors
6. sleeping bag	sheet	pillow	blanket	bedding
7. "hello"	greetings	a wave	"hi"	open arms
8. screech	noise	crash	off-key music	sirens
9. jump	command	stop	move	hurry
10. jail	hanging	suspension	fine	punishment

B. In each pair below, one idea is general and the other is specific. The general idea includes the specific one. Do two things:

(1) Underline the general idea in each pair of words.
(2) Write in one more specific idea that is covered by the general idea. Look first at the example and explanation.

Example   purple   color   _____red_____

(*Color* is the general idea; *purple* is a specific color; another specific color is *red*.)

11. bird   eagle   _____

12. furniture   table   _____

13. bus   vehicle   _____

14. sunshine   weather   _____

15. pretzels   snack   _____

16. planet   Earth   _____

17. tango   dance   _____

18. insect   bee   _____

19. lipstick   cosmetics   _____

20. job   salesclerk   _____

Moving from General to Specific

It can be helpful to arrange groups of ideas in order of how general or specific they are. For instance, which of the words below is most general, which is less general, and which is most specific?

doctor   profession   surgeon

Profession is more general than *doctor.* Why? Because a doctor is one kind of profession. Likewise, *doctor* is more general than *surgeon* because a surgeon is one type of doctor.

Try arranging the following three ideas in order of how specific they are. Put a *1* in front of the most general idea, a *2* in front of the less general idea, and a *3* in front of the most specific idea. Then read the explanation that follows.

_____ aspirin   _____ pain reliever   _____ medication

Explanation:

The most general of the three ideas is *medication. Pain reliever* is less general than *medication* because it is a type of medicine. Finally, *aspirin* is the most specific idea because it is a kind of pain reliever. So the correct answers are: *3* aspirin; *2* pain reliever; *1* medication.

➤ Practice 2

Put a *1* by the most general idea in each group, a *2* by the less general idea, and a *3* by the most specific idea.

1.   _____ machine   _____ copy machine   _____ office machine

2.   _____ candy   _____ sweets   _____ chocolate kisses

3.   _____ kitchen appliance   _____ electric appliance   _____ toaster oven

4.   _____ bow tie   _____ menswear   _____ ties

5.   _____ banana   _____ tropical fruit   _____ fruit

6.   _____ uncle   _____ man   _____ Uncle George

7.   _____ liquid   _____ coffee   _____ beverage

8.   _____ national holiday   _____ holiday   _____ Thanksgiving

9.   _____ ice cream sandwich _____ frozen dessert   _____ frozen food

10. _____ Washington, D.C.   _____ city   _____ capital city

TOPICS

Finding the topic of a paragraph can help you find the main idea. The **topic** of a paragraph is the subject that it's about. To find the topic, ask yourself this simple question:

In general, who or what is this paragraph about?

Your answer to this question will be the paragraph's topic. For example, read the paragraph below. As you do so, ask yourself, "In general, who or what is this paragraph about?"

Several remedies for too much sun can be made right in your kitchen. For instance, you can soothe a case of sunburn by spreading plain yogurt over the burnt area for ten minutes. Or you can sit in cool bath water to which you have added a cup of vinegar or baking soda. If your eyes have been irritated by the sun, cover them for five minutes with chilled tea bags or cotton soaked in milk.

Now circle the letter of the item that you think is the topic. Your answer should not be too broad or too narrow. Then read the explanation that follows.

a. Using yogurt to soothe sunburn
b. Remedies for sunburn
c. Remedies

Explanation:

The topic of the paragraph is "Remedies for sunburn"; this subject is general enough to include all of the other ideas in the paragraph. "Using yogurt to soothe sunburn" is too narrow to be the topic of the paragraph. It does not cover the other remedies, such as the one with tea bags. "Remedies" is too broad—it includes remedies other than those for sunburn.

Now try finding the topic of the paragraph below. One of the subjects shown is too broad—it is too general to be the topic. Another subject is too narrow—it is too specific to be the topic. Put a *T* by the subject that is the topic of the paragraph. Also, put a *B* by the subject that is too broad and an *N* by the topic that is too narrow. Then read and complete the explanation that follows.

It's well known that trees provide shade, beauty, and wind protection, but there are also two lesser-known benefits of trees. First, trees clean the air. Their leaves actually filter out pollution in the air. One large sugar maple, for example, can remove as much pollution as is put in the air by cars burning a thousand gallons of gas. The second lesser-known benefit of trees is that they reduce stress. Experiments show that people relax more when shown scenes with trees than when shown city scenes without natural greenery.

_____ Nature

_____ Benefits of Trees

_____ Anti-Stress Benefit of Trees

Explanation:

"Benefits of Trees" is general enough to _____ all that is said about trees in the paragraph, so it is the topic *(T)*. "Nature" is too broad *(B)* to be the topic. It includes many types of natural objects other than just trees. "Anti-Stress Benefit of Trees" is too narrow *(N)*. It covers only one of the two lesser-known _____ mentioned in the paragraph. It does not cover the other benefit, which is that trees _____.

In summary, to decide if a particular subject is the topic of a passage, ask yourself these questions:

1 Does this subject include much more than what the passage is about? If so, the subject is too broad to be the topic.

2 Is there important information in the passage that isn't covered by this subject? If so, the subject is too narrow to be the topic.

➤ Practice 3

After each paragraph are three subjects. One is the topic, another is too broad to be the topic, and a third is too narrow to be the topic. Label each subject with one of the following:

> *T*—for the topic of each paragraph
> *B*—for the subject that is too broad
> *N*—for the subject that is too narrow

Then try to fill in the missing words in the explanation that follows each paragraph.

1. People who are addicted to shopping have a high need for excitement and a low self-esteem. There seem to be two types of addicted shoppers. One is the daily shopper, who cannot miss a single day at the stores. The other is the binge buyer, who goes shopping weekly to buy huge numbers of things.

   _____ Addicts

   _____ Shopping addicts

   _____ The binge buyer

The topic of this paragraph is "Shopping addicts." "Addicts" is too broad because it includes all kinds of _____, but the paragraph discusses only shopping addicts. "The binge buyer" is too narrow; it isn't general enough to _____ the other information about shopping addicts.

2. There are two main causes of headaches. Research shows that most headaches result from muscle tension. And the most common reason for that muscle tension is continuing stress. Headaches can also be caused by changes in the supply of blood to the head. Such changes are often reactions to pollen and food chemicals.

_____   Headaches

_____   Pain

_____   Muscle tension as a cause of headaches

"Pain" is too broad to be the topic of this paragraph. A paragraph with that topic would include information about pain other than _____.
But this paragraph discusses only "headaches," which is therefore its topic. "Muscle tension as a cause of headaches" is too narrow. It doesn't _____ the information about changes in the supply of blood to the head.

3. Researchers who do surveys depend on what people tell them. People, however, sometimes lie to surveyors. In one survey, for instance, people were asked if they used seat belts. Later, researchers checked to see how many people really did use their seat belts. It turned out that almost 40 percent of those who said they buckled up did not. Also, researchers once asked people about their smoking habits. Then they tested the people's saliva to find a chemical that is found in the mouths of smokers. The tests showed that 6 percent of the women and 8 percent of the men had lied about smoking.

_____   People who are surveyed

_____   People who are surveyed about smoking

_____   Research studies

The topic of this paragraph is "People who are surveyed." "People who are surveyed about smoking" is too narrow. It doesn't include the other example in the paragraph about people who were surveyed about _____
_____. "Research studies" is too broad; it covers all types of research, not just _____.

➤ *Practice 4*

After each paragraph are three subjects. One is the topic, another is too broad, and a third is too narrow. Label each subject as follows:

> *T*—for the topic of the paragraph
> *B*—for the subject that is too broad
> *N*—for the subject that is too narrow

1. Every human body has electricity. But Pauline Shaw of England has so much electricity in her body that she is destructive. She has destroyed irons, toasters, radios, and other appliances. She has also ruined over two hundred light bulbs. One scientist at Oxford University says that Shaw can produce an electric charge as high as eighty thousand volts. He believes that a rare allergy to some foods is at fault. Shaw's system breaks down these foods in a way that affects her body's electricity.

    _____ Pauline Shaw's effect on light bulbs

    _____ Pauline Shaw's life

    _____ The electricity in Pauline Shaw's body

2. Your visit to the hospital can be a helpful experience for a patient. Comfort a patient who is ill and afraid with a warm pat or by holding his or her hand. People often wonder what they should say to patients, but it is good to remember that patients often need someone to listen to them. So be a caring listener. And remember not to stay too long—people who are seriously ill tire easily.

    _____ Your visit to a patient in the hospital

    _____ Your visit to people

    _____ Listening to a hospital patient you visit

3. The crocodile and a small bird called the plover have a surprisingly friendly relationship. A crocodile's jaws are strong, and its teeth are razor sharp. Yet the plover dares to step inside the croc's mouth. You see, after eating, the crocodile opens his mouth. This allows his "living toothbrush" to step in and clean uneaten food from his teeth. In return for his service, the plover gets a free meal.

    _____ The crocodile's habits

    _____ The crocodile and the plover

    _____ Cleaning the crocodile's teeth

TOPIC SENTENCES

Finding the topic of a paragraph prepares you to find the main idea of the paragraph. Once you have found the topic, ask yourself this question:

What is the author's main point about the topic?

The answer will be the main idea. Authors often state that main idea in a sentence called a **topic sentence**. For instance, the paragraph on sunburn remedies that you have already read contains a topic sentence:

> [1]Several remedies for too much sun can be made right in your kitchen. [2]For instance, you can soothe a case of sunburn by spreading plain yogurt over the burnt area for ten minutes. [3]Or you can sit in cool bath water to which you have added a cup of vinegar or baking soda. [4]If your eyes have been irritated by the sun, cover them for five minutes with chilled tea bags or cotton soaked in milk.

As we already know, the topic of this paragraph is "remedies for sunburn." To find the topic sentence, we must ask, "What is the author's main point about remedies for sunburn?" Sentences 2–4 give specific remedies. But sentence 1 is more general—it states that several remedies for sunburn can be made in the kitchen. All the details support this idea, describing a series of remedies that can be made in the kitchen. Sentence 1 is thus the topic sentence—the umbrella statement. The other sentences support the main idea by providing specific examples.

To become skilled at finding main ideas, you need to distinguish among a paragraph's topic, main idea, and supporting details. Below is a group of four items. One is the topic, one is the main idea, and two are details that support the main idea. Label each item with one of the following:

> *T* —for the topic
> *MI*—for the main idea
> *SD*—for the supporting details

The topic will be the subject the items are about. The main idea will be the author's main point about the topic. And the supporting details will be specific ideas that help explain and clarify the main idea. After labeling each item, read the explanation.

_____ a. Countless children have learned letters and numbers from *Sesame Street*.

_____ b. For twenty years, *Sesame Street* has taught American children a great deal.

_____ c. *Sesame Street*, the children's TV show.

_____ d. The show has also covered such important topics as love, death, and marriage.

Explanation:

All of the items are about *Sesame Street*, the children's TV show. Thus the topic *(T)* is item *c*. The main idea *(MI)* is item *b*—it gives the author's main point about the topic of *Sesame Street*. Items *a* and *d* are supporting details *(SD)*; each supports the main idea by providing specific details to explain the main idea that *Sesame Street* has taught American children a great deal.

➤ Practice 5

Each group of items below includes one topic, one main idea (topic sentence), and two supporting details. In the space provided, label each item with one of the following:

> *T* —for the topic
> *MI*—for the main idea
> *SD*—for the supporting details

In addition, try to complete the explanation that follows the first group.

Group 1

_____ a. TV has begun to deal with sex in a more realistic way.

_____ b. Couples on TV now openly discuss topics such as birth control.

_____ c. Bedroom scenes are now being shown in detail on some TV shows.

_____ d. TV's treatment of sex.

Each item is about how television handles _____. So we can conclude that item *d* is the topic *(T)*. Item *a* tells us the author's main point about that topic; thus *a* is the main idea *(MI)*. Items *b* and *c* give (*general or specific?*) _____ ideas that are examples of the main idea. Thus *b* and *c* are supporting details *(SD)*.

Group 2

_____ a. If you stop carrying matches or a lighter, you can cut down on impulse smoking.

_____ b. Quitting smoking.

_____ c. You can behave in ways that help you quit smoking.

_____ d. By keeping a record of when and where you smoke, you can avoid the most tempting situations.

Group 3

_____ a. New technology will allow people to live longer and healthier lives in the twenty-first century.

_____ b. Specialists predict that the world will be a very different place in the twenty-first century.

_____ c. The twenty-first century.

_____ d. In the twenty-first century, new means of transportation will make our jets look old-fashioned.

➤ *Practice 6*

Now that you've sharpened your skills at finding a topic and the main idea about that topic, use your skills on the following full paragraphs.

First, circle the letter of the correct topic of a paragraph. Then find the sentence in which the author states the main idea about that topic, and circle the letter of the number of that topic sentence. In addition, complete the explanations after the first paragraph.

A. ¹Work-sharing can benefit both employees and employers. ²In work-sharing, full-time jobs are divided into part-time jobs shared by two or more workers. ³Working mothers, students, and those just returning to work find these positions very appealing. ⁴Employers like work-sharing too. ⁵In a two-year work-sharing project, workers had a mere 13 percent turnover rate; the usual turnover rate is 40 percent. ⁶In addition, worker productivity was greater than expected.

1. The topic is
   a. work.
   b. work-sharing.
   c. students using work-sharing.

The subject of work is too *(broad or narrow?)* _____—it covers a great deal more than just the subject of sharing work. The subject of

students using work-sharing is too *(broad or narrow?)* _____; it does not cover the other specific details in the paragraph. Two such specific details, for example, are that mothers use work-sharing and that work-sharing workers have a low turnover rate. Thus the topic is

_____, which is general enough to cover all the other material in the paragraph.

2. The main idea is in sentence
   a. 1.
   b. 3.
   c. 6.

What is the author's main point about the topic of work-sharing? The general point is that work-sharing has _____ for both _____ and _____.

B. [1]As you speak with someone, you can gather clues as to whether he or she understands you. [2]Then you can adjust what you say accordingly. [3]But when you write, you must try to foresee the reader's reactions without such clues. [4]You also have to give stronger evidence in writing than in conversation. [5]A friend may accept an unsupported statement such as "He's a lousy boss." [6]But in most writing, the reader would expect you to back up such a statement with proof. [7]Obviously, effective writing requires more attention to detail than everyday conversation.

3. The topic is
   a. speaking.
   b. writing.
   c. effective writing.

4. The main idea is in sentence
   a. 1.
   b. 5.
   c. 7.

C. [1]Male and female children are often treated and viewed differently from birth on. [2]First, boys get a blue blanket and girls get pink. [3]Also, although more male than female babies fall ill, studies say parents are more likely to consider a baby strong if it is male. [4]Similarly, parents urge boys to take part in rough-and-tumble play. [5]But parents prefer that girls watch and talk rather than be physically active. [6]When questioned, most parents say they want their sons to be successful and independent, and they want their daughters to be loving and well-behaved.

5. The topic is
   a. males and females.
   b. male and female children.
   c. childhood illness.

6. The main idea is in sentence
   a. 1.
   b. 2.
   c. 6.

CONCLUSION

In this chapter, you did the following:

- First, you worked on recognizing the difference between general and specific ideas.

- Second, you practiced distinguishing the topic of a paragraph from subjects that are too broad or too narrow.

- The first two activities prepared you for the third and the main activity of this chapter—recognizing the main idea of a paragraph as expressed in its topic sentence.

In selections made up of many paragraphs, such as articles and chapters, the overall main idea is called the *central point*. From now on, when you read longer selections in this text, you will be given practice in finding the central point, as well as in finding the main ideas of paragraphs within the reading.

The next chapter will sharpen your understanding of the specific details that authors use to support and develop their main ideas.

➤ *Review Test 1*

A. Each group of words below consists of one general idea and four specific ideas. The general idea includes all the specific ideas. Underline the general idea in each group.

1. uncle	grandmother	relative	cousin	sister
2. vanilla	flavor	chocolate	strawberry	butterscotch
3. poker	hide and seek	baseball	Monopoly	game
4. paper plates	potato salad	ants	picnic	lemonade
5. sandals	boots	sneakers	footwear	high heels
6. ghost story	armed robbery	final exam	scary experience	horror movie
7. fingerprints	hairs	clues	blood stains	ransom notes

B. In each pair below, one idea is general and the other is specific. The general idea includes the specific one. Do two things:

  (1) Underline the idea in each pair that you think is more general.
  (2) Write in one more specific idea that is covered by the general idea.

  8. sneezing   cold symptom   _____

9. tongue   mouth   _____

10. magazine   *Time*   _____

11. infancy   life stage   _____

12. length   inch   _____

13. payment   personal check _____

14. taking a hot bath relaxing activity _____

C. Each group of three items below contains three levels of ideas. Write a *1* by the most general idea in each group, a *2* by the less general idea, and a *3* by the most specific idea.

15. _____ flower _____ plant _____ lily

16. _____ winter clothing _____ wool scarf _____ clothing

17. _____ fruit _____ dried fruit _____ raisin

18. _____ *Reading Rainbow* _____ TV show _____ children's TV show

19. _____ songs _____ "Silent Night" _____ Christmas carols

20. _____ jokes _____ humor _____ knock-knock jokes

➤ *Review Test 2*

A. After each paragraph are three subjects. Label each subject with one of the following:

> *T*—for the topic of each paragraph
> *B*—for the subject that is too broad
> *N*—for the subject that is too narrow

1-3. Riding a bicycle through busy city streets isn't dangerous if riders follow a few guidelines. One is to wear a helmet to prevent head injury in case the rider falls. Another precaution is to stay off the sidewalk. Also, riders should obey traffic rules, including respecting one-way signs.

_____ Transportation safety

_____ Wearing a biker's helmet

_____ Bicycle riding in busy city streets

4-6. Despite all the criticism it gets, television has its good points. First of all, it is educational. From *Mister Rogers* to nature programs, it teaches in a colorful and interesting way. TV is also relaxing and entertaining. After a stressful day, it's restful just to put your feet up and enjoy a favorite program or a good movie.

_____ Television

_____ The media

_____ The educational side of TV

B. (7-18.) Each group of four items includes one topic, one main idea (topic sentence), and two supporting ideas. Label each item with one of the following:

> *T* —for the topic
> *MI*—for the main idea
> *SD*—for the two supporting details

Group 1

_____ a. Eye movements.

_____ b. We blink often when we are stressed, angry, or bored.

_____ c. Our eye movements reveal our state of mind.

_____ d. When we are concentrating or very interested, we blink less.

Group 2

_____ a. An older woman has useful experiences to share.

_____ b. There are advantages to marrying an older woman.

_____ c. An older woman will be more settled in her career.

_____ d. Marrying an older woman.

Group 3

_____ a. One way to address our garbage crisis is to increase the number of home composting programs.

_____ b. Our garbage crisis.

_____ c. Laws could encourage manufacturers to make products that are more recyclable.

_____ d. We must address our garbage crisis by developing more ways to reduce garbage.

C. (19-20.) Circle the letter of the correct topic of the following paragraph. Then find the sentence in which the author states the main idea about that topic and circle the letter of that topic sentence.

> [1]Speech experts recommend various tactics for dealing with children who stutter. [2]First, say the experts, speak to children slowly. [3]This will allow them time to process what they are hearing. [4]Second, don't talk so much. [5]Too much talk may actually overstimulate a child so that his mouth can't keep up with his brain. [6]Third, allow a couple of seconds between the time the child speaks and the time you begin your response. [7]Finally, don't ask a stuttering child to recite or read a long story out loud. [8]Anxiety should be minimized to lessen the stuttering.

1. The topic is
   a. speech.
   b. dealing with children who stutter.
   c. speaking slowly to stuttering children.

2. The main idea is in sentence
   a. 1.
   b. 2.
   c. 6.

➤ Review Test 3

A. To review what you've learned in this chapter, answer each of the following questions by filling in the blank or circling the letter of the answer you think is correct.

1. The supporting details are always more *(general* or *specific?)*

   _____ than the main idea.

2. The umbrella statement that covers all of the material in a paragraph is the
   a. topic.   b. topic sentence.   c. central point.

3. _____ TRUE OR FALSE? To find the main idea of a paragraph, you may find it helpful to first look for the topic.

4. When the main idea is stated in one sentence of a paragraph, that sentence is called the
   a. topic.   b. topic sentence.   c. central point.

5. For selections made up of many paragraphs, the author's overall main point is called the
   a. central topic.   b. central point.   c. topic sentence.

B. Here is a chance to apply your understanding of main ideas to a full-length selection. First, read the following piece by a Vietnamese immigrant, Andrew Lam. Lam is associate editor for the Pacific News Service. In this article, he compares some American and Vietnamese views on life and death. After reading the selection, answer the questions that follow on topics, main ideas, and the central point. There are also vocabulary questions to help you continue working on vocabulary in context.

Words to Watch

Following are some words in the reading that do not have strong context support. Each word is followed by the number of the paragraph in which it appears and its meaning there. These words are indicated in the story by a small circle (°).

Tet (1): the Vietnamese lunar New Year festival
shield (2): cover up
reassuring (2): comforting
quips (2): jokes
disjointed (4): disconnected
pang (6): deeply felt pain
filial (6): due from a son or daughter
piety (6): devotion to and honor of family
evading (9): avoiding
feeble (9): weak
embellished (10): exaggerated
satirized (10): made fun of
monsoon rain (13): seasonal heavy rains in Asia

THEY SHUT MY GRANDMOTHER'S ROOM DOOR

Andrew Lam

When someone died in the convalescent home where my   1
grandmother lives, the nurses rush to close all the patients' doors.
Though as a policy death is not to be seen at the home, she can always
tell when it visits. The series of doors being slammed shut remind her
of the firecrackers during Tet°.

The nurses' efforts to shield° death are more comical to my   2
grandmother than reassuring°. "Those old ladies die so often," she
quips° in Vietnamese, "every day's like new year."

Still, it is lonely to die in such a place. I imagine some wasted old   3
body under a white sheet being carted silently through the empty
corridor on its way to the morgue. While in America a person may be

born surrounded by loved ones, in old age one is often left to take the last leg of life's journey alone.

Perhaps that is why my grandmother talks now mainly of her hometown, Bac-Lieu; its river and green rich rice fields. Having lost everything during the war, she can now offer me only her distant memories: Life was not disjointed° back home; one lived in a gentle rhythm with the land; people died in their homes surrounded by neighbors and relatives. And no one shut your door.

So it goes. The once gentle, connected world of the past is but the language of dreams. In this fast-paced society of disjointed lives, we are swept along and have little time left for spiritual comfort. Instead of relying on neighbors and relatives, on the river and land, we deal with the language of materialism: overtime, stress, down payment, credit cards, tax shelter. Instead of going to the temple to pray for good health we pay life and health insurance religiously.

My grandmother's children and grandchildren share a certain pang° of guilt. After a stroke which paralyzed her, we could no longer keep her at home. And although we visit her regularly, we are not living up to the filial° piety° standard expected of us in the old country. My father silently grieves and my mother suffers from headaches. (Does she see herself in such a home in a decade or two?)

Once, a long time ago, living in Vietnam we used to stare death in the face. The war in many ways had heightened our sensibilities toward living and dying. I can still hear the wails of widows and grieving mothers. Though the fear of death and dying is a universal one, the Vietnamese did not hide from it. Instead, we dwelt in its tragedy. Death pervaded our poems, novels, fairy tales and songs.

But if agony and pain are part of Vietnamese culture, pleasure is at the center of America's culture. While Vietnamese holidays are based on death anniversaries, birthdays are celebrated here. American popular culture translates death with something like nauseating humor. People laugh and scream at blood and guts movies. The wealthy freeze their dead relatives in liquid nitrogen. Cemeteries are places of big business, complete with colorful brochures. I hear there are even drive-by funerals where you don't have to get out of your own car to pay your respects to the deceased.

That America relies upon the pleasure principle and happy endings in its entertainments does not, however, assist us in evading° suffering. The reality of the suffering of old age is apparent in the convalescent home. There is an old man, once an accomplished concert pianist, now rendered helpless by arthritis. Every morning he sits staring at the piano. One feeble° woman who outlived her children keeps repeating, "My son will take me home." Then there are those mindless, bedridden bodies kept alive through a series of tubes and pulsating machines.

But despair is not newsworthy. Death itself must be embellished° 10 or satirized° or deep-frozen in order to catch the public's attention.

Last week on her eighty-second birthday I went to see my 11 grandmother. She smiled her sweet sad smile.

"Where will you end up in your old age?" she asked me, her mind 12 as sharp as ever.

The memories of monsoon rain° and tropical sun and relatives 13 and friends came to mind. Not here, not here, I wanted to tell her. But the soft moaning of a patient next door and the smell of alcohol wafting from the sterile corridor brought me back to reality.

"Anywhere is fine," I told her instead, trying to keep up with her 14 courageous spirit. "All I am asking for is that they don't shut my door."

Reading Comprehension Questions

Vocabulary in Context

1. The word *wails* in "I can still hear the wails of widows and grieving mothers" (paragraph 7) means
   a. joking.
   b. cries.
   c. delays.
   d. suggestions.

2. The word *pervaded* in "Though the fear of death and dying is a universal one, the Vietnamese did not hide from it. . . . Death pervaded our poems, novels, fairy tales, and songs" (paragraph 7) means
   a. filled.
   b. ignored.
   c. stopped.
   d. escaped.

3. The word *rendered* in "There is an old man, once an accomplished concert pianist, now rendered helpless by arthritis" (paragraph 9) means
   a. happy to be.
   b. no longer.
   c. made.
   d. willing to be.

4. The word *wafting* in "the soft moaning of a patient next door and the smell of alcohol wafting from the sterile corridor brought me back to reality" (paragraph 13) means
   a. absent.
   b. smelling pleasant.
   c. causing illness.
   d. drifting through the air.

Central Point

5. Which of the following is the topic of the entire selection?
   a. Life in Vietnam.
   b. The Vietnamese and American views of death.
   c. Escaping the suffering of old age.
   d. War's effect on a people's view of death.

6. Which sentence best expresses the central point of the selection?
   a. Dying in a convalescent home can be lonely.
   b. In Vietnam, life and death were not disconnected.
   c. The war made the Vietnamese more aware of death and dying.
   d. While death is an accepted part of life in Vietnam, in America death is hidden or altered.

Main Ideas

7. The topic of paragraph 6 is
   a. the guilt felt by the grandmother's children and grandchildren.
   b. the reason the grandmother is in a home.
   c. the number of visits made to the home.
   d. how moving to a new country changes people's behavior.

8. The main idea of paragraph 6 is expressed in its
   a. first sentence.
   b. second sentence.
   c. next-to-last sentence.
   d. last sentence.

9. The topic of paragraph 9 is
   a. the pleasure principle in America.
   b. America's escape from suffering.
   c. the reality of the suffering of old age.
   d. keeping people alive longer.

10. The main idea of paragraph 9 is expressed in its
    a. second sentence.
    b. third sentence.
    c. fourth sentence.
    d. last sentence.

Mapping Activity

The author compares the way Americans and Vietnamese view and deal with death. On the left are his main comments on death in Vietnam. On the right, fill in the two missing contrasting comments on death in America.

Central point: Americans treat death very differently than the Vietnamese.

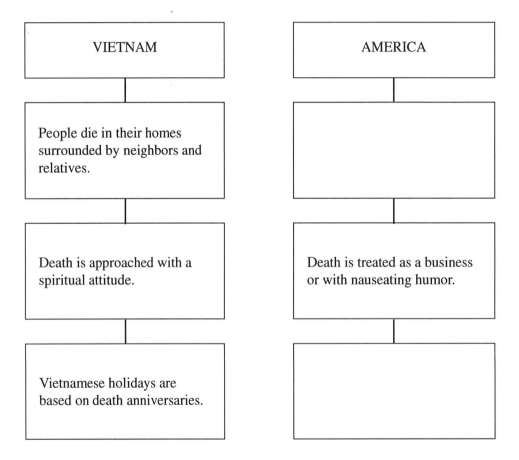

Discussion Questions

1. Do you agree that Americans try to hide death and often deal with it "with something like nauseating humor"? How has death been handled in your family?

2. Lam says that his grandmother's children and grandchildren feel guilty about putting her in a home. Should they feel guilty? What other options might there be for caring for an elderly family member?

Writing Activities

1. Lam writes that the rhythm of life in Vietnam was gentle and that people there felt connected to their neighbors and relatives. In contrast, he states, Americans live a less connected, fast-paced life. How connected do you feel to your neighbors, friends, and relatives? How fast-paced is your life? Write a paper explaining how your life does or does not fit in with Lam's observations about America. Use detailed examples throughout.

2. What would you say to the author or to his grandmother if you had the chance? Write a letter to either, explaining your thoughts and feelings about some points in the reading. Use whatever tone you feel—anger, sympathy, pity, admiration, and so on.

Check Your Performance   **MAIN IDEAS**

Activity	Number Right	Points	Total
Review Test 1 (20 items)	_____	x 1.5 =	_____
Review Test 2 (20 items)	_____	x 1.5 =	_____
Review Test 3, Part A (5 items)	_____	x 2 =	_____
Review Test 3, Part B (10 items)	_____	x 2 =	_____
Mapping (2 items)	_____	x 5 =	_____

TOTAL SCORE = _____%

Enter your total score into the reading performance chart on the inside back cover.

4

Supporting Details

The last chapter introduced you to the most important reading skill—the ability to find the main idea. This skill cannot be mastered unless you understand another essential reading skill—locating *supporting details*. These details provide the added information that is needed for you to make sense of a main idea.

WHAT ARE SUPPORTING DETAILS?

Supporting details are reasons, examples, steps, or other kinds of factual evidence that develop and support a main idea. To see how details support a given main idea, it helps to contrast them with details that do not support that main idea.

For example, read the topic sentence below. Two of the three statements under it are **reasons** that support the main idea. One statement does not support the main idea. Circle the one statement that *does not* support the main idea. Then read the explanation that follows.

Topic sentence: I prefer reading to watching television.

a. Reading excites my imagination; television does not.
b. Reading, like television, can inform me about the world.
c. Reading challenges me to think; television does not.

Explanation:

Which sentence does not support the main idea? The answer is sentence *b*. The other two sentences develop the main idea—they are reasons the author prefers reading to watching television. Sentence *b* does not state a reason for the author's preference of reading over television.

Below are another topic sentence and another list. Two of the three statements in the list are **examples** that support the main idea. One statement does not support the main idea. Circle the one statement that *does not* support the main idea. Then read the explanation that follows.

Topic sentence: When you adopt a puppy, you take on continuing financial responsibilities.

a. Dog food can easily cost more than $25 a month.
b. You will need to pay for annual shots at the vet's office.
c. A dog needs to be played with and walked during the day.

Explanation:

Which sentence does not support the main idea? The answer is sentence *c*. The other two sentences support the main idea by giving in detail two of the financial responsibilities of a dog owner. Since sentence *c* has nothing to do with financial responsibilities, it does not support the main point.

Here are a third topic sentence and another list. Two of the three statements in the list are **steps** that support the main idea. Circle the one statement that *does not* support the main idea. Then read the explanation that follows.

Topic sentence: There is a way to make peeling an onion easier.

a. First, cut off the top and bottom and put the onions in boiling water for about a minute.
b. Then drain and simply pull off the outer skin, which will now be loose.
c. The onions can then be cooked in a variety of ways, from baking to microwaving.

Explanation:

Which sentence does not support the main idea? The answer is sentence *c*. The other two sentences develop the main idea by providing two specific steps for making it easier to peel an onion. While sentence *c* is true, it has nothing to do with how to peel an onion.

The examples above should have helped you see how supporting details develop a main idea. They tell us about the main idea in more detail. The following exercises will help you better understand the relationship between a main idea and the details that support it.

➤ *Practice 1*

Each topic sentence below is followed by a list of three other sentences. Circle the letter of the one sentence that *does not* support the main idea.

Hint: To decide whether or not a sentence supports a main idea, ask yourself this question: "Does this sentence give details that make the main idea clear? Or does it introduce a completely new point?" If the sentence makes the main idea clearer, it is a supporting detail. If the sentence puts forth a new point, it does not support the main idea.

1. *Topic sentence:* Celebrities often lend support to causes they believe in.
   a. Willie Nelson has tried to help farmers with a series of concerts.
   b. Ted Danson is leading a crusade to stop polluting the oceans.
   c. There is little evidence that celebrity support does any good.

2. *Topic sentence:* Living in Los Angeles can be hazardous to your health.
   a. There are 10 million people living in Los Angeles.
   b. Smog, which can cause problems with breathing, is worse in Los Angeles than in any other city in the country.
   c. Earthquakes in Los Angeles can cause injury and even death.

3. *Topic sentence:* There are several packing tips that can make traveling easier.
   a. A poor job of packing can mean wrinkled clothes and mismatched outfits.
   b. Pack clothing to be worn first on top and clothing to be worn last on the bottom.
   c. Packing around a basic color makes shirts, ties, and socks interchangeable.

4. *Topic sentence:* It is not unusual for entertainers to change their names as they start their careers.
   a. Michael Landon's original name was Eugene Orowitz.
   b. Stefanie Powers's real name is Zofja Federkiewicz.
   c. Michelle Pfeiffer decided not to change her name.

5. *Topic sentence:* The population of the United States has been shifting from the North and Northeast to the South and Southwest.
   a. The climate in the South and Southwest is more pleasant than in the North and Northeast.
   b. The populations of Washington and Oregon have also grown in recent years.
   c. Companies have built factories in the South and Southwest, creating many jobs.

➤ *Practice 2*

The topic sentence of each of the following paragraphs is **boldfaced**. Locate and write down the number of the one sentence in each paragraph that *does not* support the main idea. Read the entire paragraph before making your decision.

1. ¹**Local clubs needing to make money can do so in many ways.** ²For instance, a baked-goods sale usually attracts many customers. ³A yard sale is also a good choice as it lets clubs offer a broad selection of items at discount prices. ⁴A talent show will let members show off their talents and provide the audience with a fun time. ⁵And remember, local clubs should not exclude members on the basis of sex.

   The sentence that *does not* support the main idea: _____

2. ¹**If you take brisk walks for exercise, there are important guidelines you should follow.** ²Your clothes should be comfortable and appropriate for the weather. ³You should walk in a safe location, away from traffic. ⁴Walking has become a popular activity, especially for older people. ⁵Finally, your shoes should fit properly and be right for the surface you will be walking on.

   The sentence that *does not* support the main idea: _____

3. ¹**Personal computers are a helpful tool for the successful college student.** ²Organizing notes can be done quickly on a personal computer. ³Computers have come down in price in recent years. ⁴Preparing essays and term papers is easier with a personal computer. ⁵Math and accounting projects take less time when a personal computer is used.

   The sentence that *does not* support the main idea: _____

4. ¹**There are important safety rules on commercial airplanes.** ²Unfortunately, many passengers pay no attention to the rules. ³Seat belts must be securely fastened. ⁴Tray tables must be locked, and seat backs must be in an upright position. ⁵If an oxygen mask appears, it must be placed over the face and fastened behind the head.

   The sentence that *does not* support the main idea: _____

5. ¹**Telephones have changed from relatively simple instruments to electronic wonders that make life easier.** ²For example, with "call-forwarding," we don't have to be home to receive a call. ³Portable phones let people talk with each other from such places as golf courses and fishing boats. ⁴Phones also come in a wide variety of colors and shapes. ⁵Thanks to cellular phones, we can even talk to people from our automobiles.

   The sentence that *does not* support the main idea: _____

READING CAREFULLY

To clearly understand the main idea of a selection, you need to carefully read the supporting details. Your understanding will also be strengthened by noting the relationship of the main idea and its supporting details.

Read the following paragraph closely, and answer the questions about it. The topic sentence (main idea) is boldfaced. Then read the explanation that follows.

> [1]Until recently, little has been done to stop the destruction of the Brazilian rain forests. [2]**Now, however, the government of Brazil is finally taking action against those who are illegally cutting down its forests.** [3]Companies that have cut down trees without a permit are being heavily fined. [4]Airplane landing strips of lawless lumber companies have been bombed. [5]Individuals caught cutting trees illegally have been jailed.

1. _____ TRUE OR FALSE? Companies illegally destroying Brazilian rain forests can now expect to be fined for their actions.

2. The answer to question 1 can be found in sentence
   a. 1.
   b. 3.
   c. 4.
   d. 5.

3. The idea below is
   a. true according to the paragraph.
   b. false according to the paragraph.
   c. not mentioned in the paragraph.

   Brazil is fighting the destruction of its rain forests because of pressure from environmental groups.

4. *Circle the letter of the missing detail:* The government of Brazil has bombed the _____ of lumber companies cutting trees illegally.
   a. trees
   b. landing strips
   c. workers

Explanation:

1. A careful reading of the paragraph reveals that the answer to this question is *true*.

2. The answer to question 1 can be found in sentence 3, which states that Brazil is heavily fining companies that have illegally cut down trees.

3. The paragraph does not say whether or not Brazil is responding to pressure from environmental groups. Thus, the answer is *c*.

4. Sentence 4 tells us that Brazil has bombed the landing strips of lumber companies cutting trees illegally. If you chose *b*, you are correct.

By now, you probably realize that finding the details which support the main idea requires careful reading on your part. The more thinking you do as you read, the easier it is to locate important supporting details.

➤ *Practice 3*

Answer the questions that follow the paragraphs. The topic sentence of each paragraph is boldfaced.

A. [1]A government study has shown that illiteracy leads to a life of crime. [2]**Therefore a new prison program encourages prisoners to improve their reading.** [3]Incoming prisoners are given a reading test. [4]Those who cannot read at an acceptable level are given classes to raise their reading ability at least to the eighth-grade level. [5]Inmates who refuse to participate have privileges taken away. [6]Prisoners who participate in the program are given the best prison jobs. [7]Those who pass the test are encouraged to enroll in college classes.

1. _____ TRUE OR FALSE? Incoming prisoners are tested to find out how well they read.

2. The answer to question 1 can be found in sentence
   a. 1.
   b. 3.
   c. 4.
   d. 7.

3. The idea below is
   a. true according to the paragraph.
   b. false according to the paragraph.
   c. not mentioned in the paragraph.

   Most prisoners refuse to participate in the reading program.

4. Prisoners who participate in the program are given
   a. the best jobs at the prison.
   b. more free time to do what they want.
   c. an early release.

5. Incoming prisoners who pass the reading test are encouraged to
   a. earn more privileges.
   b. take college classes.
   c. teach fellow prisoners.

B.   [1]**There are many causes of polluted air, which is a health hazard to humans, animals, and plants.** [2]Pollution from the smokestacks of industries that burn high-sulfur coal causes acid rain, which kills trees and lakes. [3]Auto exhaust dirties our air with chemicals. [4]Even refrigerators and air conditioners contribute to pollution. [5]They leak chemicals that destroy Earth's ozone layer. [6]This lets in harmful rays from the sun, which increases the risk of skin cancer.

6. _____ TRUE OR FALSE? Auto exhaust includes chemicals that dirty the air.

7. The answer to question 1 can be found in sentence
    a. 2.
    b. 3.
    c. 5.
    d. 6.

8. The idea below is
    a. true according to the paragraph.
    b. false according to the paragraph.
    c. not mentioned in the paragraph.

    Auto exhaust is the worst polluter of all.

9. Refrigerators leak
    a. high-sulfur coal fumes.
    b. harmful rays.
    c. chemicals that destroy the ozone layer.

10. *Circle the letter of the missing detail:* Destruction of the ozone layer lets in _____ that increase the risk of skin cancer.
    a. dirty air
    b. chemicals
    c. harmful rays from the sun

CONCLUSION

The activities in this chapter help show that better reading depends upon an awareness of a main idea *and* the details that support it. You are now ready to go on to deepen your understand of main ideas. The next two chapters will help you to do this. You will then work on a chapter that will strengthen your understanding of supporting details.

➤ *Review Test 1*

A. Each topic sentence below is followed by a list of three other sentences. Circle the letter of the one sentence that *does not* support the main idea.

1. *Topic sentence:* Parades are held on many holidays in America.
    a. Parades are often televised.
    b. Veterans' Day parades are held in cities and towns from coast to coast.
    c. Parades are common on Thanksgiving, Christmas, New Year's Day, and the Fourth of July.

2. *Topic sentence:* Because of its different climates, Hawaii's Big Island has been referred to as a "mini-continent."
    a. Skiing can be done on the slopes of the Mauna Kea mountain.
    b. The Big Island is the largest of the Hawaiian Islands.
    c. A tropical rain forest can be found on the windward side of the island.

B. The topic sentence of each of the following paragraphs is boldfaced. Choose the number of the one sentence that does *not* support the main idea. Write it in the space provided. Read the entire paragraph before making your decision.

3. ¹**Support groups can help people get over personal problems or tragedies.** ²People who run support groups often volunteer their time. ³Alcoholics Anonymous provides assistance for individuals who have a drinking problem. ⁴There are also groups for those who have been sexually abused and people suffering from drug dependency.

    The sentence that *does not* support the main idea: _____

4. ¹**Many men and women are still not entirely comfortable with the idea of females asking males out on dates.** ²Some women fear they will appear to be too "forward" if they ask a man out. ³Some men are afraid that being asked out makes them appear somehow less than masculine. ⁴Nevertheless, there are still many guys and gals who are glad it's now more socially acceptable for women to ask men on dates.

    The sentence that *does not* support the main idea: _____

5. ¹**Bats are a lot less horrible than people imagine them to be.** ²Most bats feed on insects, fruit, and nectar. ³The vampire bat, however, uses its razor-sharp teeth to nick animals and, occasionally, sleeping people. ⁴Many people believe that bats cruelly attack humans for no reason at all, yet bats are quite timid. ⁵They bite only when threatened.

    The sentence that *does not* support the main idea: _____

➤ *Review Test 2*

Answer the questions that follow the paragraphs. The topic sentence of each paragraph is boldfaced.

A.   ¹High-tension jobs have made stress a fact of life for many Americans. ²**People use various activities to combat stress.** ³Some turn to alcohol, thinking it will relax them. ⁴For others, sports such as tennis and golf help to release the tension which has built up. ⁵Still others opt for a little "quiet time," in which they do things like meditate or take a long hot bath. ⁶And then there are those who have discovered that a deep massage will relax muscles and refresh the mind and spirit.

1. _____ TRUE OR FALSE? Some people believe alcohol is relaxing.

2. The answer to question 1 can be found in sentence
   a. 3.
   b. 4.
   c. 5.
   d. 6.

3. The idea below is
   a. true according to the paragraph.
   b. false according to the paragraph.
   c. not mentioned in the paragraph.

   Some people use sports to combat stress.

4. *Circle the letter of the missing detail:* According to the paragraph, _____ will relax muscles and refresh the mind and spirit.
   a. alcohol
   b. a hot bath
   c. a deep massage

5. Quiet activities used to relieve stress include
   a. meditation.
   b. a long hot bath.
   c. both of the above.

B.   ¹The economy alternates between "good times" and "bad times." ²**Following certain financial guidelines can help people get through bad economic times.** ³Drawing up a budget and sticking to it is a big help. ⁴Paying credit card bills in full will keep debts low. ⁵Putting aside emergency cash to cover at least three months' expenses will also help. ⁶This emergency money should be in a place where it can be reached quickly, like a bank account. ⁷Finally, having a "crisis borrowing plan" is wise. ⁸Such a plan could involve borrowing money from a relative or opening a home-equity line of credit.

6. _____ TRUE OR FALSE? According to the author, paying credit card bills in full each month can help during bad economic times.

7. The answer to question 6 can be found in sentence
   a. 2.
   b. 3.
   c. 4.
   d. 5.

8. The idea below is
   a. true according to the paragraph.
   b. false according to the paragraph.
   c. not mentioned in the paragraph.

   The country is now going through difficult economic times.

9. Emergency cash should be available to cover
   a. credit card expenses.
   b. at least three months' expenses.
   c. the possibility that relatives may want to borrow money.

10. Opening a home-equity line of credit, according to the passage, would
    a. provide emergency cash for at least three months' expenses.
    b. be part of a "crisis borrowing plan."
    c. be a first step toward fixing up a home.

➤ Review Test 3

A. To review what you've learned in this chapter, answer each of the following questions. Fill in the blank, or circle the letter of the answer you think is correct.

   1. Supporting details may
      a. explain main ideas.
      b. illustrate main ideas.
      c. prove main ideas.
      d. all of the above.

   2. _____ TRUE OR FALSE? Supporting details are more specific than main ideas.

   3. Supporting details may be
      a. reasons.
      b. examples.
      c. steps.
      d. all of the above.

   4. _____ TRUE OR FALSE? Noting the main idea and supporting details helps you to see the relationship between ideas.

B. Here is a chance to apply your understanding of supporting details to a full-length selection. First, read the following true story by a woman who began her college education at age 38. She tells of frightening experiences she had to overcome in order to reach that point. After reading the selection, answer the questions that follow on supporting details. To help you continue to strengthen your work on skills taught in earlier chapters, there are also questions on vocabulary in context and main ideas.

Words to Watch

Following are some words in the reading that do not have strong context support. Each word is followed by the number of the paragraph in which it appears and its meaning there. These words are indicated in the story by a small circle (°).

> *agenda* (3): schedule
> *deranged* (4): insane
> *stalking* (4): following with the intent to do harm
> *periodically* (5): again and again

DETERMINED TO SUCCEED

Regina Lynn Rayder

I am thirty-eight years old, and I just completed my first semester   1
at Roane State Community College. I passed with a grade point average of 4.0. I have had to overcome many obstacles along the way in order to get to where I am today. I am also looking forward to my next semester in January.

To begin with, I was unable to attend high school because I had   2
been expelled for disruptive behavior when I was in junior high school. I had staged a riot because girls were not allowed to attend school wearing slacks. I had to walk about four miles to school every day, and I would get so cold that my bare legs would chap and bleed, and so I refused to wear a dress. I was expelled from school because I started wearing slacks and had gotten many of the other girls to follow my example. As a result, the rest of the students sided with me and refused to return to school. All the students in school couldn't be expelled, so we had won the battle. We were allowed to wear slacks. There was other disruptive behavior from me also. For example, I would sometimes take food from the cafeteria because my family was very poor and I never had enough to eat. The one free meal a day that I

would eat at school was all I would have until the next meal the following day. When I would get caught, I got a paddling and would have to stay after school for a week as punishment. I was very skinny and I had to be at school every day in order to eat, so I would try and take my mind off the hunger pains by concentrating on learning. I made good grades and was looking forward to high school, but I was not allowed to attend. When I went to register for high school, the principal called me into his office and said because of my disruptive behavior in junior high school that I would not be accepted.

I left school and studied on my own and was able to obtain a   3
General Equivalency Diploma. The next step on my agenda° was to go to college. I was twenty years old, and I had made all the necessary preparations in order to attend. I had taken the entry exam, which I passed, and had gotten my schedule for classes.

When I arrived home from the college that day, a deranged° man   4
was waiting on me. He had been stalking° me for a year and had raped me a few months before. He put me out of commission for the next three weeks. When he first raped me in July of 1975, I had become pregnant. Near the last week in October he broke into my home to rape me again, and he shot me through the chest and through the left wrist. I was in the hospital in intensive care for eight days. My left lung had collapsed from the .357 Magnum bullet that had penetrated it. The baby that I was pregnant with was four months matured and threatening to miscarry. I was hemorrhaging so much that I had to receive many blood transfusions. As a result, I was very weak, and it would take me about a year to regain the use of my left arm.

He raped me two weeks after my baby was born and would   5
continue to rape me periodically° for the next four years. He was always very brutal, and he always used a gun. It was impossible for me to escape this man because he was best friends with the city judge, who was very powerful, and anything he did was always "taken care of." I had called the Tennessee Bureau of Investigation, but somehow the judge found out about the call and I was "persuaded" to keep my mouth shut. Between him and the judge and a few men on the police force, I didn't have a chance. I confided in a man I knew about what was happening to me, and he tried to help. He protected me for about a month before they shot him in the back one night. I was forced to go with the murderer to get rid of the gun. The murder is still on record as unsolved. I wanted to talk with the Federal Bureau of Investigation, but I never did because they hurt me so badly when I talked with the Tennessee Bureau of Investigation. Since they found out I had talked about it, I didn't know who I could trust.

I was still trying to get an education, and I was accepted into a nursing program at an area vocational school. I had finished about four months when the rapes started again. This man was insane, and I was trapped. He would do a lot of crazy things such as put one bullet in the gun and spin the chamber, then hold it against my head and pull the trigger. He would beat me and handcuff me to the bed and put a piece of cloth in my mouth and tie another around my head to keep that one in. I was afraid I would vomit and drown or that I would start to cry and my nose would stop up so I wouldn't be able to breathe. He would keep me like this for hours while he raped and tortured me, and he would describe in detail how he was going to kill me. I was beginning to miss school because he would sometimes play his sick games for days. I was finally dismissed from school because I missed too many days. (Six months of training "down the drain" left me devastated.)

6

I decided to make another attempt to get away from this man. I wanted to live so badly, but I couldn't endure any more of his torture. The next time he pushed his way into my home and put the gun to my head, I calmly turned and walked out of the door. He had hit me with the gun, I suppose, because I was bleeding and my vision had blurred. He yelled for me to stop or he would kill me. I just kept walking. I heard him cock the gun, and I felt the bullet as it whizzed past my head. I expected at any moment for him to shoot me in the back, but I just kept walking. He fired the gun again as I opened my car door, and I got in and drove away. I got married a month after that incident, to a man I hardly knew and didn't care anything about. I just didn't want to be by myself when that monster came back. I was twenty-five years old.

7

When I turned thirty-three, I was on my own again with four children and no way to support them. I turned to government assistance and was trying to get into a position to attempt college again. Finally, after five years, my youngest child was in school and I had saved enough money for a used car. I was finally able to attend college. Now I look forward to everything, and I am determined to make my life better. I also want to help my children become productive adults. I watched my oldest child graduate last year, and my sixteen-year-old will graduate this year. My eight- and nine-year-old children have made the honor roll at school every year. I do all I can to ensure that they are intellectually motivated. For example, my nine-year-old has taken a computer class for a month each summer for the last two years. My sixteen-year-old volunteers as a substitute teacher a few hours a week during her study time at school. She has access to all the computers and other machines and knows how to operate them. I take her to the college I attend on Saturdays, and she has taught me all she knows

8

about the computer. We study at the library, and she helps me "brush up" on using the different indexes and the different machines. She does a lot of her school work at the college, and when she goes to college this fall, she will be familiar with the surroundings.

Finally, I am where I want to be, and I look forward to each day. I   9
don't worry about the man who raped me because I haven't seen him in thirteen years, and the judge who protected him is dead. All of the obstacles I have had to overcome in order to get to college have made me more determined to succeed. I am finally taking charge of my life.

Reading Comprehension Questions

Vocabulary in Context

1. The word *disruptive* in "I had been expelled for disruptive behavior. . . . I started wearing slacks and had gotten many of the other girls to follow my example" (paragraph 2) means
   a. weak.
   b. definite.
   c. disturbing.
   d. violent.

2. The words *confided in* in "I confided in a man I knew about what was happening to me, and he tried to help" (paragraph 5) mean
   a. shared secrets with.
   b. lied to.
   c. yelled at.
   d. prayed to.

3. The word *devastated* in "I was finally dismissed from school because I missed too many days. (Six months of training 'down the drain' left me devastated)" (paragraph 6) means
   a. satisfied.
   b. crushed.
   c. hopeful.
   d. unaffected.

4. The word *endure* in "I wanted to live so badly, but I couldn't endure any more of his torture" (paragraph 7) means
   a. understand.
   b. remember.
   c. refuse.
   d. bear.

Central Point

5. Which sentence from the reading comes closest to expressing the central point of the entire selection?
   a. "I have had to overcome many obstacles along the way in order to get to where I am today."
   b. "I left school and studied on my own and was able to obtain a General Equivalency Diploma."
   c. "Six months of training 'down the drain' left me devastated."
   d. "I decided to make another attempt to get away from this man."

Main Ideas

6. The main idea of paragraph 2 is expressed in its
   a. first sentence.
   b. second sentence.
   c. third sentence.
   d. fourth sentence.

Supporting Details

7. The supporting details of paragraph 2 are
   a. parts of an average day for Rayder in junior high school.
   b. Rayder's "misbehavior" in junior high school and the school's reactions.
   c. information about Rayder's taste in clothing and in food.
   d. all of the above.

8. According to the selection, the man who tried to protect Rayder
   a. fathered her child.
   b. left her.
   c. was murdered.
   d. worked for the Tennessee Bureau of Investigation.

9. At age 25, the author finally decided
   a. to shoot her attacker.
   b. not to put up with her attacker's torture any longer.
   c. to marry her attacker.
   d. to turn to government assistance to support her children.

10. According to the selection, the rapist
    a. was the father of two of the author's children.
    b. was finally caught and put in jail.
    c. killed himself.
    d. no longer worries the author.

Mapping Activity

This selection is organized by time: first one thing happened, then another, and so on. Four of the major events are scrambled in the list below. Write them in the boxes of the diagram in the correct order.

- Rayder earns her General Equivalency Diploma.
- Rayder is not allowed to enter high school.
- Rayder decides she can no longer endure her rapist's torture.
- The man who tries to protect Rayder is murdered.

Central point: Regina Lynn Rayder had to overcome some difficult obstacles in order to attend college.

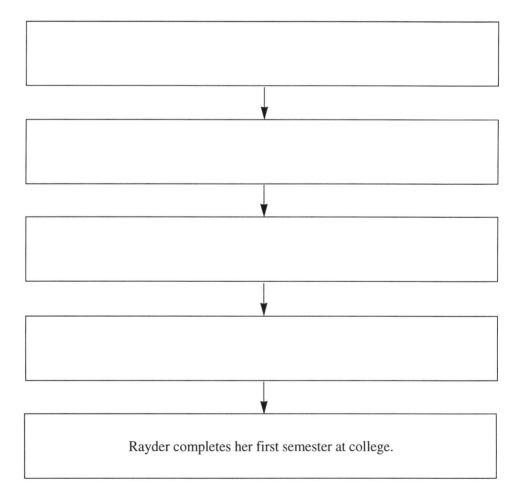

Rayder completes her first semester at college.

Discussion Questions

1. When Rayder decided that she could not endure her rapist's torture any longer, she simply walked away, even though he was shooting at her. Do you think this was the right way to handle the situation? Why or why not? Is there anything else she could have done?

2. Judging by the reading, what kind of person is Rayder? Explain which details of the reading support each quality you name.

Writing Activities

1. Write a paragraph explaining one or more ways to reduce sexual abuse in our society. Focus on what can be done by either parents, schools, or communities. Provide specific examples for each point you make. You might begin your paper like this: "Sexual abuse would probably be reduced if parents (*or* schools *or* communities) . . . "

2. Rayder had to overcome a number of obstacles in order to attend college. Write a paper about the obstacles you faced in order to get to college and how you dealt with them.

Check Your Performance   **SUPPORTING DETAILS**

Activity	Number Right	Points	Total
Review Test 1 (5 items)	_____	x 4 =	_____
Review Test 2 (10 items)	_____	x 3 =	_____
Review Test 3, Part A (4 items)	_____	x 2.5 =	_____
Review Test 3, Part B (10 items)	_____	x 3 =	_____
Mapping (4 items)	_____	x 2.5 =	_____

TOTAL SCORE = _____%

Enter your total score into the reading performance chart on the inside back cover.

5

Locations of
Main Ideas

The topic sentence, which expresses the main idea, may appear anywhere within a paragraph. Most of the topic sentences you have seen so far have been located in the first sentence of a paragraph. But the topic sentence may appear elsewhere. This chapter describes common locations of topic sentences. It then provides practice in finding the topic sentence in a series of paragraphs. By the end of the chapter, you should have a solid sense of how to locate topic sentences.

Note: Be sure to remember that a topic sentence is a general statement that covers most or all of the material in a paragraph.

TOPIC SENTENCE AT THE START OF A PARAGRAPH

Topic Sentence
Supporting Detail
Supporting Detail
Supporting Detail
Supporting Detail

Authors often begin a paragraph with the main idea. The rest of the paragraph then supports the main idea with details. Here is an example:

My desk is well organized. I keep pencils and pens in the top left drawer. Typing and writing paper are in the middle left drawer. The bottom left side has all the other supplies I might need, from paper clips to staples. The top of the desk is clear, except for a study light and a blotter. The right side of the desk has two drawers. The bottom one is a file drawer, where I keep my notes for each class. And in the top drawer? That's where I keep nuts, raisins, and M&M's that I snack on while I work.

Explanation:

> This paragraph follows a very common pattern: The first sentence is a general statement. The rest of the paragraph supports the general statement. The main idea—that the writer's desk is well organized—is in the first sentence. The rest of the sentences provide specific supporting details. They show us just how well organized the desk is.

TOPIC SENTENCE WITHIN A PARAGRAPH

> | |
> |---|
> | Introductory Detail |
> | **Topic Sentence** |
> | Supporting Detail |
> | Supporting Detail |
> | Supporting Detail |

When the topic sentence is within a paragraph, it often follows one or more introductory sentences. Those sentences lead up in some way to the main idea. They may introduce the topic of the paragraph, catch the reader's interest, relate the main idea to a previous paragraph, or give background for the main idea. Below is an example of a paragraph with a topic sentence that is not first or last. See if you can find it. Write its number in the blank space.

> [1]Do you know what to do if you have trouble sleeping? [2]In many cases, sleep problems can be avoided by following a few simple guidelines. [3]First, don't drink alcoholic beverages or drinks with caffeine close to bedtime. [4]Next, do not exercise within three hours of bedtime. [5]Finally, plan a sleep routine. [6]Go to bed at the same time and get up at the same time.

Topic sentence: _____

Explanation:

> The first sentence introduces the topic of sleep problems by asking a question. A question can *never* be a topic sentence. It is only asking something—it is not making a statement. The second sentence states the author's main idea about that topic—that sleep problems can often be avoided by following a few simple guidelines. The rest of the paragraph lists the specific guidelines referred to only generally in the topic sentence.

Topic sentences within paragraphs are often second sentences, as in the example above. But they may come even later than the second sentence. See if you can find the topic sentence in the following paragraph. Then write its number in the space provided.

¹Today we take world-wide communications for granted. ²Through TV and radio, we learn almost instantly what happens throughout the world. ³In Roman times, however, military leaders relied on a much slower, less technical method to send important messages back to headquarters—pigeons. ⁴Homing pigeons have a strong instinct to return home from just about anywhere. ⁵The birds were kept in cages at the military camps. ⁶When a message had to be sent, a soldier strapped it to the bird's leg. ⁷The bird was then released, and it flew home, delivering the message.

Topic sentence: _____

Explanation:

At first, we might think that sentence 1 states the main idea since sentence 2 gives examples of the world-wide communications. But notice what happens in sentence 3. This sentence, also a general idea, takes the reader in a different direction (as signaled by the contrast word *however*). This sentence is then supported by details in sentences 4–7. Now it becomes clear that the first two sentences are leading up to the true main idea of the paragraph, stated in sentence 3. This is clear because sentences 4–6 all give information that explains in detail the general statement in sentence 3.

TOPIC SENTENCE AT THE END OF A PARAGRAPH

Supporting Detail
Supporting Detail
Supporting Detail
Supporting Detail
Topic Sentence

When the topic sentence ends a paragraph, the previous sentences build up to the main idea. Here is an example of a paragraph in which the topic sentence comes last:

¹A museum in London has a fur-covered trout on display. ²It also has a letter written by Jesus Christ. ³Also prominent is a painting by Rembrandt. ⁴In addition, the crown jewels of England are shown. ⁵These items have one thing in common. ⁶They are all frauds. ⁷The London museum, you see, exhibits only jewelry, coins, letters, and artwork that have been proven to be fakes or forgeries.

Explanation:

When a topic sentence ends a paragraph, it often acts as a summary of the points made in the paragraph, or as a conclusion, where all of the points lead up to a final, general point. In the paragraph above, sentences 1–6 introduce and then discuss specific items on display at a museum. The last sentence is a general one that connects all the specific details that come before it.

TWO TOPIC SENTENCES: AT THE BEGINNING AND END OF A PARAGRAPH

```
┌─────────────────────────────┐
│  Topic Sentence             │
│  Supporting Detail          │
│  Supporting Detail          │
│  Supporting Detail          │
│  Topic Sentence             │
└─────────────────────────────┘
```

An author will sometimes introduce a main idea at or near the beginning of a paragraph, and then restate the idea, or make a similar general statement, at the end of the paragraph. The following paragraph is an example. Read it and the explanation that follows.

> [1]There are a number of ways to get young people involved in cutting down on the family food bill. [2]First, have your children go through newspapers to clip coupons. [3]They can also sort them into different categories and note expiration dates. [4]Next, have them help you compare generic products and brand-name products. [5]Buy each, and have a taste-testing contest. [6]If kids can't taste a difference, point out the savings there will be by buying the generic product. [7]Finally, give kids the responsibility to load the shopping cart and calculate the savings their work has produced. [8]In these ways, children can feel the pride of making an impact on their family's food budget.

Explanation:

The first sentence introduces a general idea, and sentences 2–7 provide several specific examples. Sentence 8 states a general idea similar to the one made in sentence 1. Sentences 1 and 8 each cover all the details of the passage. Thus the paragraph has two topic sentences—one at the beginning and one at the end.

➤ *Practice*

The topic sentence is in different places in the following five paragraphs. Identify each topic sentence by filling in the correct number in the blank space. For the one paragraph that has a topic sentence at the beginning *and* at the end, write in both numbers.

To find each topic sentence, do the following:

    a Identify the *topic* of the paragraph by asking yourself, "Who or what is the paragraph about?"

    b Find the *general statement* that tells you what the author's main point is about the topic.

    c Test your answer by asking yourself, "Is this general statement supported by all or most of the material in the paragraph?"

1. [1]Have you ever come across someone whose name seemed to fit his or her work? [2]There are, in fact, many people whose names match their jobs. [3]For instance, Ivan Doctor is an eye doctor, and Patience Scales is a piano teacher. [4]Then there are Sgt. Vice, a police officer, and James Judge, a superior court judge. [5]There's even a dentist named Toothaker.

   Topic sentence(s): _____

2. [1]As adoption in the United States becomes more complicated, many childless couples are going outside the country to find children to adopt. [2]In 1988, more than ten thousand foreign-born children were adopted by U.S. families. [3]That's one-fifth of all adoptions in the country that year. [4]At present, Korea and Latin America are the sources for most foreign babies adopted in the U.S. [5]A foreign adoption is often quicker than an American one. [6]In the U.S., many agencies have waiting lists of five to ten years.

   Topic sentence(s): _____

3. [1]A recent study found that over 80 percent of mountain bikers reported being injured at least once. [2]Twenty-five percent needed to see a doctor. [3]In contrast, 50 percent of on-road, or street, bikers reported an injury, with 33 percent needing medical attention. [4]The study concluded that while mountain bikers have more injuries, street bikers have more severe injuries.

   Topic sentence(s): _____

4. [1]The Council on Physical Education for Children has some suggestions on how to get children to enjoy exercise. [2]First, have children play games like soccer, where everyone is involved. [3]Next, make sure equipment is the right size. [4]Smaller and more lightweight equipment will help young children develop skills. [5]Finally, boring exercises such as jumping jacks and toe-touches should be avoided. [6]Following these suggestions from the Council on Physical Education for Children should result in better-developed skills and more enjoyment for children.

   Topic sentence(s): _____

5.   ¹Some shoppers enjoy running from sale to sale, looking for the lowest possible prices on their sheets, towels, and microwaves. ²But more shoppers today prefer stores that offer everyday low prices—not just occasional sale prices. ³These shoppers dislike waiting for a sale on an item they need. ⁴When they decide they want or need an item, they want to get it right away. ⁵Also, they hate buying something and seeing it go on sale the next week.

Topic sentence(s): _____

FINDING TOPIC SENTENCES ON FOUR LEVELS OF DIFFICULTY

As has already been said, finding the main idea is the most important of all reading skills. To give you practice in finding the main idea, the rest of this chapter presents a series of paragraphs. They are grouped into four levels of increasing difficulty, with the topic sentences appearing at varying places. Don't skip any levels. Doing the easier ones will prepare you for the more difficult ones. Finally, remember these guidelines for finding the topic sentence:

   a Identify the *topic* of the paragraph by asking yourself, "Who or what is the paragraph about?"

   b Find the *general statement* that tells you what the author's main point is about the topic.

   c Test your answer by asking yourself, "Is this general statement supported by all or most of the material in the paragraph?"

➤ *Practice: Level 1*

Write the number of each topic sentence in the space provided.

1.   ¹People who are overweight simply eat too much, right? ²Wrong. ³There are other causes for gaining weight besides eating more. ⁴One is eating the wrong kinds of food, such as fatty and sugary foods. ⁵Another may be eating at the wrong times, like just before going to bed. ⁶And a third cause of gaining weight not related to overeating is getting too little exercise.

Topic sentence: _____

2.   ¹The types of animals considered endangered or threatened are increasing. ²In 1985, there were 329 species listed by the U.S. Fish and Wildlife Service as being endangered or threatened. ³This year, there are 402 species listed. ⁴In addition, there are over 3,000 other species that officials have not had time to study. ⁵Some of these may also qualify for the list.

Topic sentence: _____

3. [1]Hannibal Hamlin was one. [2]So were George Dallas and John Breckinridge. [3]And you can add the names of Schuyler Colfax, Henry Wilson, and John Garner. [4]What do all of these men have in common? [5]Although few people know them by name, each of these men has been a vice president of the United States.

    Topic sentence: _____

4. [1]Child abuse has many tragic results. [2]A child who is abused often believes he is unworthy. [3]This low self-esteem can lead to alcoholism, drug addiction or even suicide. [4]Of course in many cases, the abuse is physically harmful and even fatal. [5]In addition, most abused children grow up to become abusers of their own children.

    Topic sentence: _____

5. [1]There is much that people can do for their pets. [2]But the opposite is also true—numerous studies have shown that owning a pet can improve a person's mental and physical well-being. [3]A pet that a person feels attached to improves the owner's frame of mind. [4]A pet gives a feeling of being needed to the person who takes care of it. [5]Pets also give an unconditional love that makes coming home after a rotten day more bearable. [6]Even being in the same room as a pet can lower one's blood pressure and heart rate.

    Topic sentence: _____

➤ Practice: Level 2

Write the number of each topic sentence in the space provided. For the one case in which there are two topic sentences, write in both numbers.

1. [1]If asked, you might say that ceramics are for pottery and plastic is for toys. [2]That may be true today. [3]In the near future, however, ceramics and plastics will be put to some very different uses. [4]New methods have produced ceramics sturdy enough to be made into scissors and knives that never rust. [5]The new ceramics can also be made into engines that run without a cooling system. [6]The new plastics can be molded into bridges, fuel tanks, and high-fidelity loudspeakers.

    Topic sentence(s): _____

2. [1]There are various types of personalized license plates. [2]Some show a person's name or, as in the case of TOOTH DR, a driver's occupation. [3]Sports enthusiasts show their love of a sport, as with license LV2GOLF, or a team: GO PHILS. [4]Others display greetings such as GDAYM8 and GR8T DAY. [5]Some license plates reveal the driver's status, as with NO MO 825,

apparently about a retired person, or the vehicle's status, as with 4 RNR, seen on a recreational vehicle.

Topic sentence(s): _____

3.   [1]Survey statistics are convincing food-makers to pay more attention to children. [2]Children influence $132 billion in annual purchases. [3]In addition, 62 percent of children visit supermarkets each week, and 50 percent participate in the choice of food or brand. [4]Fifty percent of children also say that they prefer a different salad dressing than their mothers. [5]And a full 78 percent of them claim to influence their family's choice of cold cereal. [6]Such statistics tell food-makers that appealing to children's taste can be profitable.

Topic sentence(s): _____

4.   [1]Parents have shown concern about the quality and safety of baby food. [2]As a result of parental concern, the leading baby food companies have started a strict set of safety checks. [3]First, representatives of the companies visit the farms where the produce is grown. [4]The representatives make sure that levels of pesticides are the lowest possible. [5]Next, they check every piece of incoming produce for chemicals and other impurities. [6]Finally, spot checks of the finished products are done before they are shipped to the stores.

Topic sentence(s): _____

5.   [1]Today there are summer camps for a wide variety of specialized activities, from adventure to law. [2]For instance, a ranch in Texas offers a camp where children can learn to care for exotic animals. [3]Another in Pennsylvania lets kids work on community service projects. [4]A camp in Minnesota is divided into small villages where children can learn the language and culture of China, Russia, and other countries. [5]There is even a camp in Florida where kids can learn what it is like to be a lawyer.

Topic sentence(s): _____

➤ Practice: Level 3

Write the number of each topic sentence in the space provided. For the one case in which there are two topic sentences, write in both numbers.

1.   [1]The time-honored tradition of flirting is in no danger of falling into disuse. [2]However, because of differing purposes, flirting can lead to mixed messages between participants. [3]Women often flirt just to be friendly or to meet someone new. [4]They do not necessarily expect or want further involvement. [5]Men, on the other hand, view flirting as a means to action. [6]They hope it will lead to something more than conversation.

Topic sentence(s): _____

2. [1]According to the National Education Association, there are six major problems that students bring into the high school classroom. [2]First, about a quarter of all students smoke marijuana regularly, and more than two-thirds use alcohol. [3]Forty percent of today's 14-year-old girls will get pregnant in their teens, and 80 percent of these will drop out of high school. [4]Also, 30 percent of all students now in high school will drop out. [5]One out of three girls and one out of eight boys under 18 years old have reported being sexually abused. [6]Fifth, 15 percent of girls will suffer an eating disorder during part or all of their teenage years. [7]Finally, suicide is the second most common cause of death among 15- through 19-year-olds.

Topic sentence(s): _____

3. [1]Because turnips were often eaten by the poor, people often turned up their noses at them. [2]Carrots grew wild in ancient times and were used then for medicinal purposes. [3]But they weren't considered fit for the table in Europe until the thirteenth century. [4]In the early seventeenth and eighteenth centuries, some Europeans considered potatoes fit only for animals. [5]They were thought to cause leprosy in humans. [6]Obviously, though root vegetables are delicious and easily grown, their virtues haven't always been appreciated.

Topic sentence(s): _____

4. [1]European men do it. [2]Gay men do it. [3]Some celebrities do it. [4]"It" is hugging and kissing between men, and it's something the majority of males in our society are not comfortable doing. [5]Some are afraid of being labeled as homosexual. [6]Others come from ethnic backgrounds that frown on displays of affection. [7]And for others, being affectionate toward a friend makes them feel vulnerable, something they've learned a "real man" should not be.

Topic sentence(s): _____

5. [1]According to a medical journal, there are some important guidelines for having your ears pierced. [2]First, let a professional who uses sterile instruments perform the task. [3]Second, do not pierce an ear if you have a serious medical condition, including heart disease, blood disorder, or diabetes. [4]Also, for six weeks, do not wear earrings that contain nickel or a gold alloy or that are gold-plated. [5]Next, avoid the risk of infection by washing the earlobe twice a day with cotton dipped in rubbing alcohol. [6]Finally, if a lobe becomes red, swollen, or sore, see a doctor immediately. [7]Following this advice should result in a successful ear piercing.

Topic sentence(s): _____

➤ *Practice: Level 4*

Write the number of each topic sentence in the space provided. For the one case in which there are two topic sentences, write in both numbers.

1.   [1]Being a judge may be a lofty job, but judges often face the down-to-earth problem of fighting off sleepiness during a long trial. [2]One reason is that arguments made by attorneys are usually routine. [3]They are also often long and boring. [4]A second reason is that judges are seated all during trials. [5]This can slow the body down, especially after lunch. [6]Also, courtrooms are usually stuffy. [7]Air circulation is poor, and there are no windows. [8]Lighting is dim. [9]These factors all make staying awake during trials a challenging task for judges.

   Topic sentence(s): _____

2.   [1]Marta is fourteen and lives in a village in San Salvador. [2]As in most peasant families there, every day the women prepare tortillas, thin round pancakes made from mashed corn. [3]In San Salvador, the tortillas are made in a few steps, the same way they were made hundreds of years ago. [4]Marta collects the corn and puts it in a pot of water to soak. [5]The next day, she puts the wet corn through a hand grinder. [6]Her mother then puts the ground corn on a block of stone and mashes it back and forth many times until it is a pasty dough. [7]This dough is then patted into tortillas, which are cooked on a flat griddle over an open fire. [8]They are eaten with salt and a portion of beans.

   Topic sentence(s): _____

3.   [1]Half of all Americans live within fifty miles of an ocean beach. [2]No wonder there's hardly room for a beach towel—124 million people visit the seashore annually, and the number is growing as development booms. [3]Unfortunately, all twenty-three coastal states lose two to four feet of beach a year to the ocean. [4]More people and less beach should make for some very crowded seashores in the coming years.

   Topic sentence(s): _____

4.   [1]People complain about their doctors. [2]"He rushes me through." [3]"She doesn't explain what she's doing." [4]Rather than just complain, patients need to become better managers of their own health care by asking questions and demanding answers. [5]When a patient visits a doctor, she should be prepared to describe her health problem fully and precisely. [6]She should question the doctor when she doesn't understand what he or she is doing. [7]She should make a habit of asking why certain procedures are recommended. [8]She should ask exactly how, when, and why she should take any medication. [9]If a doctor reacts badly to a patient's questions, it may be time to find a new doctor.

   Topic sentence(s): _____

5. ¹Daylight-saving time usually ends on the last weekend of October. ²This can be confusing as not all states are on daylight-saving time. ³But it is unlikely that any place has a harder time coping with time changes than Tuba City, Arizona. ⁴The state of Arizona does not observe daylight-saving time. ⁵But Tuba City is on a Navajo reservation, and the Navajo Nation does observe daylight-saving. ⁶The local school board, however, voted to return to standard time in *early* October. ⁷Yet the school's maintenance staff has a contract that states it must follow the usual daylight-saving schedule. ⁸Further, the Navajo Community College, next to the school, goes to standard time in early October. ⁹The continuing education department, in the same building, stays on the usual daylight-saving schedule.

Topic sentence(s): _____

➤ *Review Test 1*

The five paragraphs below are on the first and second levels of difficulty. Write the number of each topic sentence in the space provided. For the one case in which there are two topic sentences, write in both numbers.

1. ¹Is there a lot of stress in your life? ²Deep breathing—a simple exercise—can help you relax. ³Begin by standing or sitting up straight. ⁴Then inhale fully, until the belly is pushed out. ⁵Finally, exhale slowly, pulling the belly in and up until the lungs are empty.

Topic sentence(s): _____

2. ¹Americans have a love affair with chocolate. ²In one day, we eat six million pounds of chocolate candy—enough to make a candy bar the size of a football field and two feet thick. ³The Hershey's Chocolate company turns out a quarter million pounds of Hershey's kisses per day. ⁴That's enough to fill up the cabs of sixty full-size pickup trucks.

Topic sentence(s): _____

3. ¹There will probably be more use of home computers in the next century. ²People will use them to vote, to file taxes, and to take college exams. ³Also, there may be much more leisure time then. ⁴Experts say the work week will shrink to thirty-two hours or less. ⁵In addition, robots will take over routine service jobs and dangerous cleanups. ⁶As these expert forecasts suggest, the next century is likely to be very different from this one.

Topic sentence(s): _____

4.   [1]You can attract wildlife to your garden by following a few guidelines. [2]First, plant shrubs around your garden. [3]This will provide protection for animals and a place for birds to roost. [4]Also, plant vegetation that the birds and animals like to eat. [5]A local nursery can help you select the right vegetation. [6]Third, leave some water for the wildlife to drink. [7]Finally, keep dogs and cats away. [8]Their presence will discourage wildlife from coming around. [9]These procedures should tempt wildlife into any garden.

Topic sentence(s): _____

5.   [1]The American home can be a violent place. [2]Consider, first, that some parents punch and kick their children and even use weapons on them. [3]Evidence suggests that almost four million children are abused by their parents each year. [4]Second, husbands and wives hit, shoot and stab each other. [5]Almost two million people are abused by their spouses. [6]Finally, some adults beat, tie up, and neglect the elderly. [7]There may be over two million old people abused by their children and other caretakers.

Topic sentence(s): _____

➤ Review Test 2

The five paragraphs below are on the third and fourth levels of difficulty. Write the number of each topic sentence in the space provided. For the one case in which there are two topic sentences, write in both numbers.

1.   [1]Have you ever thought that a week in bed would do you good? [2]Well, think again. [3]Several days of bed rest can actually do harm. [4]First, just as moving around keeps bones strong, lying in bed weakens them. [5]Also, when someone is in bed for several days, blood gathers in the upper body. [6]This causes the heart to function less well and leads to more risk of blood clots. [7]Lying down also changes the position of the lungs, making breathing more difficult.

Topic sentence(s): _____

2.   [1]On an island in the Indian Ocean, people honor the dead by treating them as if they were still alive. [2]For example, they are given clean "clothing." [3]Dead bodies are often removed from their tombs and dressed in new clothes. [4]Then, before being reburied, the bodies may be danced with, sung to, and given tours of their old neighborhoods. [5]Recently, a dead soccer player was treated to three games of soccer before being placed in the family tomb.

Topic sentence(s): _____

3.   ¹Some say victimless crimes should not be illegal. ²However, the argument that some crimes have no victims is weak. ³First, whoever commits a so-called victimless crime can do himself harm. ⁴For example, a drug user may overdose. ⁵In addition, family members can be hurt. ⁶Drug addicts may be unable to properly care for their children. ⁷Finally, society can be harmed. ⁸For instance, drug addicts often need costly treatment, paid for with our tax dollars.

Topic sentence(s): _____

4.   ¹Scientists check and recheck evidence before coming to conclusions. ²But careful research hasn't stopped scientists from making big mistakes. ³In 1903, for example, n-rays were supposedly discovered. ⁴Many papers were published on such subjects as how bricks absorb n-rays and how loud noises interfere with n-rays. ⁵Several years later, scientists agreed no such ray exists. ⁶In the 1970s, scientists believed a new water called polywater had been invented. ⁷They feared that if any escaped a lab, all water would turn into polywater, ending life on earth. ⁸That danger passed when polywater was proved to be ordinary water with impurities.

Topic sentence(s): _____

5.   ¹Our lives have been enriched by inventions we might never have known about without the determination of the products' inventors. ²In 1939, for example, a professor built the first computer using "base 2," a series that was easy for a machine to identify. ³He tried to sell his idea to IBM, but was turned down. ⁴It took seven years before his idea was accepted and the first general-purpose computer was introduced. ⁵Today, all computers use the system he devised. ⁶Another example is the copy machine patented in 1939. ⁷Its inventor tried to sell his idea to twenty different companies. ⁸Because no one was interested then, the first commercial copy machine was not introduced until 1959. ⁹Through the persistence of inventors such as these, our lives have been changed.

Topic sentence(s): _____

➤ *Review Test 3*

A. To review what you've learned in this chapter, answer each of the following questions. Fill in the blank or circle the letter of the answer you think is correct.

1. The topic sentence of a paragraph states the
   a. supporting details.   b. introductory material.   c. main idea.

2. _____ TRUE OR FALSE? To find the topic sentence of a paragraph, look for a general statement.

3. _____ TRUE OR FALSE? The supporting details of a paragraph are more general than the main idea.

4. The topic sentence may appear in a paragraph *(only once* or *more than once?)* _____.

5. When the main idea is stated in the last sentence of a paragraph, it is likely to be
   a. a summary.   b. a conclusion.   c. either *a* or *b*.

B. Here is a chance to apply your understanding of topic sentences to a full-length reading. The following selection looks at a custom once followed by many families: sitting down to the dinner meal together. The author discusses the benefits of this custom and how to find time for it. After reading the selection, answer the questions that follow on the central point and main ideas. There are also vocabulary-in-context questions and a question on supporting details.

Words to Watch

Following are some words in the reading that do not have strong context support. Each word is followed by the number of the paragraph in which it appears and its meaning there. These words are indicated in the selection by a small circle (°).

> *cupa* (1): informal way of saying "a cup of" (usually meaning "a cup of coffee")
> *dissected* (2): cut apart
> *grisly* (2): horrible
> *embraced* (3): adopted
> *exorbitant* (3): extreme
> *peers* (6): people of equal standing, as in age
> *confronted* (7): faced
> *struck* (13): made by stamping or punching a material
> *sit-coms* (13): situation comedies
> *bonding* (14): forming a close relationship

DINNER WAS RESERVED FOR THE FAMILY

Maggie Isaacs

I don't know about your house, but in my home when I was a kid   1
we all met around the dinner table once a day. Usually we didn't catch
more than a glance of each other in the morning. Breakfast was a
quickie: a nod, a cupa°—and everybody's gone. Most of us weren't

---

home for lunch. But it was understood that at night we ate dinner together and shared our day.

I can still remember—and it's more than 30 years ago—explaining at the dinner table how we dissected° a frog in our high school biology class that day and, as I embellished the grisly° details for effect, secretly enjoying the look of horror on my mother's face.   2

When I had my own family, we embraced° the same custom—we ate dinner together. Sure, we sometimes had the television news on, but we talked about what was happening in the world that day. The point is, we talked. About the country, the neighborhood, the school. About our friends, teachers, the exorbitant° price of everything, the need for a new couch, the condition of the car.   3

It was here that the kids first learned about the immediate world that they were growing up in and the good and bad people in it. And they found out that you could disagree about substantial issues, like politics and religion.   4

I heard my husband ask our children at the dinner table the same question my father, years ago, had asked us: "What did you learn in school today?" And we discovered early on that we'd better have an answer to that question—as did our kids much later.   5

It now seems the family dinner hour, at least as I once knew it, is a thing of the past. And I see the results everywhere. As a college teacher, I am constantly amazed at how difficult our young adults find it to talk to anyone but their peers°. With some, every sentence contains the phrase that makes me cringe: *like, you know* . . . No, in fact, I don't know.   6

The demise of the family dinner hour has made the job of watching out for our children and spotting problems sooner than later more difficult. When we are confronted° with a teenager who uses drugs or alcohol, a high school student with poor study habits, or a youthful pregnancy, we ask ourselves, why didn't we see this coming, and we run for the experts.   7

It's admirable that our politicians are promising to do more about cracking down on drugs, improving education, and upgrading child care facilities. But we can't just turn our children over to others the way we turn a car over to a mechanic—a little adjustment here, a fine-tuning there. The middle-of-the-night stark truth is that we parents are responsible for our own children. It's time to look at ourselves to prevent the problems. Teachers, counselors, psychologists can be, at best, only our helpers.   8

No one denies that sitting down together every evening is harder today because of the two-income family. When we're dead tired, how   9 much easier to let the kids sit alone with a tray in front of the television. But it was never simple. My dad worked two jobs and somehow we managed to wait dinner for him.

My husband started his workday at 5 p.m. during the years he was 10 an editor of a newspaper. Those days we had our dinner shortly after 4 p.m. Not terribly convenient, to be sure; it meant snacks for the children before bed. At various times in my life I have served family dinner anywhere from 4 in the afternoon to 9 in the evening.

Spending "quality time" with the children, the "in" phrase today, 11 is not something that should be left to weekends. When we look at and talk to our children across the table and they look at and talk to us night after night after night, we find out all sorts of things.

My parents got an idea of whom we were spending our time with, 12 what we were doing, and how we looked. Was someone's color bad? Was someone else's appetite off? Was another youngster constantly sniffling? Had still another's personality changed; was he or she depressed?

Teenagers are a complicated lot, and any parent who sees a child 13 through those years deserves a specially struck° medal. But even with the nuisance of rearranging our schedules in order to be there at dinner-time and the knowledge that we're not likely to be a hundred percent successful in building rapport, it's more rewarding finding out about our own family than living with all the make-believe people in the TV sit-coms°.

We hear much about the bonding° that takes place between a 14 mother and newborn baby. I suggest there's another bonding that takes place at the family dinner table every night.

Reading Comprehension Questions

Vocabulary in Context

1. The word *embellished* in "I . . . remember . . . explaining how we dissected a frog . . . and, as I embellished the grisly details . . . enjoying the look of horror on my mother's face" (paragraph 2) means
   a. ignored.
   b. exaggerated.
   c. forgot.
   d. destroyed.

2. The word *substantial* in "they found out that you could disagree about substantial issues, like politics and religion" (paragraph 4) means
   a. unknown.
   b. minor.
   c. important.
   d. creative.

3. The word *demise* in "the demise of the family dinner hour has made the job of watching out for our children . . . more difficult" (paragraph 7) means
   a. beginning.
   b. decision.
   c. location.
   d. end.

4. The word *upgrading* in "our politicians are promising to do more about cracking down on drugs, improving education, and upgrading child care facilities" (paragraph 8) means
   a. improving.
   b. photographing.
   c. moving.
   d. closing.

5. The word *rapport* in "Teenagers are a complicated lot, and . . . we're not likely to be a hundred percent successful in building rapport" (paragraph 13) means
   a. confusion.
   b. resistance.
   c. understanding.
   d. education.

Central Point

6. Which of the following is the topic of the entire selection?
   a. Families eating dinner together
   b. Changes in society
   c. Family customs
   d. The two-income family

7. Which sentence best expresses the central point of the entire selection?
   a. When the author was young, her family ate dinner together at night.
   b. Changes in society are challenging our families.
   c. There are numerous two-income families today.
   d. To help prevent problems with children, families should eat dinner together.

Main Ideas

8. The topic sentence of paragraph 1 is its
   a. first sentence.
   b. second sentence.
   c. third sentence.
   d. next-to-last sentence.

Supporting Details

9. According to the author, a family dinner hour allows kids to
   a. learn more about the world in which they are growing up.
   b. ask for help with their homework.
   c. eat a well-balanced and nourishing meal.
   d. all of the above.

10. The author feels that parents should use the family dinner hour
    a. to discuss nutrition.
    b. to spot problems before they become too large to handle.
    c. to watch TV together.
    d. as an excuse to leave work early.

Mapping Activity

This selection is about a problem and a suggested solution. The main points are scrambled in the list below. Write them in the diagram where they belong.

- Parents should re-establish the family dinner hour.
- Our children need watching over.

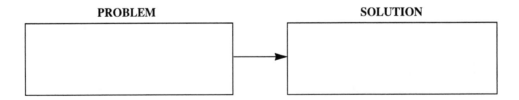

PROBLEM   SOLUTION

Discussion Questions

1. Isaacs focuses on dinner as a way for families to spend time together. What other ways are there for families to get together regularly?

2. If children aren't talking to their parents about their daily activities and problems, to whom are they talking? With what results? Should it matter if children don't talk about their lives to their parents?

Writing Activities

1. Write a paragraph beginning with this topic sentence: "Children benefit when parents spend time with them every day." Go on to explain and illustrate the benefits you think are most important.

2. Draw a line down the center of a notebook page. On the top of one side write, "Family Activities I Enjoyed Most." On top of the other side write, "Family Activities I Enjoyed Least." Under the first heading, list at least two or three of your favorite family activities as a child. Under the second heading, list some of your least favorite family activities at the time. Then write a paper with this central point: "As a child, I had several favorite and least favorite family activities."

Check Your Performance

LOCATIONS OF MAIN IDEAS

Activity	Number Right	Points	Total
Review Test 1 (5 items)	_____	x 4 =	_____
Review Test 2 (5 items)	_____	x 4 =	_____
Review Test 3, Part A (5 items)	_____	x 4 =	_____
Review Test 3, Part B (10 items)	_____	x 3 =	_____
Mapping (2 items)	_____	x 5 =	_____
		TOTAL SCORE =	_____ %

Enter your total score into the reading performance chart on the inside back cover.

6

Implied
Main Ideas

A paragraph may not have a topic sentence, but that does not mean it lacks a main idea. In this chapter, you will learn how to figure out the main idea in paragraphs that have no topic sentence.

UNDERSTANDING IMPLIED MAIN IDEAS

Below is a paragraph from an earlier chapter. This time, however, the topic sentence is missing.

> In work-sharing, full-time jobs are divided into part-time jobs shared by two or more workers. Working mothers, students, and those just returning to work find these positions very appealing. Employers like work-sharing too. In a two-year work-sharing project, workers had a mere 13 percent turnover rate; the usual turnover rate is 40 percent. In addition, worker productivity was greater than expected.

What is the main idea of the paragraph? You may remember it from reading the paragraph before. But even so, you could probably figure out the main idea. Ask yourself, "What point do all the details add up to?" After explaining work-sharing, the paragraph mentions the types of employees who like it. Then the paragraph explains that employers like work-sharing too. Putting all those ideas together, we can say the implied main idea is that work-sharing can benefit both employees and employers.

As the above passage suggests, when a paragraph has no topic sentence, the author has decided to let the supporting details suggest the main idea. The main idea is **unstated**, or **implied**, and you must figure it out by deciding upon the general point of the supporting details.

A Method for Figuring Out Implied Main Ideas

If you have trouble figuring out the implied main idea, you may find it helpful to use the following two questions:

1 What is the topic, or subject, of the paragraph? In other words, what is the whole paragraph about?
2 What is the main point being made about that topic?

For example, read the following paragraph. Note that it contains no "umbrella" statement, a general statement that covers all the others. See if you can pick out the topic and the unstated main idea. Circle the letters of your choices. Then read the explanation that follows.

> On a recent hike in the woods, I was stung by a hornet. As I tried to get away from the hornet, I fell into a thorn bush and scratched my arms. Then I got lost and had to walk an extra four miles before I found the trail. At one point I walked into a patch of shrubs which turned out to be poison ivy. Finally, I was drenched by a sudden rain shower as I was walking back to my car.

The topic of this paragraph is:
a. hiking.
b. outdoor exercise.
c. getting hurt while on a hike.
d. a hike in the woods.

The unstated main idea of this paragraph is:
a. It's easy to get lost while hiking in the woods.
b. Never go hiking into the woods alone.
c. The author's hike in the woods was filled with great dangers.
d. The author's hike in the woods was unpleasant.

Explanation:

First, what is the *topic* of the paragraph? Let's consider the four choices given above:

a. *hiking*	This is too broad to be the topic. It covers information on hiking in general, but the paragraph is about only one particular hike.
b. *outdoor exercise*	This answer is also too broad to be the topic—it covers all sorts of outdoor exercise, not just hiking.
c. *getting hurt while on a hike*	This answer is too narrow to be the topic since in addition to getting hurt, the paragraph covers getting lost and wet.

d. *a hike in the woods*

Every sentence in the paragraph is about a hike the author took in the woods. Thus, this is the correct answer.

Now that we have the topic of the paragraph, what is the author's *main point* about the topic? In other words, what is the author saying about the hike in the woods? The answer must be an idea that covers the supporting details in the paragraph. Again, let's consider the four answer choices:

a. *It's easy to get lost while hiking in the woods.*

This answer is too narrow. Only one of the sentences in the paragraph is about getting lost.

b. *Never go hiking into the woods alone.*

Nothing in the paragraph suggests that you shouldn't go hiking alone. This cannot be the answer.

c. *The author's hike in the woods was filled with great dangers.*

An insect bite, poison ivy, and a four-mile detour are inconveniences, not "great dangers." Thus, this is not the author's main point.

d. *The author's hike in the woods was unpleasant.*

The details of the paragraph tell about the problems the author had while hiking. These problems made the hike very unpleasant. This is the correct answer. It is the implied main idea of the paragraph.

By now you probably understand that to find an implied main idea, you have to become a detective. You need to look very closely at all the supporting details in the paragraph. Then you have to use this "evidence" to find the topic and the main point the author is making about the topic.

In this chapter, you will find a step-by-step guide to help you develop the skill of finding unstated main ideas. Do not skip any of the activities in this chapter. They will help you learn what you need to know about this challenging but important skill.

Step 1: Recognizing Implied General Ideas

Learning how to find unstated general ideas is a helpful step in finding implied main ideas. Look at the list of specific ideas below. Then circle the letter of the general idea that you think best covers these specific ideas. After you make your choice, read the explanation that follows.

Specific ideas: Whitney Houston, Paul Simon, Reba McEntire, Phil Collins

The general idea is:

a. men.

b. entertainers.

c. singers.

Explanation:

Since Whitney Houston is female, *men* is not general enough to cover all the specific ideas. Thus answer *a* is wrong. It's true that all the specific ideas are names of entertainers, but they are one specific kind of entertainer—they are all singers. Thus answer *b* is more broad than necessary, and answer *c* is the correct choice.

When you are looking for the general idea, remember these points:

1 The general idea must cover all of the specific ideas. (*Singers* includes *Whitney Houston, Paul Simon, Reba McEntire,* and *Phil Collins.*)

2 A general idea that covers kinds of specific ideas other than those on the list is too broad. (*Entertainers* is too broad—it covers specific ideas other than singers, such as dancers and actors.)

3 The general idea must not be so narrow that it excludes any of the specific ideas. (*Men* is too narrow—it excludes Whitney Houston.)

➤ *Practice 1*

Read each group of specific items below. Then circle the letter of the general idea that tells what the specific ideas have in common. Keep in mind that the correct general idea will not be too narrow or too broad.

1. *Specific ideas:* hat, jacket, nylon stockings, socks

   The general idea is:
   a. clothing.
   b. men's clothing.
   c. winter clothing.

2. *Specific ideas:* ice cream, yogurt, cheese, milk

   The general idea is:
   a. desserts.
   b. dairy products.
   c. foods.

3. *Specific ideas:* crayons, clay, oil paints, watercolors

   The general idea is:
   a. drawing supplies.
   b. art supplies.
   c. supplies.

4. *Specific ideas:* beer, cola, ginger ale, orange juice

   The general idea is:
   a. sodas.
   b. beverages.
   c. alcoholic beverages.

5. *Specific ideas:* retirement, marriage, graduation, funeral

   The general idea is:
   a. parties.
   b. popular events.
   c. major life events.

6. *Specific ideas:* gorilla, lion, tiger, elephant

   The general idea is:
   a. animals.
   b. pets.
   c. wild animals.

7. *Specific ideas:* volleyball, football, baseball, basketball

   The general idea is:
   a. sports.
   b. activities.
   c. team sports.

8. *Specific ideas:* lamps, candles, the sun, flashlights

   The general idea is:
   a. common household objects.
   b. sources of heat.
   c. sources of light.

9. *Specific ideas:* A+, a pay raise, a promotion, an Olympic medal

   The general idea is:
   a. lucky breaks.
   b. common achievements.
   c. rewards and awards.

10. *Specific ideas:* "It doesn't fit"; "I don't like the color"; "This tastes like paste"; "Can't you get it right just once?"

    The general idea is:
    a. comments.
    b. guesses.
    c. complaints.

Step 2: Putting Unstated General Ideas in Your Own Words

Now that you have worked on recognizing general ideas, you are ready to state such ideas on your own. Try the example below. Read the list of four specific ideas. Then think of a general idea that includes all of the specific ones. Make sure your general idea is not too broad or too narrow. Once you have written your answer, read the explanation that follows.

General idea: _____

Specific ideas: sleet
thundershowers
fog
sunshine

Explanation:

At first, you might think that the general idea is "bad weather conditions." But the fourth term, *sunshine*, does not fit into that category. So you need a broader general idea, such as "kinds of weather" or "weather conditions."

➤ *Practice 2*

In the following lists, the specific ideas are given, but the general ideas are unstated. Fill in the blanks with the unstated general ideas.

1. *General idea:* _____

   Specific ideas: fried
hard-boiled
scrambled
poached

2. *General idea:* _____

   Specific ideas: corn
broccoli
spinach
peas

3. *General idea:* _____

   Specific ideas: knives
razor blades
tacks
needles

4. *General idea:* _____

   Specific ideas: rifle
   revolver
   bow and arrow
   pistol

5. *General idea:* _____

   Specific ideas: lipstick
   Santa's suit
   blood
   stoplight

6. *General idea:* _____

   Specific ideas: bruises
   shaving nicks
   scratches
   muscle pulls

7. *General idea:* _____

   Specific ideas: pay attention in class
   take good notes
   keep up with your homework
   hand in papers on time

8. *General idea:* _____

   Specific ideas: giraffe
   skyscraper
   TV station antenna
   redwood tree

9. *General idea:* _____

   Specific ideas: Spain
   Germany
   France
   Mexico

10. *General idea:* _____

   Specific ideas: Mercedes-Benz
   Lexus
   Cadillac
   Rolls-Royce

Step 3: Recognizing Implied Main Ideas

To find an implied main idea, remember what you learned about unstated general ideas. Select a general statement that includes the specific ideas of the paragraph. The unstated main idea must not be too broad or too narrow.

The exercise that follows will help you to find unstated main ideas. Begin by reading the following group of statements. Then circle the letter of its implied main idea. Finally, read the explanation that follows.

1. Laser beams are used to guide bombs to their targets.

2. The communications industry uses lasers to carry pictures and voices through cables.

3. Medical uses of lasers include the removal of birthmarks and the unclogging of arteries.

4. Businesses use lasers to read bar codes and to guide robots through production-line tasks.

Which statement best expresses the implied main idea of the above sentences?
a. Laser beams are the best source of energy.
b. Lasers now have only limited use compared with what they will do in the future.
c. Lasers are used by the military.
d. Lasers are used in a variety of ways.

Explanation:

a. *Laser beams are the best source of energy.*

None of the first four statements compares laser beams with other sources of energy, so this cannot be the answer.

b. *Lasers now have only limited use compared with what they will do in the future.*

None of the first four statements discusses what lasers will do in the future. This cannot be the answer either.

c. *Lasers are used by the military.*

This statement is too narrow to cover all of the first four statements—only one of them has to do with the military.

d. *Lasers are used in a variety of ways.*

The first four sentences discuss a variety of uses for lasers, so this answer is correct. It is general enough to cover all of the types of uses mentioned.

➤ *Practice 3*

Read each group of four sentences. Then circle the letter of the answer that best states the implied main idea.

Group 1

1. Domestic rabbits are cute, tame, and quiet.
2. Domestic rabbits are also affectionate and playful.
3. In addition, they are easy to care for, needing a minimum of food and water.
4. Rabbits can be litter-trained, so they can be kept indoors.

Which statement best expresses the implied main idea of the above sentences?
a. More people are choosing rabbits as pets than ever before.
b. Domestic rabbits make good pets.
c. There are no disadvantages to having a domestic rabbit as a pet.
d. Domestic rabbits are easier to care for than any other pet.

Group 2

1. Smoking is a major contributor to heart disease.
2. High cholesterol due to poor diet is a major cause of heart disease.
3. High blood pressure can cause heart disease.
4. Recently it was discovered that inactivity can damage the heart.

Which statement best expresses the implied main idea of the above sentences?
a. Heart disease is the number one killer of Americans.
b. Various factors can contribute to heart disease.
c. People who exercise, don't smoke, and eat well will not get heart disease.
d. Only four factors contribute to heart disease.

Group 3

1. The English Channel is a 21.5 mile waterway between France and Great Britain.
2. The English Channel is known for its frigid waters, dangerous currents, and stinging jellyfish that can paralyze a swimmer.
3. Over 4,300 long-distance swimmers have tried to swim the English Channel.
4. Fewer than 20 percent of the swimmers who have tried to swim the English Channel have succeeded, and three have died in the attempt.

Which statement best expresses the implied main idea of the above sentences?
a. The English Channel is the most dangerous channel in the world.
b. A long-distance swimmer is not considered successful until he or she has swum the English Channel.
c. The English Channel poses tremendous challenges for long-distance swimmers.
d. More men than women have swum the English Channel successfully.

Step 4: Recognizing Implied Main Ideas in Paragraphs

You have practiced finding implied main ideas in a group of statements. The next step is to find unstated main ideas in paragraphs. Read the paragraph below, and see if you can circle the letter of its unstated main idea. Then read the explanation that follows.

Americans' favorite pizza toppings include pepperoni and sausage. In Japan, people put tuna on their pizzas. Australians like to top their pizza with shrimp and pineapple. And many British prefer their pizza with sweet corn sprinkled on top.

The implied main idea is:
a. Pizza is eaten all over the world.
b. Most people feel that pepperoni and sausage are the best toppings for pizza.
c. People in different countries have very different ideas of what goes well on pizza.
d. Some people enjoy eating pizza with a fish topping.

Explanation:

a. *Pizza is eaten all over the world.*

This statement is too broad. The sentences mention different countries, but not countries all over the world.

b. *Most people feel that pepperoni and sausage are the best toppings for pizza.*

This statement is not supported by the facts given in the passage. The passage states only that pepperoni and sausage are among the favorite pizza toppings of Americans.

c. *People in different countries have very different ideas of what goes well on pizza.*

This statement is supported by the facts. All four sentences in the passage discuss the various pizza toppings enjoyed in different countries. So this is the correct answer. It is the unstated main idea of the paragraph.

d. *Some people enjoy eating pizza with a fish topping.*

This statement is too narrow. It covers only the detail about what the Japanese like on their pizza.

➤ *Practice 4*

Read each passage carefully, and then circle the letter of the statement that best expresses the main idea of the paragraph. Remember to ask these two questions:

(1) What topic is the whole paragraph about?
(2) What is the author saying about this topic?

The answer to the second question will be the unstated main idea of the paragraph.

1. Why do some people avoid crossing the path of a black cat? The reason is centuries old. People in the Middle Ages believed that witches were very dangerous creatures who could change themselves into black cats. Witches were also thought to be easily upset. So, if you wanted to avoid trouble, the safest thing to do was simply avoid all black cats.

    The unstated main idea is:
    a. Some people avoid crossing the path of a black cat.
    b. Superstitions have interesting historical backgrounds.
    c. The fear of crossing the path of a black cat comes from beliefs about witches in the Middle Ages.
    d. During the Middle Ages, people believed that witches were dangerous and could change themselves into black cats.

2. Two workers on the twentieth floor of a building saw a bird banging its head against the outside of their office window. They rescued the bird and took it to a nearby animal hospital. The vet explained that what had happened was not unusual. The bird had eaten berries which had been on the vine long enough to ferment. The sugar had partially turned to alcohol. The bird, in other words, was drunk. The vet gave it time to sober up and then released it.

    The unstated main idea is:
    a. Two office workers learned that birds can get drunk.
    b. Workers in skyscrapers often rescue birds.
    c. Birds like to bang their heads against windows.
    d. A drunken bird should be taken to an animal hospital.

3. First it was racquetball. Next it was jogging. Then it was aerobic exercises. What will the next exercise craze be? Many people are turning to walking. Walking can give the same benefits to the heart that any exercise can. And just about anybody can walk, regardless of age or location. Also, walking will burn off the same number of calories as aerobics or running. But perhaps the best advantage of walking is that it is almost completely injury-free.

    The unstated main idea is:

a. People keep changing the exercises they do.
b. There are several good reasons for exercising.
c. Walking benefits the heart and uses up the same number of calories as running.
d. There are good reasons why walking may become the next exercise craze.

Step 5: Putting Implied Main Ideas into Your Own Words

You are now ready to try putting the unstated main idea of a paragraph into your own words. This involves three steps:

1 First look for the topic.
2 Then decide on what point the author is making about that topic.
3 State this idea in your own words.

➤ *Practice 5*

After reading each paragraph below, write what you think is the unstated main idea of the paragraph. For help in figuring out the main idea, complete the hint that follows each paragraph.

1. Do not struggle, or you will be sucked down into the quicksand even faster. Fall on your back, sticking your arms out, so that you will float on the surface. Roll your legs slowly back and forth to free them from the quicksand. Once your legs are free, begin rolling toward solid ground.

   What is the unstated main idea of this paragraph?_____

   _____

   Hint: The paragraph is about how to _____ quicksand.

2. For city walking, any really comfortable walking shoe will work. Mountain trails, however, require hiking boots, which support the ankles. And in wet areas, fabric shoes, which won't stretch, are better than leather ones. Finally, thick-soled shoes give more protection on rough surfaces such as gravel roads.

   What is the unstated main idea of this paragraph?_____

   _____

   Hint: The paragraph gives examples of different _____ for different _____.

3.   When threatened by a dog, a cat will stand on stiffened legs, push its ears back and arch its back. Also, the cat's hairs will "bulk up," making it look larger. "Looking for trouble?" the cat seems to be saying. "Well, you have found it." A cat angered by human teasing will flick its tail as if to say, "You are pushing me too far." If the person keeps teasing, the cat will fold its ears back and hiss. It's as though the cat is saying, "Stupid human! This is your final warning before I bury my claws in you." On a more loving note, cats will rub against their owners. This is a cat's way of saying, "You belong to me as much as I belong to you. We are family."

What is the unstated main idea of this paragraph? _____

_____

Hint: The paragraph gives examples of how cats _____ their feelings.

➤ *Review Test 1*

A. Read each group of specific items below. Then circle the letter of the general idea that tells what the specific ideas have in common. Remember that the general idea should not be too broad or too narrow.

   1. *Specific ideas:* stamps, coins, baseball cards, antiques

      The general idea is:
      a. practical items.
      b. useless items.
      c. items people collect.

   2. *Specific ideas:* orange, lime, lemon, grapefruit

      The general idea is:
      a. fruit.
      b. citrus fruit.
      c. food.

   3. *Specific ideas:* Los Angeles, San Diego, Seattle, San Francisco

      The general idea is:
      a. cities.
      b. cities on the West Coast.
      c. cities in California.

   4. *Specific ideas:* Mickey Mouse, Bugs Bunny, Lassie, Cinderella

      The general idea is:
      a. cartoon characters.
      b. fictional characters.
      c. fictional animals.

5. *Specific ideas:* swollen sinuses, strained eyes, a neighbor who plays drums, a nearby jackhammer

The general idea is:
a. health problems.
b. causes of headaches.
c. noisy activities.

B. In the following lists, the specific ideas are given, but the general idea is unstated. Fill in the blanks with the unstated main idea. Make sure your answer is not too broad or too narrow.

6. *General idea:* _____

Specific ideas: Atlantic Ocean
Delaware River
Lake Erie
Dead Sea

7. *General idea:* _____

Specific ideas: books
magazines
newspapers
comic books

8. *General idea*: _____

Specific ideas: lukewarm
cold
boiling
hot

9. *General idea:* _____

Specific ideas: dentist
nurse
doctor
lab technician

10. *General idea:* _____

Specific ideas: eat out less often
rent movies instead of going to the theater
buy clothes on sale
use coupons at the supermarket

➤ Review Test 2

A. Read each passage carefully. Then circle the letter of the sentence that best states the implied main idea.

1.   One way to tell if your houseplant needs water is to put your dry fingertip on top of the soil. If the soil sticks to your finger and the surface of the soil seems springy, the plant probably does not need water. Another way to check is to use the "done cake" test. Stick a toothpick into the soil. If it comes out clean, it's time to water your plant. Finally, you can try the "listen" test. Hit the side of the pot with your knuckles or with a stick. A hollow sound means that your plant needs water. A dull sound means the plant is moist enough for now.

The unstated main idea of this paragraph is:
a. Houseplants need to be watered regularly.
b. If a plant's soil is springy and doesn't stick to a toothpick, the plant doesn't need watering.
c. Watering a houseplant too frequently can harm the plant.
d. There are several ways to tell if a plant needs to be watered.

2.   In 1919, the city of Enterprise, Alabama, built a monument to an insect. The boll weevil was a destructive insect. It had eaten so much of the cotton crop planted by farmers that the farmers seemed ruined. In a desperate attempt to survive, they planted vegetable crops. They discovered that the harmful insect wouldn't touch these crops. The vegetable crops became so successful that the farmers found themselves three times richer than when they had planted cotton. They continued planting the new crops. They also decided the bug should be honored.

The unstated main idea of this paragraph is:
a. Farmers worldwide honor the boll weevil.
b. The boll weevil destroyed the cotton industry for Enterprise farmers.
c. When the boll weevil destroyed the cotton industry for Enterprise farmers, the farmers thought they were ruined.
d. Enterprise farmers honored the boll weevil because it forced them into growing more profitable crops than cotton.

3.   Before the twentieth century, millions of people died needlessly in hospitals. Back then, doctors didn't wash their hands between tasks. Little was known about germs and how they were spread. Doctors would finish one operation, then immediately start on another operation. Then they would examine patients, never realizing that they were carrying bacteria from one person to another. In many cases, they seriously infected the very people they were trying to cure.

The unstated main idea of this paragraph is:
a. Before the twentieth century, doctors knew very little about disease.
b. When little was known about germs, people's cleanliness habits were poor.
c. Before much was known about germs, doctors unknowingly caused much illness and death by spreading germs.
d. Before the twentieth century, doctors would finish one operation and go on to another without washing their hands.

B. Read each paragraph below. Then write what you think is the unstated main idea of the paragraph.

4. One excuse that gets in many students' way is "I can't do it." Instead of making an honest effort to do the work, the "I can't do it" type gives up before even starting. Then there is the "I'm too tired" excuse. Many students use this as a reason to give in to the temptation to nap when there is work to be done. Another common excuse for low achievement is "The instructor is boring." Students fond of this excuse expect every course to be highly entertaining and claim that they can't be expected to learn anything otherwise.

   What is the unstated main idea of this paragraph? _____

   _____

5. Very young infants enjoy big, bright toys to look at and chew. Colorful mobiles, squeaky animals, and strings of hard rubber beads are good choices for them. Older babies who can sit up enjoy toys they can grasp and explore with their hands. Cloth picture books, cups that nest inside each other, and balls covered with textured fabric will please a child of this age. Children between the ages of eighteen months and three years like toys matched to their increasing freedom of movement. Toy shopping carts, lawn mowers, wagons, and other push-and-pull toys are popular with children of this age.

   What is the unstated main idea of this paragraph? _____

   _____

➤ *Review Test 3*

A. To review what you've learned in this chapter, answer each of the following questions. Fill in the blank or circle the letter of the answer you think is correct.

   1. A paragraph without a topic sentence may have a(n) _____ main idea.

   2. _____ TRUE OR FALSE? In a paragraph without a topic sentence, the main idea is suggested by the supporting details.

   3. An implied main idea is
       a. a narrow idea.   b. unstated by the author.   c. stated by the author.

   4. To find the implied main idea of a paragraph, you may find it helpful to first decide on the paragraph's
       a. topic.   b. length.   c. topic sentence.

   5. Finding the implied main idea of a paragraph requires
       a. a dictionary.   b. reasoning.   c. topic sentences.

B. Here is a chance to apply your understanding of implied main ideas to a full-length reading. People who need help often don't ask for it directly. Some may shout at strangers or threaten to hurt someone. One woman in Chicago used a less violent but perhaps more shocking means to signal that things were not okay with her. The reactions of people around her were of special interest to newspaper columnist Bob Greene. Read his account of what happened. Then answer the questions that follow on the implied central point and main ideas and on the other reading comprehension skills you have learned.

Words to Watch

Following are some words in the reading that do not have strong context support. Each word is followed by the number of the paragraph in which it appears and its meaning there. These words are indicated in the article by a small circle (°).

   accounts (6): descriptions of the events
   titillation (7): excitement
   violating (8): disobeying
   fabric (8): structure
   rustle (9): move with a soft fluttering or crackling sound
   fault (9): a break in a rock
   avalanche (9): the slide or fall of a large mass
   resigned (9): accepting without a struggle
   trifling (9): unimportant
   assessment (9): tax

blissful (10): joyful
jeered (11): shouted with scorn
lewd (12): indecent
fragile (12): delicate
juvenile (15): childish

HANDLED WITH CARE

Bob Greene

The day the lady took her clothes off on Michigan Avenue, people   1
were leaving downtown as usual. The workday had come to an end;
men and women were heading for bus and train stations, in a hurry to
get home.

She walked south on Michigan; she was wearing a white robe, as   2
if she had been to the beach. She was blond and in her thirties.

As she passed the Radisson Hotel, Roosevelt Williams, a   3
doorman, was opening the door of a cab for one of the hotel's guests.
The woman did not really pause while she walked; she merely
shrugged the robe off, and it fell to the sidewalk.

She was wearing what appeared to be the bottom of a blue bikini   4
bathing suit, although one woman who was directly next to her said it
was just underwear. She wore nothing else.

Williams at first did not believe what he was seeing. If you hang   5
around long enough, you will see everything: robberies, muggings,
street fights, murders. But a naked woman on North Michigan Avenue?
Williams had not seen that before and neither, apparently, had the other
people on the street.

It was strange; her white robe lay on the sidewalk, and by all   6
accounts° she was smiling. But no one spoke to her. A report in the
newspaper the next day quoted someone: "The cars were stopping, the
people on the buses were staring, people were shouting, and people
were taking pictures." But that is not what other people who were there
that afternoon said.

The atmosphere was not carnival-like, they said. Rather, they said,   7
it was as if something very sad was taking place. It took only a moment
for people to realize that this was not some stunt designed to promote a
product or a movie. Without anything telling them, they understood
that the woman was troubled, and that what she was doing had nothing
to do with sexual titillation°; it was more of a cry for help.

The cry for help came in a way that such cries often come. The 8 woman was violating° one of the basic premises of the social fabric°. She was doing something that is not done. She was not shooting anyone, or breaking a window, or shouting in anger. Rather, in a way that everyone understood, she was signaling that things were not right.

The line is so thin between matters being manageable and being 9 out of hand. One day a person may be barely all right; the next the same person may have crossed over. Here is something from the author John Barth:

> She paused amid the kitchen to drink a glass of water; at that instant, losing a grip of fifty years, the next-room-ceiling plaster crashed. Or he merely sat in an empty study, in March-day glare, listening to the universe rustle° in his head, when suddenly a five-foot shelf let go. For ages the fault° creeps secret through the rock; in a second, ledge and railings, tourists and turbines all thunder over Niagara. Which snowflake triggers the avalanche°? A house explodes; a star. In your spouse, so apparently resigned°, murder twitches like a fetus. At some trifling° new assessment°, all the colonies rebel.

The woman continued to walk past Tribune Tower. People who 10 saw her said that the look on her face was almost peaceful. She did not seem to think she was doing anything unusual; she was described as appearing "blissful°." Whatever the reaction on the street was, she seemed calm, as if she believed herself to be in control.

She walked over the Michigan Avenue bridge. Again, people who 11 were there report that no one harassed her; no one jeered° at her or attempted to touch her. At some point on the bridge, she removed her bikini bottom. Now she was completely undressed, and still she walked.

"It was as if people knew not to bother her," said one woman who 12 was there. "To tell it, it sounds like something very lewd° and sensational was going on. But it wasn't like that at all. It was as if people knew that something very . . . fragile° . . . was taking place. I was impressed with the maturity with which people were handling it. No one spoke to her, but you could tell that they wished someone would help her."

Back in front of the Radisson, a police officer had picked up the 13 woman's robe. He was on his portable radio, advising his colleagues that the woman was walking over the bridge.

When the police caught up with the woman, she was just standing 14 there, naked in downtown Chicago, still smiling. The first thing the police did was hand her some covering and ask her to put it on; the show was over.

People who were there said that there was no reaction from the   15
people who were watching. They said that the juvenile° behavior you
might expect in such a situation just didn't happen. After all, when a
man walks out on a ledge in a suicide attempt, there are always people
down below who call for him to jump. But this day, by all accounts,
nothing like that took place. No one called for her to stay undressed; no
one cursed the police officers for stopping her.

"It was as if everyone was relieved," said a woman who saw it.   16
"They were embarrassed by it; it made them feel bad. They were glad
that someone had stopped her. And she was still smiling. She seemed to
be off somewhere."

The police charged her with no crime; they took her to Read   17
Mental Health Center, where she was reported to have signed herself in
voluntarily. Within minutes things were back to as they always are on
Michigan Avenue; there was no reminder of the naked lady who had
reminded people how fragile is the everyday world in which we live.

Reading Comprehension Questions

Vocabulary in Context

1. The word *stunt* in "It took only a moment for people to realize that this was
   not some stunt designed to promote a product or a movie" (paragraph 7)
   means
   a. trick.
   b. danger.
   c. accident.
   d. race.

2. The word *premises* in "The woman was violating one of the basic premises
   of the social fabric. She was doing something that is not done" (paragraph 8)
   means
   a. deep cuts.
   b. tests of friendship.
   c. assumptions or rules.
   d. crimes.

3. The phrase *out of hand* in "The line is so thin between matters being
   manageable and being out of hand" (paragraph 9) means
   a. frightening.
   b. outdoors.
   c. close by.
   d. unmanageable.

4. The word *harassed* in "no one harassed her; no one jeered at her or attempted to touch her" (paragraph 11) means
   a. imitated.
   b. ignored.
   c. bothered.
   d. hired.

5. The word *colleagues* in "a police officer . . . was on his portable radio, advising his colleagues that the woman was walking over the bridge. When the police caught up with the woman, she was just standing there" (paragraphs 13–14) refers to
   a. friends.
   b. relatives.
   c. fellow police officers.
   d. nearby witnesses.

Central Point

6. Which sentence best expresses the implied central point of the entire selection?
   a. The police can be counted on to help someone who has lost control of her life.
   b. People can be sympathetic when someone loses control of her life.
   c. Mentally ill people can behave in very strange ways.
   d. People are expected to wear clothing in public.

Main Ideas

7. Which sentence best expresses the implied main idea of paragraphs 6 and 7?
   a. Nobody spoke to the woman.
   b. According to a newspaper report, people shouted and took pictures of the woman.
   c. Contrary to a newspaper account, people realized the woman was disturbed, and they behaved sympathetically.
   d. At first people thought the woman's behavior might be a stunt to promote a product or a movie.

8. The implied main idea of paragraph 15 is
   a. Spectators often behave badly toward people who are going through a crisis.
   b. Nobody shouted for the woman to stay undressed.
   c. People were not annoyed when the police stopped the woman.
   d. People did not react immaturely to the woman's nudity.

9. The implied main idea of paragraph 17 is
   a. The woman was taken to a mental health center, and things quickly got back to normal on Michigan Avenue.
   b. The police decided that the woman had not committed a crime.
   c. The police had more to worry about than a mentally ill woman.
   d. The woman signed herself into the Read Mental Health Center.

Supporting Details

　　10. ＿＿＿＿＿ TRUE OR FALSE? Spectators asked if they could help the woman.

Mapping Activity

In general, this selection is organized by time: first one thing happened, then another, next another, and so on. Four of the major events are scrambled in the list below. Write them in the diagram in their correct order.

- She continued walking, removing her bikini bottom as she crossed a bridge.
- The police caught up with the woman and had her get dressed.
- As a woman walked past a hotel, she dropped her robe; she was wearing only a bikini bottom.
- The police took the woman to a mental health center, where she signed herself in.

Central point: When a woman showed her need for help by violating one of society's basic rules, people responded sympathetically.

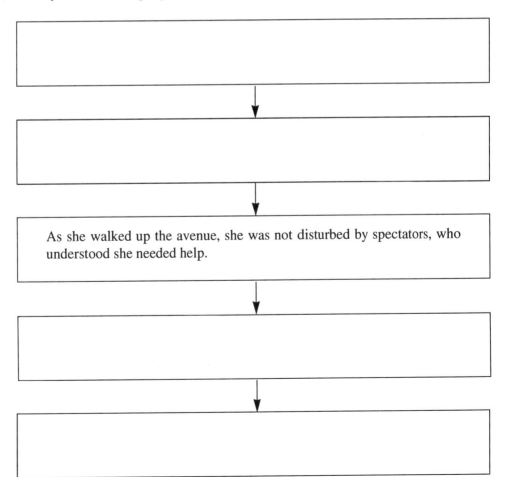

Discussion Questions

1.   Most of us never experience loss of control as great as that of the woman in the selection. But we all have times when we lose some of our control. What can cause you to stop studying on a regular basis, or to stop eating or sleeping well, or to stop being respectful of others?

2.   Greene states that the woman who took off her clothes was "doing something that is not done." What are some other things that are definitely "not done" in public? For instance, what are our unspoken rules about dress at school and work, interaction with strangers on the street, and restaurant manners?

Writing Activities

1.   The author tells us that when the woman took her clothes off, "she was signaling that something was not right." Write about a time in your life, or in the life of someone you know, when things were "not right," or out of control. What caused the crisis? What happened as a result? You might, for instance, write about one of the following: (1) the loss of a loved one; (2) a time when you were having trouble on the job or in school; (3) a serious illness (yours or that of someone you know); (4) a situation involving drug, alcohol, or sexual abuse.

2.   Most of us have not done something as socially unacceptable as the woman in Chicago. But we've all done something "crazy," such as punching a hole in the wall or putting an ad in the local paper proposing marriage. Write a paper telling about a time you did something very out of the ordinary. Your central point might begin: "The craziest thing I ever did was . . . " Include your reasons for doing what you did and the consequences of your actions.

Check Your Performance			IMPLIED MAIN IDEAS
Activity	*Number Right*	*Points*	*Total*
Review Test 1 (10 items)	_____	x 3 =	_____
Review Test 2 (5 items)	_____	x 3 =	_____
Review Test 3, Part A (5 items)	_____	x 3 =	_____
Review Test 3, Part B (10 items)	_____	x 3 =	_____
Mapping (4 items)	_____	x 2.5 =	_____
		TOTAL SCORE =	_____%

Enter your total score into the reading performance chart on the inside back cover.

7

More About
Supporting Details

Chapter 4 explained supporting details and gave you practice with the careful reading needed to understand those details. This chapter will explain the difference between two types of supporting details: major and minor. It will also describe two helpful ways to locate both kinds of supporting details.

UNDERSTANDING MAJOR AND MINOR SUPPORTING DETAILS

There are two types of supporting details, major and minor. To understand the difference between the two, look at a paragraph you've already seen. Below is the main idea of the paragraph.

Main Idea

There are two main causes of headaches.

How much do we learn from that general sentence? Not much. If the author named the two causes, we would have a better understanding of the general idea. Those two causes would then be the major supporting details of the paragraph. **Major details** are the separate, chief points that support the main idea. Below is the same main idea with two major details.

Main Idea with Major Details

There are two main causes of headaches. Research shows that most headaches result from muscle tension. Headaches can also be caused by changes in the supply of blood to the head.

Now there is some meat on the bare bones of the main idea. The author has provided major details (the two main causes of headaches) to support the main idea. Together, the main idea and the major supporting details form the basic framework of paragraphs.

These major details are often more fully explained, and that's where minor supporting details come in. Major details provide more information about the main idea, and **minor supporting details** provide added information about the major details.

The paragraph on the causes of headaches can be filled out even more with some minor details. The result would be a paragraph like the one below.

Main Idea with Major and Minor Details

There are two main causes of headaches. Research shows that most headaches result from muscle tension. And the most common reason for that muscle tension is continuing stress. Headaches can also be caused by changes in the supply of blood to the head. Such changes are often reactions to pollen and food chemicals.

Just as the major details expanded on the main idea, the minor details have further explained the major details. Now the main idea has even more meaning for us.

Here is an umbrella design like the ones in the first chapter on the main idea. It shows the main idea and the major and minor supporting details that fit under the main idea.

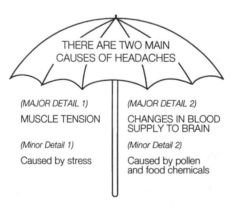

Sometimes paragraphs contain only major details, as in the paragraph on greeting cards. Reread that paragraph (on p. 52), and you will see that each sentence presents one major detail, one fact to support the main idea. More often, however, paragraphs include both major and minor details. When this happens, you should be able to identify the major details and any minor details that support them.

A Model Paragraph

Try your hand at separating major from minor support in the paragraph below. The first sentence gives the main idea. Then the paragraph goes on to present three major details in support of the main idea. In the spaces following the paragraph, write the three major details. Then read the explanation that follows.

As you read, watch for words that commonly introduce new points, such as *first, secondly, also, next,* and *finally.* Such words are sometimes called **addition words**.

> During the 1950s, when television became a part of American family life, television audiences preferred three kinds of shows. First, comedy shows were popular. *I Love Lucy* and *The Texaco Star Theater* were among the most loved comedy shows. Also, variety shows were common. *The Ed Sullivan Show* and *Arthur Godfrey's Talent Scouts* are examples of popular variety shows of the time. Finally, viewers of the 50s loved game shows. *Beat the Clock* and *The $64,000 Question* were two of the most popular.

Main idea: During the 1950s, when television became a part of family life, television audiences preferred three kinds of shows.

Major supporting detail 1: _____

Major supporting detail 2: _____

Major supporting detail 3: _____

Explanation:

The first major detail is introduced by the word *first:* "First, comedy shows were popular."

The second major detail is introduced by the word *also:* "Also, variety shows were common."

The third major detail is introduced by the addition word *finally:* "Finally, viewers of the 50s loved game shows."

Now go back to the paragraph and look for the minor supporting details—the details that support the major ideas. Fill those details into the blanks below. (One has been filled in for you.) Then read the explanation that follows.

Main idea: During the 1950s, when television became a part of American family life, television audiences preferred three kinds of shows.

Major supporting detail 1: Comedy shows

Minor details: a. *I Love Lucy*

b. _____

Major supporting detail 2: Variety shows

Minor details: a. _____

b. _____

Major supporting detail 3: Game shows

Minor details: a. _____

b. _____

Explanation:

The minor supporting details illustrate the major details. The first two minor details are examples of comedy shows: a) *I Love Lucy* and b) *The Texaco Star Theater*. The second two minor details are examples of variety shows: a) *The Ed Sullivan Show* and b) *Arthur Godfrey's Talent Scouts*. The third set of details are examples of game shows: a) *Beat the Clock* and b) *The $64,000 Question*.

A fully stated version of each major and minor detail would be in sentence form. For example, one way to fully state the first major detail of the outline is: "Comedy shows were popular in the 1950s." The first minor detail could be stated like this: "*I Love Lucy* was among the most popular comedy shows." In outlines, however, it is often useful to summarize a statement in a word or phrase.

➤ *Practice 1*

Major and minor supporting details are mixed together in the lists that follow. The details of each list support a given main idea. Separate the major supporting details from the minor ones by filling in the outlines. Some details have already been filled in. Remember that the major supporting details will be more general than the minor details.

List 1

Main idea: People enjoy different kinds of pets.

- Snakes
- Dogs
- Cats
- Rats
- Traditional pets

Major detail: 1. Unusual pets

Minor details: a. _____

                b. Spiders

                c. _____

Major detail: 2. _____

Minor details: a. _____

                b. _____

                c. Birds

List 2

Main idea: Snacks can be divided into two types.

- Junk food
- Apples
- Healthy food
- Strawberries
- Potato chips
- Candy

Major detail: 1. _____

Minor details: a. _____

                b. Cake

                c. _____

Major detail: 2. _____

Minor details: a. _____

                b. _____

                c. Carrot sticks

List 3

Main idea: Popular vacation destinations can be found across the country.

- New Orleans is especially popular during Mardi Gras.
- The South has much to offer.
- California's beaches attract people year-round.
- Boston has sites that date back to the Revolutionary War.
- Florida has beautiful beaches and many theme parks.
- Las Vegas, Nevada, has gambling and shows featuring famous stars.
- The East has a wealth of historical sites.
- Philadelphia has attractions such as the Liberty Bell.

Major detail: 1. The West has many distinct attractions.

Minor details: a. _____

_____

b. Arizona is known for its scenic deserts.

c. _____

_____

Major detail: 2. _____

_____

Minor details: a. _____

_____

b. San Antonio, Texas, blends the cultures of Texas and Mexico.

c. _____

_____

Major detail: 3. _____

_____

Minor details: a. Washington, D.C., has been the nation's capital for almost 200 years.

b. _____

_____

c. _____

_____

TWO HELPFUL WAYS TO LOCATE MAJOR DETAILS

Two common ways in which authors alert you to the major details of a passage are by using:

1 An opening phrase

2 Addition words, such as *first, second,* and *next.*

An *opening phrase* often tells you that a particular series of details is coming. And *addition words* often introduce each of the details. You can use each of these clues to help you find the major details of a passage. Often a paragraph contains both an opening phrase and one or more addition words. Following is a look at each technique.

Opening Phrases

Paragraphs often contain a main idea and a list of supporting details—a list of reasons, examples, steps, and so on. Opening phrases often signal what type of detail to watch for. Here are some typical opening phrases:

Opening Phrases

several kinds of	a few causes of	two advantages
a few reasons	several characteristics	four steps
various factors	three types	a number of ways

When you see phrases like those above, you can expect a list of major supporting details to follow.

Note that each of the opening phrases in the box above includes a word that ends in the letter *s*. These are plurals that refer to the kinds of details that will be listed, such as kind*s*, characteristic*s*, reason*s*, step*s*, and factor*s*. These plurals will help you identify the major details that are listed. At times, you will even know *how many* major details to expect. For example, opening phrases may "tell" you to look for *two* advantages, *three* types, or *four* steps.

Opening phrases are often part of the topic sentence. Following, for example, are two typical topic sentences:

1. There are four main causes of heart disease.

   (The opening phrase *four main causes of heart disease* suggests that the author will list the four causes.)

2. Five magazines have a circulation of over ten million a month.

   (The opening phrase *five magazines* suggests that the author is going to list these magazines.)

To help you understand opening phrases, read the paragraph below. Then complete the outline: First write down the opening phrase that is used as a heading, being sure to include the word that ends in *s*. Next, list the three major details. Then read the explanation that follows the outline.

Psychologists have suggested three methods for helping people overcome test anxiety. Writing out answers and imagining a test situation when you are completely relaxed can help make you less nervous. The second suggestion is to overlearn. Even when you think you understand and know the information completely, keep studying. This will increase your confidence. It will also keep the answers more available when anxiety strikes. The third technique is to put yourself into a relaxed state before entering the examination room. Think of something soothing, perhaps the sounds of waves splashing on the shore as you sit on the sand soaking up sunshine. This method is useful only if you tend toward high anxiety.

Heading: _____s for helping people
    overcome test anxiety

List of major details:

1. _____

_____

2. _____

3. _____

_____

Explanation:

The topic sentence of the paragraph is the first one: "Psychologists have suggested three methods for helping people overcome test anxiety." The opening phrase that describes the type of detail being listed is "three methods for helping people overcome test anxiety." Those methods are the three major details:

1. Writing out answers and imagining a test situation when you are completely relaxed
2. Overlearning
3. Putting yourself in a relaxed state before entering the exam room

Addition Words

Addition words often introduce supporting details. Here are some common addition words:

Addition Words

first	third	next	finally
first of all	also	in addition	last
one	another	additionally	last of all
second	moreover	furthermore	

In the paragraph above on overcoming test anxiety, the last two major details are introduced with addition words. The second major detail is introduced with the addition word *second* ("The second suggestion is to overlearn"). The third major detail is introduced with the addition word *third* ("The third technique is to put yourself into a relaxed state before entering the examination room").

To check your understanding, read the paragraph below. Underline the opening phrase that tells you a list is coming. Next, complete the outline that follows by filling in the major details. Then read the explanation.

> ¹In our busy lives, there are several ways we manage to save time. ²First, we use modern inventions that help us do more in less time. ³We use a microwave oven, for instance, to cook a baked potato at least ten times faster than once possible. ⁴We also save time by doing more than one thing at once. ⁵For example, a student may finish writing a paper, eat breakfast, and put on his or her shoes all at the same time. ⁶Finally, of course, we may simply rush. ⁷We may save time by gulping a meal or running to catch a bus.

Main idea: There are several ways we manage to save time.

Major supporting details:

1. _____

2. _____

3. _____

Explanation:

The main idea of this paragraph is in the first sentence. It includes the opening phrase "several ways." We learn right away that the paragraph will list several ways we save time.

In sentence 2, the addition word *first* introduces the first major detail: "we use modern inventions that help us do more in less time." Sentence 3 gives a minor detail, in the form of an example about the microwave oven. (Remember, minor details do not introduce new points; minor details make major details more clear.)

In sentence 4, the addition word *also* signals the second major detail: "we save time by doing more than one thing at once." Sentence 5 gives a minor detail—an example of saving time by doing two or more things at once.

In sentence 6, the addition word *finally* introduces the third and last major detail: "we may simply rush." Sentence 7 gives examples, the minor details about gulping food and rushing for a bus.

The opening phrase and the addition words have helped us identify the major details. Here is an outline showing the main idea and major details:

Main idea: There are several ways we manage to save time.

1. We use modern inventions that help us do more in less time.
2. We save time by doing more than one thing at once.
3. We may simply rush.

Be on the lookout, then, for opening phrases. They signal the topic sentence, and they suggest what kind of major detail to look for in a paragraph. Also look for addition words, which often indicate that major details will follow.

CONCLUSION

To get the most out of your reading, you must read attentively. Look for the main idea and the details that support it. Notice which details are the separate, chief points that support the main idea. Those are the major supporting details. The points that clarify the major details are the minor details. Be on the lookout for opening phrases that signal that a list of major details will follow. And look for addition words that often help you locate individual major details.

The rest of this chapter is made up of exercises giving you practice in finding main ideas and supporting details. When you finish, you should have a good understanding of the difference between major and minor details.

➤ *Practice 2*

In the spaces provided, complete the notes on each paragraph: First complete the headings, being sure to include the word that ends in *s*. Then fill in the missing major details.

In each paragraph, the topic sentence is boldfaced, and the addition words that signal major details are set off in italics.

A.   **In any high school, almost every student belongs to one of three subcultures.** *One* subculture is the delinquent group, the least popular of the subcultures. Members of this group hate school, the faculty, and any other authority figures. The *next* step up the ladder of popularity is the academic subculture. Hard-working students who value their education belong to this group. The *third* subculture is the most popular—the fun subculture. Looks, clothes, cars, dates and social status are what interest members of this group.

Heading: _____s in Any High School

List of major details:

1. _____
2. _____
3. _____

B. **Various types of remedies have been developed for snoring.** *One* common type of remedy tries to keep people from sleeping on their backs, the usual position for snoring. Such remedies include gadgets like the "snore ball whistle," a rubber ball clipped to the seat of the snorer's pajamas. The ball whistles when the snorer rolls onto his or her back. There are *also* various anti-snoring chin straps. They are based on the fact that people can't snore if they don't open their mouths. A *third*, less common remedy is surgery. That works only in the rare cases where the snoring is caused by growths of tissue in the sinus area.

Heading: _____s of Remedies for Snoring

List of major details:

1. _____
2. _____
3. _____

➤ *Practice 3*

In the spaces provided, complete the notes on each paragraph: First complete the headings, being sure to include the word that ends in *s*. Then fill in the missing major details.

In each paragraph, the topic sentence is boldfaced, but the addition words are *not* in italics.

A. **Although smoking cigarettes is never healthy, there are three ways to reduce the risk involved.** First of all, switch to a low-tar and low-nicotine brand. Some cigarettes have twice as much of these dangerous ingredients as others. Secondly, allow less smoke to enter your lungs. Instead of inhaling deeply, take short, shallow puffs of the cigarette. And finally, put out the cigarette when it's half gone. The last half of each cigarette contains 60 percent of its tar and nicotine.

Heading: _____s to Reduce the Risks of Smoking

List of major details:

1. _____
2. _____
3. _____

B.   **You will do better on tests if you follow a few simple suggestions.** First, study experts say that slow and steady preparation for exams is best. Cramming the night before is less effective and more stressful. Another helpful method is to arrive early for a test. It's calming to have a few minutes to sit down in the classroom, collect one's thoughts, and find a pen. Third, once the test begins, answer the easier questions first. Then go back and tackle the hard ones. Finally, you will do better on essay questions if you make a brief outline before beginning to write.

Heading: _____s for Doing Better on Tests

List of major details:

1. _____

2. _____

3. _____

4. _____

➤ Practice 4

Answer the questions that follow each paragraph. The topic sentence of each paragraph is boldfaced.

A.   Science fiction writer Arthur C. Clarke correctly predicted when a rocket would first go to the moon. **Clarke has also made many interesting predictions for later in this century.** One of these predictions is that we'll have cars without wheels. He feels cars will be made that can float on air instead of rolling on the ground. He has also predicted that there will be settlements on the moon. They will exist under air-conditioned domes, where food will be grown. Materials for the buildings in these settlements will be mined from the moon itself, he says.

1. The main idea suggests that this paragraph will list certain
   a. writings.
   b. times.
   c. predictions.

2. The major details of this paragraph are
   a. 1) predictions, 2) cars, and 3) settlements on the moon.
   b. 1) cars without wheels and 2) settlements on the moon.
   c. 1) food grown under domes and 2) building materials mined on the moon.

3. The first major detail is introduced with the transition
   a. *one.*
   b. *these.*
   c. *also.*

4. *Fill in the blank:* Clarke feels cars will one day move by _____

_____ .

5. *Fill in the blank:* Clarke predicts that people will live on the moon under

_____ .

B. [1]Prescription drugs can be just as dangerous as illegal drugs if used carelessly. [2]**To avoid the dangers of prescribed drugs, consumers should follow several guidelines.** [3]One is to become aware of a drug's possible side effects. [4]Unexpected side effects, such as dizziness, can be frightening and even dangerous. [5]The patient should also find out if it is safe to take the medicine along with other drugs he or she is using. [6]Some combinations of drugs can be deadly. [7]Finally, medicine should always be stored in its own labeled bottle. [8]Accidental mix-ups of drugs can have tragic results.

1. The opening phrase that tells what type of major detail to watch for is
   a. *prescribed drugs.*
   b. *consumers.*
   c. *several guidelines.*

2. The last major detail is introduced by the addition word
   a. *one.*
   b. *also.*
   c. *finally.*

3. *Fill in the missing major detail:* The major details of the paragraph are 1) know a drug's side effects, 2) know if a drug can be taken with one's other

   medicines, and 3) _____

_____

4. A minor detail of the paragraph is presented in sentence
   a. 2.
   b. 5.
   c. 6.

5. *Fill in the blank:* Drugs can be deadly if combined with _____

_____

➤ *Review Test 1*

A. (1-5.) Major and minor supporting details are mixed together in the list that follows. The details of this list support the given main idea. Separate the major, more general details from the minor ones by filling in the outline. Some details have been filled in for you.

Main idea: Building materials can be classified in two groups.

- Manufactured materials
- Natural materials
- Clay
- Glass
- Wood

Major detail: 1. _____

Minor details: a. Straw

                    b. _____

                    c. _____

Major detail: 2. _____

Minor details: a. Concrete

                    b. Plastic

                    c. _____

B. (6-10.) In the spaces provided, complete the notes on each paragraph: First complete the headings, being sure to include the word that ends in *s*. Then fill in the missing major details. The topic sentence of each paragraph is set off in boldface.

1.   **Good speakers talk with their bodies in several ways.** First, they use eye contact. Eye contact helps speakers build a warm bond with the audience. It also tells them whether or not they are keeping the audience's interest. Facial expressions are another way speakers use their bodies. Good speakers use facial expressions to stress their words. Last are hand movements, which good speakers also use to accent what is being said.

    Heading: _____s That Good Speakers Talk with
                Their Bodies

    List of major details:

    1. Eye contact

    2. Facial expressions

    3. _____

2. **There are four kinds of employee behavior that bosses dislike, says a recent survey.** First is dishonesty. If a boss thinks an employee cannot be trusted, nothing else about that worker will matter. The second thing bosses dislike is irresponsibility. They hate when workers waste time or do personal business during the workday. Bosses also dislike lateness. One employer said, "It doesn't matter when we start—9 a.m. or 10 a.m. Some people will still be fifteen minutes late." Finally, bosses, of course, dislike many absences.

Heading: _____s of Employee Behavior That
   Bosses Dislike

List of major details:

1. Dishonesty

2. _____

3. _____

4. Many absences

➤ *Review Test 2*

Answer the questions that follow the paragraphs. The topic sentence of each paragraph is set off in boldface.

A. **In addition to fresh vegetables, gardening offers several health benefits.** One study found that gardeners have fewer heart attacks than others. The reasons seem to be that being around plants lowers blood pressure and helps people better resist stress. Another benefit of gardening is harder bones. For women, who are at risk of weak bones, this benefit is especially important. Experts feel that work such as pushing a wheelbarrow or lugging bags of manure slows bone loss. A third benefit of gardening is that it provides safe exercise.

1. As the topic sentence suggests, the major details of the paragraph are
   a. fresh vegetables.
   b. health benefits of gardening.
   c. reasons that gardeners have fewer heart attacks.

2. Specifically, the major details of this paragraph are
   a. 1) blood pressure and 2) resistance to stress.
   b. 1) the pleasures of fresh vegetables and 2) health benefits.
   c. 1) fewer heart attacks, 2) harder bones, and 3) safe exercise.

3-4. According to some researchers, what are the two reasons that being among

plants may lower heart attacks? _____

5. Experts feel that bones benefit from
   a. fewer heart attacks.
   b. low blood pressure.
   c. certain work.

B.   [1]**The word** *spinster* **has had different meanings throughout history.** [2]In the 1600s, this word referred to any female. [3]Spinning thread or yarn for cloth was something every woman did at home. [4]By 1700, *spinster* had become a legal term for an unmarried woman. [5]Such women had to work to survive, and spinning was their most common job. [6]Before long, however, spinning was done in factories. [7]*Spinster* then suggested someone who was "left over" or "dried up," just as the job of home spinning had dried up for women. [8]Today, with so many women working, most single women consider the word *spinster* an insult.

6. In general, the major supporting details in this paragraph are
   a. important events in the history of women's work.
   b. events in the history of spinning thread and yarn.
   c. different meanings of the word *spinster* throughout history.

7. Fill in the blank: In the 1600s, the word *spinster* referred to _____

   _____

8. The answer to question 7 can be found in sentence
   a. 1.
   b. 2.
   c. 4.

9. By 1700, single women were called spinsters because
   a. spinning was done by all women.
   b. most single women made their livings by spinning.
   c. spinning was no longer done at home.

10. When spinning was done in factories, *spinster* came to mean
    a. any woman.
    b. a woman who spins.
    c. a "left over" or "dried up" woman.

➤ *Review Test 3*

A. To review what you've learned in this chapter, answer each of the following questions. Fill in the blank, or circle the letter of the answer you think is correct.

1. _____ TRUE OR FALSE? Major supporting details are more general than minor supporting details.

2. Opening phrases can tell us
   a. that a list of some type will follow.
   b. how many major details will follow.
   c. both of the above.

3. An addition word can tell us
   a. how many major details to expect.
   b. that a new major detail is being introduced.
   c. both of the above.

4-5. Fill in each blank with an addition word or phrase:

   _____   _____

6-10. Label each part of the outline form below with one of the following:

   • Main idea
   • Major supporting detail
   • Minor supporting detail

   _____

   1. _____

      a. _____

      b. _____

   2. _____

B. Here is a chance to apply your understanding of supporting details to a full-length reading. First, read the following selection by a college student who has had a tough time figuring out her life. She has had to move between countries and adjust to their cultures, and she has had a difficult time making friends. Yet she is determined to succeed. After reading the selection, answer the supporting detail questions that follow. There are also other comprehension questions to help you continue practicing the skills you learned in earlier chapters.

Words to Watch

Following are some words in the reading that do not have strong context support. Each word is followed by the number of the paragraph in which it appears and its meaning there. These words are indicated in the story by a small circle (°).

shuttled (1): sent back and forth
detested (5): hated
prescribed (5): required
perennial (5): continual
ironic (5): opposite to what might be expected
snobbish (6): self-satisfied and superior
on a much smaller scale (10): to a smaller degree
grapple (11): struggle
expectant (12): looking forward

MY OWN TWO FEET

Irina Marjan

Sometimes in my life, I have felt like the world's orphan. I have 1 been shuttled° between two countries, yet I don't fully belong to either one. I speak their languages, but I sound "foreign" to the native speakers of both. I have had two sets of parents, yet neither set has really wanted or accepted me. I turned 18, and I just started attending college. Even if neither of my two sets of parents has truly helped me, I am finding that I have my own two feet, and I'm beginning to stand on them.

In the beginning, I didn't know who my parents were or where I 2 belonged. I was born in Queens, New York, and shipped off at nine months to Belgrade, Yugoslavia. My parents had their own problems and couldn't take proper care of me.

I lived with my grandparents and aunt and uncle in Lokve, 3

Yugoslavia. For a long time, I thought that my aunt and uncle were my parents, so when my mother came to see me, I ran away from her because I didn't know who she was. My foster parents had never told me that they were not my parents, much less who my parents were. They didn't like my mother, so they didn't say a word to help me to understand who this strange visitor was. My mother was upset because I didn't want to talk to her. One day, she caught me by my hair and made me listen. "You listen," said the woman, "I'm your mother." After that, she brought me back to the U.S., where I stayed with my parents for a year but was sent back to Yugoslavia because they still didn't get along, and I wasn't welcome any more.

At the age of five, when it was time to start school in Yugoslavia, 4 the children in kindergarten were rude. I only had one friend, and we used to cry together because no one liked us. We would run out the door as soon as the teacher went on her break. I would run home, and my grandfather would bring me back to school. It was the "highlight" of every school day. My schoolmates reminded me about this till I was in seventh grade.

If this was not enough, then there was the obstacle of learning to 5 speak Serbian. The Serbian language was the official language of Yugoslavia even though there were many other languages spoken regionally. For example, the school I attended was the school for the children of Romanian-speaking people living in the area. All of my classes were in Romanian except for my Serbian language class. At that school, the only foreign language offered was French. I had to make a decision whether to stay in that school and learn French or transfer to a Serbian school which had more foreign languages, including English, which I wanted to learn. If I'd transferred, then I'd have had to take all my classes in Serbian, which I hated. What I already detested° in my Serbian language class were the prescribed° essays that I had to write, in particular the perennial° favorite "Moja domovina"—"My country." This was ironic° because it wasn't even my country!

There was a Serbian school nearby, but the Serbians who attended 6 it were arrogant and had snobbish° attitudes toward non-Serbians who wanted to go to their school. Therefore, I decided to stay and learn French. I never did learn English.

In the summer of 1988, at 14, I came to the U.S. to visit my 7 parents. At that point, there was nothing for me to go back to in Yugoslavia because I had gotten to be too much of a responsibility for my aunt and uncle since I'd entered puberty. But ultimately I didn't want to go back because I knew I would have to attend a high school where classes were taught entirely in Serbian.

At that moment, I decided that I ought to remain in the U.S. My   8
father still wanted to send me back, but that's when I started taking
charge of my life. I told him that I wanted to stay in the U.S. and make
something out of my life. I decided that I would go to school here and
reach high. I would graduate with a master's degree in business some
day. And I would speak and write perfect English.

A dream and the realization of a dream may be separated by many   9
years and many hurdles. One hurdle for me was graduating from high
school. High school was hard. I had to learn English. I had to make
new friends. I had to work to make money. In English my biggest
problem was my accent. I will never forget my first oral report. It was a
health class, and we had to do a report on drugs and alcohol. I listened
to everyone's report, but no one listened to mine. The whole class was
laughing instead of listening. I had a strong accent, and I was reading
very fast because I was nervous. It was funny for my classmates, but
for me it was one of the worst experiences in my life. I had to talk to
people who didn't care what I had to say about drugs and alcohol. Also,
these rude people were the very people that I had to become friends
with. I cried every day because I was lonely and had no one to call a
friend. I had an accent, and I was different than everyone else.
Therefore, it was hard for them to accept me. As my English improved,
they began to accept me. I could feel that my life was getting better. I
did better in my classes and became friends with many people. Still, I
was working from 4 to 8 p.m. I had to stay up till 2 a.m. to finish my
school work; I had to learn English and do well in my classes in order
to graduate.

On a much smaller scale°, even when things were improving, they   10
had a way of making me stumble. The silly matter of my hair almost
held me back from going to college this fall. I had damaged my hair
badly with chemical processes, and I couldn't do anything to fix it
because it was far too damaged. It was mixed gray, yellow straw, and
brown. I was scared because I lost a lot of hair when I brushed it.
Handfuls of the tangled colors came out. I didn't know how I could
start college with so little and such hair. Finally, I cut it all to the roots
and bravely started college with a boy's crew cut. I was not going to let
anything push me aside in my path to a degree.

Now that I'm here in an English-speaking college on this side of   11
the Atlantic at last, I foresee a rough road financially, but at 18 and with
my sense that I can grapple° with hardship and come out on my feet, I
think I can do it. I work twenty-five hours a week for five dollars an
hour and have scheduled a full college load. I don't play around with
perms or hair color, but I do keep my eyes on the prize. I'm beginning

to feel as American as my passport declares, and I'm told by my teachers that I'm a real student.

I guess I had to learn who I was, where I came from, where I 12 belonged, what I wanted to do with my life, and where I would want to live it before I could start taking charge of it. Now at 18, I've started taking charge of my life, and I'm trying to make the best of it. I can look back and see the long road from the tears in my first grade class to the hopeful and expectant° attitude I bring to college, and to the rest of my life.

Reading Comprehension Questions

Vocabulary in Context

1. The word *arrogant* in "There was a Serbian school nearby, but the Serbians who attended it were arrogant and had snobbish attitudes toward non-Serbians" (paragraph 6) means
   a. conceited.
   b. pleasant.
   c. intelligent.
   d. normal.

2. The word *foresee* in "Now that I'm here in an English-speaking college on this side of the Atlantic at last, I foresee a rough road financially" (paragraph 11) means
   a. forget.
   b. predict.
   c. appreciate.
   d. want.

Central Point and Main Ideas

3. Which sentence best expresses the central point of the selection?
   a. Sometimes Marjan felt like "the world's orphan."
   b. Marjan did not want to go back to Yugoslavia because she knew she would have to attend a high school there where classes were taught entirely in Serbian.
   c. From her childhood on, Marjan overcome many obstacles to eventually take charge of her life and aim for success.
   d. It was during her high school years that Marjan had to learn English, make new friends, and work hard to earn money.

4. Which sentence best expresses the implied main idea of paragraphs 4–6?
   a. The author found her school life in Yugoslavia to be pleasant.
   b. The author had big social problems.
   c. The author's grandfather was her best friend.
   d. The author had great challenges to deal with in Yugoslavian schools.

5. The main idea of paragraph 10 is expressed in its
   a. second sentence.
   b. third sentence.
   c. fourth sentence.
   d. fifth sentence.

Supporting Details

6. _____ TRUE OR FALSE? The author never found out who her parents were.

7. _____ TRUE OR FALSE? At age 14, the author did not want to return to Yugoslavia because the classes were taught in Serbian.

8. Marjan feels she began taking charge of her life when she
   a. lived in Yugoslavia.
   b. decided not to attend the Serbian school.
   c. decided at age fourteen to stay in the U.S.
   d. bravely started college with a boy's crew cut.

9. The major details of paragraphs 4–6 are
   a. the author's Yugoslavian friends and family.
   b. the languages the author knew as a child.
   c. the author's schoolmates and neighbors in Yugoslavia.
   d. the challenges of dealing with rude classmates and the Serbian language in school.

10. A central point is supported by major details, just as main ideas are. The major details of the entire selection are
    a. obstacles the author faced in Yugoslavia.
    b. the author's family problems.
    c. challenges the author has met on the way to taking charge of her life.
    d. obstacles the author has faced in all of her school work.

Mapping Activity

This selection follows Marjan's life in two countries. The major events described by the author are written below. Circle the name of the country she was in when each incident occurred.

- Marjan is born in (Yugoslavia; the United States).

- At nine months, Marjan is sent to (Yugoslavia; the United States).

- Marjan starts kindergarten in (Yugoslavia; the United States).

- At age 14, Marjan visits her parents in (Yugoslavia; the United States).

- Marjan graduates from high school in (Yugoslavia; the United States).

Discussion Questions

1. Marjan writes that at the age of fourteen, she decided that she should remain in the U.S. Do you think this is old enough to decide where you want to live? What types of decisions were you making at the age of fourteen?

2. Marjan states that she had trouble making friends in high school because "I had an accent, and I was different than everyone else." What could the school have done to make life easier for a foreign student like Marjan? What could her fellow students have done?

Writing Activities

1. We might conclude from the reading that one of Marjan's struggles was to build her self-esteem. Write a paragraph telling what steps people can take to strengthen their self-esteem. Your topic sentence will be "There are a number of things people can do to build up their own self-esteem." Where possible, use examples to illustrate your points.

2. In paragraph 9, Marjan discusses the difficulties she had to face in high school. Write a paper describing the difficulties you had to face in high school. If you eventually overcame them, explain how. To illustrate the points you make, include detailed descriptions of incidents.

    Alternatively, write a paper about the challenges you had to face as a young child or as an elementary school student.

Check Your Performance   MORE ABOUT SUPPORTING DETAILS

Activity	*Number Right*	*Points*	*Total*
Review Test 1 (10 items)	_____	x 2.5 =	_____
Review Test 2 (10 items)	_____	x 2.5 =	_____
Review Test 3, Part A (10 items)	_____	x 2 =	_____
Review Test 3, Part B (10 items)	_____	x 2 =	_____
Mapping (5 items)	_____	x 2 =	_____
		TOTAL SCORE =	_____%

Enter your total score into the reading performance chart on the inside back cover.

8

Transitions

Read the following sentences:

I love drinking coffee. It keeps me awake at night.

The author's point in these two sentences is unclear. Does the writer love drinking coffee *because* it keeps him awake at night? Or does he like drinking coffee *although* it keeps him awake at night? To make the author's point clear, a *transition* is needed. **Transitions** are words and phrases (like *because* and *although*) that show the connections between ideas. They guide readers in the same way that signposts inform travelers. To show how transitions direct us, here are the same two ideas, but this time with a transition:

I love drinking coffee *even though* it keeps me awake at night.

Now the writer's point is clear: he loves drinking coffee *in spite of* its keeping him awake at night. The transition has provided a bridge between the two ideas. In Latin, *trans* means "across," and transitions live up to their name by carrying the reader "across" from one idea to another.

SIX COMMON TYPES OF TRANSITIONS

There are six major types of transitions:

1 Words that show addition
2 Words that show time
3 Words that show contrast
4 Words that show comparison
5 Words that show illustration
6 Words that show cause and effect

Each of these transitions will be explained on the pages that follow.

1   WORDS THAT SHOW ADDITION

Put a check beside the item that is easier to read and understand:

_____   The sound on our TV set is distorted. The picture keeps jumping out of focus.

_____   The sound on our TV set is distorted. Also, the picture keeps jumping out of focus.

The first item makes us wonder if the picture's jumping has something to do with the sound being distorted. The word *also* in the second item makes the relationship between the sentences clear. The author is discussing two separate problems with the TV set. One problem is that the sound is distorted. An *additional* problem is that the picture keeps jumping out of focus. *Also* and words like it are known as addition words.

Addition words show you that the author is continuing in the same train of thought. They introduce ideas that *add to* what has already been mentioned. Here are some common addition words:

Addition Words

first	third	next	finally
first of all	also	in addition	last
one	another	additionally	last of all
second	moreover	furthermore	

Examples

The following examples contain addition words. Notice how these words introduce ideas that *add to* what has already been said.

A lively workout at the end of a long day relaxes me. *Furthermore*, it makes my problems seem smaller.

Hippos give birth underwater. They *also* nurse their young there.

I hate the job because of the long hours. *Moreover*, my boss treats me rudely.

➤ Practice 1

Complete each sentence with a suitable transition from the above box. Try to use a variety of transitions.

1. _____ to spoiling our softball game, the rainstorm flooded our basement.

2. Cigarettes stain your teeth, burn holes in your clothes, and give you bad breath. _____, they can kill you.

3. The human body has six pounds of skin. _____, it contains sixty thousand miles of blood vessels.

4. Julius takes turns cooking dinner with his wife. He _____ does the laundry every other week.

5. My car badly needs a tuneup. _____, the muffler needs to be replaced.

2 WORDS THAT SHOW TIME

Put a check beside the item that is easier to read and understand.

_____ Mitch went for the job interview. He got a haircut and shaved off his mustache.

_____ Before Mitch went for the job interview, he got a haircut and shaved off his mustache.

The first item isn't clear about when Mitch got a haircut and shaved off his mustache—before or after the interview. The word *before* in the second item makes the order of the two events clear. Mitch got a shave and haircut *before* he went for the job interview. *Before* and words like it are time words.

Time words help us to understand the order in which events occur. They tell us *when* something happened in relation to something else. Here are some common time words:

Time Words

first	during	often	then
second	in the past	following	since
after	before	later	while
next	earlier	afterward	as

Examples

The following examples contain time words. Notice how these words show us *when* something takes place.

I carefully inserted a disk into the computer. *Next*, I turned on the power switch.

As I listened, Sally's story became more and more believeable. *After* she finished, I was sure she had told the truth.

Following the accident, Rob was questioned by the police but was not given a ticket.

Helpful Points About Transitions

Here are two helpful points to keep in mind about transitions:

1 Certain words within a group mean very much the same thing.

   For example, *also* and *moreover* both mean "in addition." Authors often use different transitions simply for the sake of variety.

2 In some cases, the same word can serve as two different types of transitions, depending on how it is used.

   For example, the word *first* may be an *addition* word, as in the following sentence:

   > My brother has some strange kitchen habits. *First*, he loves to cook with the radio on full blast. *Moreover*, . . .

   First may also be used to signal a *time* sequence, as in this sentence:

   > Our English class had several interruptions this morning. *First*, the radiator began squeaking. *Then*, . . .

➤ *Practice 2*

Complete each sentence with a suitable transition from the list on the previous page. Try to use a variety of transitions.

1. When someone makes me angry, I _____ count to ten, and then I yell.

2. A change in routine _____ upsets my grandfather.

3. _____ the death of its beloved president, the whole country mourned.

4. _____ A.J. pumped the gas, Mario checked the oil, and Richard put air in the tires.

5. Phil was furious when the TV broke _____ the final game of the World Series.

3   WORDS THAT SHOW CONTRAST

Put a check beside the item that is easier to read and understand.

_____   I went to college registration early in the day. The lines were very long.

_____   I went to college registration early in the day, but the lines were very long.

In the first item, we're not sure if the lines were long as expected or in contrast to what was expected. The transition *but* in the second item shows that the author expected short lines—the lines were long *despite* the author's early arrival. *But* and words like it are known as contrast words.

Contrast words show that two things *differ* in one or more ways. Here are some common contrast words:

Contrast Words

in contrast	on the other hand	despite	instead
differ	however	nevertheless	unlike
even though	although	yet	but

Examples

The following examples contain contrast words. Notice how these words signal that one thing is *different from* another thing.

> The test results I got in my science lab experiment were *unlike* those reached by everyone else in the class.

> Mike was angry when he didn't get a raise. His wife, *however*, took the news calmly.

> My brother wanted to go to Burger King, *but* the rest of the family voted for Pizza Hut.

➤ Practice 3

Complete each sentence with a suitable transition from the above box. Try to use a variety of transitions.

1. _____ he is short, John is a star basketball player.

2. I know that eating this last piece of pizza is not good for my waist, _____ I can't let it go to waste.

3. _____ the penguin can't fly, this bird can swim faster than any fish.

4. _____ the cold weather, my parents took their usual daily walk in the park.

5. Skeet is the kind of cat who waits patiently to be fed. _____, Tabby follows us around the house meowing when he's hungry.

4 WORDS THAT SHOW COMPARISON

Put a check beside the item that is easier to read and understand.

_____ For many people, the first day on a new job is a scary experience. The first class in college can be a frightening event.

_____ For many people, the first day on a new job is a scary experience. Similarly, the first class in college can be a frightening event.

The word *similarly* in the second item makes the relationship between the sentences clear. Just as the first day on a new job can be frightening, so can the first time in a college class. *Similarly* and words like it are known as comparison words.

Comparison words signal that the author is pointing out a similarity between two subjects. The words tell us that the second subject is *like* the first one in some way. Here are some common comparison words:

Comparison Words

like	equal	likewise	alike
similarly	equally	in the same way	comparable
just as	identical	similar	the same as

Examples

The following three sentences contain comparison words. Notice how these words show that things are *alike* in some way.

Four-year-old Kevin watched his older brother Tommy swing the bat and then tried to do it in the *same* way.

The nervous young actor stood stiffly in the center of the stage, looking *like* a frightened pup.

I can't stand the sound of brakes screeching. *Equally* annoying is hearing chalk squeaking on a blackboard.

➤ Practice 4

Complete each sentence with a suitable transition from the above box. Try to use a variety of transitions.

1. I was surprised when I tried a frozen banana—it tastes just _____ banana ice cream.

2. When Karen and Mac went shopping for a new car, they found _____ features on several models.

3. Pollen in the air makes me sneeze. Cat hair affects my brother
_____.

4. Eddie admires his father greatly and tries to be _____ him in all ways.

5. The two necklaces looked almost _____, yet one was worth thousands of dollars and the other cost $8.95.

5 WORDS THAT SHOW ILLUSTRATION

Put a check beside the item that is easier to read and understand.

_____ There is too much stress in my life. I am working overtime three days a week.

_____ There is too much stress in my life. For instance, I am working overtime three days a week.

The first item makes us think that the only cause for stress is too much overtime work. The words *for instance* in the second item make it clear that the overtime work is only one of the causes of stress. *For instance* and words and phrases like it are known as illustration words.

Illustration words tell us that one or more examples will be used to explain a point. Here are some common illustration words:

Illustration Words

for example	to illustrate	once
for instance	such as	including

Examples

The following examples contain illustration words. Notice how these words signal that one or more *examples* are coming.

Nine states got their names from rivers that flow through them. *For example*, Minnesota is named after the Minnesota River.

Some Canadians, *including* Michael J. Fox and Peter Jennings, moved to the United States to seek their fame and fortune.

When Cesar and Mary bought an old farmhouse, they ran into many problems. *For instance*, some plumbing had rotted, and the roof leaked.

➤ *Practice 5*

Complete each sentence with a suitable transition from the box on the previous page. Try to use a variety of transitions.

1. City problems, _____ crime, lack of good schools, and pollution, seem to have gotten worse in recent years.

2. The sun is Earth's main energy source. _____, the sun causes seasons to change and winds to blow.

3. Some doctors feel laughing helps people who are ill. _____, one doctor reported that patients who joined a weekly "humor group" had less pain.

4. Nita's parents speak Spanish at times they don't want the children to understand them, _____ when they plan a birthday surprise.

5. Abraham Lincoln was famous for his honesty. _____, when he worked at a store, he once walked several miles to return a nickel to a customer.

6   WORDS THAT SHOW CAUSE AND EFFECT

Put a check beside the item that is easier to read and understand:

_____   The baby refused to eat her breakfast. I was in a bad mood all morning.

_____   The baby refused to eat her breakfast. As a result, I was in a bad mood all morning.

In the first item, we are not sure of the relationship between the two sentences. Were there two problems: the baby's refusing to eat and the bad mood? The words *as a result* show that the bad mood was *caused* by the baby refusing to eat. *As a result* and words and phrases like it are known as cause-and-effect words.

Cause-and-effect words show that the author is discussing the *reason or reasons* something happened or the *results* of something. They signal that one event *caused* another to happen. Here are some common cause-and-effect words:

Cause-and-Effect Words

because	as a result	reason	thus
cause	effect	since	on account of
lead to	so	therefore	consequently

Examples

The following examples contain cause-and-effect words. Notice how these words introduce a *reason* for something or the *results* of something.

> I sleep for an hour before going to night class *because* I'm very tired after work.

> *Since* we seldom use our air conditioner, our electric bill is never too high.

> The play was terrible. *Therefore,* when a phone rang on stage, one member of the audience said, "That must be for me," and left.

➤ Practice 6

Complete each sentence with a suitable transition from the box on the previous page. Try to use a variety of transitions.

1. The teams were not finished with the game, but it had to be called _____ darkness.

2. Drinking enormous amounts of carrot juice can _____ one's skin to turn orange.

3. The lifeguard thought he spotted a shark. _____, the beach was closed for the day.

4. People in the Antarctic no longer wear fur _____ quilted, layered clothing is warmer.

5. My husband likes the house to look neat. _____, when things pile up on his dresser, he scrapes them all into the top drawer.

PRACTICE WITH A VARIETY OF TRANSITIONS

As you read, keep in mind that transitions provide logical connections between ideas. Each of the three sentences below needs a transition word to connect two ideas. Write one of the transitions below into each sentence. Use each transition once. Then read the explanations that follow.

and (meaning *in addition*)   but (meaning *however*)   so (meaning *as a result*)

1. A raccoon has gotten into our attic, _____ flying ants have invaded our basement.

2. I don't feel like studying, _____ I know I have to in order to get good grades.

3. Pete left his wallet at home, _____ he wasn't able to buy anything to eat at the ballpark.

Explanations:

1. The transition that logically connects the two parts of the first sentence is *and:*

   A raccoon has gotten into our attic, *and* (meaning "in addition") flying ants have invaded our basement.

   One idea is being *added* to a similar idea.

2. The transition that logically connects the two parts of the second sentence is *but:*

   I don't feel like studying, *but* (meaning "however") I know I have to in order to get good grades.

   How the writer feels is *contrasted* with what he knows he has to do.

3. The transition that best connects the two parts of the third sentence is *so:*

   Pete left his wallet at home, *so* (meaning "as a result") he wasn't able to buy anything to eat at the ballpark.

   The second situation is *caused* by the first one.

Now see if you can fill in a correct longer transition in each sentence below. Use each of the following transitions once. Then read the explanations.

moreover (meaning *in addition*)
however (meaning *but*)
therefore (meaning *as a result*)

1. We refer to the inside of a pencil as "lead"; _____, it is really a mixture of graphite and clay.

2. The sky will be very cloudy tonight; _____, we won't get a good view of the eclipse of the moon.

3. Our company sponsors a day-care center for employees' children; _____, it runs a free health club for employees.

Explanations:

1. The transition that logically connects the two parts of the sentence is *however:*

   We refer to the inside of a pencil as "lead"; *however* (meaning "but"), it is really a mixture of graphite and clay.

   The second idea *contrasts* with the first one.

2. The transition that logically connects the two parts of the sentence is *therefore:*

   The sky will be very cloudy tonight; *therefore* (meaning "as a result"), we won't get a good view of the eclipse of the moon.

   The second situation *results* from the first one.

3. The transition that logically connects the two parts of this sentence is *moreoever:*

   Our company sponsors a day-care center for employees' children; *moreover* (meaning "in addition"), it runs a free health club for employees.

   A second company benefit is *added* to the first one.

Keeping in mind the meanings of transitions can help you while you read. Here is a list of some common transitions and their meanings:

Common Transitions and Their Meanings

Transition Word	Meaning	Transition Word(s)	Meaning
and	in addition	on the other hand	however
also	in addition	nevertheless	however
moreover	in addition	so	as a result
furthermore	in addition	therefore	as a result
but	however	thus	as a result
yet	however	consequently	as a result

➤ Practice 7

In each blank space, write the transition in parentheses that logically fits the item. Read carefully to make sure you understand the logical relationship between ideas.

1. The tennis class you recommended was full, *(and, but, so)* _____ I was forced to sign up for a basketball class.

2. Jim and Edna wanted to go to Hawaii for vacation, *(and, but, so)* _____ they didn't have the money.

3. Vandals smashed the car's headlights, *(and, but, so)* _____ they slashed the tires as well.

4. Roberto has had difficulties learning English grammar. *(Furthermore, Therefore, On the other hand)* _____, he has had very few problems with calculus.

5. I've never liked getting up early. *(Yet, Moreover, Therefore)* _____, I have had to since I started working the early morning shift.

6. Dan felt that winters in his hometown in North Dakota were too long and too cold. *(Consequently, Moreover, On the other hand)* _____, he decided to move to Arizona.

7. I got a bad report card and was late coming home from a date. *(Therefore, Nevertheless, Furthermore)* _____, Dad told me I was grounded, with no TV or visits from friends.

8. Dawn learned to ice-skate at age three. *(Consequently, Nevertheless, Moreover)* _____, she could beat her older brothers at pool at age five.

9. Almost twenty million people try to quit smoking each year. *(Therefore, Yet, Furthermore)* _____ only about one million are successful.

10. My mother and I wanted for me to become a teacher. *(Therefore, On the other hand, Furthermore)* _____, my father and my grandparents wanted me to become a lawyer.

TRANSITIONS IN PARAGRAPHS

Since a paragraph may express a variety of relationships, various types of transitions may be used. Below is a brief example. This paragraph begins with a sentence you saw at the beginning of this chapter. Complete the paragraph by filling in each blank with one of the transitions below. Use each transition once. Then read the explanation that follows.

since	next	just like	but

I like drinking coffee even though it keeps me awake. Once I tried decaffeinated coffee, (1)_____ I didn't like it. (2)_____, I tried regular tea. However, I discovered that tea kept me awake (3)_____ coffee. (4)_____ decaf coffee and tea didn't work out, I went back to drinking regular coffee.

Explanation:

1. The first blank needs to be filled in with a *contrast* transition to show the contrast between what the writer expected and what happened: Once I tried decaffeinated coffee, *but* I didn't like it.

2. The second transition shows a *time* relationship: *Next,* I tried regular tea.

3. The third transition indicates a *comparison* between tea and coffee: However, I discovered that tea kept me awake *just like* coffee.

4. The last transition introduces the *cause* of the writer going back to regular coffee: *Since* decaf coffee and tea didn't work out, I went back to drinking regular coffee.

➤ Practice 8

For each of the following two paragraphs, fill in each blank with one of the transitions from the box above it. Use each word once.

but	second	last
instead	first of all	

A. Doctors recommend a few tips for parents to follow to prevent ear problems in children. (1)_____, cotton swabs should never be used to wash out the ear. Swabs can push ear wax inside the ear and cause temporary hearing loss. (2)_____, the volume on stereos and television should not be blaring. (3)_____, the volume should be set at the same level as normal speech. (4)_____, if a child has an earache, he or she should be taken to see a doctor. It could be a temporary problem, (5)_____ it could also be a symptom of a serious problem.

consequently	finally	furthermore
however	since	

B. The fuel burned by automobiles and trucks is a major cause of air pollution. (6)_____, automobile manufacturers are looking at different ways to fuel cars. One fuel being tried is hydrogen. Hydrogen is clean-burning. (7)_____, there is a lot of it, (8)_____ hydrogen is one part of water. (9)_____, there are problems that have to be worked out. Hydrogen burns seven times faster than gasoline. It is also highly flammable. (10)_____, removing hydrogen from water is difficult, time-consuming, and expensive.

➤ *Review Test 1*

A. Fill in each blank with one of the transitions from the box below. Use each word once.

so	moreover	even though
such as	before	

1. My ten-year-old car needs transmission work. _____, it could use a whole new set of tires.

2. Cheryl hasn't received a raise _____ she has worked at the company now for three years.

3. The first telephone booths were mistaken for other things, _____ elevators.

4. _____ Ella leaves her apartment, she makes sure the answering machine is turned on.

5. No one did well on the test. _____ the teacher decided to spend more class time on the material.

B. Fill in each blank with one of the transitions from the box below. Use each word once.

however	leads to	like
second	therefore	

Many women have the goal of a "perfect" body. Fitness centers know this fact. (6)_____, they run ads that feature tall, shapely models who suggest this message: "Join our center, and you'll look (7)_____ me." Such a message is disturbing for two reasons. First, it sets up a goal that few women can reach. And (8)_____, the main point of fitness centers should be health, not looks. It is true that physical fitness (9)_____ improved looks. (10)_____, the ads should show fit women with many types of shapes. Then more women will come to like their own body type.

➤ Review Test 2

Complete each sentence with the appropriate transition word or phrase shown in the margin. Then circle the kind of transition you have used.

1. a. An active volcano offers some amazing sights, _____ red-hot fountains that may burst 150 feet into the air.

   likewise
   even though
   including

   b. The transition shows:
   illustration   comparison   contrast

2. a. _____ Tom is a so-so student himself, he pushes his little brother to study hard.

   Although
   Often
   Since

   b. The transition shows:
   time   contrast   cause and effect

3. a. First it started to rain. _____ the weather

   reporter said showers were likely.

   b. The transition shows:

   time   contrast   illustration

However
For instance
Then

4. a. _____ Marta liked the teacher, she decided

   to take her for another course.

   b. The transition shows:

   comparison   time   cause and effect

Although
Because
Just like

5. a. To avoid drunk drivers, I stay home on New Year's

   Eve. I _____ stay off the road late at night.

   b. The transition shows:

   addition   time   contrast

however
also
in contrast

6. a. Bad habits _____ nail biting and overeating

   often begin in childhood.

   b. The transition shows:

   time   contrast   illustration

in contrast
such as
before

7. a. I hung up the phone and _____ I

   began to cry.

   b. The transition shows:

   time   contrast   cause and effect

therefore
then
instead

8. a. The wife of the inventor of the telephone couldn't use

   her husband's invention _____ she

   was deaf.

   b. The transition shows:

   addition   contrast   cause and effect

and
because
yet

9. a. Stainless steel never rusts or cracks. _____,

   it can take great changes in temperature.

   b. The transition shows:

   addition   time   illustration

Moreover
After
However

10. a. The   sailboat   sped   through   the   water   *despite*
      _____ a hot knife cutting through   *like*
      warm butter.   *because*

    b. The transition shows:
       contrast   cause and effect   comparison

➤ Review Test 3

A. To review what you've learned in this chapter, answer each of the following questions. Fill in the blank, or circle the letter of the answer you think is correct.

1. Transitions are words or phrases that signal
   a. main ideas.
   b. relationships between ideas.
   c. importance of ideas.

2. _____ TRUE OR FALSE? An illustration transition shows that two things differ.

3. _____ TRUE OR FALSE? A cause-and-effect transition signals the reason that something happened or the result of something.

4. The transitions *likewise* and *similarly* are _____ words.

5. The transitions *another* and *furthermore* are _____ words.

B. Here is a chance to apply your understanding of transitions to a full-length reading. This selection is about an insect most of us probably take for granted: the monarch butterfly. The author describes the monarch's remarkable annual journey and the problems it is facing. Read the selection and then answer the questions that follow on transitions and the relationships they signal. There are also other comprehension questions to help you continue practicing the skills you learned in earlier chapters.

Words to Watch

Following are some words in the reading that do not have strong context support. Each word is followed by the number of the paragraph in which it appears and its meaning there. These words are indicated in the article by a small circle (°).

   shimmered (1): sparkled
   larvae (3): the wingless, newly-hatched insects
   cocoons (4): the silky case spun by the larvae of insects
   ancestors (6): parents and grandparents
   aerial (6): from the air

hibernation (6): a state similar to sleep that many animals enter during winter
migration (7): seasonal journey
sanctuary (11): a place offering shelter and protection

THE AMAZING MONARCH BUTTERFLY

Peter Sanchez

On a January day in 1975, Ken and Catalina Brugger wandered   1
through an ancient forest in Mexico. The forest sat on a high mountain
slope eighty miles west of Mexico City. The air was damp and cool. The
sky was cloudy, so little light reached through the trees. As the Bruggers
walked along, they realized they were hearing a quiet, constant noise. It
was like rain falling on the fir trees. But there was no rain. They looked
around for the source of the sound. Suddenly, sunlight broke through the
clouds and lit up the forest. The Bruggers gasped in delight. All around
them, the trees shimmered° with the beating of brilliant orange and
black wings. The Bruggers were surrounded by millions of monarch
butterflies, resting in their winter home.

The Bruggers' discovery was important in the world of butterfly   2
study. Butterfly lovers knew that, late every summer, hordes of
monarchs migrate from Canada into Mexico. More than 300 million of
the fragile creatures make the 2,500-mile flight. But no one knew what
became of the butterflies once they reached Mexico. Within the next
few years, twelve more monarch roosts were discovered. They were all
along the same mountain range where the Bruggers had made their
find. Now the mystery was solved.

The monarchs' stay in Mexico is just one part of an amazing life   3
cycle. Every spring, in Mexico, female monarchs lay enormous
numbers of eggs. One female may lay more than four hundred a month.
She attaches her eggs to milkweed plants. The milkweed provides a
perfect first home for the young monarchs. Because milkweed is
poisonous to most creatures, birds and other butterfly enemies avoid it.
But monarchs love milkweed. The eggs hatch in three to twelve days,
and out come worm-like larvae° which feast on the weed. The poison
does not hurt them. But it does have an important effect. It makes the
monarch as poisonous as the plant was. A bird that eats a monarch will
become very sick—and never eat another one.

After living for two weeks as larvae, the monarchs attach   4
themselves to leaves. Then they spin cocoons°. After a week, the

cocoons open and the butterflies emerge, soon to begin their 2,500-mile flight northwards. Many of them die as they pass through such southern states as Texas and Louisiana. But first they lay more eggs. After a few weeks, a new generation of monarchs is ready to continue the journey. They—or their children or grandchildren—will finally reach Canada, where they spend the summer.

In late August, the monarchs begin the return trip from Canada to Mexico. Flying along southbound breezes, the butterflies travel as fast as thirty-five miles per hour. Most make the trip in about six weeks.

No one knows how the young butterflies find their way to Mexico. Yet they do. They arrive at the same stands of fir trees their ancestors° rested in months before. There they crowd onto the trees in enormous numbers. Their weight sometimes breaks branches. Aerial° photographs of the monarch roosts show the normally green forest turned bright orange. The monarchs rest in the Mexican forests for about seven months. They survive in a state that is similar to hibernation°. The forests' cool, damp air slows all the butterflies' bodily functions. The insects rest, using very little energy.

Then in March, responding to some mysterious signal, the butterflies revive, and the process begins again. They take to the air again and head north. Again, most of them die while they pass through southern states. But first they lay their eggs. After a few weeks, a new generation of monarchs is continuing the migration° to Canada through the U.S.

The monarch butterfly has been making its amazing migration for perhaps ten million years. Along the way, the beautiful insect has thrilled countless humans. Sadly, the day of the monarch may be ending.

The actions of human beings are threatening the survival of the monarch butterfly. Cars crush millions of monarchs every year. Weedkillers destroy milkweed, without which the monarch cannot survive. The wildflowers that give them nectar are also being wiped out. Insect poisons contaminate the water that the monarchs drink. Worst of all, timber companies are threatening the Mexican forests where the monarchs winter. One sanctuary has already been destroyed, and others are targeted for large-scale logging.

So far, it is not too late to save the monarch. Environmental groups in Mexico, the U.S., and Canada are trying to stop logging in the monarch's rest areas. U.S. seed companies have produced a "monarch mixture" of milkweed and wildflowers for schoolchildren to plant in meadows. But such efforts must proceed quickly if the beautiful monarch is to survive.

The Mexican organization Monarca A.C. is one of the groups

trying to save the butterfly. Its president, Carlos Gottfried, says that no effort is too great. "If we lose the monarch," he explains, "we lose a link with something mysterious and everlasting. When you stand in a monarch sanctuary°, your soul is shaken and your life is changed."

Reading Comprehension Questions

Vocabulary in Context

1. The word *hordes* in "Butterfly lovers knew that, late every summer, hordes of monarchs migrate from Canada into Mexico. More than 300 million . . . make the 2,500 mile flight" (paragraph 2) means
   a. a few.
   b. neighbors.
   c. large groups.
   d. admirers.

2. The word *roosts* in "no one knew what became of the butterflies once they reached Mexico. Within the next few years, twelve more monarch roosts were discovered. They were all along the same mountain range. . . . Now the mystery was solved" (paragraph 2) means
   a. resting places.
   b. types of butterfly.
   c. chickens.
   d. photos.

3. The word *revive* in "The insects rest. . . . Then in March, responding to some mysterious signal, the butterflies revive. . . . They take to the air again and head north" (paragraphs 6–7) means
   a. go back to sleep.
   b. begin to die.
   c. become active again.
   d. become confused.

Central Point and Main Ideas

4. Which of the following sentences best expresses the central point of the entire selection?
   a. The actions of human beings are making it difficult for many insects and animals to survive.
   b. Millions of monarch butterflies migrate annually from Canada to Mexico.
   c. Accidentally finding the winter home of the monarch butterfly may cause the butterfly to become extinct.
   d. The monarch butterfly, a beautiful insect with an amazing life cycle, may not survive without more help from humans.

5. A topic sentence may cover the supporting details of more than one paragraph. Which sentence best expresses the main idea of paragraphs 3–7?
   a. The first sentence of paragraph 3
   b. The second sentence of paragraph 3
   c. The first sentence of paragraph 4
   d. The first sentence of paragraph 7

6. The main idea of paragraph 9 is expressed in its
   a. first sentence.
   b. second sentence.
   c. third sentence.
   d. last sentence.

Supporting Details

7. In general, the supporting details of paragraphs 3–7 are
   a. the numbers of monarch butterflies that migrate each year.
   b. the stages in the monarch butterfly's life cycle.
   c. the places where monarch butterflies are seen.
   d. the mysteries of the monarch butterfly.

Transitions

8. The statement below expresses a relationship of
   a. time.
   b. contrast.
   c. illustration.
   d. cause and effect.

   Because milkweed is poisonous to most creatures, birds and other butterfly enemies avoid it. (Paragraph 3)

9. The sentence below expresses a relationship of
   a. time.
   b. addition.
   c. comparison.
   d. cause and effect.

   They survive in a state that is similar to hibernation. (Paragraph 6)

10. Fill in each blank with one of the time transitions in paragraph 7.

    _____   _____

Mapping Activity

The major events in the life cycle of a monarch butterfly are scrambled below. Write them in the diagram in their correct order. Two items have been filled in for you.

Main idea: The monarch butterfly's amazing life cycle spans many months and many miles.

- The monarchs rest for seven months.
- Larvae hatch from the eggs and feed on milkweed for two weeks.
- Butterflies emerge from the cocoons.
- The monarchs take to the air and head north, they or their children or grandchildren reaching Canada.
- The larvae attach themselves to leaves and spin cocoons.

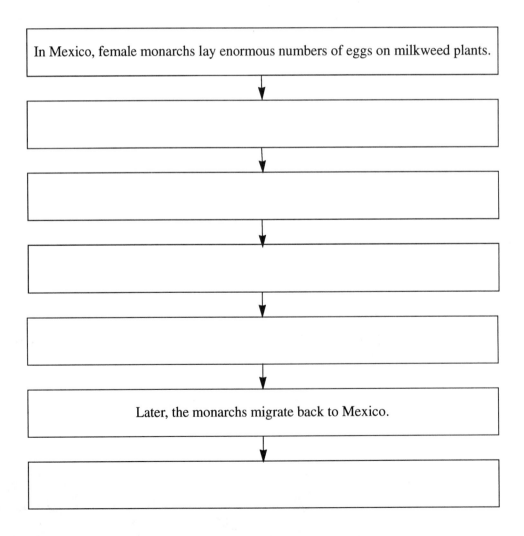

In Mexico, female monarchs lay enormous numbers of eggs on milkweed plants.

↓

↓

↓

↓

Later, the monarchs migrate back to Mexico.

↓

Discussion Questions

1. The author and some people he mentions in the article believe it is important to save the monarch butterfly. What reasons are given? Do you agree that it is important to save the butterfly? Why or why not?

2. The author mentions two mysteries associated with the monarch butterfly. Which mystery has been solved? Which mystery remains to be solved? What possible answers to that mystery can you think of?

Writing Activities

1. Like the Bruggers, most of us have had dramatic experiences of one sort or another with insects or animals. Write a paper describing one such experience. In addition to telling in detail what happened, explain how the experience made you feel.

2. The president of a Mexican organization trying to save the monarch butterfly implies that a monarch sanctuary is a magical place, one people cannot forget. Write a paragraph about a place that you will never forget. Describe this place, and explain why it is so special to you.

Check Your Performance   TRANSITIONS

Activity	Number Right	Points	Total
Review Test 1 (10 items)		x 2 =	
Review Test 2 (20 items)		x 2 =	
Review Test 3, Part A (5 items)		x 2 =	
Review Test 3, Part B (10 items)		x 2 =	
Mapping (5 items)		x 2 =	

TOTAL SCORE = _____ %

Enter your total score into the reading performance chart on the inside back cover.

9

Patterns of Organization

To help readers understand main ideas, authors try to present supporting details in a clearly organized way. Details might be arranged in any of several common patterns. By recognizing these patterns, you will be able to make better sense of what you read. You will also be able to remember more of what you read.

THE FIVE BASIC PATTERNS OF ORGANIZATION

Here are the most commonly used patterns of organization:

1 Time order

2 List of Items

3 Comparison and/or Contrast

4 Cause and Effect

5 Definition and Example

How Patterns of Organization Use Transitions

Each of the five patterns is based on a relationship you learned about in the chapter on transitions. The patterns therefore involve transition words that you probably recognize by now. In the "List of Items" pattern, for example, the ideas that are listed are often connected by transitions that show addition: *also, another, moreover,* and so on. The following list shows the kinds of transitions commonly used with each pattern.

Pattern	Transitions Most Often Used
Time order	Words that show time (*then, next, after* . . .)
List of items	Words that show addition (*also, another, moreover* . . .)
Comparison and/or contrast	Words that show how things are alike (*like, similar to, just as* . . .) or different (*unlike, however, in contrast* . . .)
Cause and effect	Words that show cause and effect (*because, as a result, since* . . .)
Definition and example	Words that illustrate (*for example, to illustrate* . . .)

The following pages provide explanations and examples of each pattern.

1 TIME ORDER

Authors usually present events in the order in which they happened. This results in the **time order** pattern of organization.

To get a sense of the time order pattern, arrange the following group of sentences into an order that makes sense. A *1* has been put in front of the sentence that comes first. Put a *2* in front of the sentence that comes second, a *3* in front of the sentence that should come next, and a *4* in front of the sentence that should be last. Then read the explanation which follows.

_____ Next, you stop in New Zealand.

__1__ A plane trip to Australia is a long one.

_____ Finally, you arrive in "the land down under."

_____ First you stop in Honolulu.

Explanation:

Clues to the pattern of the above sentences are transitions that show time: *first, next,* and *finally.* The sentences should read as follows:

A plane trip to Australia is a long one. First you stop in Honolulu. Next, you stop in New Zealand. Finally, you arrive in "the land down under."

As a student, you will see time order used frequently. Textbooks in all fields describe events and processes, such as the events leading to the Battle of Bunker Hill, the process involved in making steel, or the stages of a frog's life. In addition, time order is involved in any directions you have to follow.

The following transition words often signal that a paragraph or selection is organized according to time order.

Time Transitions

first	next	as	while
second	before	now	during
then	after	until	when
since	soon	later	finally

Other signals for this pattern are dates, times, and such words as *stages, series, steps,* and *process.*

The two most common kinds of time order involve *a series of events or stages* and *a series of steps* (directions). Each is discussed below.

Series of Events or Stages

Below is a paragraph in which a series of events is organized according to time order. Complete the outline of the paragraph by listing the events in the order in which they happened. The main idea is provided for you. Also, one point has been filled in, and a second has been started. When you're done, read the explanation that follows.

> The Model T, manufactured for about twenty years, was a great success for the Ford Motor Company and for mass production. In 1903, Henry Ford organized the company, which was profitable from the start. However, it became even more profitable when, in 1908, he introduced the Model T. That year, the company turned out 10,607 cars, each selling for $850. Ford gradually developed the principle of the assembly line, and by 1913, mass production made it possible for the company to produce more cars and lower the selling price. As a result, the Model T was the first car within reach of the average American. In 1916, the company produced 730,041 cars and sold them for $360 each. By the time production of the Model T stopped in 1927, a total of fifteen million had been produced.

Main idea: The Model T, manufactured for about twenty years, was a great success for the Ford Motor Company and for mass production.

1. The Model T was introduced in 1908, when almost 11,000 were made and sold for $850 each.

2. By 1913, _____

_____

3. In 1916, the company made over 730,000 Model T's, sold at less than half the original price.

4. _____

_____

Explanation:

The second point of the outline should have been finished with the second important point in the Model T's history. One way of wording that point is: "By 1913, mass production made it possible to produce more cars and lower the selling price." The last point of the outline could be worded like this: "By 1927, when production of the Model T stopped, fifteen million had been made."

➤ Practice 1a

The following passage describes a sequence of events. Complete the outline below the paragraph.

In January of 1848, while building a sawmill along the American River, carpenter and engineer James Marshall saw gold flecks in the water. California then had a population of only about 14,000. By spring, many would-be miners were rushing to the area to look for the precious metal. Word about the gold gradually spread eastward, and by 1849, there were over 80,000 "forty-niners" in California in hopes of striking it rich. By 1860, California's population had grown to 380,000.

Implied main idea: The discovery of gold led to a rapid population growth in California.

1. Gold was discovered in California in January of 1848, when the state's population was at about 14,000.

2. By 1849, _____

3. _____

Series of Steps (Directions)

Directions use time order to explain a series of steps toward a particular goal. You need to be able to follow directions in order to succeed at many activities at school and throughout life. Below is a paragraph in which directions are given. Read it and number in correct order the steps listed after the paragraph. Then read the explanation that follows.

Do you have a noticeable stain or burn in your carpeting? It's easy to correct the problem. First, use a sharp utility knife to cut out the damaged area (but not the padding underneath). Then cut a patch the same size and shape from a leftover piece of carpet or a spot of carpeting that's not noticeable, such as under a radiator. Next, cut a piece of burlap the same size as the patch. Place the burlap where you cut out the damaged piece of carpet. Finally, glue the carpet patch to the burlap.

Type of directions: Steps to eliminating a stain or burn in carpeting

_____ Cut a piece of burlap the same size as the patch.

_____ Glue the carpet patch to the burlap.

_____ Place the burlap where the damaged carpeting was.

_____ Cut out the damaged area of carpeting.

_____ Cut out a patch the same size and shape from a leftover piece of carpet or a spot of carpeting that's not noticeable.

Explanation:

This is the order in which you should have put the points: (1) Cut out the damaged area of carpeting. (2) Cut out a patch the same size and shape from a leftover piece of carpet or a spot of carpeting that's not noticeable. (3) Cut a piece of burlap the same size as the patch. (4) Place the burlap where the damaged carpeting was. (5) Glue the carpet patch to the burlap.

➤ *Practice 1b*

The following passage gives directions involving several steps that must be done in order. Read it, and number in correct order the steps listed below the paragraph.

Flavored honey not only tastes good, but it is also easy to make. Start with one pound of honey. Add one tablespoon of grated lemon, lime, or orange peel. Heat the mixture over a low flame. Then let the honey stand for two hours. Next, strain the honey, and pour it into an eight-ounce jar. Store the flavored honey at room temperature, and enjoy it whenever you are in the mood for a special treat.

Type of directions: Steps to making flavored honey

_____ Heat up over a low flame.

_____ Strain and pour into an eight-ounce jar.

_____ Add one tablespoon grated lemon, lime, or orange peel.

_____ Store at room temperature.

_____ Let stand for two hours.

_____ Start with one pound of honey.

2 LIST OF ITEMS

A **list of items** refers to a simple series of details, such as reasons, examples, or facts, that support a point. The items are listed in any order the author feels is important.

Arrange the following group of sentences into the order signaled by the addition transitions. Put a _1_ in front of the sentence that should come first, a _2_ in front of the sentence that comes second, and a _3_ in front of the sentence that should be last. Then read the explanation which follows.

_____ In addition, a brisk walk is an excellent and inexpensive form of exercise.

_____ Walking can be a rewarding experience.

_____ For one thing, walking lets you see firsthand what's going on in your neighborhood.

Explanation:

The paragraph would begin with the main idea: "Walking can be a rewarding experience." The next two sentences go on to list two of the rewards of walking. The transitional phrases _for one thing_ and _in addition_ introduce the rewards and tell you the order in which the author has chosen to list them. The paragraph should read as follows:

> Walking can be a rewarding experience. For one thing, walking lets you see firsthand what's going on in your neighborhood. In addition, a brisk walk is an excellent and inexpensive form of exercise.

The following transition words often signal that a paragraph or selection is organized according to a list of items:

Addition Transitions

and	for one thing	another	furthermore
also	second	in addition	finally
first	next	moreover	last of all

A List of Items Paragraph

Find the main idea in the passage below. As is often the case with lists of items, the main idea will indicate what the author is listing. Count the *number* of items that the author has listed, and identify the *type* of item being listed. Look for the transitions that will help you find the items. Then read the explanation that follows the passage.

> A videotape called "How to Have a Moneymaking Garage Sale" lists these tips for success. First, check with your insurance company to be sure that you are covered for unforeseen events such as accidents. Second, price your articles reasonably. Clothes should sell for about 10 percent of their original value, and appliances for 20 percent. Finally, never publish a phone number in your advertisements. This is a good security measure and will prevent nuisance calls.

1. How many items are listed?
   a. One
   b. Two
   c. Three
   d. Four

2. What type of item is listed?
   a. Garage sales
   b. Unforeseen events
   c. Ways to price clothing and appliances
   d. Tips for success

Explanation:

The main idea of the paragraph (the first sentence) tells us that the paragraph will list "tips for success" with a garage sale. Three tips are given: "First, check with your insurance company. . . ," "Second, price your articles reasonably," and "Finally, never publish a phone number in your advertisements." The addition transitions *first, second,* and *finally* introduce the three items listed.

➤ *Practice 2*

The following two passages are organized using a list of items pattern. Underline each main idea and answer the questions that follow each passage.

A.   A recent study suggested that parents should be on the lookout for stress in their children. There are several signs of stress in young people. Unusual tiredness in a child is one sign. Another is temper tantrums. And a third is the child forgetting known facts, which may result from mental exhaustion.

How many items are listed? _____

What type of item is listed? _____

B.   Most people think of pizza as junk food, but pizza contains many healthful ingredients. First of all, the crust is rich in B vitamins, which keep the nervous system humming smoothly. Also, the tomato sauce is an excellent source of vitamin A, which is essential for good vision, among other things. And finally, the mozzarella cheese contains protein and calcium, each of which supports good health in many ways, including keeping bones strong.

How many items are listed? _____

What type of item is listed? _____

3   COMPARISON AND/OR CONTRAST

The **comparison and/or contrast** pattern shows how two things are like each other, or how they are different, or both. When things are *compared*, you are shown how they are *alike*. When things are *contrasted*, you are shown how they *differ*.

To get a sense of the comparison and/or contrast pattern, arrange the following group of sentences into an order that makes sense. Put a *1* in front of the sentence that should come first, a *2* in front of the sentence that comes second, and a *3* in front of the sentence that should be last. Transition words will help you find the correct order. Finally, read the explanation which follows.

_____   Both city and country dwellers give good reasons for where they live.

_____   On the other hand, people who live in the country talk about a slower pace of life, clean air and water, and friendly neighbors.

_____   People who live in cities mention good-paying jobs and closeness to cultural events.

Explanation:

The first sentence states the main idea: "Both city and country dwellers give good reasons for where they live." This sentence hints that a comparison and/or contrast pattern will follow. That is, it suggests that the reasons city dwellers give for where they live will contrast with those of country dwellers. The transitional phrase *on the other hand* signals that a contrast is being made. The paragraph should read as follows:

Both city and country dwellers give good reasons for where they live. People who live in cities mention good-paying jobs and closeness to cultural events. On the other hand, people who live in the country talk about a slower pace of life, clean air and water, and friendly neighbors.

We often compare and contrast, even though we may not be aware of it. For example, a simple decision on what to do on a Saturday night requires us to compare and contrast possible choices. Do we want to go to the movies or rent a video? Do we feel like having friends over or do we prefer being alone?

Here are some common transitions showing comparison:

Comparison Transitions

like	likewise	similarly
also	just like	equally
same	resembles	similarities
alike	similar	just as

Here are transitions which show contrast:

Contrast Transitions

however	different	on the other hand
in contrast	differently	as opposed to
instead	unlike	differs from

A Comparison and/or Contrast Paragraph

Read the following passage and answer the questions that follow. Then read the explanation.

There are differences of opinion on the value of computers in the classroom. Some people feel that computers will soon replace many of teachers' duties. One writer states, "Computers make do-it-yourself education downright efficient. Your child can probably learn spelling or arithmetic or a foreign language faster on a computer than in a crowded classroom." However, others warn that too much technology may harm children. One psychologist warns that computers, as well as video games and TV, may weaken children's language skills.

1. Is this paragraph comparing, contrasting, or both? _____

2. What is being compared and/or contrasted?_____

_____

3. Which comparison and/or contrast signal words or phrases are used in the paragraph? _____

Explanation:

This paragraph contrasts opinions on the value of computers in the classroom. The transition words *differences* and *however* signal that a contrast is being discussed.

➤ Practice 3

The following passages use the pattern of comparison and/or contrast. Read each passage and answer the questions that follow.

A. Stepfamilies and "natural" families have interesting similarities and differences. Both types of families have a similar range of everyday values, and both types have backgrounds that tend to be alike as well. But the stepfamily includes more people—ex-husbands, ex-wives, ex-in-laws, and various other relatives on both sides. In addition, the stepfamily has anger, guilt, and conflicts that "natural" families don't face. For example, stepchildren are likely to have bitter feelings toward their stepparents that don't surface in relationships between children and their natural parents.

1. Is this paragraph comparing, contrasting, or both? _____

2. What is being compared and/or contrasted?_____

_____

B. According to the record books, men and women can be equally bad drivers. On the female side is the Arkansas woman who needed 104 attempts before passing her driver's test. A similar driver is the Texas man who received ten tickets, drove on the wrong side of the road four times, and was involved in four hit-and-run accidents. He accomplished all this in just one year.

1. Is this paragraph comparing, contrasting, or both? _____

2. What is being compared and/or contrasted?_____

_____

4   CAUSE AND EFFECT

Paragraphs using the **cause-and-effect** pattern address questions such as "Why did this event happen?" or "What would be the result of doing this?" In other words, they discuss the *causes* and/or the *effects* of an event.

To get a sense of the cause-and-effect pattern, arrange the following group of sentences into an order that makes sense. Put a *1* in front of the sentence that should come first, the sentence with the main idea. Put a *2* in front of the sentence that comes second and a *3* in front of the sentence that should be last. Then read the explanation which follows.

_____ For example, it commonly results in great relaxation.

_____ Meditation has been found to have a wide variety of effects.

_____ It has also occasionally been found to cause such negative effects as anxiety and even depression.

Explanation:

The transition words *results, effects,* and *cause* suggest the cause-and-effect pattern. In paragraph form, the sentences would read as follows:

> Meditation has been found to have a wide variety of effects. For example, it commonly results in great relaxation. It has also occasionally been found to cause such negative effects as anxiety and even depression.

Authors usually explore events by using a cause-and-effect pattern. They don't just tell you *what* happened; they tell you *why* it happened as well. For example, a textbook account of the Boston Tea Party would be incomplete without giving its cause: The colonists threw 342 chests of a British tea into the water of Boston's harbor *because* the British company was allowed to sell the tea without paying taxes. An important part of any effort to understand events and processes includes learning about cause-and-effect relationships.

Here are common transitions used in the cause-and-effect pattern:

Cause-and-Effect Transitions

because	as a result	therefore	thus
reason	since	leading to	result
leads to	causes	effects	brings about

A Cause-and-Effect Paragraph

Read the passage below; then answer the questions about cause and effect. Finally, read the explanation that follows.

> Do you often raid the refrigerator at midnight? Research has shown that nighttime eating has effects most people would prefer to avoid. According to one researcher, "Eating at night . . . burns fewer calories than eating a snack in the morning." Burning fewer calories, in turn, leads to putting on more weight. On any one evening, this process may put very little weight on a person. Over time, however, the results may be significant.

1. What is one *cause* described in this paragraph? _____

_____

2. What are two *effects*?

a. _____

b. _____

3. What three cause-effect transitions are used?

_____

Explanation:

The cause in this paragraph is eating at night. The two effects are burning fewer calories and putting on more weight. The cause-effect transitions are *effects, leads to,* and *results.*

➤ *Practice 4*

A. Each of the following items describes a cause-and-effect relationship. For each item, identify both the cause and effect. The first one is done for you as an example.

1. A woman in England recently received her driver's license after forty attempts. Unfortunately, she had spent so much money on driving lessons that she could not afford a car.

   Cause: The woman spent a lot of money on driving lessons.
   Effect: She could not afford a car.

2. Because the contract offer did not satisfy them, major league baseball players decided to go on strike.

   Cause: _____

   Effect: _____

3. Cindy and Tomas have realized that they argue constantly; therefore, they have decided to go to a marriage counselor.

   Cause: _____

   Effect: _____

4. When a researcher purposely put bacteria into mashed bananas, the bananas refused to spoil. The reason turned out to be that mashed banana fights certain germs that spoil food.

   Cause: _____

   Effect: _____

5. The amount of waste being produced by plastic food containers is worrying scientists, businesses, and consumers. As a result, an effort is being made to produce packaging which will not be thrown away—it will be edible.

Cause: _____

Effect: _____

B. The following passages list both causes and effects. Write *C* in front of each item that is a cause and *E* in front of each item that is an effect.

6. When you awaken in the morning, you are about one-half inch taller than when you went to bed. The reason for this change stems from the fact that you have fluid-filled discs in your spine. When you are upright—either sitting or standing—gravity squeezes down the fluid, making your back shorter. During the night, when you are lying down, the discs gradually spring back to their regular "unsquashed" size.

_____ You are about one-half inch taller in the morning than when you went to bed at night.

_____ When you're lying down at night, the discs in your spine spring back to their full size, after being "squashed" by gravity during the day.

7. Typhoons are violent hurricanes that occur in the western Pacific Ocean. Since these storms have winds of more than seventy-five miles per hour, they can be enormously destructive. A recent typhoon which hit the Philippine Islands left over 300 people dead and 370,000 homeless. It also resulted in tens of millions of dollars in damage.

_____ A typhoon

_____ 300 people dead

_____ 370,000 homeless

_____ Tens of millions of dollars in damage

8. Go ahead and laugh—it's good for you. Laughing relaxes the facial muscles, causing you to look and feel less tense. It also increases the oxygen in the brain, resulting in a light-headed sense of well-being. In addition, laughing is a proven stress-reducer; thus it decreases your chances of getting stress-related illnesses.

_____ Laughing

_____ Looking and feeling less tense

_____ A light-headed sense of well-being

_____ Decreased chances of getting stress-related illnesses

5   DEFINITION AND EXAMPLE

If a textbook author uses a term that readers may not understand, the author may take the time to provide a **definition**. Then, to make sure the definition is fully understand, the author may give one or more **examples** to explain it.

To get a sense of the definition and example pattern, arrange the following group of sentences into a paragraph that makes sense. Put a *1* in front of the sentence that should come first, a *2* in front of the sentence that comes second, and a *3* in front of the sentence that should be last. Then read the explanation which follows.

_____   Other common phobias include fears of snakes, water, and enclosed places.

_____   When people are so afraid of heights, for example, that they cannot cross a bridge without trembling, they would be said to have a phobia.

_____   A phobia is an irrational and extreme fear of some object or situation.

Explanation:

The paragraph would begin by defining the term *phobia*. An example that is explained in some detail comes next, followed by a list of other examples. A total of four examples (fears of heights, snakes, water, and enclosed places) are used to illustrate the term *phobia*. The paragraph should read as follows:

> A phobia is an irrational and extreme fear of some object or situation. When people are so afraid of heights, for example, that they cannot cross a bridge without trembling, they would be said to have a phobia. Other common phobias include fears of snakes, water, and enclosed places.

The examples that follow a definition are often introduced by these transitions:

Example Transitions

for example	such as	illustration
for instance	to illustrate	one
including		

Note: Keep in mind that example transitions are used in *all* types of patterns, not just in the definition and example pattern. Authors use examples to illustrate general ideas as well as definitions. The focus here, of course, is on examples used with definitions.

A Definition and Example Paragraph

The following paragraph defines a term, explains it, and gives examples of it. Read the paragraph; then answer the questions. Finally, read the explanation which follows.

> [1]Functional illiteracy is the inability to read and write at a level required for success in daily life. [2]The problem is wide-ranging. [3]To illustrate, it is estimated that one in five adults is unable to read warning labels on containers of harmful substances. [4]In addition, they cannot read the headlines in a newspaper or fill out a job application. [5]Furthermore, half of the adult population in the country is unable to read a book written at an eighth-grade level.

1. What term is being defined? _____

2. Which sentence gives the definition? _____

3. Which sentence explains how common the problem is?_____

4. In which sentence does the first example appear? _____

5. How many examples are given in all? _____

Explanation:

The term *functional illiteracy* is defined in the first sentence. The second sentence tells us how common the problem is: "wide-ranging." The first example—the inability to read warning labels—is introduced in the third sentence. Three other examples are given in sentences 4–5 (the inability to read headlines, to fill out a job application, or "to read a book written at an eighth-grade level"), making a total of four examples given.

➤ *Practice 5*

The following passages each include a definition and one or more examples. In the spaces provided, write the number of the sentence that gives the definition, and then write the number of the sentence where each example begins.

A.   [1]Regeneration is the ability which some animals have to renew lost body parts. [2]For instance, an octopus can regrow lost tentacles. [3]And a spider can regrow lost legs. [4]This can come in very handy when a limb is lost in an accident or in a fight.

Definition: _____   Example 1: _____   Example 2: _____

B.   [1]A kleptomaniac is a person with the psychological disorder in which there is a strong impulse to steal. [2]Unlike other people who steal, kleptomaniacs rarely do so for financial reasons. [3]The head of security at a famous department store says that one kleptomaniac caught shoplifting there wore a mink coat and a diamond ring. [4]She was married to a prominent doctor in town. [5]She is typical of many people who can afford to buy what they steal, but do not. [6]Psychologists suggest that kleptomaniacs steal because they feel emotionally deprived. [7]They have money, but they lack love. [8]Since they cannot steal affection, they steal things—to help "settle the score" and make them feel less cheated.

Definition: _____   Example: _____

C.   [1]People who have charisma have a special charm or appeal that draws other people to them. [2]They are not always the best-looking people, the smartest, or the best-dressed. [3]But they have sparkling personalities and the ability to make the people near them feel special. [4]The late President John F. Kennedy is one well-known example of a person with charisma. [5]One admirer said of him, "When you spoke with him, he looked at you as though you were the most important person in the world." [6]A good illustration of a fictional character with charisma is Tracey, the overweight and charming teenager in the movie *Hairspray*. [7]She steals the most handsome boy in town from his "perfectly" built—and perfectly boring—girlfriend.

Definition: _____   Example 1: _____   Example 2: _____

TOPIC SENTENCES AND PATTERNS OF ORGANIZATION

The topic sentence of a paragraph often suggests its pattern of organization. For instance, here is the topic sentence of a paragraph you worked on earlier: "A videotape called 'How to Have a Moneymaking Garage Sale' lists these tips for success." This sentence strongly suggests that the paragraph will go on to list a number of tips. Even before finishing the paragraph, you can expect that it will be organized as a list of items.

Here are two more topic sentences. Write in the blank space the pattern of organization you think each one suggests. Then read the explanations that follow.

1.   Building a cage for a rabbit involves several steps.

Pattern of organization: _____

2.   There are a number of differences between southern California and northern California.

Pattern of organization: _____

Explanations:

The first sentence suggests that a series of steps for building a rabbit cage will follow. The paragraph is likely to be arranged in a time order.

The second sentence suggests that the paragraph will discuss the differences between southern California and northern California. In all likelihood, the paragraph will have a contrast pattern.

Keep in mind, then, that the topic sentence often signals how the paragraph will be organized.

➤ Practice 6

Circle the letter of the pattern of organization that each topic sentence suggests.

1. The National Restaurant Association recently put together a list of the most popular take-out foods in the nation.

   a. Cause and effect   b. Time order   c. List of items

2. The loss of a job has been found to affect different age groups in different ways.

   a. Time order   b. Comparison and/or contrast   c. List of items

3. Defense mechanisms are the psychological methods people use to protect their self-esteem.

   a. Comparison and/or contrast   b. Time order   c. Definition and example

4. Smoking is on the decline in America because of government efforts to educate people on the unfavorable effects of the habit.

   a. Time order   b. Comparison and/or contrast   c. Cause and effect

5. You can successfully plant your new tree by following a few simple steps.

   a. Time order   b. Comparison and/or contrast   c. Cause and effect

➤ Review Test 1

Identify the pattern used in each item below. Write the letter of one of the following patterns of organization in the space provided. Each pattern is used twice.

a Time order
b List of items
c Comparison and/or contrast
d Cause and effect
e Definition and example

_____ 1. Because he wanted to prove that he was an exceptional athlete, Deion Sanders decided to play both professional baseball and professional football.

_____ 2. In geography, a panhandle is a strip of territory extending like the handle of a pan. The Oklahoma panhandle, for example, is a narrow part of the state that projects westward over Texas.

_____ 3. Famous lawman Wyatt Earp was born in Monmouth, Illinois, in 1848. In 1881, he was involved in the controversial gunfight at the OK Corral. Earp died in 1929 in Los Angeles, California.

_____ 4. I've always wanted to learn to play the piano. However, my parents insisted that I take violin lessons.

_____ 5. Blanchard's Furniture Store is having a super sale on sofas, dining room sets, and bedroom furnishings. Coffee tables are also on sale.

_____ 6. A stereotype is an overly generalized image of members of a group. One common stereotype, for instance, is the image of all professors as being absentminded.

_____ 7. Glossy and flat paints have different virtues. A glossy paint is easier to keep clean than a flat paint, but a flat paint covers flaws in the wall better than a glossy one does.

_____ 8. Toby decided he needed a day off. He stayed in bed until noon, watched game shows on TV all afternoon, called out for a pizza for dinner, then read until it was time for bed.

_____ 9. Mark's family believes in volunteering. His mother delivers food to shut-ins, and his father works with the Boy Scouts. In addition, his older sister plays the piano at nursing homes.

_____ 10. A professor of hearing sciences at Ohio University has discovered that the reason for some people's speech problems is that they lack feeling in their tongues. Thus they have trouble placing their tongues in the correct position for certain sounds.

➤ *Review Test 2*

Circle the letter of the main pattern of organization in each of the following passages.

1. There are adventurous outdoor sports to appeal to almost anyone. For example, one such sport, hiking, can be done by just about anyone. Another, mountain biking, can be enjoyed by entire families. Yet another, mountain climbing, calls for participants who have good powers of concentration and are in excellent shape.

    The paragraph's main pattern of organization:
    a. List of items
    b. Time order
    c. Cause and effect

2. A Los Angeles lawyer named Steve is happy about the one time he didn't go to court. On a cross-country flight, the movie came on. He reached into his carry-on bag and pulled out a set of headphones. He was told by a flight attendant that he could not use them. The flight attendant said that he had to "rent" the airline's headphones. The lawyer insisted this was not fair, and continued to watch the movie with his own headphones. When the plane landed, airport police arrested him and charged him with "theft of the movie's soundtrack." The lawyer was detained briefly, then released. The case was turned over to the local district attorney, who decided not to prosecute.

    The paragraph's main pattern of organization:
    a. Time order
    b. List of items
    c. Comparison and/or contrast

3. Many people without a job must do without life's necessities. So it is no surprise that being unemployed can have harmful effects on health. In poor countries especially, unemployment may mean having little or no medical care. Also, the experience of unemployment itself can affect one's health. Studies have shown anxiety and depression can result from the loss of a job. Alcohol and tranquilizer abuse increase with unemployment. One study showed that when unemployment rises, the death rate for heart disease also rises.

    The paragraph's main pattern of organization:
    a. Time order
    b. Comparison and/or contrast
    c. Cause and effect

4. A *mutant* is a plant or animal that has brand-new characteristics. It can be the beginning of an entirely new group of plants or animals. For instance, a mutant—a dwarf orange cauliflower—was recently found in a field of normal white cauliflower. The mutant was crossed with a regular-sized cauliflower to produce a new vegetable—a full-sized orange cauliflower.

The paragraph's main pattern of organization:
a. Time order
b. List of items
c. Definition and example

5. A recent survey indicated that the cities which are growing fastest are the least pleasant to live in. Lagos, Nigeria; Lima, Peru; and Mexico City, Mexico are among the fastest-growing cities in the world. They are growing so fast that the quality of life there has suffered. In contrast, cities such as Melbourne, Australia; Toronto, Ontario, Canada; and Seattle, Washington, are growing at a much slower pace. They are considered to be among the most livable cities in the world.

The paragraph's main pattern of organization:
a. Time order
b. Comparison and/or contrast
c. Definition and example

➤ *Review Test 3*

A. To review what you've learned in this chapter, answer each of the following questions. Fill in the blank, or circle the letter of each answer you think is correct.

1. *Fill in the blank with one of the answers in parentheses:* A paragraph's pattern of organization is the pattern in which its (*main ideas, supporting details, implied main ideas*) _____ are organized.

2. _____ TRUE OR FALSE? When a passage provides a series of directions, it uses a comparison and/or contrast pattern.

3. _____ TRUE OR FALSE? The pattern in which a series of details are presented in any order the author considers best is called a list of items.

4. Which pattern of organization is often signaled by such transitions as *because, as a result* and *since*?
a. Comparison and/or contrast
b. Cause and effect
c. Time order

5. Which pattern of organization is often signaled by such transitions as *similarly* and *on the other hand*?
   a. List of items
   b. Comparison and/or contrast
   c. Definition and example

B. Here is a chance to apply your understanding of patterns of organization to a to a full-length reading. In this selection, the author tells about a young man who had to overcome more and work harder than most people to reach his goals. Tri Lee's story shows just how long a journey we can make if we are determined enough.

Following the reading are questions on patterns of organization. There are also other reading comprehension questions to help you continue to reinforce the skills taught in previous chapters.

Words to Watch

Following are some words in the reading that do not have strong context support. Each word is followed by the number of the paragraph in which it appears and its meaning there. These words are indicated in the story by a small circle (°).

> *valedictorian* (12): student with the highest grades in a class who gives a graduation speech
> *paranoid* (22): overly suspicious
> *immersed* (23): deeply involved
> *protagonist* (26): the main character of a story
> *antagonist* (26): opponent
> *irony* (26): the contrast between what is said and what is meant
> *persevered* (27): kept on trying
> *diverse* (28): varied

THE VOYAGE OF TRI LEE

John Kellmayer

Tri Lee came a long way in six years.   1

In 1983, at the age of twelve, Tri Lee boarded a small fishing boat,   2
about ninety feet long. There were eighty-four other Vietnamese refugees
on the boat when it departed from Cantho, Vietnam, at 4 a.m. The sea
was rough and choppy, and waves splashed over the side of the boat. The
fishing boat towed another, much smaller boat. No one was in the second
boat, only some clothes and supplies. The night was bitingly cold, and
the moon was hidden by thick clouds. The fishing boat's destination was

international waters, off the coast of Malaysia. Communist patrol boats fired at the fishing boat as it pulled out of the harbor.

More frightened than ever, Tri watched with sad brown eyes as the coast of his homeland, Vietnam, slowly disappeared from sight.   3

Tri, separated from his parents, was accompanied by two male cousins, seventeen and eighteen years old. He had no money and few belongings. Neither he nor his cousins spoke English. The other people on the boat were strangers to him.   4

It took four days before the two boats reached their destination. The eighty-five refugees then were forced to enter the smaller boat, about forty feet long. The boat people had paid the owners of the larger fishing boat to transport them to international waters. Once there, they were on their own.   5

The eighty-five refugees crowded in the small boat faced a perilous situation. Their supply of food and drinking water was limited. There was a good chance they might never see land again.   6

After a few days at sea, however, they spotted a British oil rig. At first, the British refused to pick up the Vietnamese. The British were headed toward another destination and didn't want to be bothered with the refugees. Instead, they offered only supplies and directions to Malaysia. Then, after wishing the refugees good luck, the British got under way.   7

A desperate young Vietnamese woman picked up an axe and smashed a hole in the fishing boat, which immediately began to fill with water.   8

The fishing boat was rapidly sinking. Tri said a silent prayer and prepared himself for the worst. Faced with witnessing eighty-five humans drown, the English sailors then relented. The oil rig turned around, and the Vietnamese refugees were picked up.   9

Tri climbed aboard the oil rig. Standing on its deck, he looked back to watch the fishing boat disappear under water.   10

He would never look back again.   11

Six years later, Tri Lee stood on a much different platform and looked out onto a much different scene. He had been named co-valedictorian° of the senior class of a high school in a New Jersey suburb. Tri told his classmates, their parents, families, and friends about his experiences in Vietnam. He spoke about freedom, opportunities, goals, believing in yourself, and the value of hard work.   12

"I'm just a person with average ability who works as hard as I can," said Tri with a noticeable accent. "I'm not a hero by any stretch of the imagination. I'm just determined to take advantage of the   13 opportunities that are there for me. Anybody can accomplish what I did. They just have to want it badly enough."

The rest of Tri Lee's story shows just how motivated he was.   14

After being rescued by the British oil rig, Tri was sent to a United   15
Nations refugee camp on a small island called Bindong, in Malaysia. There were twenty thousand other Vietnamese refugees in the camp. Tri was separated from his cousins, who were sent to a U.N. camp in the Phillipines.

Tri lived in the Bindong camp for four months. He describes life   16
there as "horrible" and recalls unsanitary conditions, unappetizing foods, and sleeping on the wooden floor of a crowded hut. And there was so much conflict and fighting among the refugees that armed guards had to patrol the camp twenty-four hours a day.

Tri spent most of his time at Bindong studying English and trying   17
to convince the authorities that he should be allowed to enter America. Many refugees had been turned down, but Tri had three factors in his favor. First, two older sisters had followed the same route out of Vietnam a year earlier. They, too, had passed through the camp at Bindong and had been allowed to immigrate to America. Second, Tri, who studied most of the day and much of the night, had quickly learned some English. He impressed the authorities with his intelligence and motivation. Third, Tri's age was an advantage. United States immigration officials realized that it would be much easier for a twelve-year-old than for a middle-aged person to make a new start in America.

Eventually, Tri's request to enter America was granted. However,   18
he was first sent to another refugee camp in the Phillipines for a few months. There he was reunited with his two cousins. He was then put on flights from Malaysia to Hong Kong, San Francisco, and Philadelphia.

The Catholic Church arranged for Tri to be placed with a foster   19
family in Voorhees, New Jersey. His two sisters were already living there with another family and attending Eastern Regional High School. Tri enrolled at the Voorhees Middle School.

Although Tri had excelled in English at the refugee camps,   20
attempting to speak and understand English well enough to fit in with American teenagers proved very difficult. As a result of his language difficulties and the problems of adjusting to a much different culture, Tri withdrew and kept to himself. In the beginning, he had few friends. He was homesick and lonely and wondered if his parents, who were still in Vietnam, were alive.

"It was a rough time for me," Tri recalls. "Back in the refugee   21
camps, we were taught sentence structure, grammar, punctuation, and
formal conversational English. Everything changed, though, when I
arrived in America. When people spoke fast, I had problems
understanding what they were saying. Also, I couldn't begin to
understand slang or street English. And American teenagers use a lot of
slang and street English," he says with a smile. "In addition, I missed
my home and my parents an awful lot, especially in the beginning . . .
Still, as rough a time as I went through, it couldn't compare to what I
had gone through in Vietnam, on the boat, and in the refugee camps.

"Anyhow, when I didn't understand, I thought people were   22
talking about me, maybe saying bad things about me. I thought they
didn't like me, or they didn't think I belonged in their country. I
suppose I got a little paranoid° for a while."

Tri was placed in a class for non-English-speaking students. He   23
received intensive instruction in reading, writing, and speaking English.
Determined to overcome the language barrier, Tri excelled in his
lessons and studied constantly at home. Also, he became a voracious
reader. "I would read anything I could get my hands on," explains Tri.
"I particularly liked reading the classics. Even today, I still prefer to
read serious literature. Two of my favorite books are *All Quiet on the
Western Front* and *Lord of the Flies*. I remember I read a lot of books
about sports, hunting and fishing, and airplanes, too. In addition, my
foster parents spoke only English. . . . In order to survive in America, I
had to learn English. I was totally immersed° in the language. In fact, if
I had to give one bit of advice to non-English-speaking students, it's get
rid of your native language dictionaries as soon as you can. Don't let
them become too much of a crutch for you."

Once Tri felt more comfortable with informal English, he became   24
more trusting and started to make friends. Also, athletics helped Tri
gain acceptance among his American classmates. An outstanding
runner, Tri joined the track and cross-country teams.

When Tri entered Eastern Regional High School, his special   25
English classes were discontinued, and he was placed in the college
preparatory curriculum. Tri will always remember the day during his
freshman year when he realized he was finally completely comfortable
with English. "I listen to the radio a lot. The way I look at it, the more
English I hear, the better. In addition, I like rock music. I enjoy groups
such as Van Halen and U2. . . . Anyhow, one morning when I was in
the ninth grade, I was listening to the radio and it dawned on me that I
had stopped translating everything from Vietnamese into English. I had
actually started *thinking in English!*"

When Tri entered his sophomore year at Eastern Regional, he 26
signed up for all honors classes. He remembers his first homework
assignment in honors English II. "We had to read five short stories and
identify the protagonist°, the antagonist°, the conflict, and the irony° in
each story. The assignment was due the following morning. I kept
going over and over those stories, afraid that I didn't know what I was
doing and that I was making a lot of stupid mistakes. I put at least six
hours into that assignment. I had other homework that night, too.
Needless to say, I didn't get a whole lot of sleep that night."

But Tri persevered°. He continued to sign up for the most difficult 27
honors courses. And in order to devote himself exclusively to his studies,
he quit the track and football teams. His course schedule was the most
rigorous that the school could offer. In his senior year, Tri's schedule
included honors English and French, Advanced Physics, Advanced
Placement Calculus, and Pascal (a computer language course).

And Tri was no longer withdrawn. He became so popular with his 28
classmates that he was elected Student Council treasurer in his junior
and senior years. He had a diverse° group of friends in high school and
became a close observer of Western culture.

He noticed three significant differences between American and 29
Asian students. First, Tri was surprised at the way American young
people speak to their elders. He recalls being startled at how some of
his classmates would talk about, and sometimes to, their parents or
teachers. Also, he wasn't used to the ease with which Americans
express their feelings. Class discussions in which classmates shared
personal feelings were a completely new experience for him.
According to Tri, Vietnamese children are taught to keep their feelings
to themselves. Finally, Tri believes that American high school students
don't place the same value on education as do Asian students.

"American teenagers have so much given to them—new cars, 30
nice clothes, a comfortable place to live—that some of them get
spoiled. They take too many things for granted. My parents constantly
stressed how important school was to my sisters and me. They told me
that education is the most important thing in the world. In addition, my
background as a Vietnamese boat person makes me appreciate the
opportunities I have in America. I don't mean to criticize American
young people; they just don't know what it's like to live in a country
that was torn apart by war. They don't know what it's like to be a
refugee, to have to leave your homeland, to have your father arrested
by the Communists. They don't know how good they have it here."

Tri admits that math and science come easily to him, but he still 31
has to struggle sometimes with English. Consequently, he continues to

work hard to improve his language skills. "I make sure I read the newspaper every day. And I'm always reading a book or magazine. The best English teachers I've ever had have been my friends. They'll go out of their way to help me improve my English. All along, even back when I was struggling in junior high school, I had friends who would tutor me and give me extra help with assignments.

"There were times I probably aggravated my friends, always 32 asking them what something meant. But they never got tired of my questions. They never got impatient with me. As a result, I gained more confidence. I think the confidence I acquired with my use of English carried over to all the other areas of my life."

What was the end result of Tri's devotion to his studies? Over 33 four years at Eastern Regional High, Tri received straight A's in all subjects. He was named to the National Honor Society during his junior and senior years. And, of course, he was then chosen co-valedictorian of his class.

Eventually, Tri's family was reunited in America. The 34 Communists had arrested Tri's father, an army surgeon, and placed him in a "reeducation camp" for two years. When Tri's father was released, he and his wife joined the growing numbers of Vietnamese boat people and followed their children to America.

Tri feels he's been changed by his experiences in America. Like 35 many American teenagers, he prefers to wear T-shirts, jeans, and sneakers. Also, he enjoys many of the same activities his American friends do. For instance, Tri goes to a lot of movies. He particularly likes the James Bond films. He attends rock concerts and major league baseball games. Tri likes to shop at the malls and enjoys talking to friends on the phone.

Tri's Americanization, however, has occasionally created conflict 36 with his parents. "My parents were close to fifty years old when they immigrated to America. When I left Viet Nam, I was a little boy. When our family was reunited in America, I had become a teenager—an American teenager. Sometimes I'll say or do something that I know makes my parents wonder about me . . . Still, they understand that I've been exposed to a much different culture and that some of my ideas have changed a lot. We still have a real good relationship, though. They've always been very supporting of me. And one thing that hasn't changed is that my parents constantly stress the importance of education."

Today, Tri attends Princeton University, where he is majoring in 37 mechanical engineering. His journey from a small fishing boat adrift in international waters to the Princeton campus shows the value of a firm will and hard work.

> Tri shares his story on these pages in hopes that others,   38
> immigrants or native-born Americans, may be uplifted and encouraged
> when they face hardship.
>
> It's his way of saying thanks to America.   39

Vocabulary Questions

A. Use context clues to help you decide on the best definition for each italicized word. Then circle the letter of each choice.

1. The word *perilous* in "The eighty-five refugees crowded in the small boat faced a perilous situation. Their supply of food and drinking water was limited" (paragraph 6) means
   a. weather.
   b. dangerous.
   c. calm.
   d. guilty.

2. The word *relented* in "Faced with witnessing eighty-five humans drown, the English sailors then relented. The oil rig turned around, and the Vietnamese refugees were picked up" (paragraph 9) means
   a. cheered.
   b. turned away.
   c. hardened in attitude.
   d. gave in.

3. The word *voracious* in "he became a voracious reader. 'I would read anything I could get my hands on,' explains Tri" (paragraph 23) means
   a. science.
   b. careless.
   c. confused.
   d. eager.

4. The word *rigorous* in "His course schedule was the most rigorous that the school could offer. In his senior year, Tri's schedule included honors English and French, Advanced Physics, Advanced Placement Calculus, and Pascal (a computer language course)" (paragraph 27) means
   a. difficult.
   b. necessary.
   c. expensive.
   d. clear.

5. The word *acquired* in "the confidence I acquired with my use of English carried over to all the other areas of my life" (paragraph 32) means
   a. avoided.
   b. gained.
   c. designed.
   d. remembered.

B. Below are words from "Words to Watch." Write in the one that best completes each sentence.

diverse	immersed	paranoid
persevere	valedictorian	

6. Hawaii boasts of its _____ ethnic groups living together in harmony.

7. Julie's long hours of study have made her the top student in the class so far. She is therefore a candidate for class _____.

8. Peter doesn't seem to trust anyone anymore—he's become completely

   _____.

9. Tanya was so _____ in playing the piano that she didn't hear the fire alarm go off.

10. To reach a worthwhile goal, one must often _____, for there may be many obstacles and setbacks.

Reading Comprehension Questions

Central Point and Main Ideas

1. Which sentence best expresses the central point of the selection?
   a. Tri Lee still has to struggle with his English at times.
   b. In just six years, Tri Lee went from a non-English-speaking refugee to the top of his high school class.
   c. Tri Lee is studying mechanical engineering at Princeton University.
   d. Many immigrants become successful Americans.

2. The main idea of paragraph 29 is expressed in its
   a. first sentence.
   b. second sentence.
   c. next-to-last sentence.
   d. last sentence.

3. Which sentence best expresses the main idea of paragraph 36?
    a. Tri's parents were almost fifty years old when they came to live in America.
    b. Tri had grown up a lot during the time he and his parents were separated.
    c. Tri's relationship with his parents remains good, but they are uncomfortable with some of his Americanization.
    d. Tri's parents realize that he has been exposed to a very different culture than the one he was brought up with in Vietnam.

Supporting Details

4. Tri Lee came to the United States
    a. after a few days at sea in a small boat.
    b. soon after being rescued by a British oil rig.
    c. with his entire family.
    d. after escaping from Vietnam and spending months in refugee camps.

5. According to Tri Lee, in comparison with Asian students, American students
    a. take less for granted.
    b. place greater value on their education.
    c. have an easier time expressing their feelings.
    d. speak more respectfully to and about their elders.

Transitions

6. The relationship of the two sentences below is one of
    a. addition.
    b. time.
    c. illustration.
    d. cause and effect.

    . . . he still has to struggle sometimes with English. Consequently, he continues to work hard to improve his language skills. (Paragraph 31)

7. Each of the three differences between American and Asian students explained in paragraph 29 is introduced with an addition transition. Write those transitions below.

    _____   _____   _____

Patterns of Organization

8. The pattern of organization of paragraph 9 is
    a. time order.
    b. comparison and/or contrast.
    c. list of items.
    d. definition and example.

9. The pattern of organization of paragraph 16 is
    a. time order.
    b. comparison and/or contrast.
    c. cause and effect.
    d. list of items.

10. The pattern of organization of paragraph 29 is
    a. time order.
    b. comparison and/or contrast.
    c. cause and effect.
    d. definition and example.

Mapping Activity

This selection is organized by time: first one thing happened, then another, then another, and so on. We can divide those events into three main parts. Two parts are summarized in the diagram below. In the empty box, write a summary of the missing part of Tri Lee's story.

Central point: With hard work and dedication, Tri Lee overcame hardships to change himself from a refugee who knew no English to a star American student.

Tri Lee escaped from Vietnam as a boat person and was rescued by a British ship.

$\downarrow$

$\downarrow$

In New Jersey, Tri Lee became an excellent student and adjusted to American teenage life.

Discussion Questions

1. Tri Lee did whatever he had to—study for hours, get little sleep, quit sports—to get good grades. What goal are you determined to reach? How do you intend to reach it?

2. Many have come to America to escape their native countries. For some like Tri Lee, the journey was difficult, even dangerous. How and when did your family (or your ancestors) come to America? What hardships, if any, did they face?

Writing Activities

1. What special goal are you determined to reach? Write a paper explaining that goal and how you intend to reach it. List the steps you plan to take and what difficulties you are prepared to face in order to make your plan a success.

2. Tri Lee faced great dangers and discomforts during his journey to America. Have you ever been in a dangerous situation? A very uncomfortable one? Write a narrative (a description of a series of events) of a time when you were in an unusual situation of danger and/or discomfort. Before starting your narrative, reread paragraphs 1–11. Note how the author uses specific details to recreate the events in Tri Lee's dramatic escape from Vietnam. Then try to include the same type of specific details in your narrative.

Check Your Performance		**PATTERNS OF ORGANIZATION**	
Activity	*Number Right*	*Points*	*Total*
Review Test 1 (10 items)	_____	x 3 =	_____
Review Test 2 (5 items)	_____	x 3 =	_____
Review Test 3, Part A (5 items)	_____	x 2 =	_____
Review Test 3, Part B (20 items)	_____	x 2 =	_____
Mapping (1 item)	_____	x 5 =	_____
		TOTAL SCORE =	_____%

Enter your total score into the reading performance chart on the inside back cover.

10

Inferences

You have probably heard the expression "to read between the lines." When you "read between the lines," you pick up ideas that are suggested but that are not directly stated in what you are reading. The ideas you pick up are implied and are often important for a full understanding of a passage. Discovering the ideas that are not stated directly is called **making inferences**, or **drawing conclusions**.

UNDERSTANDING INFERENCES

We make inferences every day. Consider the following situations:

- If you are inside a building and see a person come in who is folding a wet umbrella, you infer that it is raining outside.
- If you hear a siren while driving and see through the rearview mirror that a police car is behind you, you infer that the officer wants you to pull over.
- If you bite into an apple and see half a worm, you infer that the other half is in your mouth.

In many cases like those above, we evaluate the evidence given to us and reach a sensible conclusion. In other words, we make inferences.

We also make inferences as we read. You have already done some inferring while using this book. Here are sentences from an item in the "Vocabulary in Context" chapter:

The adverse weather conditions forced us to stay inside for most of our vacation. The day the weather finally turned nice, we had to leave.

The sentences do not tell us what *adverse* means. But they do strongly suggest that *adverse* means the opposite of "nice." So we can reasonably assume that, at least in this context, *adverse* means "bad."

You also made inferences in the "Implied Main Ideas" chapter. That chapter taught you how to find main ideas which were not directly stated. You used information in a paragraph to figure out its main idea. In other words, you inferred the main idea of the paragraph.

In this chapter, you will get more practice in drawing inferences. Start by reading the paragraph below and answering the question that follows. Then read the explanation.

> In 1901, a popular sandwich was called a "dachshund sausage." (A dachshund is a dog with a long, round body.) A cartoonist drawing a picture of a dachshund sausage discovered that he could not spell *dachshund*. He then invented a new term, one that caught on. As a result, we now refer to this sandwich as a "hot dog."

Which one of the following inferences is most strongly suggested by the information in the passage?

    a. The cartoonist loved hot dogs.
    b. The cartoonist made a lot of money from inventing the term "hot dog."
    c. The cartoonist had a low level of education.
    d. People preferred the term "hot dog" over "dachshund sausage."

Explanation:

> An inference must be supported by the facts in a passage or by experience. There is no evidence that the cartoonist loved hot dogs or made money from inventing the term "hot dog." Therefore *a* and *b* are not correct. Nor is item *c* supported by the facts. Just because the cartoonist was unable to spell *dachshund* does not mean he had a low level of education. Most people have trouble spelling a word now and then. Item *d*, however, is supported by the passage. If the term "dachshund sandwich" had been preferred, today we would not be referring to the sandwich as a "hot dog."

Now look at the cartoon on the next page from *The New Yorker* magazine. It shows the front of the New York City Public Library, which in real life is a large building with statues of lions in front. The statues have been there for many years. The heads of the lions face the street.

Understanding a cartoon's message often involves good inference skills. Can you infer the meaning of this cartoon? Look at it, and then check what you believe is its message. Then read the explanation that follows.

What message can you infer from the cartoon? Put a check by the **one** inference that is most logically based on the information given in the cartoon.

____ 1. The cartoonist feels libraries are so boring that even the lions would rather watch television than read.

____ 2. The cartoonist is making the observation that television competes with books for people's attention.

____ 3. The cartoonist is making the observation that lions cannot read.

Explanation:

Since libraries are filled with interesting books, we can assume that the cartoonist is not saying that libraries are boring. So inference *1* is incorrect. Also, the fact that lions cannot read is not particularly interesting or funny. So we can assume the cartoonist would not bother to imply inference *3*. To get the message of this cartoon, we have to think about the fact that the lions are watching TV in front of a building devoted to reading. This tells us that the cartoonist is highlighting the fact that television strongly competes with books for people's attention.

INFERENCES IN EVERYDAY READING

Authors do not always spell out exactly what they want readers to know. Therefore in order to read well, you must infer. Here are some guidelines to understanding important ideas that are not directly stated:

1   Consider all the information and clues provided by the author. To do this, you must read attentively.

2   Use your own experiences to help you make sense of what you read. In other words, try to identify with the point the author is trying to get across.

3   Use common sense. Don't read too much into what is being discussed. By the same token, don't be afraid to reason out what is happening. Let logic dictate how far you can go.

Keep these points in mind as you read the passage below. Answer each of the questions that follow by circling the letter of the most reasonable inference. To help you, hints are provided to help you think through the choices. The hints show the type of reasoning process involved in making inferences. Finally, read the explanation that follows.

> In 1892, Lizzy Borden's parents were found brutally murdered. They had been hacked to death, as if with an axe. But did their accused daughter Lizzy really do it? Lizzy Borden herself testified that she had bought a small axe just two days before the crime. And she was caught burning a dress that was stained with blood. In spite of this evidence, the jury found Lizzy innocent.

1. The passage suggests that Lizzy Borden
    a. hated her parents.
    b. killed her parents.
    c. might have killed her parents.

    Hint: The passage states that Lizzy's parents were found "hacked to death, as if with an axe."

2. We can assume that the bloodstained dress
    a. was something Lizzy did not want to keep.
    b. had belonged to Lizzy.
    c. was worn by Lizzy on the day her parents died.

    Hint: All the passage says about the dress is that Lizzy was caught burning it.

3. We can infer that
    a. the jury was sure Lizzy was innocent.
    b. the jury was sure Lizzy was guilty.
    c. the jury felt there wasn't enough evidence against Lizzy to convict her.

Hint: The author writes that the jury found Lizzy innocent "in spite of" the evidence of the axe and the bloodstained dress.

Have you made your choices? If so, read the explanation below.

Explanation:

1. The answer is *c*. The author doesn't mention how Lizzy felt about her parents. Thus we don't have enough information to choose answer *a*. All we know is that her parents were murdered and that their wounds could have been made by an axe. Since Lizzy had bought an axe two days earlier, she might have been the murderer, but not necessarily. After all, the jury, which had more information about the case than what is given in the passage, found her innocent. Logic tells us, then, that the best answer is *c*.

2. The passage does not reveal whose dress it was or who wore it. Thus there is no evidence that answer *b* is correct. Also, although Lizzy's burning the dress looks suspicious, there is no evidence in the passage that she wore the dress or that the stains on it are her parents' blood. Lizzy might even have burned the dress to protect someone else. Thus answer *c* is incorrect. The choice best supported by the paragraph is *a*. We know that Lizzy was burning the dress, so she obviously did not want to keep it.

3. The evidence of the burned dress and the axe might have made jurors think Lizzy was guilty. Yet, since they found her innocent, we can conclude they at least had doubts about her guilt for some reason. The correct answer, then, is *c*.

➤ *Practice 1*

Read each passage below. Then put a check by the **two** inferences that are most strongly supported by the information in the passage, logic, and your experience.

1.   This morning, our cat was waiting at our doorstep. He was purring. Next to him was a dead mouse.

  ___ a. The cat had caught the mouse.

  ___ b. There are mice in the house.

  ___ c. The cat was pleased with what he had done.

  ___ d. The speaker will no longer let the cat outside.

2. Recently, a well-known mall store chained all its coats and jackets to the racks. To try one on, a customer has to ask a clerk to unlock it. Also, a security guard is posted just inside the doorway.

___ a. Other stores in the mall have also chained their coats and jackets to racks.

___ b. The store is trying to discourge shoplifters.

___ c. The coats and jackets are valuable.

___ d. The mall store is in a poor neighborhood.

3. At dinner, Shawna did not eat any of the homemade apple pie, even though everyone else enjoyed the rich dessert. Four hours later, when other people in the family were ready to go to bed, Shawna helped herself to a big piece of pie.

___ a. Shawna was cheating on her diet.

___ b. Shawna had gotten hungry.

___ c. Shawna enjoys apple pie.

___ d. Shawna was in a bad mood during dinner.

4. At 3:00, Curtis stomped into his office and slammed the door. A few minutes later, he pulled open all the drawers of his desk and started tossing their contents into an empty carton. At 3:15, he marched out of the office, carrying the carton. "You can send my final check to my home address," he yelled to the secretary on his way out the door.

___ a. Curtis has been fired.

___ b. Curtis will be moving to a better office.

___ c. Curtis is upset.

___ d. Curtis does not plan to return to his office.

5. A recent survey of 1,000 business people revealed that 89 percent take work home with them. In addition, 85 percent work more than 45 hours a week, and 65 percent work more than one weekend a month. According to the survey, 81 percent of these people suffer from stress, and 48 percent feel stress every day.

___ a. Nobody works harder than people in business.

___ b. A business career can be demanding.

___ c. Careers in business often involve a lot of stress.

___ d. Business people can handle stress better than other people.

> *Practice 2*

Read each passage below. Then circle the letter of the most logical answer to each question, based on the information given. Use the clues in the passage, your own experience, and logic to help you infer the answer.

A. Sometimes what a student learns in class is not what the teacher had in mind. One example is the case of the science professor who wished to demonstrate the effects of alcohol to her class. On the lab table, she set two beakers—one containing water and the other filled with grain alcohol. Then she dropped an earthworm into each. The worm in the alcohol beaker wriggled violently, trying to escape, and quickly died. The worm in the water beaker moved slowly and gracefully, seeming to enjoy its new environment. The professor smiled with satisfaction and looked at the roomful of students. Then she asked, "What lesson can be learned from this demonstration?" One student quickly raised his hand. "If you drink alcohol," he answered, "you'll never have worms."

   1. We can infer that alcohol
      a. is good for earthworms.
      b. is deadly to earthworms.
      c. does not harm earthworms.

      Hint: Sentence 5 says, "The worm in the alcohol beaker wriggled violently, trying to escape, and quickly died."

   2. We can assume that the science professor
      a. was opposed to alcoholic beverages.
      b. wanted to show that alcohol can hurt living beings.
      c. wanted to show that earthworms can swim.

      Hint: Sentence 2 says the science professor "wished to demonstrate the effects of alcohol to her class."

   3. We can infer that the student who answered the question
      a. may have missed the teacher's point.
      b. was very observant.
      c. often drank alcoholic beverages.

      Hint: What message would the teacher be most likely to have in mind?

B. In wedding ceremonies today, the groom relies on his best man to carry out many important duties. However, in earlier times, the role of the best man had nothing to do with the groom at all. The best man's sole duty was to stick like glue to the bride. His only purpose was to protect her from any tribes that might interrupt the ceremony and kidnap her for marriage to one of their villagers. Only after the ceremony was over, and the bride safely married, could the best man relax. Then he could turn his attention to the groom and—more importantly—to the celebration in progress.

4. We can infer that in earlier times,
   a. there were dangers to getting married.
   b. wedding ceremonies took longer than they do today.
   c. the best man was selected by the bride's father.

   Hint: The author clearly implies that the bride was at risk of being kidnapped.

5. We can assume that the best man
   a. in earlier times was a member of the groom's family.
   b. was once chosen for strength and devotion.
   c. is more important today than in the past.

   Hint: The passage states that the best man had to stick like glue to the bride and protect her.

6. We can infer that in those earlier times
   a. there were no bridesmaids.
   b. neighboring tribes would not kidnap a married woman.
   c. women were often attracted to men from neighboring tribes.

   Hint: The passage says that the best man could relax once the bride was safely married.

➤ *Practice 3*

Read each passage below. Then circle the letter of the most logical answer to each question. Use the clues in the passage, your own experience, and logic to choose each answer.

A.   A U.S. District Court judge recently was listening to closing arguments in a felony trial when his usual court clerk noticed something strange. The judge was furiously writing on a legal pad. When the arguments ended and the judge called for a recess, the curious clerk looked to see what the judge had written. Scribbled repeatedly on the pad were the words "Don't go to sleep. You must not go to sleep!" When the clerk entered the judge's chambers, she found him sound asleep on the couch.

1. We can infer that
   a. the judge was old.
   b. the judge had a sleeping disorder.
   c. the judge was trying hard not to fall asleep in court.

2. We can also infer that
   a. the judge was bored by the trial's proceedings.
   b. the judge did not normally write such comments during a trial.
   c. the judge was embarrassed when the court clerk entered his chambers.

B.   People whose noses run during a romantic embrace shouldn't worry that they are allergic to their true love. Researchers say that it is perfectly normal for men and women to get a stuffed or runny nose during passionate moments. The congestion is caused by changes in hormones that can occur during pleasurable excitement. Such changes can happen at any stage of life. Men, however, are most likely to experience this condition during adolescence or old age. This is because their hormone levels are in a state of change during those times. For the same reason, women are especially prone to romance-related stuffy noses during pregnancy.

3. We can assume that
    a. in most people, hormone levels remain constant.
    b. our hormone levels vary, especially at certain times in our lives.
    c. changes in hormones are more drastic in men than in women.

4. We can infer that
    a. if we get runny noses during romantic activities, we must stop what we are doing.
    b. hormones influence our noses.
    c. it is easier to catch a cold when passionate than during any other activity.

5. The passage suggests that
    a. everyone experiences a runny nose during passion at some time in his or her life.
    b. men should not engage in romantic embraces during adolescence or old age.
    c. a runny nose during passion can happen to anyone.

➤ *Review Test 1*

Read each passage below. Then put a check by the **two** inferences that are most strongly supported by the information in the passage, logic, and your experience.

1.   Many expressions that we use make little sense unless you know the stories behind them. To illustrate, consider what we say when someone gets fired from a job."Hey, did you hear? Joe got sacked on Friday." "Getting sacked" is a phrase with its roots in ancient Rome. The Romans punished certain criminals by tying them in sacks and throwing them into the river. "Getting sacked" eventually came to mean getting "thrown out" of a job.

____ a. An expression's meaning can change over the years.

____ b. English was once the main language in Rome.

____ c. The history of words and phrases may go back many years.

____ d. At one time, people who were fired from their jobs were put in sacks.

2.   People who can't write their names usually sign with an "X." There is a reason for this. The "X," of course, is so simple to write that even a child could do it. But, more importantly, when an "X" is tipped on its side, it forms a cross, a sacred religious symbol. This symbol once implied that the person signing could be trusted.

____ a. An "X" is one of the easiest letters to make.

____ b. More people sign their names with an "X" today than in the past.

____ c. The "X" signature was supposed to make people think of a cross.

____ d. "X" was used only in signing religious documents.

3.   One of Japan's greatest delicacies can also kill you. The blowfish, prized for its delicious and tender flesh, also contains a quick paralyzing poison. In Japan, the blowfish is never served unless it is prepared by specially trained and licensed chefs who know how to remove all of the poison. Even so, the only way to know if all of the poison has been removed is to see if the diner survives.

____ a. Eating a blowfish can be dangerous.

____ b. The blowfish is the most poisonous fish in Japan.

____ c. The blowfish should be prepared only by specialists.

____ d. Many people die soon after eating a blowfish.

4.   Beauty sometimes can be painful. The members of one tribe in Africa think a large lower lip is beautiful. To achieve it, they must stretch their lips out with plates positioned in between their lower lip and gums. Ancient Chinese thought tiny feet were very pretty. They would bind the feet of their girls to ensure the smallest feet possible. And in nineteenth-century America, small waists were in fashion. Women who wanted tiny waists would lace themselves in corsets so tight that they would sometimes faint from lack of breath.

____ a. Standards of beauty rarely change.

____ b. Today, the Chinese consider tiny feet ugly.

____ c. Standards of beauty vary from culture to culture.

____ d. Chinese no longer bind young girls' feet.

5.   Lightning doesn't always strike outdoors. In fact, people can be killed inside their homes. Lightning can come in through an open window or door and then bounce around a room until it finds a way outside again. Also, any electrical appliance which conducts electricity can act as a magnet for dangerous lightning. Lightning can even be conducted through telephone wires and electrocute a person talking on the phone.

___ a. Nothing's more dangerous than lightning.

___ b. A lightning storm can be harmful whether you are inside or outside.

___ c. Lightning has killed more people using electrical appliances than people talking on the phone.

___ d. During a lightning storm, it is safer not to use the telephone or electrical appliances.

➤ *Review Test 2*

Read each passage below. Then circle the letter of the most logical inference. Use the clues in the passage, your own experience, and logic to choose your answers. Hints are given for each item after the first passage.

A. The minimum daily requirement of water for an adult has been set by the government at eight glasses. If you think you need to slurp down eight glasses of water to meet this requirement, think again. We get a lot of the water we need from a variety of other sources. For example, approximately 250,000 of us get more than five glasses of water from our morning cups of coffee alone. Others get water from soft drinks. Even solid foods have water content. About 200,000 Americans eat enough potatoes to provide them with 10 ounces of water per day. Indeed, almost half of our water intake comes from solid foods such as meats and vegetables.

1. We can infer that
   a. there is more water in solid foods than in liquid foods.
   b. there is water in almost everything we eat.
   c. people who don't eat meat are in danger of getting too little water.

   Hint: The passage tells us that we get a lot of the water our bodies need from a variety of sources and that even solid foods have water content.

2. We can assume that
   a. the more coffee we drink, the more water we take in.
   b. soft drinks and coffee contain exactly the same amount of water.
   c. more people drink coffee than soft drinks.

   Hint: All the passage says is that we can get water from coffee and from soft drinks.

3. We can infer that
   a. it's okay to take in more than eight glasses of water a day.
   b. it's quite difficult to get our minimum daily requirement of water.
   c. we get more water from meat than from vegetables.

   Hint: The passage is about a minimum requirement.

B.   The mole, depending on its species, has eyes that are completely hidden or barely visible. The animal sees little more than changes in the amount of light. Its forelimbs, which stick out at the side, have large digging muscles. A fifth of its weight is due to huge lungs, which enable it to breathe air that is not rich in oxygen. The mole makes its living digging an elaborate system of tunnels, some of which bulge out on the surface of the ground. Worms actually drop in the tunnels, as one wit has put it, "like bacon and eggs on the ceiling." Since insects and worms are always passing through the earth, the mole only has to scout its tunnels to "harvest" a meal.

4. We can infer that the mole
   a. works underwater.
   b. is a good digger.
   c. has keen eyesight.

5. We can also infer that the mole
   a. generally has plenty to eat.
   b. often comes above ground to seek food.
   c. would be welcome in yards to keep lawns free of worms.

➤ *Review Test 3*

A.   To review what you've learned in this chapter, answer each of the following questions. Fill in the blank, or circle the letter of the answer you think is correct.

1. An inference is an idea that is *(directly stated, implied, not referred to)*

   _____ by an author.

2. _____ TRUE OR FALSE? Making an inference and drawing a conclusion are the same thing.

3. _____ TRUE OR FALSE? It is logical for an inference to contradict the facts of a passage.

4. To understand inferences, you must
   a. use the clues provided by the author.
   b. use your experience.
   c. use logic.
   d. all of the above.

5. Reading between the lines involves
   a. reading attentively.
   b. reading a lot.
   c. reading slowly.
   d. all of the above.

B. Here is a chance to apply your understanding of inferences to a full-length reading about how one woman turned her life around. While terrified at the thought of going back to school, she struggled through scholarship forms and an assessment test. She went on to overcome her fear of college and gain a new self-image and sense of optimism.

Following the reading are questions on inferences. There are also other reading comprehension questions to help you continue to reinforce the skills taught in previous chapters.

Words to Watch

Following are some words in the reading that do not have strong context support. Each word is followed by the number of the paragraph in which it appears and its meaning there. These words are indicated in the article by a small circle (°).

> *humiliation* (2): shame or dishonor
> *documented* (4): proven
> *Richter scale* (11): a scale that measures the intensity of an earthquake
> *Pell grant* (12): a government grant for those who need financial assistance
> to attend college
> *peer pressure* (18): the influence of people belonging to the same group (in
> age, status, etc.) in society
> *second nature* (19): a quality or behavior that has been used for so long that
> it seems automatic
> *perspective* (19): mental view
> *self-maintaining* (22): able to take care of oneself
> *forged* (25): formed

THE DREAM INSIDE

Ruth Norris

Wash the dishes! Clean your room! Mow the grass! Phooey! 1
When I grow up, I'm going to run my own life. Isn't that what all children say? Starting at around the age of ten, my goal was to live my own life my own way. By the age of seventeen I was married. I had freedom at last.

Just when everything seemed to be going my way, I realized that 2
the love of my life was secretly a Nazi dictator who took his schooling on the right-hand side of Hitler. At least that's how it seemed to me. As if that wasn't enough, I learned the cold hard facts of divorce and the humiliation° of having to move back in with my parents.

At the age of twenty-one, Mr. Stork brought me a bouncing baby   3
boy. It only took me about a week to figure out that a child is not
something you can just leave in the toy box when you are done playing.
Years went by as I watched my son grow and my paychecks shrink. I
was alone and in charge of my life, and boy was I having fun.

The answer to all my problems came while I was watching a soap   4
opera: every family needs a father figure. I was married again. Now I
was raising two boys. Which one actually had the higher I.Q. never was
documented°. But I decided that a husband, unlike a child, could be left
in his toy box and never played with again. This put my seven-year-old
and me back into the single parent group.

A person doesn't need much to be in this group: just sign up on   5
welfare. Unfortunately, in this group, a person doesn't get much. While
it seemed to be working for us, somehow I had completely lost what I
had always wanted. Now the Department of Human Services was in
charge of my life.

School had still not entered my mind. I guess I thought since I had   6
a high-school diploma, from 1977, who needed more? Maybe I did. I
found this out when it came time to help my ten-year-old with his math
homework. I don't remember doing that kind of math when I was
young. I'll just make him study harder; that way I won't look so stupid.

The next year or so I don't really have any memory of. I did try   7
marriage number three, but that was a very short one. I ended up just
settling back in front of the television and accepting my fate.

My fate seemed to be the knowledge of the street. This had many   8
good points. It gave me the know-how to survive. Book knowledge, on
the other hand, is a lot different; for this I needed school. While I was
having a hard time money-wise, keeping my son dressed properly and
school supplies replenished, the need for my education entered my
mind but was just a faraway dream.

I sat and watched the world go by. Many of my friends were   9
going back to school, but they had more money and time to waste than
I did. All my time was needed to impress the welfare system with my
lack of worldly possessions. That in itself was a full-time job, and I was
good at it. This became my big accomplishment. I was in control now.
It's funny how things look when I keep my eyes closed.

While sitting—my most perfected art—and watching television   10
one night, I was dreaming of all the things I would not be able to get
my son for his thirteenth birthday. Thirteen, he was no longer a baby.
He was turning into a teenager before my eyes. It won't be long before
he becomes a young adult. Then he becomes completely independent.
Next, he'll move into an apartment of his own. Oh my God! Then he

will fall in love, get married, and have children! I'm going to be a lonely, old, fat grandmother facing the rest of my life with nothing to fill the void! Wake up, Ruth! Take charge of your life before it's over!

Who said that? Is it really possible that there is a little voice inside 11 my head that can scream loud enough to register on a Richter scale°? I had read about it in children's books, and I had watched it happen on television, but now it was happening to me. My inner self was wanting to come out. Most of all, my inner self was wanting to learn, to grow, and to become something.

After another week or two, I decided to check into the possibility 12 of furthering my education. What could it hurt? I'll send for a Pell grant° form, and if I'm accepted, maybe I'll go.

The application is here. I thought surely they would have lost my 13 address. No problem; I'll just fill it out and see what happens. What is all this? A person has to have a college degree to understand the forms. How will I ever make it through school if I can't make it through the forms? Boy, am I in trouble.

Well, that chore is done and over. The papers are in the mail. It's 14 in the hands of the U.S. Post Office now. I'm glad I don't have to worry about it anymore.

I can't believe it. They accepted me! Don't panic. The next step is 15 the Assessment Test. The secretary has assured me that I cannot flunk. That's a relief. Great, what am I going to wear? How do school kids dress these days? I hope it's not like my son. What am I doing? I'm thirty-three years old. I'm too old for this! Calm down; it's just a test, not a fashion show.

Everything is going pretty well. I have made it through the first 16 part of the test without much trouble. The only part left is the math portion. I'll do okay unless there are a lot of fractions. What is all this shorthand-looking number stuff? This can't be math. I'm doomed!

Well, the results are in. I'm not as dumb as I thought. My worst 17 hurdle is going to be math. All my scores made it almost to college level. I'll be starting my first math class with the other four-year-olds at Noah's Ark Preschool.

What a feeling there is inside me. I have a sense of 18 accomplishment and a sense of worth. The hardest part is yet to come. The toughest obstacle of all, I have found, is fear. That one little four-letter word has such an impact on me. It covers such a large variety of areas: failure, fitting in, acceptance, peer pressure°, and rejection.

What will it be like if I can't make the grade? How will I handle 19 sitting next to students who are fifteen years my junior and not knowing as much as they do? How will I watch some people do their work with what seems like second nature°, while I pull at my gray hairs trying to make the simplest things come into perspective°? What will they think of me? These questions ran through my head a million times before I ever set one foot in my first classroom.

The first day is here. Sitting outside the school with all my new books, pencils, paper, and wearing the new outfit my mother had bought me, I almost had a change of mind. "Start the car and drive away," I told myself out loud. Instead, I opened the car door and walked into class.

This is great! I'm not the oldest person here. I'm not even the fattest! This is going to be all right. Even my clothes are up to date with my age group. I feel good.

Time out. Maybe this isn't so great. It averages out for every hour I spend in school, I have three hours of homework. Time is going to be an important factor for the first time in a lot of years. Maybe it is a good thing my son is now a self-maintaining° individual. The days are long, and television is now a luxury. This is so different, but I think I'm going to make it.

Who made up these rules? Mid-term tests? I'm not ready! Just when everything is going smoothly, someone throws in another test! I hope they don't make a habit of this. Let me guess, this is what school is, right? Right.

I'm actually doing it. I'm changing my life. Although it will take me until I am sixty-five to get through my math courses, everything else is falling into place. I used to think I would be just another Roseanne Arnold, but since I have enrolled in school, I see myself more as a Murphy Brown. Journalism has aroused my attention since I now feel intelligent enough to read a newspaper. I have a lot to share with people, and journalism can be my tool. I ended my first semester with a 3.6 grade point average. Pretty darn good for a woman of thirty-four.

All in all I believe I have finally done it. I am now in charge of my life. The funny part is, it has been a lot easier than I thought it would be. What I was so afraid of I will probably never really know. My future is not forged° in steel, but it looks brighter than it used to. It makes me think of the yellow brick road in *The Wizard of Oz*. Even with a well-laid path, there will still be flying monkeys or a wicked witch trying to stop me. But with the dream inside me now a reality, the future looks pretty good. What seems so ironic to me is now I tell my son to wash the dishes, clean his room, and mow the grass. I only hope and pray it doesn't take him thirty-four years to find what I have.

Vocabulary Questions

A. Use context clues to help you decide on the best definition for each italicized word. Then circle the letter of each choice.

1. The word *replenished* in "While I was having a hard time money-wise, keeping my son dressed properly and school supplies replenished, the need for my education entered my mind but was just a faraway dream" (paragraph 8) means
   a. restocked.
   b. in style.
   c. straight.
   d. well-sharpened.

2. The word *void* in "It won't be long before he becomes a young adult . . . I'm going to be a lonely, old, fat grandmother facing the rest of my life with nothing to fill the void!" (paragraph 10) means
   a. stomach.
   b. emptiness.
   c. past.
   d. questions.

3. The word *hurdle* in "Well, the results are in. I'm not as dumb as I thought. My worst hurdle is going to be math" (paragraph 17) means
   a. test question.
   b. teacher.
   c. hope.
   d. difficulty to overcome.

4. The word *impact* in "The toughest obstacle of all, I have found, is fear. That one little four-letter word has such an impact on me" (paragraph 18) means
   a. encouragement.
   b. pity.
   c. effect.
   d. head start.

5. The expression *forged in steel* in "My future is not forged in steel, but it looks brighter than it used to" (paragraph 25) means
   a. high technology.
   b. long.
   c. firmly set.
   d. bent.

B. Below are words and phrases from "Words to Watch." Write in the one that best completes each sentence.

documented	humiliation	peer pressure
perspective	second nature	

6. It is now well _____ by various studies that smoking is one cause of lung cancer.

7. For teenagers, _____ is often more important than the influence of the family.

8. My parents have been arguing for so many years that it is _____ for them—they do it automatically.

9. You can't imagine the _____ I felt when the slip under my wedding gown slid off.

10. It is often a long while after I live through a difficult time before I am able to get a clear _____ on the experience.

Reading Comprehension Questions

Central Point and Main Ideas

1. Which sentence best expresses the central point of the entire selection?
   a. Overcoming her fears, Norris turned her life around by enrolling in college.
   b. Norris felt freedom at the early age of seventeen.
   c. With government assistance, taking charge of her life was easy for Norris.
   d. Many people have to wait until they are in their thirties before they can take charge of their lives.

2. The main idea of paragraph 19 is best expressed in its
   a. first sentence.
   b. second sentence.
   c. next-to-the-last sentence.
   d. last sentence.

Supporting Details

3. Once in college, Norris discovered that
   a. she was the oldest student in her classes.
   b. her wardrobe needed updating.
   c. doing a good job in college requires a lot of time.
   d. all of the above.

Transitions

4. The relationship of the second sentence below to the first is one of
   a. addition.
   b. time.
   c. illustration.
   d. contrast.

   > "Start the car and drive away," I told myself out loud. Instead, I opened the car door and walked into class. (Paragraph 20)

Patterns of Organization

5. The main pattern of organization of paragraph 10 is
   a. time order.
   b. comparison and/or contrast.
   c. definition and example.
   d. list of items.

6. The pattern of organization of paragraph 19 is
   a. time order.
   b. list of items.
   c. comparison and/or contrast.
   d. cause and effect.

Inferences

7. In paragraph 2, the author's description of her husband suggests that he
   a. was German.
   b. had a secret life.
   c. expected her to do as he commanded.
   d. rarely worked.

8. Norris suggests in paragraph 9 that she was
   a. very busy at that time.
   b. planning even then to go back to school.
   c. pleased not to have too much money.
   d. fooling herself into believing she was accomplishing something.

9. From paragraphs 19 and 20 we can infer that
   a. Norris really did not want to go to school.
   b. Norris's first day at college required some courage.
   c. the author had tried once before to begin college.
   d. Norris's family did not support her going back to school.

10. From the reading, we might infer that
    a. early marriage can be beneficial.
    b. it is never too late to take charge of your life.
    c. schools should eliminate assessment tests.
    d. it is best to wait until your thirties to take charge of your life.

Mapping Activity

In general, this selection is organized according to time. Major events in Norris's life are presented in the order in which they occurred. Five of those events are scrambled in the list below. Write them in their correct order in the diagram that follows.

- Norris takes the assessment test for college.
- Norris marries and divorces for the first time.
- Norris very successfully completes her first semester of college.
- After Norris's second and third marriages, she goes on welfare.
- Norris has a baby.

Central point: In her thirties, Ruth Norris took charge of her life by enrolling in college.

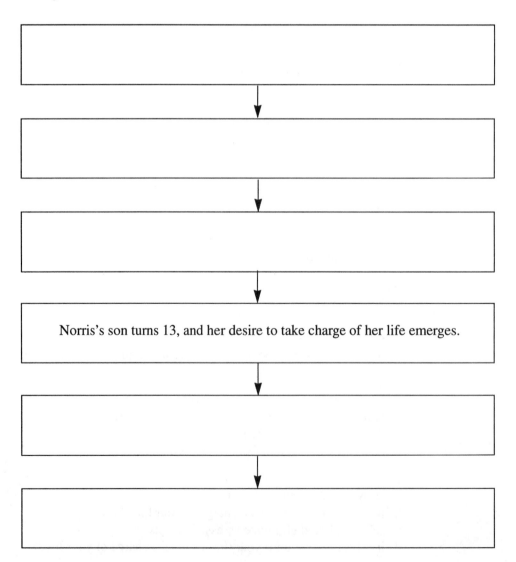

Norris's son turns 13, and her desire to take charge of her life emerges.

Discussion Questions

1. Norris writes, "I used to think I would be just another Roseanne Arnold, but since I have enrolled in school, I see myself more as Murphy Brown." What contrast does she mean to imply by naming these two characters?

2. Norris starts her essay with orders that were given to her when she was a child: "Wash the dishes! Clean your room! Mow the grass!" She then states in the conclusion of her essay, "What seems so ironic to me is now I tell my son to wash the dishes, clean his room, and mow the grass." Why do you think she finds this ironic?

Writing Activities

1. Doing well on her assessment test gave Norris "a sense of worth." Think about the experiences that have contributed to your self-esteem, and then write a paragraph about one of those experiences. Use the following topic sentence (or something like it): "One special experience greatly strengthened my sense of self-worth."

2. Norris tells of many difficult experiences, including the humiliation of having to move back with her parents after her first divorce. What is one of the most difficult situations you have had to face? Write a paper describing that experience in detail, including how you dealt with it.

Check Your Performance			**INFERENCES**
Activity	*Number Right*	*Points*	*Total*
Review Test 1 (10 items)	_____	x 2.5 =	_____
Review Test 2 (5 items)	_____	x 3 =	_____
Review Test 3, Part A (5 items)	_____	x 2 =	_____
Review Test 3, Part B (20 items)	_____	x 2 =	_____
Mapping (5 items)	_____	x 2 =	_____
		TOTAL SCORE =	_____%

Enter your total score into the reading performance chart on the inside back cover.

Part II

MASTERY TESTS

DICTIONARY USE: Test 1

A. Use your dictionary and the spelling hints on page 12 to find the correct spelling of the following words.

1. hury   _____   4. eazy   _____

2. sertain _____   5. chappel _____

3. blead   _____   6. beleive _____

B. Below are three pairs of dictionary guidewords followed by other words. Circle the two words in each series which would be found on the page with the guidewords.

7-8. **cooler / coral**

    color   cool-headed   cookbook   copy   cord

9-10. **fever / field**

    feud   fight   fiend   fiber   few

11-12. **jilt / joint**

    jog   jolly   jiggle   jingle   joke

C. Use the pronunciation key below to answer the questions that follow.

Pronunciation Key

ă pat	ā pay	â care	ä father	ĕ pet	ē be	ĭ pit
ī tie	î pier	ŏ pot	ō toe	ô paw, for		oi noise
ŏŏ took	ōō boot	ou out	th thin	*th* this		ŭ cut
û urge	yōō abuse	zh vision	ə about, item, edible, gallop, circus			

13. In *elbow* (ĕl′bō′), the *e* is pronounced like the *e* in
    a. *pet.*   b. *be.*

14. In *elbow* (ĕl′bō′), the *o* is pronounced like the *o* in
    a. *pot.*   b. *toe.*   c. *for.*

15. In *blooper* (blōō′pər), the *oo* is pronounced like the *oo* in
    a. *took.*   b. *boot.*

16. In *blooper* (blōō′pər), the *e* is pronounced like
    a. the *e* in *pet.*   b. the *e* in *be.*   c. the *e* in *item.*

(Continues on next page)

D. Answer the questions below about the following dictionary entry for *cite*.

cite (sīt) *v.* **cit•ed, cit•ing. 1.** To mention in support of or as proof of a point. **2.** To praise for worthy action, esp. in military service. **3.** To call before a court of law.

17. The part of speech of *cite* is
    a. verb.
    b. noun.
    c. adjective.

18. The past tense of *cite* has
    a. one syllable.
    b. two syllables.
    c. three syllables.

19. The definition of *cite* that fits the sentence below is
    a. definition 1.
    b. definition 2.
    c. definition 3.

    The judge himself is on trial; he was cited for taking bribes from local union officials.

20. The definition of *cite* that fits the sentence below is
    a. definition 1.
    b. definition 2.
    c. definition 3.

    To back up my point that homemakers work hard, I cited a study which shows that most spend over fifty hours a week on household chores.

DICTIONARY USE: Test 2

Use your dictionary to find the information needed for sections A–D of this test.

A. List the parts of speech for the following words.

    1. fluid _____

    2. most _____

    3. one _____

B. Write the irregular forms for the following words.

    4. life _____

    5. city _____

    6. wear _____

C. Write in the dictionary definition of *cell* that fits the following sentences.

    7. Many prisons are so overcrowded that a cell designed for one inmate has two
       or three occupants.

    _____

    8. The honeybee emerging from its cell startled the bear.

    _____

D. Write three synonyms given by your dictionary for each of the following words.

    9. hot _____

    10. ordinary _____

(Continues on next page)

E. Answer the questions that follow the dictionary entries. Use the pronunciation guide below to answer the questions on pronunciation.

Pronunciation Key

ă pat	ā pay	â care	ä father	ĕ pet	ē be	ĭ pit
ī tie	î pier	ŏ pot	ō toe	ô paw, for		oi noise
ŏŏ took	ōō boot	ou out	th thin	*th* this		ŭ cut
û urge	yōō abuse	zh vision	ə about, item, edible, gallop, circus			

flock (flŏk) *n.* **1.** A group of animals, as birds or sheep, that live, travel, or feed together. **2.** A group of people under the leadership of one person. **3.** A large crowd or number. —*v.* To congregate or travel in a crowd.

11. *Flock* would be found on the dictionary page with which guidewords?
    a. **float / flower**   b. **flower girl / fluoroscope**   c. **flurry / fob**

12. The *o* in *flock* sounds like the *o* in *(pot, toe* or *for?)* _____

13. What parts of speech is *flock*? _____

14. Which definition of *flock* best fits the sentence below, 1, 2, 3 or the last one?

    _____

    The shepherd spent an hour looking for the lamb that had become separated from the flock.

15. Which definition of *flock* best fits the sentence below, 1, 2, 3 or the last one?

    _____

    When the weather turns hot, people flock to the beaches and lakes.

mix•er (mĭk′sər) *n.* **1.** A person or thing that blends elements, esp. a mechanical device that combines substances or ingredients. **2.** A sociable person. **3.** An informal party arranged to give people an opportunity to get acquainted. **4.** A beverage, as ginger ale, added to an alcoholic drink.

16. How many syllables are in *mixer*? _____

17. The *i* in *mixer* sounds like the *i* in *(pit, tie* or *pier?)* _____

18. Which syllable is accented in *mixer*? _____

19. Which definition of *mixer* best fits the sentence below, 1, 2, 3 or 4? _____
    When Ginger arrived at college, she was invited to a number of mixers.

20. Which definition of *mixer* best fits the sentence below, 1, 2, 3 or 4? _____
    Ted disliked the taste of alcohol, even when a mixer was added.

DICTIONARY USE: Test 3

A. Use your dictionary and the spelling hints on page 12 to find the correct spelling of the following words.

1. reciept   _____
2. writting   _____
3. dicide   _____
4. klean   _____
5. wispor   _____
6. actshun   _____

B. Below are three pairs of dictionary guidewords followed by other words. Circle the two words in each series which would be found on the page with the guidewords.

7-8. **distaste / dive**

distance   distinct   dissect   ditch   divide

9-10. **garment / gauge**

garter   garden   gave   gear   gate

11-12. **tiptop / toddle**

tipsy   to   together   tireless   tomboy

C. Use the pronunciation key below to answer the questions that follow.

Pronunciation Key

ă pat	ā pay	â care	ä father	ĕ pet	ē be	ĭ pit
ī tie	î pier	ŏ pot	ō toe	ô paw, for		oi noise
ŏŏ took	ōō boot	ou out	th thin	*th* this		ŭ cut
û urge	yōō abuse	zh vision	ə about, item, edible, gallop, circus			

13. In **dignity** (dĭg'nĭ-tē), the *y* is pronounced like the *e* in which word in the pronunciation key? _____

14. In **dignity** (dĭg'nĭ-tē), the *i*'s are pronounced like the *i* in which word in the pronunciation key? _____

15. In **firetrap** (fīr'trăp'), the *i* is pronounced like the *i* in which word in the pronunciation key? _____

16. In **firetrap** (fīr'trăp'), the *a* is pronounced like *a* in which word in the pronunciation key? _____

(Continues on next page)

239

D. Answer the questions below about the following dictionary entry for *baby*.

ba•by (bā′bē) *n., pl.* **-bies. 1.** A very young child; infant. **2.** The youngest member of a family or group. **3.** Someone who acts like a baby. **4.** *Slang.* A young woman or girl.

17. *Baby* is accented on
    a. its first syllable.
    b. its second syllable.
    c. both syllables.

18. *Fill in the blank:* The plural of *baby* is _____.

19. The definition of *baby* that applies to the sentence below is
    a. definition 1.
    b. definition 2.
    c. definition 3.
    d. definition 4.

    "You're such a baby," screamed Rhonda. "You always want your own way."

20. The definition of *baby* that fits the sentence below is
    a. definition 1.
    b. definition 2.
    c. definition 3.
    d. definition 4.

    It's hard to believe that Elena, the baby in our family, just became a teenager.

DICTIONARY USE: Test 4

Use your dictionary to find the information needed for sections A–D of this test.

A. List the parts of speech for the following words.

      1. chill _____

      2. plain _____

      3. double _____

B. Write the irregular forms for the following words.

      4. do _____

      5. phony _____

      6. know _____

C. Write in the dictionary definition of *groom* that fits the following sentences.

      7. The owner of that stable of horses hired a new groom.

      _____

      8. The head of the company plans to groom his son to take over the company one day.

      _____

D. Write four synonyms given by your dictionary for each of the following words.

      9. last _____

      10. sell _____

E. Answer the questions that follow the dictionary entries. Use the pronunciation guide below to answer the questions on pronunciation.

Pronunciation Key

ă pat	ā pay	â care	ä father	ĕ pet	ē be	ĭ pit
ī tie	î pier	ŏ pot	ō toe	ô paw, for		oi noise
o͝o took	o͞o boot	ou out	th thin	*th* this		ŭ cut
û urge	yo͞o abuse	zh vision	ə about, item, edible, gallop, circus			

(Continues on next page)

flesh (flĕsh) *n.* **1.** The soft tissue of the body, esp. the skeletal muscles. **2.** The meat of animals as distinguished from the edible tissue of fish or fowl. **3.** The pulpy part of a fruit or a vegetable. **4.** The body as distinguished from the mind or soul. **5.** Mankind in general; humanity. —*v.* To fill out (a structure or framework).

11. What parts of speech is *flesh*? _____

12. *Flesh* would be found on the dictionary page with which guidewords?
     a. **financier / firebox**   b. **flock / flower**   c. **flee / float**

13. The *e* in *flesh* sounds like the *e* in which word in the pronunciation key?

     _____

14. Which definition of *flesh* best fits the sentence below—1, 2, 3, 4, 5, or the

     last one? _____

     Vegetarians do not eat animal flesh.

15. Which definition of *flesh* best fits the sentence below—1, 2, 3, 4, 5, or the

     last one? _____

     When planning your paper, first decide on the main points, and then flesh
     out the details.

col•o•ny (kŏl′ə-nē) *n., pl.* **-nies. 1.** A group of people who settle in a distant land but remain subject to a parent country. **2.** A territory ruled by a distant power. **3.** A group of people with similar interests concentrated in one area: *the American colony in Paris.* **4.** A group of the same kind of organisms living or growing together.

16. *Colony* would be found in the dictionary page with which guidewords?
     a. **colloquy / comatose**   b. **comb / coming**   c. **coffer / cold turkey**

17. The first *o* in *colony* sounds like the *o* in which word in the pronunciation

     key? _____

18. The accent in *colony* is on which syllable? _____

19. The plural of *colony* is _____.

20. Which definition of *colony* best fits the sentence below—1, 2, 3, or 4? _____

     A large colony of retired Americans has settled in Guadalajara, Mexico,
     where the cost of living is reasonable and the crime rate is low.

DICTIONARY USE: Test 5

Use your dictionary to answer the questions that follow.

A. Place dots between the syllables in the following words. Then write the correct pronunciation symbols, including the accent marks.

    1. c r e d i t _____

    2. l e g a l _____

    3. n e e d l e _____

    4. p l e a s a n t _____

B. List the parts of speech for the following words.

    5. mobile _____

    6. once _____

C. Write in the irregular form for the following words.

    7. half _____

    8. parenthesis _____

D. Write the dictionary definition of *crush* that fits each of the following sentences.

    9. Grapes must be crushed if they are to be made into wine.

    _____

    10. The crush of people who turned out to watch the fireworks was more than the area was meant to handle.

    _____

E. Write four synonyms given by your dictionary for each of the following words.

    11. level _____

    12. cheerful _____

(Continues on next page)

F. Answer the following questions about the dictionary entry for *bittersweet*.

13. What parts of speech are given for *bittersweet*? _____

14. How many schwa sounds are in *bittersweet*? _____

15. Which syllable in *bittersweet* gets the strongest accent? _____

16. Write the dictionary definition of *bittersweet* that fits the sentence below.

Jana's relationship with Jeremy was bittersweet. Sometimes they got along wonderfully, while at other times they had terrible fights.

_____

G. Answer the following questions about the dictionary entry for *manifold*.

17. What parts of speech are given for *manifold*? _____

18. The *o* in *manifold* sounds like the *o* in which word in the pronunciation key?

_____

19. Write the dictionary definition of *manifold* that fits the sentence below.

The manifold in Richie's car needed replacing.

_____

20. Write the dictionary definition of *manifold* that fits the sentence below.

Alex had manifold talents, including speaking three languages and playing the guitar well enough to be in a rock group.

_____

DICTIONARY USE: Test 6

Use your dictionary to answer the questions that follow.

A. Place dots between the syllables in the following words. Then write the correct pronunciation symbols, including the accent marks.

    1. e x e r c i s e _____

    2. i n q u i r e _____

    3. m o d i f y _____

    4. s u s p e n s e _____

B. List the parts of speech for the following words.

    5. loose _____

    6. so _____

C. Write in the irregular forms for the following words.

    7. jelly _____

    8. steal_____

D. Write the dictionary definition of *quick* that fits each of the following sentences.

    9. Brian's quick feet helped to make him a star soccer player.

    _____

    10. I have only time for a quick lunch before I go to my Spanish class.

    _____

E. Write four synonyms given by your dictionary for each of the following words.

    11. make _____

    12. poor _____

(Continues on next page)

F. Answer the following questions about the dictionary entry for *legitimate*.

13. What parts of speech are given for *legitimate*? _____

14. How many schwa sounds are in *legitimate*? _____

15. Which syllable in *legitimate* gets the strongest accent? _____

16. Write the dictionary definition of *legitimate* that fits the sentence below.

    The writing expert confirmed that the signature of George Washington was legitimate.

    _____

G. Answer the following questions about the dictionary entry for *season*.

17. What parts of speech are given for *season*? _____

18. Write the dictionary definition of *season* that fits the sentence below.

    A hospital emergency room will quickly season a young doctor.

    _____

19. Write the dictionary definition of *season* that fits the sentence below.

    Ty was always saddened by the last game of the World Series because it signaled the end of the baseball season.

    _____

20. *Season* comes from a Latin word that means _____

VOCABULARY IN CONTEXT: Test 1

A. Using context clues for help, circle the letter of the meaning of each word in italics.

1. Cleo is a *chronic* complainer. She even complains if I say she complains too much.

   Chronic means

   a. rare. b. constant. c. messy.

2. In a hospital emergency room, it is common to see such *gruesome* sights as burned skin and bleeding wounds.

   Gruesome means

   a. shocking. b. common. c. false.

3. "Your paper should be more *coherent*," my English teacher wrote. "In places, it is poorly organized and lacking in logic."

   Coherent means

   a. disorganized. b. detailed. c. organized and logical.

4. Would weeds make a good *supplement* to your diet? Yes, a daily addition of certain weeds would give you all you need of vitamins A and C.

   Supplement means

   a. substitute. b. addition. c. flavoring.

5. Sometimes people with *contrary* qualities are attracted to each other. For example, quiet Loni goes steady with Ken, who is loud.

   Contrary means

   a. similar. b. unusual. c. opposite.

(Continues on next page)

B. Using context clues for help, write the definition of each word in italics. Choose the meanings from the words in the box below. Each meaning will be used once.

pieces of business	make longer	start
brief and clear	difficult experience	

6. To *prolong* your life, get married. Married people tend to live longer than singles.

   Prolong means to _____

7. Everyday *transactions* include buying food and clothing and signing papers to rent an apartment.

   Transactions are _____

8. Our mayor has decided to *initiate* a recycling program. Soon our newspapers, bottles, and cans will be re-used instead of dumped.

   Initiate means to _____

9. There is a special chair that eases the *ordeal* of giving birth. Most women who use the chair say they feel less pain and give birth more quickly than when lying down.

   An *ordeal* is a _____

10. My wordy cousin said, "It is my opinion that the level of heat has gone beyond what I am able to consider comfortable." Why can't he just be more *concise* and say, "I'm hot"?

    Concise means _____

VOCABULARY IN CONTEXT: Test 2

Figure out the meanings of the following five words by studying them in context. Then complete the matching and fill-in test that follows.

1 **apathy**
   (ap′-ə-thē)

When the topic of taxes came up, Carmen's *apathy* about elections changed to sharp interest.

The students showed all the signs of *apathy*, including doodling and writing notes to one another.

2 **appropriate**
   (ə-prō′prē-ĭt)

It is not *appropriate* to wear cut-off jeans to most job interviews.

Today it is thought *appropriate* for a woman to ask a man on a date, yet most women don't do it.

3 **illusion**
   (ĭ-loo′zhən)

Soap opera is a made-for-TV *illusion*. Yet many fans of one show were so convinced of its reality that they sent gifts when a character got married.

My aunt has no wish to create the *illusion* of never-ending youth. Why should she hide her silver hair or the smile wrinkles around her eyes?

4 **phobia**
   (fō′bē-ə)

Rosie has a *phobia* about heights. She can't look down from the top of a tall building without feeling terror.

Perhaps no *phobia* is stranger than the fear of having peanut butter stick to the roof of your mouth.

5 **vigorous**
   (vĭg′ər-əs)

Healthy elderly people can enjoy *vigorous* activities, such as jogging and biking.

I felt so lazy today that the most *vigorous* thing I did all day was brush my teeth.

Note: A key to pronunciation is on page 14.

A. Match each word with its definition.

1. apathy   _____ proper

2. appropriate   _____ lively; energetic

3. illusion   _____ a continuing abnormal fear

4. phobia   _____ lack of interest

5. vigorous   _____ a false impression; an unreal appearance

(Continues on next page)

B. Fill in each blank with one of the words from the box. Use each word once.

apathy	appropriate	illusion
phobia	vigorous	

6. I can't understand why it's not considered _____ to put one's elbows on the dinner table.

7. To get your heart beating, a slow stroll won't do; your walk must be

   _____.

8. I thought I saw my mother walk past my apartment window, but it was just an _____ caused by moving shadows and my own imagination.

9. The _____ of parents is often one reason behind juvenile crime. Parents should pay more attention to their children's activities.

10. There are many odd _____s. One cabdriver, for example, had to change his job because of a deep fear of red lights.

VOCABULARY IN CONTEXT: Test 3

A. Using context clues for help, circle the letter of the meaning of each word in italics.

1. Sports seem to be as *vital* to my husband as are food and air.

   Vital means

   a. difficult.   b. necessary.   c. unimportant.

2. When an Asian volcano burst in 1883, the sound was *audible* 3,000 miles away.

   Audible means

   a. able to be seen.   b. able to be heard.   c. able to be felt.

3. Ms. Landis is a very easy teacher. Her idea of being *severe* is refusing to accept a paper that is more than a month late.

   Severe means

   a. strict.   b. in charge.   c. gentle.

4. One usually *rational* football fan became so crazy when his team lost the Super Bowl that he shot the TV.

   Rational means

   a. insane.   b. very popular.   c. reasonable.

5. It was said that no *obstacle*—whether extreme heat, snow, or rocky land—could keep the Pony Express from delivering the mail on time. When Indians killed one rider, the horse even went on to deliver the mail alone.

   Obstacle means

   a. something that   b. temperature.   c. animal.
   gets in the way.

(Continues on next page)

B. Using context clues for help, write the definition of each word in italics. Choose the meanings from the words in the box below. Each meaning will be used once.

unskilled	telling of a story	similar
fate	lack of basic needs and comforts	

6. Ice is harder than most people think; its hardness is *comparable* to that of concrete.

   Comparable means _____

7. My sister is such an *inept* cook that she never needs to call the family to supper. We just come to the table when the smoke alarm goes off.

   Inept means _____

8. As a boy, my grandfather suffered great *deprivation*. For example, his shoes always had holes in them, and meat was a rare treat.

   Deprivation means a _____

9. Whenever something bad happens to Jane, she says it's the fault of *destiny*. But I prefer to take charge of my own life rather than simply blaming fate.

   Destiny means _____

10. My father died when I was a baby, but Mom told me so many stories about him that I feel I knew him. For example, one *anecdote* was about how he cried with joy when I was born.

    Anecdote means a _____

VOCABULARY IN CONTEXT: Test 4

Figure out the meanings of the following five words by studying them in context. Then complete the matching and fill-in test that follows.

1 **accelerate**
   (ăk-sĕl′ə-rāt′)

Tidal waves sometimes *accelerate* until reaching a speed of 450 miles an hour.

I thought I put my foot on the brake, but the car *accelerated* instead of stopping.

2 **controversy**
   (kŏn′trə-vûr′sē)

Whether or not smoking should be illegal in all public places is a matter of *controversy.* I heard two people arguing about it on TV just the other day.

There aren't many topics of greater *controversy* in our country than abortion.

3 **data**
   (dāt′ə)

Data about the moon's surface includes information gained from photos and soil samples.

According to scientific *data,* laughing is good for us. For example, evidence shows that laughing exercises the heart.

4 **immunity**
   (ĭ-myoo′nĭ-tē)

Certain foreign officials in this country have *immunity* to our laws; they can't even be arrested for murder.

It's not fair that supervisors have *immunity* from the rule against smoking in the restrooms.

5 **versatile**
   (vûr′sə-təl)

A *versatile* food processor does everything but cook—it slices, chops, shreds, and blends.

Ivan is a wonderful piano player. But Joel is more *versatile*; he sings, acts, and plays the piano.

Note: A key to pronunciation is on page 14.

A. Match each word with its definition.

1. accelerate   _____ information

2. controversy   _____ able to do many things well

3. data   _____ speed up

4. immunity   _____ argument

5. versatile   _____ freedom from something required of others

(Continues on next page)

B. Fill in each blank with one of the words from the box. Use each word once.

accelerate	controversy	data
immunity	versatile	

6. According to one researcher's _____, all pregnant woman tend to dream about the same things.

7. As the roller coaster headed downward and began to _____, the entire carload of passengers screamed at once.

8. The kids wanted to stay outside even though it was raining. But after the first flash of lightning, there was no _____. They all agreed we should move the picnic indoors.

9. With just a few pieces of clothing, Ling has put together a _____ wardrobe. By matching just the right pieces and jewelry, she has casual, work, and dressy outfits.

10. After I failed the driving test, I asked for _____ from the required ten-day wait before taking it again. My license was about to run out, so I needed a new one quickly.

VOCABULARY IN CONTEXT: Test 5

Using context clues for help, circle the letter of the meaning of each word in italics.

1. Senator Blanchford claims to be an *advocate* of a clean environment, but she has yet to vote for any bills to clean up polluted waterways in her state.

   An *advocate* is a person who

   a. gets elected.   b. supports something.   c. cleans things up.

2. Because certain plants are poisonous to animals, pet owners should keep *antidotes* handy to prevent their pets from suffering and perhaps dying.

   An *antidote* is a

   a. medicine.   b. weapon.   c. poison.

3. When asked about possible scandals, most politicians are less than *candid*. They will say anything to convince voters that their behavior has not been improper.

   Candid means

   a. pleasing.   b. happy.   c. honest.

4. Anyone who *encounters* a wild animal in the woods should stay calm and leave as quickly as possible.

   To *encounter* means to

   a. admire.   b. meet.   c. get away from.

5. A complicated lecture can be *illuminated* with logical examples and clear-cut explanations.

   Illuminated means

   a. made clear.   b. practiced.   c. confused.

6. It is hard to be *impartial* when you listen to two people arguing. Usually you want to take one person's side.

   Impartial means

   a. interested.   b. friendly.   c. not favoring one side over another.

(Continues on next page)

7. Reiko figured she had only two *options*: either stay in college or work for minimum wages the rest of her life.

   Options means

   a. choices.   b. wishes.   c. habits.

8. The decision Veronica made to study instead of going out for pizza with her friends was *prudent*. She got an A on the exam, while her friends all got D's.

   Prudent means

   a. generous.   b. wise.   c. unfortunate.

9. I *procrastinated* so long in getting a babysitter for New Year's Eve that all of our sitters were busy for that night by the time I called.

   Procrastinated means

   a. worked.   b. changed.   c. delayed.

10. Because the prisoner showed no *remorse* at committing the crime, the judge sentenced him to the longest possible prison term.

    Remorse means

    a. regret.   b. pleasure.   c. purpose.

VOCABULARY IN CONTEXT: Test 6

Figure out the meanings of the following five words by studying them in context. Then complete the matching and fill-in test that follows.

1 ambivalent
(ăm-bĭv′ə-lənt)

Heidi was *ambivalent* about her career choice. She wasn't sure if she should study to be a nurse or an accountant.

Horace is not usually *ambivalent*, but this evening he can't make up his mind about what he wants for dinner.

2 apprehensive
(ăp′rĭ-hĕn′sĭv)

People are often *apprehensive* about new situations. Their fear lessens as they become more familiar with the situation.

Ed was *apprehensive* about the upcoming final exam. Unless he did well, he would be disqualified from playing football.

3 elated
(ĭ-lā′tĭd)

My sister was *elated* when she heard she was finally pregnant.

Ramon was *elated* when he was offered a promotion and a big raise.

4 nostalgia
(nŏ-stăl′jə)

Music from the 1960s fills my parents with *nostalgia* because it reminds them of when they first met.

Willis has feelings of *nostalgia* when he thinks about the happy days of his childhood, before his father died.

5 vivid
(vĭv′ĭd)

It is common to have *vivid* memories of a special event. You can almost see yourself reliving the occasion.

Thelma's recollection of the car crash was all too *vivid*. She could recall all the terrible details of the impact and the resulting injuries.

Note: A key to pronunciation is on page 14.

A. Match each word with its definition.

1. ambivalent   _____ a desire for something in the past

2. apprehensive   _____ delighted; overjoyed

3. elated   _____ uncertain

4. nostalgia   _____ afraid; anxious

5. vivid   _____ full of lifelike images

(Continues on next page)

257

B. Fill in each blank with one of the words from the box. Use each word once. Read through the passage at least once before starting to fill in the blanks.

ambivalent	apprehensive	elated
nostalgia	vivid	

Marta was (6)_____ about her upcoming trip. On the one hand, she was (7)_____ because she had never been on an airplane before. She would be flying all the way from Los Angeles to Miami. On the other hand, she was (8)_____ at the thought of seeing Aunt Cristina again. She had not seen her aunt for ten years, but Marta's memories of this special woman were (9)_____. Marta could still see Cristina gathering Marta's brothers and sisters and entertaining them with stories about life in the old country. Such memories usually filled Marta with great (10)_____, but now they only made her more excited about her visit to Miami.

MAIN IDEAS: Test 1

A. Each group of words below consists of one general idea and four specific ideas. The general idea includes all the specific ideas. Underline the general idea in each group.

1. jazz	blues	rap	music	rock
2. science	biology	physics	chemistry	zoology
3. fry	boil	cook	bake	steam
4. chapter	contents	book	index	page
5. murder	crime	stealing	speeding	kidnapping
6. bonnet	turban	hat	baseball cap	helmet
7. granola	oatmeal	raisin bran	cereal	bran flakes
8. pants	cuffs	pockets	buttons	zipper
9. mortgage	VISA bill	debt	child support	car loan

B. In each pair below, one idea is general and the other is specific. The general idea includes the specific one. Do two things:

    a Underline the idea in each pair that you think is more general.

    b Then write in one more specific idea that is covered by the general idea.

10. Mexican food	taco	_____
11. comics section	newspaper	_____
12. Miami	city	_____
13. weapon	knife	_____
14. iron	metal	_____
15. monster	Dracula	_____
16. high chair	children's furniture	_____
17. poker	card game	_____
18. good-luck charm	four-leaf clover	_____

(Continues on next page)

C. Each group of three items below contains three levels of ideas. Write a *1* by the most general idea in each group, a *2* by the less general idea, and a *3* by the most specific idea.

19. _____ Mariah Carey   _____ singer   _____ pop singer

20. _____ color   _____ red   _____ bright color

21. _____ lawn mower   _____ garden tool   _____ tool

22. _____ *The Tonight Show* _____ TV program   _____ talk show

23. _____ oak floor   _____ flooring   _____ wood floor

24. _____ store   _____ department store   _____ K-Mart

25. _____ telephone call   _____ long-distance call _____ communication

MAIN IDEAS: Test 2

A. Each group of words below consists of one general idea and four specific ideas. The general idea includes all the specific ideas. Underline the general idea in each group.

1. envelope	can	box	container	bottle
2. banana	ice cream	syrup	cherries	banana split
3. high-risk job	astronaut	firefighter	policeman	miner
4. insurance	dead bolt	guard dog	protection	suntan lotion
5. microwaves	take-out food	high-speed trains	time savers	express mail
6. burnt toast	minor problems	boring date	flat tire	a cold

B. After each paragraph are three subjects. Label each subject with one of the following:

> *T*—for the topic of the paragraph
> *B*—for the subject that is too broad
> *N*—for the subject that is too narrow

7-9. The United States accepts close to two million legal immigrants each year. California is the top destination. It accepts almost 40 percent. Texas is next, accepting 12 percent. These two states are followed by New York, Florida, and Illinois as favorite destinations.

_____ Immigration

_____ Legal immigrants in California

_____ Legal immigrants to the United States

(Continues on next page)

10-12. People who favor laws against handguns have several reasons. They argue, for example, that handguns make it easier to kill people. Other weapons, such as knives, may cause less damage. Also, people who own guns could leave a loaded handgun within reach of a small child. Children do not know the difference between a toy gun and the real thing. Finally, half of all the guns used in crimes have been stolen. This means that criminals get many of their weapons from people who bought guns to protect themselves.

_____ Weapons

_____ Handgun laws

_____ One way criminals get handguns

C. (13-20.) Each group of items below includes one topic, one main idea (topic sentence), and two supporting details. Label each item with one of the following:

        T —for the topic
        MI—for the main idea
        SD—for the supporting details

Group 1

_____ Eating buttercups or irises can give someone extreme indigestion.

_____ If eaten, certain common garden plants can make people very ill.

_____ If eaten, lilies of the valley cause an irregular heartbeat.

_____ Certain common garden plants.

Group 2

_____ Imagine your former sweetheart wearing a diaper or covered with smelly garbage.

_____ Recovering from a broken romance.

_____ Certain methods can help you recover from a broken romance.

_____ Each time you find yourself thinking of the other person, stop yourself by banging a fist on the table.

MAIN IDEAS: Test 3

A. In each pair below, one idea is general and the other is specific. The general idea includes the specific one. Do two things:

   a Underline the idea in each pair that you think is more general.

   b Then write in one more specific idea that is covered by the general idea.

1. hot beverage	tea	_____
2. senator	elected official	_____
3. reading material	news magazine	_____
4. sweat pants	exercise clothing	_____
5. baseball player	catcher	_____
6. achievement	grade of A in a course	_____

B. After each paragraph are three subjects. Label each subject with one of the following:

> *T*—for the topic of the paragraph
> *B*—for the subject that is too broad
> *N*—for the subject that is too narrow

7-9. Many employees steal small items from their workplaces. The most common stolen goods are office supplies. People who would never steal a pen from a supermarket shelf think nothing of taking one home from work. Also, many office workers consider personal use of the office copying machine a benefit of the job. And then there are specialists. One famous story concerns an appliance plant worker. He regularly helped himself to parts from the assembly line. Eventually, he had enough to build his own refrigerator.

_____ Crime

_____ Employee theft

_____ Employee theft of office supplies

(Continues on next page)

10-12. Although people dream of being celebrities, the disadvantages of fame are great. First, the famous must look perfect all the time. There's always someone ready to photograph a celebrity looking dumpy in old clothes. The famous also give up their privacy. Their divorces and other problems end up on the evening news and in headlines. Even worse, famous people are often in danger. They get threatening letters and are sometimes attacked.

_____ The dangers of fame

_____ The disadvantages of fame

_____ The advantages and disadvantages of fame

C. (13-20.) Each group of items below includes one topic, one main idea (topic sentence), and two supporting details. Label each item with one of the following:

T —for the topic
MI—for the main idea
SD—for the supporting details

Group 1

_____ Occupations and walking.

_____ Nurses walk the most, over five miles a day.

_____ One study found occupations influence how much people walk.

_____ Dentists walk the least, under a mile each day.

Group 2

_____ Staying in the sun too long can cause sunstroke.

_____ People develop skin cancer after years of working on their suntans.

_____ Being in the sun.

_____ Spending time in the sun can be dangerous.

MAIN IDEAS: Test 4

A. Each group of three items contains three levels of ideas. Write a *1* by the most general idea in each group, a *2* by the less general idea, and a *3* by the most specific idea.

1. _____ Ireland   _____ country   _____ European country

2. _____ sentence   _____ paragraph   _____ word

3. _____ organizations   _____ Four-H Clubs   _____ youth organizations

4. _____ buildings   _____ church   _____ houses of worship

5. _____ *Jurassic Park*   _____ entertainment   _____ movie

6. _____ household chores _____ washing floors   _____ cleaning

B. After each paragraph are three subjects. Label each subject with one of the following:

> *T*—for the topic of the paragraph
> *B*—for the subject that is too broad
> *N*—for the subject that is too narrow

7-9. Flea markets and garage sales appeal to people for a couple of reasons. First, of course, a used item costs less than a new one. Many people on a budget have wonderful wardrobes they have assembled with good used clothing. Second, many who shop at flea markets and garage sales are collectors. There are people who collect old hats, 1950s toasters, toaster covers, salt and pepper shakers, comic books, and just about anything else you can think of.

_____ Collecting items sold at flea markets and garage sales

_____ Flea markets and garage sales

_____ Places to shop

(Continues on next page)

10-12. Some people think an only child is lucky because of the material goods and attention he or she receives. But only children have their problems too. For one thing, they have no privacy. Parents always feel entitled to know everything that's going on in an only child's life. Also, only children miss the companionship of brothers and sisters. They can be lonely, and they may have trouble making friends later in life because they never learned to get along with a brother or sister.

_____ Only children

_____ Children

_____ The loneliness of only children

C. (13-20.) Each group of items below includes one topic, one main idea (topic sentence), and two supporting details. Label each item with one of the following:

        T —for the topic
        MI—for the main idea
        SD—for the supporting details

Group 1

_____ Fresh vegetables in season cost less than canned or frozen vegetables.

_____ Fresh, frozen, and canned vegetables.

_____ Canning and freezing vegetables robs them of important vitamins and minerals.

_____ Fresh vegetables have advantages over frozen and canned vegetables.

Group 2

_____ The word *trombone* comes from the French word for *pull* and *push*.

_____ The names of many musical instruments come from the way they are played.

_____ The names of musical instruments.

_____ *Violin* is Latin for "to skip like a calf."

MAIN IDEAS: Test 5

A. After each paragraph are three subjects. Label each with one of the following:

> *T*—for the topic of the paragraph
> *B*—for the subject that is too broad
> *N*—for the subject that is too narrow

1-3. Losers in presidential elections often fade away after one attempt at the White House. But some unsuccessful presidential nominees try more than once. Richard Nixon was defeated by John F. Kennedy in 1961, yet was successful six years later. Adlai Stevenson lost to Dwight Eisenhower in 1954 and then tried again in 1958. He was unsuccessful again. But Henry Clay and William Jennings Bryan can top that. Each was nominated three times and lost each time.

_____ Some unsuccessful presidential nominees

_____ Richard Nixon and John F. Kennedy

_____ Nominees for the presidency

4-6. Herding dogs share certain characteristics that make them excellent watchdogs. They are large dogs. Among the purebreds classified as herding dogs by the American Kennel Club are collies, sheepdogs, and German shepherds. Also, herding dogs are bred to work closely with humans. They are fast learners, eager to please, and like to dominate situations.

_____ Herding dogs

_____ Dogs

_____ Collies, sheepdogs, and German shepherds

(Continues on next page)

B. Circle the letter of the correct topic of each of the following paragraphs. Then find the sentence in which the author states the main idea about that topic, and circle the number of that sentence.

> ¹Businesses leaving the United States do so for various reasons. ²Lower cost for plants and labor is a major reason. ³Being purchased by a foreign company is another reason for a business to leave the U.S. ⁴Other reasons are high taxes in the U.S. and special incentives offered by a host country.

7. The topic is
   a. businesses that are leaving the United States.
   b. American businesses.
   c. businesses that leave the U.S. because they are purchased by a foreign company.

8. The main idea is stated in sentence
   a. 1.
   b. 2.
   c. 4.

> ¹The average monthly earnings of people who don't complete high school are less than $500. ²A high school graduate averages slightly more than $1,000 per month. ³A college graduate averages over $2,000 per month. ⁴A person with a master's degree makes even more. ⁵These statistics from the U.S. Census Bureau show that the more education you get, the more you are likely to earn.

9. The topic is
   a. education and earning power.
   b. our system of education.
   c. the earning power of a master's degree.

10. The main idea is stated in sentence
    a. 1.
    b. 2.
    c. 5.

MAIN IDEAS: Test 6

A. After each paragraph are three subjects. Label each with one of the following:

> *T*—for the topic of the paragraph
> *B*—for the subject that is too broad
> *N*—for the subject that is too narrow

1-3. The television audience during prime time is divided up unevenly among all the available channels. During those hours, most people watch the national networks. Over 70 percent of sets are tuned to ABC, CBS, NBC, or Fox. Cable stations account for 20 percent of viewers. Pay TV takes up another 5 percent. Public TV is viewed by only 3 percent of the public during prime time.

_____ The television audience

_____ The television audience during prime time

_____ The prime time audience for cable stations

4-6. Secondhand smoke—smoke from someone else's cigar or cigarette—can cause breathing illnesses and even lung cancer. According to the government, there are several ways to avoid the dangers of secondhand smoke. First, don't allow smoking at all in your home. Second, if someone smokes outdoors, it should not be in areas where nonsmokers pass by. Third, in restaurants that allow smoking, ask to be seated as far away from the smoking area as possible.

_____ Smoking

_____ Sitting far from the smoking area in restaurants

_____ Secondhand smoke

(Continues on next page)

B. Circle the letter of the correct topic of each of the following paragraphs. Then find the sentence in which the author states the main idea about that topic, and circle the number of that sentence.

[1]Gasoline is the most common product made from petroleum. [2]However, about three thousand products other than gasoline are also made from petroleum. [3]Some of the others are bubble gum, crayons, floor polish, house paint, and eyeglasses. [4]Ping-pong paddles and loudspeakers also contain petroleum.

7. The topic is
   a. gasoline as a product of petroleum.
   b. products.
   c. products made from petroleum.

8. The main idea is stated in sentence
   a. 1.
   b. 2.
   c. 4.

[1]Children who don't read during summer vacation will lose six months of their reading level by September. [2]There are several things parents can do to help children maintain their reading levels during summer vacation. [3]First, turn the TV off when it is not being watched. [4]Second, set up a daily reading time for children. [5]Third, be a role model by reading novels, magazines, or newspapers. [6]Leave them around the house so that children will see reading materials around. [7]Fourth, show an interest in what your child is reading by asking questions or by taking turns reading out loud. [8]Also remember that writing and reading go together. [9]Leave notes for your child that require a written response. [10]Buy a notebook for children to write a journal that shows their activities and thoughts.

9. The topic is
   a. reading.
   b. maintaining children's reading levels during summer vacation.
   c. being a good role model for reading during summer vacation.

10. The main idea is stated in sentence
    a. 1.
    b. 2.
    c. 3.

SUPPORTING DETAILS: Test 1

Each topic sentence below is followed by a list of three other sentences. Circle the letter of the one sentence that *does not* support the main idea.

1. *Topic sentence:* "Designer checks"—personal bank checks which reflect the check-writer's interests—are becoming more and more popular.

   a. A growing number of animal lovers are ordering checks with pictures of endangered animals.
   b. Designer checks are more expensive than regular checks.
   c. Many people with a sense of humor have put Daffy Duck and Bugs Bunny on their checks.

2. *Topic sentence:* Martial arts such as judo and aikido are becoming popular in the United States for several reasons.

   a. A martial arts workout is good exercise.
   b. Learning martial arts can help one defend against personal attacks.
   c. People can get hurt practicing martial arts.

3. *Topic sentence:* There are various things you can do to prevent your car from being stolen.

   a. Police report auto thefts have risen dramatically in recent years.
   b. When parking your car, keep it locked with the keys out of sight.
   c. Install a burglar alarm on your car.

4. *Topic sentence:* Zippers had various early uses.

   a. One of the first uses of the zipper was as a fastener for overshoes.
   b. Zippers once held together the canvas coverings of early airplanes.
   c. The word *zipper* was originally a B.F. Goodrich trademark.

(Continues on next page)

5. *Topic sentence:* In a town in Thailand, there is a rodeo that uses elephants instead of horses.

   a. The elephants are found throughout Thailand.
   b. Elephants compete in contests such as log-pulling.
   c. The most popular event is a tug-of-war in which one elephant competes against (and always beats) a hundred men.

SUPPORTING DETAILS: Test 2

A. Each topic sentence below is followed by a list of three other sentences. Circle the letter of the one sentence that *does not* support the main idea.

1. *Topic sentence:* The major political parties in the U.S. have animals as their symbols.

   a. The Republican party has an elephant as its symbol.
   b. The Republican party was organized in 1854 to oppose slavery.
   c. The symbol used by the Democratic party is a donkey.

2. *Topic sentence:* Waxing your car can be made easier if you follow a few guidelines.

   a. First make sure your car has been washed and is dry.
   b. Waxing your car frequently will protect its paint.
   c. Also, don't wax your car in the hot sun.

B. The main idea of each of the following paragraphs is boldfaced. Locate and write down the number of the one sentence in each paragraph that *does not* support the main idea. Read the entire paragraph before making your decision.

3. [1]**Although chocolate candy tastes good, too much of it can be bad for you.** [2]First of all, it contains caffeine, which makes some people uncomfortably nervous. [3]Chocolate can also be found in ice cream and pastries. [4]Chocolate candy contains sugar and fat, which can put on unwelcome pounds. [5]It can also contribute to tooth decay.

   The sentence that *does not* support the main idea: _____

4. [1]**Many have discovered that weekend vacations can be more practical than longer vacations.** [2]Such vacations make it possible to get away from it all more often than just once or twice a year. [3]They also require less planning than a typical one- or two-week vacation. [4]Weekend vacations are especially good for parents who don't want to be away from their family for very long. [5]Many parents feel that children should never be taken on weekend vacations.

   The sentence that *does not* support the main idea: _____

(Continues on next page)

5.   **¹High schools that have adopted a year-round schedule have found advantages to their new timetable.** ²For instance, year-round schedules reduce overcrowding at schools. ³In addition, students may be able to complete their course work faster than in a nine-month schedule. ⁴Nevertheless, year-round schedules should not be tried in hot climates. ⁵Finally, students and teachers report that learning becomes more of a habit on a year-round schedule than on a traditional schedule.

The sentence that *does not* support the main idea: _____

SUPPORTING DETAILS: Test 3

The main idea of each of the following paragraphs is boldfaced. Locate and write down the number of the one sentence in each paragraph that *does not* support the main idea. Read the entire paragraph before making your decision.

1.   ¹**There are several things we must do to take proper care of our pets.** ²Feeding them food low in fat and high in vitamins will help keep them healthy. ³This is good advice for the human diet as well. ⁴Regular trips to the vet are also important. ⁵Exercise on a regular basis will prevent boredom and provide mental and physical stimulation.

The sentence that *does not* support the main idea: _____

2.   ¹**The largest fruits and vegetables ever grown are much larger than anything you'll find in the supermarket.** ²The largest carrot ever grown, for instance, weighed over fifteen pounds. ³The biggest lemon on record came off a California tree and weighed eight and a half pounds. ⁴The largest tomato weighed almost eight pounds. ⁵And a North Carolina gardener grew the largest watermelon on record—a whopping 279 pounds. ⁶More fruits and vegetables are grown in the United States than any other country in the world.

The sentence that *does not* support the main idea: _____

3.   ¹**Every day of the year has a special name.** ²People, however, pay little attention to these "special" days. ³For instance, March 1 is Mother Goose Day. ⁴Rat-Catchers' Day, in honor of the Pied Piper of Hamelin, is on July 22. ⁵Be Late for Something Day is September 5. ⁶Be Bald and Be Free Day is celebrated on October 14, and November 19 has been designated as "Have a Bad Day" Day.

The sentence that *does not* support the main idea: _____

4.   ¹**Parents who help children with their schoolwork should follow a few simple guidelines.** ²First of all, it is important to be patient in explaining lessons and encourage children to ask questions. ³Schoolwork is so difficult these days that most parents probably shouldn't help their children at all. ⁴In addition, children should never be ridiculed or embarrassed. ⁵Finally, parents should not bluff answers. ⁶If they don't know an answer, they should admit it and look up the answer with the child.

The sentence that *does not* support the main idea: _____

(Continues on next page)

5. [1]**To help make your garage or yard sale successful, display your merchandise wisely.** [2]First, don't put merchandise on the ground—people don't like to have to bend or step over things. [3]Put clothes on hangers and hang them on bars so they are easy to inspect. [4]Other merchandise should be on tables. [5]Remember that you will sell more if you are willing to negotiate prices. [6]Finally, place popular items, like exercise equipment and bicycles, in plain view.

The sentence that *does not* support the main idea: _____

SUPPORTING DETAILS: Test 4

The main idea of each of the following paragraphs is boldfaced. Locate and write down the number of the one sentence in each paragraph that *does not* support the main idea. Read the entire paragraph before making your decision.

1. **¹People who are taking medication must watch for unexpected side effects.** ²These effects may include eye problems such as bloodshot eyes or blurred vision. ³Other possible undesired effects are hearing loss, ringing in the ears, dizziness, and rashes. ⁴Many people experiencing such unexpected side effects neglect to call a doctor.

   The sentence that *does not* support the main idea: _____

2. **¹The Gorilla Foundation tries to make life full and interesting for its gorilla residents.** ²The Foundation is located in Woodside, California. ³In the morning, a gorilla might spend some time painting designs on paper. ⁴One female gorilla, Koko, enjoys daily visits with her pet cat. ⁵Since gorillas in the wild spend much of their time eating, gorillas at the Foundation are fed seven meals throughout the day. ⁶There are also plenty of opportunities for them to relax and to play in an outdoor enclosure.

   The sentence that *does not* support the main idea: _____

3. **¹Inventions often end up being used in unintended ways.** ²For instance, paper clips have been used as tie clips. ³In addition, they have been known to hold up people's pants cuffs. ⁴The Post-it Note was originally invented as a nonslip bookmark, but now it is often used to post notes on doors and stick notes onto documents. ⁵The paper note is backed with a special glue that makes it stick on and pull off easily.

   The sentence that *does not* support the main idea: _____

4. **¹The American Kennel Club divides purebred dogs into eight divisions.** ²Sporting breeds include retrievers and setters. ³Nonsporting dogs include bulldogs and poodles. ⁴There are more nonsporting dogs than any other breed. ⁵Hounds include greyhounds and bloodhounds. ⁶Terriers contain such dogs as Irish and Scottish. ⁷Toy dogs include Shih Tzus and Chihuahuas. ⁸German shepherds and sheepdogs are part of the "herding" group. ⁹Working dogs include malamutes and Rottweilers. ¹⁰Miscellaneous breeds, the eighth division, include such dogs as border collies and Australian shepherds.

   The sentence that *does not* support the main idea: _____

(Continues on next page)

5.   [1]**When you buy plants, follow certain guidelines to ensure that they stay healthy on the trip home.** [2]First, make sure you buy plants at a nursery instead of a discount store. [3]Next, get them home as soon as possible. [4]Moving from one location to another can cause stress in a plant. [5]Third, keep plants out of your trunk, which is usually hotter than the passenger section of a car or van. [6]Fourth, make sure the plants stay upright so they do not lose leaves. [7]Also, if possible, moisten the leaves and soil before you transport the plants, to relieve stress. [8]Finally, if your plants stick out of your car, drive slowly so you don't damage the leaves or break the branches.

The sentence that *does not* support the main idea: _____

SUPPORTING DETAILS: Test 5

Answer the questions that follow each paragraph. The topic sentence of each paragraph is boldfaced.

A.   [1]**Various pests destroy vegetation across the country.** [2]The Mediterranean fruit fly attacks over 250 types of fruits and vegetables nationwide. [3]Its cousin, the Mexican fruit fly, can cause damage to over 50 varieties of vegetation. [4]The boll weevil, which once did enormous damage to the cotton industry in the South, is still active in some areas. [5]It attacks cotton only. [6]The gypsy moth strips the leaves off over 500 kinds of trees, shrubs, and garden plants. [7]Also destructive is the Japanese beetle, which strikes over 250 kinds of trees, fruits, and vegetables.

1. _____ TRUE OR FALSE? The Mexican fruit fly is related to the Mediterranean fruit fly.

2. _____ TRUE OR FALSE? According to the passage, the cotton industry in the South was greatly damaged by the Mexican fruit fly.

3. The idea below is
   a. true according to the paragraph.
   b. false according to the paragraph.
   c. not mentioned in the paragraph.

   The Japanese beetle came from Japan.

4. *Circle the letter of the missing detail:* The _____ damages over 500 kinds of trees, shrubs, and garden plants.
   a. Mediterranean fruit fly
   b. boll weevil
   c. gypsy moth

5. The answer to question 4 can be found in sentence
   a. 4.
   b. 5.
   c. 6.
   d. 7.

(Continues on next page)

B.   ¹When winter approaches, influenza (the flu) is not far behind. ²**To protect against influenza, doctors recommend that people—especially those in high-risk groups—get vaccinated as early as possible.** ³An early shot gives the body time to develop the antibodies necessary to fight the flu. ⁴Among the groups at greater than average risk of getting the flu are senior citizens and children. ⁵People with long-term health problems are in danger, as well. ⁶Those who belong to these high-risk groups should get a flu shot every year.

6. _____ TRUE OR FALSE? Children are at greater than average risk of getting influenza.

7. The answer to question 1 can be found in sentence
   a. 4.
   b. 5.
   c. 6.
   d. 8.

8. The idea below is
   a. true according to the paragraph.
   b. false according to the paragraph.
   c. not mentioned in the paragraph.

   Senior citizens do not need a flu shot every year.

9. *Circle the letter of the missing detail:* _____ will let your body develop antibodies in time to fight the flu.
   a. A yearly flu shot
   b. An early flu shot
   c. Several flu shots

10. *Complete the sentence:* People in _____ groups would benefit from a yearly flu shot.

SUPPORTING DETAILS: Test 6

Answer the questions that follow each paragraph. The topic sentence of each paragraph is boldfaced.

A.   [1]**In both fiction and reality, ventriloquists become quite attached to their dummies.** [2]In the 1929 movie *The Great Gabbo*, a ventriloquist goes mad and destroys his dummy. [3]He spends the rest of his life on the run, believing he is wanted for murder. [4]There are real-life stories of ventriloquists who are buried with their dummies. [5]Other accounts tell of ventriloquists who left money to their dummies in their wills. [6]One ventriloquist, Herbert Dexter, spent more time with his dummy, Charlie, than with his wife and used it to cruelly mock her. [7]In the 1930s, his wife sued him for divorce, naming Charlie as having successfully competed for her husband's affections. [8]She claimed that she had thoughts of "murdering" Charlie. [9]"I would have thrown him out of the window had I been able to unlock the coffin-like trunk in which he was kept," she testified. [10]The divorce was granted.

1. The movie *The Great Gabbo* is about a ventriloquist who
   a. is buried with his dummy.
   b. is wanted for murder.
   c. destroys his dummy.

2. _____ TRUE OR FALSE? According to the author, some ventriloquists are buried with their dummies.

3. Some real-life ventriloquists have supposedly
   a. destroyed their dummies.
   b. committed murder.
   c. left money in their wills to their dummies.

4. The answer to question 3 can be found in sentence
   a. 4.
   b. 5.
   c. 6.
   d. 7.

5. Herbert Dexter
   a. was buried with his dummy, Charlie.
   b. sued his wife for divorce.
   c. used his dummy to make fun of his wife.

(Continues on next page)

B.   [1]**Adults can teach children to handle money well by helping them to follow a money management plan.** [2]First, children should be taught ways to earn money. [3]Baby-sitting, newspaper routes, or household chores may be options. [4]Then, children should be shown how to save money for something special. [5]A plan can be developed that allows them to use a little of the money they earn for minor purchases, such as birthday cards and candy. [6]The rest of the money they earn can be put in the bank. [7]When there is enough, the child can make that special purchase. [8]A money management plan taught early can prevent children from wasting money later in life.

6. _____ TRUE OR FALSE? According to the author, children should be taught how to save money for a special purchase.

7. The answer to question 6 can be found in sentence
    a. 2.
    b. 3.
    c. 4.
    d. 6.

8. The idea below is
    a. true according to the paragraph.
    b. false according to the paragraph.
    c. not mentioned in the paragraph.

    Children can be permitted to use some of the money they earn for minor purchases.

9. The author considers birthday cards to be
    a. expensive.
    b. useless.
    c. minor purchases.

10. _____ TRUE OR FALSE? The author feels early training in money management can help children handle their money well as adults.

LOCATIONS OF MAIN IDEAS: Test 1

The five paragraphs that follow are on the first level of difficulty. Write the number of each topic sentence in the space provided.

1. ¹In many homes, the refrigerator door is the family bulletin board. ²On it, people place things they don't want to lose. ³These may include the phone number of the local police or of a favorite baby sitter. ⁴Also kept there are reminders, including notes about social events. ⁵Finally, the refrigerator is a favorite spot to display things, such as a child's art work.

    Topic sentence: _____

2. ¹Do you want to lose weight? ²Then try eating in only one place and at regular times. ³This will help you cut down on snacking. ⁴Also, eat slowly. ⁵The trick is to get as much pleasure as possible from the smallest amount of food. ⁶You want to give your body time to let you know when you've had enough. ⁷Last, make exercise part of your daily schedule. ⁸You will have more success losing weight if you follow these diet guidelines.

    Topic sentence: _____

3. ¹Few things are more boring than standing in line. ²Luckily, ways have been found to make some otherwise boring waits more bearable. ³Airlines now hire people to make sure customers don't waste time in the wrong lines. ⁴In some places, live entertainment cheers customers in long lines. ⁵It seems that being able to look at oneself also makes waiting easier. ⁶In large buildings, complaints about slow elevators decrease when mirrors are put up nearby.

    Topic sentence: _____

4. ¹When their costs go up, gas stations try new ways of making a profit. ²To stir up business, some have gone back to giving away free glasses with a fill-up. ³Also, at some stations, customers can have their cars washed, rent a video, or leave film to be developed. ⁴There are even stations with stores that sell many quick-stop needs, from doughnuts to dog food.

    Topic sentence: _____

(Continues on next page)

5. ¹Have you ever wondered why we are attracted to certain people as friends and lovers? ²One key is physical closeness. ³We are more likely to be interested in people we see often. ⁴What we think of as good looks are also important. ⁵We tend to like people whose looks we like. ⁶We also are drawn to people with whom we share similar backgrounds, interests, and values. ⁷Several factors, then, help explain our attractions to other people.

Topic sentence: _____

LOCATIONS OF MAIN IDEAS: Test 2

The five paragraphs below are on the first and second levels of difficulty. Write the number of each topic sentence in the space provided. For the one case in which there are two topic sentences, write in both numbers.

1.   [1]Do you keep your eyes open when you kiss? [2]If so, you're in the minority. [3]There are several explanations for the fact that most people close their eyes when kissing. [4]One explanation is that it is simply tradition. [5]We learned to kiss that way and continue. [6]Another is that closing our eyes helps us focus on our sense of touch. [7]A third explanation says that when we kiss we are so close that we could not look at each other without crossing our eyes.

   Topic sentence(s): _____

2.   [1]William Henry Harrison had one of the most fascinating careers of all the presidents of the United States. [2]He was the only president to study medicine. [3]Before getting his degree, he left school and joined the Army, where he rose to the rank of general. [4]He was elected president at age sixty-eight. [5]Until Ronald Reagan, this was the oldest a man had been elected president. [6]He gave one of the longest inaugural addresses on record, close to two hours. [7]Shortly after his speech, he caught pneumonia. [8]Harrison died a little more than a month after taking office.

   Topic sentence(s): _____

3.   [1]Hot dogs are as American as any food. [2]Unfortunately, they are also high in fat and salt. [3]Since the country has become more health-conscious, some companies have introduced hot dogs that are more nutritious. [4]First came chicken and turkey frankfurters, which have been on the market for some time. [5]These are lower in fat than the traditional beef and pork hot dogs. [6]There are now also franks that have tofu added to them to reduce fat 20 percent or more. [7]Some companies have cut out nitrates, preservatives that have been linked to cancer. [8]Still others have lowered the salt content of their hot dogs.

   Topic sentence(s): _____

(Continues on next page)

4.   ¹The traditional American dream has included getting married, buying a home, and raising a family. ²While marriage may still be the goal of most men, an Ohio University survey suggests that it appeals to fewer women. ³The survey asked single men and women between the ages of eighteen and thirty-four if they ever wanted to get married. ⁴Two out of three men said they wanted to get married. ⁵Only 50 percent of the women surveyed indicated a desire to get married.

Topic sentence(s): _____

5.   ¹It is often difficult for foreign students to adjust to life in America. ²For one thing, they may be uncomfortable with the casual relationship that exists between American teachers and students. ³In many countries, students treat teachers much more formally. ⁴In addition, foreign students have the language problem to deal with. ⁵Their English classes may not have prepared them to understand fast-paced conversation filled with slang expressions. ⁶Foreign students' social lives can be difficult as well. ⁷Having a background so different from that of other students can make it hard to find friends. ⁸For various reasons, then, life in America can be hard on foreign students.

Topic sentence(s): _____

LOCATIONS OF MAIN IDEAS: Test 3

The five paragraphs below are on the second level of difficulty. Write the number of each topic sentence in the space provided. For the one case in which there are two topic sentences, write in both numbers.

1. [1]The ease in opening and closing Velcro has given it some interesting uses. [2]For instance, astronauts have used it to keep objects—and themselves—from falling into space. [3]They also have had small pieces of Velcro stuck inside their helmets so they could scratch an itchy nose. [4]Today, the fabric is used to fasten the fireproof suits of race-car drivers. [5]This allows a driver to jump out of a suit in seconds if necessary. [6]Velcro is also used to join two parts of the artificial heart.

    Topic sentence(s): _____

2. [1]Studies show that a dog or cat creates a more relaxed home environment which can help to end family arguments. [2]In addition, pets often serve as an emotional outlet for older men. [3]The men share thoughts and feelings with the pets that they don't share with the rest of the family. [4]Pets also ease life's stressful times, including the death of a loved one. [5]Furthermore, pets have been used with proven success in increasing the will to live among older people. [6]Clearly, pets can be good for our mental health.

    Topic sentence(s): _____

3. [1]If you want to improve your running ability, lifting weights will help. [2]Weight training increases strength, which will help propel you forward more efficiently. [3]Weights will also prepare you to run longer distances, since muscle is where fuel is stored. [4]And, combined with stretching activities, weights will cut down on injuries. [5]Even though you may not see many muscle-bound runners, working with weights will help you run.

    Topic sentence(s): _____

4. [1]Every week, guns kill several hundred Americans. [2]To cut down on these deaths, some say we should stop the sale of guns, or at least of the worst kinds. [3]Since so many people already own guns, others suggest we require a permit to carry a gun outside the home. [4]Many gun owners call for yet another solution: tough penalties for those who use guns in crimes. [5]These are just a few of the many ideas on how to reduce the dangers of guns in America.

    Topic sentence(s): _____

(Continues on next page)

5.   ¹The reason we shiver and get goosebumps when we are shocked has to do with our animal nature. ²When animals see or hear something threatening, their fur stands on end. ³This reaction makes them look larger and thus more dangerous to an enemy. ⁴In addition, extra blood flows to their muscles, getting them ready for action. ⁵Humans react in the same way. ⁶When we sense danger, goosebumps appear where our fur would stand on end if we had any. ⁷Also, the blood flow to our skin is reduced in favor of our muscles, making us feel cold. ⁸Unlike other animals, we have no fur to warm us, so we shiver to get warm.

Topic sentence(s): _____

LOCATIONS OF MAIN IDEAS: Test 4

The five paragraphs below are on the third level of difficulty. Write the number of each topic sentence in the space provided. For the one case in which there are two topic sentences, write in both numbers.

1. [1]Can watching television influence how we think? [2]Research shows that people who watch a lot of TV are influenced by its unrealistic representation of sex roles. [3]For example, male characters outnumber females by three to one in prime-time TV. [4]Also, men play a far greater variety of roles than women. [5]And fewer than 20 percent of married mothers on television work outside the home; in real life, over 50 percent do. [6]No wonder so many heavy TV viewers agree that "women should take care of running their homes and leave running the country to men."

   Topic sentence(s): _____

2. [1]The question of who holds the power in a marriage is more complex than it used to be. [2]Husbands once had more power in marriages. [3]They earned more, were better educated, and had jobs with more prestige. [4]But as women get better jobs and earn more, they gain power at home. [5]Another factor in the balance of power is whether or not both partners care the same about the marriage. [6]If the husband, for example, cares more about staying married than the wife does, the wife will have more power. [7]That is because the husband will do more to please her. [8]Thus the power structure of marriage has become more complicated in recent years.

   Topic sentence(s): _____

3. [1]What steps can you take if you turn an ankle or strain a muscle? [2]Many sports physicians recommend the "RICE" formula for sprains and strains: Rest, Ice, Compression, and Elevation. [3]First, rest the joint or muscle that hurts. [4]Secondly, apply ice to the injured area. [5]Ice may be used at regular times for two days. [6]A compression bandage, such as an Ace bandage, will also ease the pain. [7]Finally, elevating an injured ankle or knee will keep pressure off it and prevent further damage. [8]Of course, if the pain stays or if the injury swells, you should see a doctor at once.

   Topic sentence(s): _____

(Continues on next page)

4. [1]Until recently, the mountain town of Katy, West Virginia, was too far away to pick up television signals. [2]But then cable TV was installed. [3]Now all but three of the 170 houses in Katy have television. [4]The introduction of TV to Katy has influenced local students in both helpful and harmful ways. [5]On the plus side, students now express themselves better. [6]They also understand others and world events better. [7]But on the minus side, students' attention span has shortened. [8]And they are now so used to a TV being on that they have trouble working in quiet classrooms.

    Topic sentence(s): _____

5. [1]The distance we like to keep between ourselves and others depends on the other people, according to one researcher. [2]The space within about one foot from us is "intimate" space. [3]We share it willingly only with loved ones. [4]If forced to share it with strangers (in a crowded elevator, for instance), we feel uncomfortable. [5]Between one and four feet away is our "personal" space, which we share with friends. [6]This is about how far apart we sit at a restaurant, for example. [7]Between about four and ten feet away is "social" space. [8]This is the distance we keep from strangers at parties and other gatherings. [9]Finally, over ten feet away is "public" space, a distance at which we can pretty much ignore others.

    Topic sentence(s): _____

LOCATIONS OF MAIN IDEAS: Test 5

The five paragraphs below are on the third and fourth levels of difficulty. Write the number of each topic sentence in the space provided. For the one case in which there are two topic sentences, write in both numbers.

1. ¹Home burglar alarms often go off even when no trespasser is entering the house. ²False alarms in home security systems occur for a variety of reasons. ³Police in Texas report that cockroaches sometimes get into systems and trigger the alarm. ⁴A firm in Arkansas learned that a system that kept going off was home to a spider. ⁵Whenever the spider moved by a sensing device, the alarm went off. ⁶A company in Dallas discovered that a system was continually being set off by a banner set up to motivate salespeople. ⁷Whenever the air conditioning came on, the banner blew back and forth, setting off a motion detector. ⁸Almost all companies report that the most common cause is human error. ⁹Two out of three false alarms occur when people forget their code or open doors and windows without turning off the system.

    Topic sentence(s): _____

2. ¹Our life stages may be set by biology, but how we view those stages is shaped by society. ²During the Middle Ages, for example, children dressed—and were expected to act—like little adults. ³Adolescence became a separate stage of life only fairly recently, when a teenage subculture appeared. ⁴Before that, young people were "children" until about age sixteen. ⁵Then they went to work, married, and had their own children. ⁶Today, young adulthood has become a new stage of life, covering about ages twenty to thirty. ⁷And now that people live longer and spend years in active retirement, older adulthood has also become a distinct life stage.

    Topic sentence(s): _____

3. ¹In California, a "Victim's Bill of Rights" was passed recently. ²This law broadened the type of evidence that could be used in court. ³The idea was to keep criminals from going free due to legal loopholes. ⁴But defense lawyers soon learned that they, too, could use this law. ⁵In rape trials especially, the new law could be used to move part of the blame onto the victim. ⁶This was done by presenting evidence, not permitted before, that the victim was careless or sexually "loose." ⁷A law intended to protect crime victims thus turned out to have just the opposite effect.

    Topic sentence(s): _____

(Continues on next page)

4.   [1]Zoos used to be places where unhappy-looking animals paced back and forth in small cages. [2]But today, many zoos have large "natural" areas in which animals can live as if they were in the wild. [3]In some zoos, for example, chimpanzees and gorillas live in large areas that look like rain forests. [4]Huge animals such as elephants wander freely on "African plains" in the heart of New York City and San Diego. [5]Zookeepers sometimes use such environments to allow animals to work for their food, as in the wild. [6]In one zoo, for instance, honey is hidden in a fake anthill. [7]Chimpanzees scoop the honey out with a stiff piece of hay, a process similar to how they "fish" for insects in Africa.

Topic sentence(s): _____

5.   [1]While parents of different countries use different languages, parental speech patterns appear to be much the same throughout the world. [2]A Stanford University study found that when mothers want to warn their babies, they use short, sharp words such as *no* in English and *nyet* in Russian. [3]When parents want to praise their babies, the message first rises in pitch and then falls. [4]American mothers, for instance, stretch the word good into *"Goo-ood!"* [5]When the baby needs comforting, a long, soothing sound such as *shhh* is used. [6]And to call attention to something, parents begin with a low tone and end on a high note, as in "Look at THIS!" [7]When it comes to communicating with children, there is apparently a universal language.

Topic sentence(s): _____

LOCATIONS OF MAIN IDEAS: Test 6

The five paragraphs below are on the fourth level of difficulty. Write the number of each topic sentence in the space provided. For the one case in which there are two topic sentences, write in both numbers.

1. [1]Photo radar is increasing the efficiency of ticket giving. [2]With photo radar, a beam is directed at oncoming traffic. [3]When a speeder is detected, a picture of the front of the vehicle is taken. [4]The license number is matched with the car's owner, and a ticket is sent. [5]The arresting officer does not have to take time explaining the situation to one motorist while others speed by. [6]Also, the load on traffic courts is lessened since people are sent a copy of the picture that was taken. [7]Photo radar has shown itself to be a practical and effective means of enforcing speed limits.

   Topic sentence(s): _____

2. [1]It is not uncommon for depression to set in after a divorce. [2]A recent study shows that a condition called "move down" contributes to post-divorce depression. [3]"Move down" refers to the economizing that is done by the person moving out of the residence. [4]The person who moves out has a tendency to move into a house or apartment that is of lower quality. [5]The study compared divorced people who moved down with those who maintained a home of the same quality. [6]Those who did not move down were less stressed and had less chance of depression setting in.

   Topic sentence(s): _____

3. [1]A bullfighter usually kneels in front of the bull before a fight begins. [2]Audience members are amazed at his courage. [3]However, the truth is that by kneeling, the bullfighter tricks the bull into being gentle. [4]Among animals, when two males fight, one can signal he gives up by taking a yielding position. [5]The animal drops to the ground and raises his backside. [6]This position tells the other male that he has won and thus reduces his instinct to fight. [7]For this reason, the bull thinks the kneeling bullfighter is giving up. [8]Therefore the bull does not attack.

   Topic sentence(s): _____

(Continues on next page)

4.   [1]The Great Flood of 1993 caused extreme destruction in states along the Mississippi River. [2]There is strong evidence that humans were a major contributor to the destruction during the Great Flood. [3]The longest river in the U.S., the Mississippi begins in Minnesota and empties into the Gulf of Mexico in Louisiana. [4]Before Europeans settled along its banks, the river responded to floods by widening. [5]Workers changed that by building levees to protect the towns along the river's banks. [6]Engineers straightened the river. [7]Both changes made the river move faster. [8]When floods come, the water has no place to go and presses against the levees. [9]When the pressure becomes too great, the levees break, flooding towns. [10]If the levees hold, there is a danger that the water will become higher than the levees, and this results in floods as well.

Topic sentence(s): _____

5.   [1]There are 170 million acres of federally owned land used by ranchers to graze cattle and sheep. [2]The government recognizes that two-thirds of that land is overgrazed. [3]A new technique called "holistic resource management" may put an end to overgrazing and return lands to their original state. [4]The technique, called HRM for short, is modeled on a pattern that existed before cattle herds trampled the prairies. [5]Buffalo used to move into an area, consume grasses and plant life, fertilize the area, then move on to new areas. [6]Followers of HRM try to imitate this pattern by moving herds along at a set speed and time.

Topic sentence(s): _____

IMPLIED MAIN IDEAS: Test 1

A. Circle the letter of the general idea that best covers the specific ideas. Remember that the correct general idea will not be too narrow or too broad. It will describe what the specific ideas have in common.

1. *Specific ideas:* popcorn, apple, potato chips, cheese and crackers

    The general idea is:
    a. foods.
    b. snack foods.
    c. foods eaten at the movies.

2. *Specific ideas:* Washington, Lincoln, Columbus, New York

    The general idea is:
    a. presidents.
    b. famous men from history.
    c. cities.

3. *Specific ideas:* Scrabble, checkers, Monopoly, chess

    The general idea is:
    a. board games.
    b. games.
    c. games only two people can play.

4. *Specific ideas:* runny nose, coughing, sneezing, sore throat

    The general idea is:
    a. cold symptoms.
    b. symptoms.
    c. throat problems.

5. *Specific ideas:* 2, 4, 5, 18, 644

    The general idea is:
    a. numbers.
    b. even numbers.
    c. clothing sizes.

(Continues on next page)

B. In the following lists, the specific ideas are given, but the general idea is unstated. Fill in the blanks with the unstated general idea. Make sure your answer is not too broad or too narrow.

6. *General idea:* _____

   Specific ideas: French
   Italian
   Thousand Island
   blue cheese

7. *General idea:* _____

   Specific ideas: house
   apartment
   condominium
   mansion

8. *General idea:* _____

   Specific ideas: minute
   month
   decade
   century

9. *General idea:* _____

   Specific ideas: fear
   hate
   love
   jealousy

10. *General idea:* _____

   Specific ideas: Marine Corps
   Army
   Navy
   Air Force

IMPLIED MAIN IDEAS: Test 2

A. Circle the letter of the general idea that best covers the specific ideas. Remember that the correct general idea will not be too narrow or too broad. It will describe what the specific ideas have in common.

1. *Specific ideas:* hide and seek, tag, jacks, hopscotch

   The general idea is:
   a. games.
   b. toys.
   c. children's games.

2. *Specific ideas:* yes, no, maybe, OK

   The general idea is:
   a. negative answers.
   b. positive answers.
   c. answers.

3. *Specific ideas:* traffic jam, ingrown toenail, burnt toast, stiff neck

   The general idea is:
   a. disasters.
   b. rare conditions.
   c. minor problems.

4. *Specific ideas:* yes/no, male/female, famous/unknown, asleep/awake

   The general idea is:
   a. opposites.
   b. pairs.
   c. synonyms.

5. *Specific ideas:* convince your roommate that cleaning the house is good exercise, move to a new apartment, never look too closely at your surroundings

   The general idea is:
   a. ways to get along with others.
   b. ways to relax.
   c. ways to do as little cleaning as possible.

(Continues on next page)

B. In the following lists, the specific ideas are given, but the general idea is unstated. Fill in the blanks with the unstated general idea. Make sure your answer is not too broad or too narrow.

6. *General idea:* _____

   Specific ideas: doughnuts
   cereal
   bacon and eggs
   pancakes

7. *General idea:* _____

   Specific ideas: comma
   dash
   colon
   period

8. *General idea:* _____

   Specific ideas: *Time*
   People
   TV Guide
   Reader's Digest

9. *General idea:* _____

   Specific ideas: Finding a ten-dollar bill on the sidewalk
   Having a teacher cancel a test you're not ready for
   Being too late for a flight on an airplane that crashes
   Winning a lottery

10. *General idea:* _____

    Specific ideas: treadmill
    stationary bike
    rowing machine
    stair stepper

IMPLIED MAIN IDEAS: Test 3

Circle the letter of the statement that best expresses the implied main idea of each group.

Group 1

1. Switzerland is known for its chocolates.
2. Ireland is famous for potatoes.
3. Argentina is well known for its beef.
4. Japan is famed for raw fish dishes.

    The unstated main idea of these sentences is:
    a. Certain countries can produce only particular foods.
    b. Certain countries are associated with particular foods.
    c. Certain countries are known for the products they make.
    d. European countries are associated with particular foods.

Group 2

1. Halogen lights burn more brightly than regular bulbs.
2. They also last longer than traditional bulbs.
3. Halogen lights use less energy than standard bulbs.
4. Halogen lights are less expensive than other bulbs.

    The unstated main idea of these sentences is:
    a. In the future, people will use halogen lights more than any other.
    b. There are no disadvantages to halogen lights.
    c. There are various reasons to use halogen lights.
    d. Halogen lights are stronger than regular light bulbs.

Group 3

1. To become president of the United States, a person must be at least thirty-five years old.
2. He or she must have lived in the U.S. for the last fourteen years.
3. In addition, he or she must be American-born.
4. A convicted felon cannot be president of the U.S.

    The unstated main idea of these sentences is:
    a. There is an age limit to becoming president of the U.S.
    b. To become president of the U.S., a person must have been born a U.S. citizen and live in the country.
    c. All countries have requirements for their presidential candidates.
    d. There are certain requirements for becoming president of the U.S.

(Continues on next page)

Group 4

1. Earthquakes occur in the western U.S.
2. Hurricanes can be expected if you live in the South.
3. Tornadoes are common in the Plains States.
4. Flooding occurs in states with large rivers.

The unstated main idea of these sentences is:
a. Natural disasters occur in various regions around the country.
b. The South and the Plains States are especially dangerous places to live.
c. There are only four kinds of natural disasters that hit the U.S.
d. Flooding is the most dangerous natural disaster in the U.S.

Group 5

1. When you begin to exercise, make sure you warm up to increase flexibility and get your heart ready for what follows.
2. Make sure you drink plenty of fluids to replace those lost.
3. Forget the old saying "No pain, no gain"—if your body is hurting, stop.
4. When you finish exercising, take some time to cool down, so your heart can readjust to a slower pace and your muscles won't stiffen up.

The unstated main idea of these sentences is:
a. The most important step in exercising is warming up properly.
b. Certain guidelines must be followed to avoid stiff muscles.
c. Certain guidelines will make your exercise program easier on your body.
d. Exercising properly takes a lot of time.

IMPLIED MAIN IDEAS: Test 4

Circle the letter of the implied main idea in each of the following paragraphs.

1. The first frost in Montana occurs around September 15. Colorado gets its first frost about October 1. Oklahoma's first frost is near the end of October. Louisiana can expect a frost around the middle of November. And Florida can look for a frost about the middle of December.

    The unstated main idea of this paragraph is:
    a. The first frost date varies from state to state.
    b. There is no frost in Texas.
    c. All states can expect to get a frost.
    d. Winter comes to Colorado before it hits Oklahoma.

2. Did you ever wonder why baby boys wear blue? The answer comes from centuries ago. Once, people thought that evil spirits could harm newborn boys. They believed that only a very forceful color could offer protection. Blue, the color of Heaven, was thought to be the most powerful color. Boys began to be wrapped up in blue blankets. It seemed that no baby boy wearing blue was being harmed by evil spirits. Thus, the tradition was continued, and it still exists today.

    The unstated main idea of this paragraph is:
    a. People associate certain powers and qualities with colors.
    b. Centuries ago, people believed evil spirits could harm newborn boys.
    c. The tradition of dressing boys in blue began with an ancient superstition.
    d. Because blue seemed to be the color of Heaven, people once thought it was the most powerful color.

3. A woman in Texas found an abandoned litter of young kittens and decided to bring them home. She was not sure how her female dachshund would respond to them. The response was rare and unexpected. The dachshund experienced a false pregnancy. She lay down on her side and encouraged the kittens to nurse. She even began producing milk. A local veterinarian said there was no harm to the kittens. He also said he had never seen anything like it.

    The unstated main idea of this paragraph is:
    a. Dogs and cats of all types get along better than you'd expect.
    b. A dachshund had a surprisingly motherly response to a litter of young kittens.
    c. A kind woman saved the lives of several abandoned kittens.
    d. A dachshund once shared a home with some kittens.

(Continues on next page)

4.   In 1910, twenty-eight-year-old Franklin D. Roosevelt was elected to the New York Senate. It was his first elected office. After serving as United States Secretary of the Navy, he was elected governor of New York in 1928. He was re-elected in 1930. In 1932, he was elected president of the United States. He remained president until his death in 1945. No one has served as president as long as "F.D.R."

The unstated main idea of this paragraph is:
a. Franklin D. Roosevelt had a long career in state and national politics.
b. No one has served as president as long as Franklin D. Roosevelt.
c. Franklin D. Roosevelt's first elected position was state senator.
d. Many interesting Americans have had political careers.

5.   As a prank, an eighth grade class in Iowa made up the name Jeff Schuman for a fictitious classmate. They continued the gag into high school, nominating Jeff for student body president and homecoming king. One student entered Jeff in a national test on international affairs. After filling out his own test, the student filled out Jeff's test by randomly selecting answers. The imaginary student got a better score than the real student. In fact, the contest organizers notified the school that Jeff Schuman had won third place.

The unstated main idea of this paragraph is:
a. Students should not play pranks.
b. "Jeff Schuman" was an imaginary student.
c. A long-term school prank ended up producing surprising results.
d. High school students play numerous pranks.

IMPLIED MAIN IDEAS: Test 5

Write out what you think is the unstated main idea of each of the following five paragraphs. Hints will help you figure out a couple of the implied main ideas.

1. Polynesians once believed that a total eclipse of the sun occurred when the sun and moon made love. The stars were the offspring. Some North American Indian tribes believed that an eclipse signaled the death of a celestial body. Other tribes believed that coyotes that roamed the stars hunted during an eclipse. In China eclipses were so significant that three thousand years ago, two astronomers who failed to predict an eclipse were beheaded.

    What is the unstated main idea of this paragraph? _____

    _____

    Hint: The topic of this paragraph is eclipses. What is the author's main point about eclipses?

2. Flowers such as the morning glory and the buttercup are lovely to look at. But they are poisonous as well. Eating any part of a buttercup can cause injury to the digestive system. The seeds in a morning glory can cause severe mental disturbances. Poinsettia and mistletoe, two plants popular around Christmas, can be fatal if swallowed. Even garden plants can be dangerous. If eaten, tomato vines and the leaves around potatoes can cause severe nervous disorders. And many wild mushrooms are so poisonous they can kill if eaten.

    What is the unstated main idea of this paragraph? _____

    _____

3. Chocolate causes pimples. If you are bitten by a snake, you should suck the snakebite to prevent poisoning from the venom. If you have an ulcer, you should drink milk. What do all of these common medical beliefs have in common? They are all false. Breakouts of pimples are linked with an increase in the body's production of a certain hormone, and there may be a genetic link as well. The bacteria present in your mouth will increase the risk of infecting a snakebite wound. Milk contains lactic acid, which stimulates the acid in the stomach and causes an ulcer to become irritated.

    What is the unstated main idea of this paragraph? _____

    _____

    Hint: The topic of this paragraph is certain common medical beliefs. What is the author's main point *about* these common medical beliefs?

(Continues on next page)

4. Are you going to a garage or yard sale? If so, try to be early. The best buys are the first ones to go. Also, if you see just what you are looking for, buy it. If you think about it too long or think you can come back later, you may lose a good purchase. Finally, don't be afraid to bargain. If items are priced, ask if the seller will take 25 percent less than the marked price. If items aren't priced, get a figure in your mind that you are willing to pay; then ask the seller if he will take 25 percent less than that figure.

    What is the unstated main idea of this paragraph? _____

    _____

5. When you're sick, remember to drink plenty of fluids to keep from becoming dehydrated. Also, eat small, frequent meals. Small meals may tire you out less and minimize stomach problems. Also useful is a low-fat diet, which is easier on your digestive system. A low-fat diet may also increase the activity of your body's cells that fight illness. A final dietary guideline for when you're sick is to drink a fruit smoothie when you're hungry. Smoothies are easy to swallow and digest and full of healing vitamins and minerals. They are also easy to make—just throw strawberries, bananas, orange juice, plain yogurt, a pinch of wheat germ and some ice into a blender.

    What is the unstated main idea of this paragraph? _____

    _____

    Hint: The topic of this paragraph is dietary guidelines. What is the author's main point *about* these dietary guidelines?

IMPLIED MAIN IDEAS: Test 6

Write out what you think is the unstated main idea of each of the following five paragraphs.

1. Good college students will read an assigned textbook chapter before class. During lectures, they will take extensive notes. Another study technique they will practice is to budget their time carefully. By studying each subject every week, they will make themselves ready for midterm and final examinations. And they will prepare essays, term papers and speeches well in advance of when they are due.

   What is the unstated main idea of this paragraph?_____

   _____

2. The United States calls its currency the "dollar." Australia and New Zealand have also named their currency "dollar." The money in Great Britain is called the "pound." Korea uses the "won." In Russia you spend "rubles." Mexico and the Philippines use a "peso." And the country of Zaire calls its money unit a "zaire."

   What is the unstated main idea of this paragraph?_____

   _____

3. To begin with, sit in an upright position while driving on long trips. To prevent yourself from getting stiff or beginning to relax, shift your position frequently. In addition, turn on the radio to something which holds your attention. If the other passengers in the car will be asleep, appoint one person to stay awake and keep you company. Finally, if you are just too tired to continue, find a safe place to get off the road and rest.

   What is the unstated main idea of this paragraph?_____

   _____

(Continues on next page)

4.   Let's say you are taking a trip with time off from work. In America, you would be going on vacation; in Great Britain, you would be going on "holiday." Do you need a prescription filled before leaving? In America, you would go to a drugstore. In Britain, you'd look for a "chemist." Start packing your luggage. What Americans call an "undershirt" the British refer to as a "vest." (An American vest is called a "waistcoat" in England.) Now, where will you put your luggage? If you are an American, it goes in the car's trunk. A Briton puts it in the "boot." And before leaving, don't forget to check the car's oil and water levels. To do so, an American looks under the car's hood. In the U.K., one looks under the "bonnet." Does the car need fuel? In America, you'd ask for gas. In Britain, you'd want "petrol."

What is the unstated main idea of this paragraph? _____

_____

5.   Some actors and rock stars are paid almost a hundred times as much per year as school teachers are. Not to downgrade the role of entertainment in our lives, but certainly these performers do not do work that is many times more important than those who teach and guide our nation's students. Indeed, the opposite is true. As another example, professional athletes earn vastly more than firefighters. Athletes bring enjoyable diversion to our lives, but firefighters save lives. Again, there can be little doubt that the lower-paid group, firefighters, make the more important contribution to society. As a last example, most high-fashion designers, who can make up to $50,000 for a single gown, far out-earn police officers. We can surely live without high-fashion clothes, but a society without law-enforcement officers would be unlivable for all of us.

What is the unstated main idea of this paragraph? _____

_____

MORE ABOUT SUPPORTING DETAILS: Test 1

A. (1-5.) Major and minor supporting details are mixed together in the list below. The details of this list support the main idea shown. Separate the major, more general details from the minor ones by filling in the outline. One detail has been filled in for you.

Main idea: Garage sales have both advantages and disadvantages.

- You will make some money.
- There are disadvantages to a garage sale.
- There are advantages to a garage sale.
- Your neighbors will see all the junk you've acquired.
- Getting everything ready will take a lot of time.

Major detail: 1. _____

Minor details: a. _____

               b. _____

Major detail: 2. _____

Minor details: a. You will meet many interesting people.

               b. _____

B. (6-10.) In the spaces provided, complete the notes on each paragraph: For the first paragraph, complete the heading. Then fill in the missing major details. For the second paragraph, fill in the missing major details.

In each paragraph, the topic sentence is boldfaced, and the addition words that signal major details are set off in italics.

1.   **You can cut down the amount of fat in your diet in several ways.** *First,* eat less red meat, which has high amounts of fat. *Also,* use low-fat or non-fat dairy products. Low-fat and non-fat products are available for milk, cheese, and yogurt. *Another* way to limit the fat in your diet is to bake, broil, or boil your food instead of frying it in fat.

Heading: Several Ways to _____

List of major details:

1. _____

2. _____

3. Bake, broil, or boil your food.

(Continues on next page)

2.   **Instincts are animal behaviors that don't need learning.** *One* example is the way birds build nests. Birds don't stop to think about which type of nest to build. All robins, for instance, build their nests the same way. *Also,* ants don't think about how to get food. Without lessons, they gather food as every other ant in the hill does. A *third* example is that all cats lick themselves clean without learning to do it.

Heading: Animal Behaviors That Don't Need Learning

List of major details:

1. _____

2. _____

3. Cats lick themselves clean.

MORE ABOUT SUPPORTING DETAILS: Test 2

A. (1-5.) Major and minor supporting details are mixed together in the list below. The details of this list support the main idea shown. Separate the major, more general details from the minor ones by filling in the outline. One detail has been filled in for you.

Main idea: There are a number of things to remember when filling out a job application.

- Have the names and dates of your educational background in mind or on paper.
- Make sure the application is easy to read.
- Print or write clearly.
- Be prepared to provide names and dates of your previous jobs.
- Use a pen.

Major detail: 1. _____

Minor details: a. _____

_____

      b. _____

_____

Major detail: 2. Come prepared to fill in certain commonly requested information.

Minor details: a. _____

_____

      b. _____

_____

(Continues on next page)

B. (6-10.) In the spaces provided, complete the notes on each paragraph: For the first paragraph, complete the heading, including the word that ends in *s*. Then fill in the two missing major details. For the second paragraph, fill in the two missing major details. In each paragraph, the topic sentence is boldfaced.

1.   A respectful parent guides and instructs more than he or she punishes. **To be a respectful parent, there are several don'ts you should remember.** First, don't yell a lot at children. Yelling will tell a child that the parent is out of control. Or it will result in a shouting match that loses respect. Second, don't lay down too many rules. Growing up is not a boot camp. Too many rules will prevent children from understanding what is really important. Third, don't show disrespect to a child. This will create resentment. Fourth, don't order children around. They will not learn responsibility if they feel they have to do what you want at the instant you command it. Finally, don't neglect to acknowledge good behavior. Praise and hugs work wonders in promoting responsibility and respect.

Heading: _____s for Parents to Remember

List of major details:

1. Don't yell a lot at children.

2. Don't lay down too many rules.

3. _____

4. Don't order children around.

5. _____

2.   **For various reasons, veterinarians are implanting computer microchips under the skin of pets.** First, the chips can be used to recognize an animal that has been lost or stolen. Second, they can be used to identify purebred animals that have come from breeders. Breeders who guarantee that an animal is free from defects can identify the animal later in life. And third, the animal's history can be kept on the chip. This means that if a pet changes vets, the new doctor can see what treatments the animal has undergone.

Heading: Various Reasons Vets Are Implanting Computer Microchips Under the Skin of Pets

List of major details:

1. _____

2. Implanted microchips can identify animals for breeders.

3. _____

MORE ABOUT SUPPORTING DETAILS: Test 3

A. (1-4.) In the spaces provided, complete the notes on each paragraph: For the first paragraph, complete the heading, including the word that ends in *s*. Then fill in the missing major detail. For the second paragraph, fill in the two missing major details. In each paragraph, the topic sentence is boldfaced.

1. **There are a couple of important steps to take when choosing a puppy.** One is to check out a pup's physical condition carefully. Being cute isn't enough. The animal's eyes should be clear and bright, and its gums should be pink and firm. Also, get an idea of the puppy's personality. Watch it play with other pups. If it's very timid or aggressive, it might not make a good pet.

   Heading: _____s to Take When Choosing
   a Puppy

   List of major details:

   1. Check out a pup's physical condition carefully.

   2. _____

2. Many people continue to work after "retiring." **There are two main reasons many senior citizens continue to work after "retiring."** First, of course, some work mainly for the money. According to one survey, 32 percent of older workers fall into this category. The others, however, work mainly because they like to. One retired mechanic, for instance, loves his $4.75-an-hour job at a fast-food restaurant. And a teacher who had always wanted to be a doctor went into medicine after "retirement," as a nurse.

   Heading: Two Main Reasons "Retired" People Continue to Work

   List of major details:

   1. _____

   2. _____

(Continues on next page)

B. Read the paragraph below and then answer the questions that follow. To help you focus on the details, the topic sentence has been boldfaced.

> **While we lack the instincts of animals, humans do share several powerful motives.** One is the drive to achieve. This desire is what urges us to set athletic records or to try out for the starring role in a play. Another human motive is the urge to use power. People with a strong power drive may join a campus activity in order to become its leader. The desire to associate with other people is a third powerful motive. This motive brings people to join organizations, work on committees, socialize, and marry.

5. The major details of this paragraph involve several
   a. instincts that people share.
   b. motives that people share.
   c. habits that people share.

6. The major details are indicated by the signal words
   a. *one, another,* and *third.*
   b. *first, second,* and *finally.*
   c. *achieve, power,* and *associate.*

7. The major details of this paragraph are human drives to
   a. set records, star in plays, and join organizations.
   b. achieve, use power, and associate with others.
   c. join organizations, work on committees, socialize, and marry.

8. When people join a campus activity in order to become its leader, they are motivated by the drive to
   a. achieve.
   b. use power.
   c. socialize.

9. The desire to associate with others motivates people to
   a. set athletic records.
   b. lead a campus activity.
   c. socialize and marry.

10. When people try out for a play, they are motivated by the drive to
    a. achieve.
    b. use power.
    c. socialize.

MORE ABOUT SUPPORTING DETAILS: Test 4

A. (1-6.) In the spaces provided, complete the notes on each paragraph: For the first paragraph, complete the heading, including the word that ends in *s*. Then fill in the two missing major details. For the second paragraph, fill in the three missing major details. In each paragraph, the topic sentence is boldfaced.

1. **If you have trouble sleeping, there are several methods to help you grow tired.** Some people find that relaxing the muscles quickly leads to sleep. A simple stretching exercise or a long hot bath can do the trick. Or settle your mind by doing a nagging task. For instance, clean out a drawer, or sew buttons on a coat. You might also relax with something pleasant and familiar. Try listening to soft music or enjoying the family photo album.

   Heading: _____s to Help You Get Sleepy

   List of major details:

   1. Relax the muscles

   2. _____

   3. _____

2. **There are various ways to stay informed of important events in the world today.** One is to read newspapers. Good daily papers such as *The New York Times* and the *Los Angeles Times* are available in many cities across the country. *USA Today* is sold nationally and provides state and national coverage. Another way is to subscribe to a weekly newsmagazine. *Time* and *Newsweek* are the most popular. A third way to keep informed is to watch TV news shows. Each network broadcasts morning and evening news shows. ABC has a late-night newscast. And for those with no set schedule, Cable News Network (CNN) broadcasts news twenty-four hours a day.

   Heading: Various Ways to Stay Informed About Important Events

   List of major details:

   1. _____

   2. _____

   3. _____

(Continues on next page)

B. Read the paragraph below and then answer the questions that follow. To help you focus on the details, the topic sentence is boldfaced.

> **Several kinds of changes can warn that a teenager is considering suicide.** Some changes are physical. The youngster may have no energy or may show a sudden gain or loss in weight. Other changes are emotional. There can be sudden outbursts, usually for no apparent reason. Also, the youngster may stop communicating with family or may even withdraw from people in general. The most dramatic signs of suicide are changes in old habits and interests. These signs often include new sleeping patterns and giving away favorite possessions.

7. In general, the major details of this paragraph are changes that
   a. are physical.
   b. can warn of suicide.
   c. affect sleep.

8. Specifically, the major details of this paragraph are
   a. weight gain, withdrawal, and giving away of possessions.
   b. no energy, actions for no apparent reason, and dramatic signs.
   c. physical changes, emotional changes, and shifts in habits and interests.

9. An example of a physical change is
   a. loss of energy.
   b. lack of communication.
   c. new sleep patterns.

10. The last sentence of the paragraph provides
    a. a major detail.
    b. minor details.
    c. both a major and a minor detail.

MORE ABOUT SUPPORTING DETAILS: Test 5

Read each paragraph below and then answer the questions that follow it. To help you focus on the details of each paragraph, the topic sentences have been boldfaced.

A.   [1]**Parts of our environment affect the way we behave and feel.** [2]First, there is temperature. [3]Most people prefer temperatures in the 70s. [4]When it is hotter than the 70s, they become less active and less alert. [5]Lighting also affects us. [6]In the classroom or on the job, bright light encourages work. [7]In contrast, the low lighting of a restaurant relaxes us and encourages informal conversation. [8]Last is color. [9]For example, red is felt as exciting, blue as calming, and yellow as cheerful.

1. As the topic sentence suggests, the major details of this paragraph are
   a. various temperatures.
   b. places where we work and relax.
   c. parts of our environment that affect our behavior and moods.

2. Specifically, the major details of this paragraph are
   a. cool, hot, and just-right temperatures.
   b. the classroom, the job, and the restaurant.
   c. temperature, lighting, and color.

3. The signal words that introduce the major details are
   a. *first, also,* and *last.*
   b. *most, when,* and *and.*
   c. *in contrast, for example,* and *as.*

4. Most people become less alert
   a. in bright light.
   b. in temperatures over the 70s.
   c. in restaurants with low lighting.

5. The last sentence of the paragraph provides
   a. a major detail.
   b. minor details.
   c. both major and minor details.

(Continues on next page)

B. ¹**Intelligence includes several basic mental abilities.** ²One is language skill. ³People strong in this ability do well on reading tests and have large vocabularies. ⁴Another such ability is a quick memory. ⁵People talented in this skill may learn the words to a popular song after hearing it only once or twice. ⁶A third basic mental skill allows us to make sense of visual information. ⁷People strong in this ability can quickly see similarities and differences between designs and pictures.

6. The major details of this paragraph are
    a. types of mental abilities.
    b. types of language abilities.
    c. types of similarities and differences.

7. The signal words that introduce the major details are
    a. *several, mental,* and *abilities.*
    b. *one, another,* and *third.*
    c. *first, also,* and *another.*

8. Specifically, the major details of this paragraph are
    a. designs and pictures.
    b. language, memory, and visual abilities.
    c. reading tests, large vocabularies, and unscrambling mixed-up sentences.

9. The ability to learn quickly the words to a popular song shows a strong
    a. language ability.
    b. memorizing ability.
    c. visual ability.

10. The ability to see quickly how designs and pictures are alike shows a strong
    a. language ability.
    b. memorizing ability.
    c. visual ability.

MORE ABOUT SUPPORTING DETAILS: Test 6

Read each paragraph below and then answer the questions that follow it. To help you focus on the details of each paragraph, the topic sentences have been boldfaced.

A. **¹The National Board of Medical Examiners recently released a number of alarming facts about doctors.** ²First, the amount of time doctors spend examining patients is down dramatically from previous years. ³Twenty years ago, doctors spent eleven minutes with patients. ⁴Today they take only seven minutes. ⁵Second, it was found that a large number of patients have been switching doctors. ⁶Within the past year, for instance, 25 percent of patients reported changing doctors. ⁷The most common reason given was that patients did not feel comfortable with the doctor they left. ⁸Finally, medical students' reasons for wanting to become a doctor were unexpected. ⁹The most common reason given was to make a good living. ¹⁰Working with people ranked third.

1. The opening phrase that describes the major supporting details is
   a. "The National Board of Medical Examiners."
   b. "a number of alarming facts about doctors."
   c. "the amount of time doctors spend examining patients."

2. The first major supporting detail is signaled by the addition word or words
   a. *a number of.*
   b. *only.*
   c. *first.*

3. The second major detail is introduced in sentence
   a. 3.
   b. 5.
   c. 6.

4. The third major detail is introduced in sentence
   a. 7.
   b. 8.
   c. 9.

5. Circle the letter of the outline that best reflects the paragraph.

   A. Main idea: The National Board of Medical Examiners recently released a number of alarming facts about doctors.
      1. Twenty years ago, doctors spent eleven minutes examining patients.
      2. Today, on the average, doctors spend seven minutes examining patients.
      3. Within the past year, 25 percent of patients reported changing doctors, in most cases because of discomfort with the doctor.
      4. The reasons medical students give for wanting to become a doctor were unexpected.

(Continues on next page)

B. Main idea: The National Board of Medical Examiners recently released a number of alarming facts about doctors.

    1. Doctors today spend less time examining patients than they did twenty years ago.

    2. A large number of patients have been switching doctors.

    3. Medical students rank making a good living as a more important reason to become a doctor than working with people.

B. ¹**There are different ways to handle embarrassing moments.** ²One way is to reduce the significance of the embarrassing moment. ³For instance, if you don't make a big deal about spilling your coffee, other people probably won't. ⁴Another way is to disown your behavior. ⁵After the embarrassing moment, say something like "That's not the real me, you know." ⁶And a third way to handle an embarrassing moment is to get help. ⁷For example, if you spill food at a restaurant, don't try to clean it up yourself. ⁸Have a friend or a waiter help you to clean up the mess.

6. The major supporting details for this paragraph are
   a. 1) embarrassing moments, 2) disowning yourself, and 3) spilling food at a restaurant.
   b. 1) reduce the significance of the event, 2) disown your behavior, and 3) get help.
   c. 1) don't make a big deal out of spilling your coffee, 2) say, "That's not the real me, you know," and 3) let somebody else clean up a spill at a restaurant.

7. The first major supporting detail is signaled by the addition word or words
   a. *one.*
   b. *also.*
   c. *another.*

8. The last major supporting detail is signaled by the addition word or words
   a. *another.*
   b. *third.*
   c. *for example.*

9. Sentence 3 provides
   a. a major detail.
   b. a minor detail.

10. Sentence 4 provides
    a. a major detail.
    b. a minor detail.

TRANSITIONS: Test 1

A. Fill in each blank with the appropriate transition in the box. Use each transition once.

Note: You may find it helpful to check (✓) each transition after you insert it into a sentence.

also	during	for instance
because	similar	

1. At 21, Claudia saw a photo of her mother at the same age. She was amazed to see how _____ they looked.

2. I'm not going to invite Brad and Gerry to the same party _____ they are not on speaking terms.

3. Some animals can regrow lost limbs. _____, the starfish grows back a lost arm in a few weeks.

4. In his forties, Chun's hairline started to move back. He _____ had more trouble than ever losing weight.

5. _____ an interview, former President Jimmy Carter was asked how he would feel if his daughter had a love affair. He answered, "Shocked. She's only seven."

(Continues on next page)

B. Fill in each blank with the appropriate transition in the box. Use each transition once.

Note: You may find it helpful to check (✓) each transition after you insert it into a sentence.

because	but	such as
first	when	

There are some interesting facts about the peanut butter in your pantry. (6)_____, about 63 percent of all the peanuts grown are made into peanut butter. Second, over 500 million pounds of peanut butter are made in the United States alone. That would make 7 billion peanut-butter-and-jelly sandwiches! It's true we use some peanut butter for other things, (7)_____ cookies, candies, and eating right out of the jar when nobody is looking. (8)_____ there's still enough left for a lot of sandwiches. Those sandwiches are good for you (9)_____ peanut butter is full of protein. Most people, however, don't even think about this nutritional benefit. They just know that (10)_____ they spread peanut butter on bread, their tastebuds are about to be happy.

TRANSITIONS: Test 2

Fill in each blank with the appropriate transition word or phrase. Then circle the kind of transition you have used.

1. a. _____ digging in his garden, Lonnie discovered an old tin box full of coins.

   b. The transition signals

   time.   contrast.   addition.

   To illustrate
   Although
   While

2. a. Both Presidents Lincoln and Kennedy were killed on a Friday. _____, each was in a large crowd and with his wife when killed.

   b. The relationship of the second sentence to the first is one of

   cause and effect.   illustration.   addition.

   Furthermore
   In contrast
   As a result

3. a. _____ human infants suck their thumbs, baby elephants suck their trunks.

   b. The relationship between the two parts of the sentence is one of

   cause and effect.   time.   comparison.

   Although
   Just as
   Because

4. a. The chef stuffed steel wool into the cracks of the restaurant _____ mice could no longer get into the kitchen.

   b. The transition shows

   comparison.   cause and effect.   time.

   so
   similarly
   in contrast

5. a. Nita planned to become a stewardess _____ she discovered she got airsick.

   b. The transition shows

   cause and effect.   time.   contrast.

   because
   in the same way
   until

(Continues on next page)

6. a. Arnie's recent camping trip was a disaster. _____, one morning he scared a skunk and sat in poison ivy.

   As a result
   For example
   In addition

   b. The transition signals a relationship of
   addition.   cause and effect.   illustration.

7. a. Roberto was so hungry that he ordered two Whoppers. _____, he asked for a large chocolate shake.

   In contrast
   For example
   Also

   b. The transition shows
   contrast.   illustration.   addition.

8. a. Movie audiences usually dislike film monsters. _____, filmgoers pitied King Kong and even shed tears at his death.

   In addition
   However
   Likewise

   b. The relationship of the two sentences is one of
   contrast.   comparison.   addition.

9. a. You can be insured against just about anything. _____, comedians Abbott and Costello once insured themselves against any member of their audience dying of laughter.

   In addition
   On the other hand
   For instance

   b. The relationship of the second sentence to the first sentence is one of
   addition.   contrast.   illustration.

10. a. The zookeeper put a large mirror in the peacock's cage. _____, the bird spread its tail and showed off for the "other" peacock.

    As a result
    Furthermore
    In the same way

    b. The transition signals a relationship of
    addition.   comparison.   cause and effect.

TRANSITIONS: Test 3

A. Fill in each blank with a suitable transition from the box. Use each transition once. *Note:* You may find it helpful to check (✓) each transition after you insert it into a sentence.

even though	for example	now
because	moreover	

1. In rodeos, a horse jumps and bucks _____ it is in pain from the sharp spurs on the cowboy's boots and the strap pulled tight around its groin.

2. Colleges have started to serve the needs of handicapped students. _____, some schools provide tutors and notetakers for the handicapped.

3. _____ many diseases are closely tied to eating habits, the average U.S. doctor receives less than three hours of training in nutrition.

4. In the past, fingerprints were needed to positively identify a criminal. _____, the genetic code of a single cell is enough to do the same.

5. Widespread drug use by athletes has led to calls for random testing. _____, some authorities are proposing much stiffer penalties for athletes who abuse drugs.

(Continues on next page)

B. Fill in each blank with the appropriate transition from the box. Use each transition once.

Note: You may find it helpful to check (✓) each transition as you insert it into a sentence.

although	also	such as
therefore	however	

Mark Twain, creator of colorful characters (6)_____ Tom Sawyer, loved to tell stories. He (7)_____ loved an audience. But did you know he spent hours telling tales to someone who never heard a single word he said? He probably never had a better audience than his special young friend, Helen Keller. Helen was both blind and deaf. (8)_____, she could feel the shapes and movements of his lips and (9)_____ could make out the words. Her enjoyment of his tales was clear. "She interrupted all along and in the right places, with chuckles and bursts of laughter," Twain recalled. He admired Helen's patience and skill in learning to read, write, and speak. (10)_____ Twain was forty-five years older than Helen, they became good friends.

TRANSITIONS: Test 4

Fill in each blank with the appropriate transition word or phrase. Then circle the kind of transition you have used.

1. a. The first apartment that we looked at was dirty, _____ the second one had been recently painted.

   furthermore
   but
   so

   b. The transition shows
   addition.   cause and effect.   contrast.

2. a. Wind whipped the ocean around, _____ huge, rough waves.

   resulting in
   despite
   instead of

   b. The transition signals a relationship of
   contrast.   time.   cause and effect.

3. a. My rabbit, Jack, has definite food preferences. _____, he'll ignore an apple if there are peanuts in his dish.

   Similarly
   For example
   However

   b. The relationship of the second sentence to the first is one of
   illustration.   contrast.   comparison.

4. a. _____ the 1960s, American college students protested against the Vietnam War.

   Like
   Instead of
   During

   b. The transition shows
   comparison.   time.   contrast.

5. a. Jan was happy with the clock radio he won in the contest _____ he would rather have won the portable TV.

   even though
   because
   additionally

   b. The transition signals a(n)
   comparison.   contrast.   addition.

(Continues on next page)

6. a. The river had overflowed onto the road I take to school. _____, I had to drive out of my way to get to my class.

In addition
As a result
Similarly

b. The relationship between the two sentences is one of
addition.   cause and effect.   comparison.

7. a. The great magician Houdini claimed to be extremely strong. _____, he would invite members of the audience to hit him in the stomach with all their strength.

Furthermore
On the other hand
To illustrate

b. The relationship of the second sentence to the first is one of
illustration.   contrast.   addition.

8. a. Oil spills in rivers and lakes cause great problems for wildlife. _____, the oil is a threat to our own water supply.

Moreover
Instead
To illustrate

b. The relationship of the second sentence to the first is one of
addition.   illustration.   contrast.

9. a. A newborn tiger and a newborn domestic cat are _____ in some ways. Both are born with their eyes closed, and both are dependent upon their mother for a long time.

in contrast
similar
next

b. The transition signals
contrast.   time.   comparison.

10. a. Computers can determine how poisonous something is by examining its makeup. _____, computers can predict which part of the body a poison will affect.

Furthermore
However
For example

b. The relationship of the second sentence to the first is one of
contrast.   illustration.   addition.

TRANSITIONS: Test 5

A. This part of the test will check your ability to recognize the relationships (signaled by transitions) within and between sentences. Read each passage and answer the questions that follow.

Passage 1

¹Travel by airplane is safer than travel by car. ²Yet I am still nervous whenever I fly. ³When I get on a plane, I make sure I know where all the safety features are on the plane. ⁴I look for my life raft and the fire extinguishers. ⁵I also look around to spot all of the emergency exits.

1. The relationship of sentence 2 to sentence 1 is one of
   a. illustration.   c. addition.
   b. time.   d. contrast.

2. The relationship of sentence 5 to sentence 4 is one of
   a. cause and effect.   c. illustration.
   b. addition.   d. comparison.

Passage 2

¹McDonald's is the largest fast-food chain in the United States. ²McDonald's can also be found in Mexico, throughout Europe, and even in Russia. ³In fact, the busiest McDonald's in the world is in Moscow. ⁴To illustrate how busy this restaurant is, it serves more than 40,000 customers a day. ⁵In three weeks, this restaurant sells more food than the average McDonald's does in a year.

3. The relationship of sentence 2 to sentence 1 is one of
   a. addition.   c. illustration.
   b. contrast.   d. cause and effect.

4. The relationship expressed by sentence 4 is one of
   a. addition.   c. illustration.
   b. time.   d. contrast.

(Continues on next page)

Passage 3

[1]The world's population grows by 250,000 each day. [2]Most births occur in the poorest parts of the world. [3]For instance, almost 140,000 people are born each day in Asia. [4]An additional 75,000 are born daily in Africa. [5]However, on any one day in North America, Europe and Australia, only 13,000 will be born.

5. The relationship of sentence 3 to sentence 2 is one of
   a. illustration.   c. cause and effect.
   b. contrast.   d. time.

6. The relationship of sentence 5 to sentence 4 is one of
   a. addition.   c. illustration.
   b. comparison.   d. contrast.

B. Fill in each blank with the appropriate transition from the box. Use each transition once.

Note: You may find it helpful to check (✓) each transition as you insert it into a sentence.

as a result	another	although
for example		

(7)_____ environmental news is not usually very good, there are some success stories worth noting. (8)_____, many companies in Tokyo, Japan, are allowing workers to use computers to work from home. (9)_____, there is less pollution from automobiles. Similar success stories are being reported in the U.S. The air quality in Los Angeles has improved greatly in the past twenty years. (10)_____ example is a river in Cleveland that was once so polluted that it routinely caught fire. It has been cleaned up and is no longer a fire hazard.

TRANSITIONS: Test 6

A. This part of the test will check your ability to recognize the relationships (signaled by transitions) within and between sentences. Read each passage and answer the questions that follow.

Passage 1

[1]We may curse honeybees while we are having a picnic, but we should be thankful for them as we eat. [2]Honeybees are responsible for pollinating 60 percent of the fruit and vegetables we eat. [3]For instance, honeybees routinely pollinate apple and orange trees, tomatoes, and carrots. [4]Without them, lettuce might sell for five dollars a head, and fruit would be an occasional luxury.

1. The relationship of the last part of sentence 1 to the first part is one of
   a. time.   c. addition.
   b. cause and effect.   d. contrast.

2. The relationship of sentence 3 to sentence 2 is one of
   a. addition.   c. cause and effect.
   b. illustration.   d. time.

Passage 2

[1]Bicycle riding can be a good way to get exercise. [2]It can also be a pleasant way to see the countryside. [3]Not so pleasant is getting a flat tire miles from home. [4]A new product may change that. [5]An airless tire is now available for biking enthusiasts. [6]Made of polyurethane, it is lightweight and durable. [7]Moreover, it comes with a lifetime guarantee that the tire will never go flat.

3. The relationship of sentence 2 to sentence 1 is one of
   a. addition.   c. cause and effect.
   b. illustration.   d. comparison.

4. The relationship of sentence 7 to sentence 6 is one of
   a. time.   c. addition.
   b. cause and effect.   d. contrast.

(Continues on next page)

Passage 3

¹Some officials in California recently released water from a dam down a river. ²They wanted to improve the environment for wildlife. ³Instead of helping wildlife, however, they harmed it. ⁴Over five thousand fish were killed, including salmon, trout and catfish. ⁵A study revealed that the water which was released carried more sediment and waste than officials had realized.

5. The relationship of sentence 3 to sentence 2 is one of
   a. time.   c. contrast.
   b. addition.   d. comparison.

6. The relationship of the last half of sentence 4 to the first part is one of
   a. addition.   c. illustration.
   b. contrast.   d. time.

B. Fill in each blank with the appropriate transition from the box. Use each transition once.

Note: You may find it helpful to check (✓) each transition as you insert it into a sentence.

in addition	another	however
often		

The Philippine Islands have some of the richest coral reefs in the world. (7)_____, scientists are concerned that fishermen are destroying the reefs. One common practice used to catch a large number of fish is to throw explosives into the water. This kills schools of fish and destroys the reef where they live. (8)_____ practice is used to catch certain fish for use in aquariums overseas. Fishermen throw poison into the water around the reef. The poison stuns the fish, which float to the surface and are easily netted. The poison destroys the reef. (9)_____, it is fatal to the fish, which are poisoned slowly. It (10)_____ takes as long as three months for the fish to die. By that time, the fish are in aquariums of unsuspecting fish collectors who wonder what they did wrong.

PATTERNS OF ORGANIZATION: Test 1

Arrange the groups of scrambled sentences below into logical paragraphs by numbering the sentences in an order that makes sense. (Remember that transitions often help indicate the correct order.) Then circle the letter of the main pattern of organization used.

Group 1

_____ Some strong cleaning products can cause headaches and dizziness.

_____ Therefore it makes sense to use such wholesome products as white vinegar, lemon juice, and baking soda.

_____ That's because they give off poisonous fumes.

Main pattern of organization used:
a. Time order
b. List of items
c. Cause and effect
d. Definition and example

Group 2

_____ One reason is that the garage is often used by salespeople as an office.

_____ Another is that, with no driveway, the lawn looks a lot bigger than it actually is.

_____ If you ever visit a model home, you will notice that it does not have a driveway.

Main pattern of organization used:
a. Time order
b. List of items
c. Comparison and/or contrast
d. Definition and example

Group 3

_____ Then he plotted a way to get even with her.

_____ Finally, he decided it wasn't worth the effort.

_____ When Jennifer told Lenny their relationship was over, he was furious.

Main pattern of organization used:
a. Time order
b. List of items
c. Cause and effect
d. Definition and example

(Continues on next page)

Group 4

_____ If there's more than one such body circling a planet, they are all called moons.

_____ Any natural body circling around a planet is called a moon.

_____ Jupiter, for instance, has twelve moons, the name of the largest being Ganymede.

Main pattern of organization used:
a. Time order
b. Comparison and/or contrast
c. Cause and effect
d. Definition and example

Group 5

_____ Most people have strong memories of what life was like for them in high school.

_____ Some remember high school as a happy, exciting, and carefree time of life.

_____ On the other hand, some people remember only embarrassment, loneliness, and a sad confusion.

Main pattern of organization used:
a. Time order
b. Comparison and/or contrast
c. Cause and effect
d. Definition and example

PATTERNS OF ORGANIZATION: Test 2

Write the letter of the main pattern of organization for each item below. Each pattern is used twice.

a Time order
b List of items
c Comparison and/or contrast
d Cause and effect
e Definition and example

_____ 1. Soon after the movie began, my friend fell asleep. An hour later, he was snoring loudly. When five minutes were left, he woke up suddenly and said, "Did I miss anything?"

_____ 2. Cetaceans (sĭ-tā′shənz) are marine mammals that never leave the water. Included in this group of animals are whales and dolphins.

_____ 3. An ideal apartment will have three features. To begin with, it will be close to school or work. Second, it will be in a safe area. Third, it will have a reasonable price.

_____ 4. When Dee met Mark's parents, she discovered that both were friendly, but his father was much more sociable than his mother.

_____ 5. The reason there are fewer than a hundred panda bears living in the wild is that the bamboo forests which they use for protection and food are dying.

_____ 6. A star is any heavenly body that has continuous nuclear reactions which give off light and heat in all directions. Our sun, for instance, is a star.

_____ 7. Covering a stain that paint won't hide is a simple two-step process. First brush a coat of shellac over the stain. Then, after the shellac dries, repaint the area.

_____ 8. A typical U.S. family saves less than 6 percent of its income. In contrast, the average Japanese family saves more than 15 percent of its income.

(Continues on next page)

_____ 9. My neighbor wants his home entertainment to be "state of the art." He has a satellite disk on his rooftop. In his den there is a large screen projection TV. He also has a hi-fi VCR as well as a CD and laser disk player.

_____ 10. An enormous Arizona cactus is called the "apartment house of the desert" because it provides a home for numerous birds and other animals.

PATTERNS OF ORGANIZATION: Test 3

Read each paragraph below. Then circle the letter of the chief pattern of organization used in the passage.

1. Obsessive-compulsive people have repeated thoughts and behaviors they cannot control. A common example of their mental illness is an extreme fear of germs. A man who once had such a fear said, "After doing a routine thing like opening a textbook, I would wash my hands for fifteen to twenty minutes."

    Main pattern of organization used:
    a. Time order   c. Comparison and/or contrast
    b. List of items   d. Definition and example

2. Motion picture and television director David Lynch is famous for creative, exciting, yet weird works. In addition to his well-known TV series *Twin Peaks*, he created and directed such strange movies as *Dune, Blue Velvet,* and *Wild at Heart.*

    Main pattern of organization used:
    a. List of items   c. Cause and effect
    b. Comparison and/or contrast d. Definition and example

3. There are significant differences between sugar and honey. Not only does honey have a higher sweetening power than sugar, but it also keeps baked goods moist longer than sugar does.

    Main pattern of organization used:
    a. Time order   c. Cause and effect
    b. Comparison and/or contrast d. Definition and example

4. Some people seem to be affected by the short, dark days of winter. The shorter days bring about sadness and depression in them. Also, they become fatigued easily, and they sleep for long periods of time.

    Main pattern of organization used:
    a. Time order   c. Cause and effect
    b. Comparison and/or contrast d. Definition and example

(Continues on next page)

5. What should you do if you buy a used car which has been recalled by the manufacturer but was never taken in for repair? First, make sure the recall was not for a major repair. If it was, you may want to try to get your money back. If you decide to keep the car, your next step is to call the National Highway Traffic Safety Administration for instructions on how to get the needed work done.

Main pattern of organization used:
a. Time order
b. Definition and example
c. Comparison and/or contrast
d. Cause and effect

PATTERNS OF ORGANIZATION: Test 4

Read each paragraph and then circle the letter of the chief pattern of organization used in the passage.

1. Vitamins are substances that are needed in small amounts for normal bodily growth and health. They are found in plant and animal foods. Vitamin C, for instance, is thought to have many roles in the body, such as fighting infection and healing wounds. In addition, studies indicate that vitamin C may be helpful in cancer prevention. Foods that contain significant amounts of vitamin C include strawberries, citrus fruits, and liver.

   Main pattern of organization used:
   a. List of items
   b. Comparison and/or contrast
   c. Definition and example

2. An African-American cavalry unit called Buffalo Soldiers patrolled the American frontier between 1866 and 1944. These horsemen were given their name by Native Americans who came to respect the soldiers' bravery. Buffalo Soldiers rode with Teddy Roosevelt into Cuba in 1898. They chased Mexican bandit Pancho Villa to his homeland in 1916. And they patrolled the U.S.-Mexican border on horseback until 1944. The brigade was disbanded when soldiers were needed for World War II.

   Main pattern of organization used:
   a. Time order
   b. List of items
   c. Comparison and/or contrast

3. In 1912, the Nabisco Biscuit Company introduced three new products that they called "The Trio." One was called Mother Goose. It was a rich-tasting cookie made in the shapes of famous Mother Goose characters. The second new product was the Veronese Biscuit. It was a hard, high-quality biscuit with a detailed design. Both were discontinued within ten years. The third product was a cream filling between two chocolate-flavored wafers. Today it is the top-selling cookie in the United States, with annual sales over five billion. Its name is Oreo.

   Main pattern of organization used:
   a. Time order
   b. List of items
   c. Cause and effect

(Continues on next page)

4. People in small groups are much more likely to cooperate with each other than those in large groups. In small groups, each person feels more responsible for the group's success. In contrast, individuals in large groups feel weak ties to most others in the group, be it a large corporation or a large city. Also, people in small groups are more likely to take no more than their share of available resources. For instance, a few families in a small neighborhood in Washington state took care to conserve water when the water supply got low. However, in large cities, many residents do not voluntarily conserve resources such as water.

Main pattern of organization used:
a. Time order
b. Comparison and/or contrast
c. Definition and example

5. White socks are traditionally worn during sports activities from running to racquetball. The reason goes back to the tragic death of a president's son. When Calvin Coolidge was president, his son died after playing tennis. He accidentally broke his skin as he played, and a dye in his sock entered his bloodstream. Poisons present in the dye are thought to have killed him. Because of the publicity from this tragedy, the public became convinced that only white socks should be worn during athletic events.

Main pattern of organization used:
a. List of items
b. Comparison and/or contrast
c. Cause and effect

PATTERNS OF ORGANIZATION: Test 5

For each paragraph, write the number of the sentence that contains the main idea. Then circle the letter of the chief pattern of organization used in the passage.

1. [1]Driving long distances on vacations can be dangerous unless you follow guidelines prepared by the National Safety Council. [2]First, plan your driving so you avoid fatigue. [3]Don't drive at times you are likely to be tired, and take breaks at regular intervals. [4]Second, make sure your blood is circulating. [5]Stretch from time to time. [6]Push your legs against the floorboard to keep blood moving. [7]Third, keep alert. [8]Keep the car cool. [9]Keep talking with a passenger, or turn on music you don't ordinarily listen to and sing along.

   Sentence with the main idea: _____

   Main pattern of organization used:
   a. List of items
   b. Time order
   c. Comparison and/or contrast

2. [1]A new species of ant was discovered in the office of the president of the World Wildlife Fund. [2]The president, Kathryn Fuller, came into her office one day and found a number of ants in a plant. [3]She did not recognize the ants as any species she had ever seen. [4]She then called an expert, who studied the ants for several months. [5]The expert eventually concluded that such ants had never been seen by scientists before and should be considered a new species.

   Sentence with the main idea: _____

   Main pattern of organization used:
   a. Comparison and/or contrast
   b. Definition and example
   c. Time order

3. [1]During the Middle Ages, people in Europe hated and feared ordinary housecats, which they thought were used by witches to contact demons. [2]Unfortunately, this fear of cats resulted in many more deaths from the terrible illness bubonic plague than otherwise would have occurred. [3]Because of their fear, people drove cats away from their houses and villages. [4]Rats were thus totally free to breed there and spread disease. [5]Millions of people died from the bubonic plague, which was carried by diseased rats. [6]If more cats had been allowed to stay, they could have killed many of these rats.

   (Continues on next page)

Sentence with the main idea: _____

Main pattern of organization used:
a. List of items
b. Cause and effect
c. Comparison and/or contrast

4.   [1]Many former runners have abandoned the aches and pains of jogging for the enjoyment of biking. [2]The question for many is this: which kind of biking should I do? [3]The choice for bikers is between mountain bikes and racing bikes, which differ considerably. [4]Mountain bikes are meant to be used off roads. [5]They are very durable, and they have wide tires, fifteen to twenty-four gears, and straight-across handlebars for upright riding. [6]Racing bikes are meant to be ridden on streets. [7]They are extremely light and built for speed, with comfort less of a concern. [8]They have ten to fourteen gears, very narrow tires, and curved handlebars which are turned down so there is less wind resistance against the rider.

Sentence with the main idea: _____

Main pattern of organization used:
a. Comparison and/or contrast
b. Definition and example
c. Cause and effect

5.   [1]A computer virus is an unwanted program that generally causes a problem of some sort with a computer. [2]One, the Ping-Pong virus, has a ball bouncing on the screen. [3]The ball erases characters from the screen as it bounces. [4]Another example is the Falling-Letter virus, which takes characters from the screen and drops them to the bottom of the monitor. [5]Datacrime is a virus that reformats the computer's disk and adds unwanted material to it. [6]Yet another virus, the Disk Killer, wipes out parts of the computer's hard disk. [7]Before doing so, it provides a message on-screen that the disk will be wiped out if the user turns off the computer.

Sentence with the main idea: _____

Main pattern of organization used:
a. Time order
b. Comparison
c. Definition and example

PATTERNS OF ORGANIZATION: Test 6

For each paragraph, write the number of the sentence that contains the main idea. Then circle the letter of the chief pattern of organization used in the passage.

1. ¹It isn't uncommon for a flight to carry people across several time zones. ²Our systems, however, are used to one time zone. ³Suddenly crossing several of them throws our bodies off their usual rhythm. ⁴The result is jet lag. ⁵Once jet lag strikes, it may take as much as a week or longer for the body's clock to reset itself. ⁶Consequently, we have a week or so of feeling awful, performing poorly, and sleeping poorly. ⁷Thus a single airplane flight can have relatively long-lasting physical effects.

    Sentence with the main idea: _____

    Main pattern of organization used:
    a. List of items
    b. Comparison and/or contrast
    c. Cause and effect

2. ¹Multiple personality is a rare condition in which more than one personality seems present in a single person. ²The distinct personalities appear at different times. ³One famous example of a multiple personality is the case of Maud and Sara K., two personalities that existed in one woman. ⁴Maud walked with a bounce, and Sara moved more calmly. ⁵Maud was excited and happy. ⁶Sara was depressed. ⁷Even their IQ's differed because Sara was an adult and Maud had the mentality of a child.

    Sentence with the main idea: _____

    Main pattern of organization used:
    a. Time order
    b. Cause and effect
    c. Definition and example

3. ¹Americans and the English do not view burial in the same way. ²English churchyards are often maintained in a rather wild state, with plenty of wildflowers and weeds. ³In American cemeteries, the lawns are kept mowed and neatly trimmed. ⁴Also, the English don't try to protect their mourners and coffins from close contact with raw earth. ⁵Americans, on the other hand, cover the dirt near a grave with plastic grass, and they lower the casket onto a protective wooden shell. ⁶Finally, the British accept the fact that the dead and

(Continues on next page)

their caskets will decay. [7]In America, embalming fluid makes the dead look alive, and casket catalogues emphasize that their products will last for years.

Sentence with the main idea: _____

Main pattern of organization used:
a. Time order
b. Comparison and/or contrast
c. Definition and example

4.   [1]Chemical pesticides do a great job of getting rid of pests. [2]However, they may also be a threat to human health. [3]Chemical pesticides can be replaced by various natural pest-control measures. [4]For instance, a natural way to fight garden pests is to introduce other bugs to a garden. [5]Insects such as ladybugs and dragonflies feed on other insects that harm crops. [6]There are also several natural substances that repel insects. [7]For example, citronella oil, which comes from a certain grass, keeps some insects away. [8]Also, some people claim to discourage visits from ants by planting mint around the house.

Sentence with the main idea: _____

Main pattern of organization used:
a. Time order
b. List of items
c. Cause and effect

5.   [1]One of the most celebrated robberies of the century occurred in Great Britain over thirty years ago. [2]In August 1963, fourteen robbers stopped a mail train that was moving from Glasgow, Scotland, to London, England. [3]They made off with over seven million dollars. [4]This started a national search for the criminals. [5]Almost all were caught and sentenced to thirty years in prison. [6]One, Ronald Biggs, escaped in 1965 and made his way to Brazil. [7]When he was discovered there in 1974, British officials requested his return. [8]Brazil refused, and Biggs is still living there.

Sentence with the main idea: _____

Main pattern of organization used:
a. Time order
b. List of items
c. Comparison and/or contrast

INFERENCES: Test 1

After reading each passage, put a check by the **two** inferences that are most firmly based on the given information, logic, and your experience.

1. Very early one Sunday morning, I was awakened by loud, banging noises on one of my walls. I dragged myself out of bed and rang my neighbor's doorbell. "Are you hammering?" I asked in amazement.
   "Why, yes," she replied. "Is the noise coming through?"

   ____ a. The narrator likes to sleep late on Sundays.

   ____ b. The narrator may live in an apartment building.

   ____ c. The narrator and the neighbor do not get along.

   ____ d. The neighbor did not realize how much noise she was making.

2. The Big Wave Surf Shop is located in Redondo Beach, in southern California. On a recent hot, sunny day, its customers were disappointed to find the shop closed. A sign hanging on the door said the store was "Closed Due to Snow."

   ____ a. The owner of the surf shop has no sense of humor.

   ____ b. The surf shop had never been closed before.

   ____ c. The owner of the surf shop is not desperate for business.

   ____ d. The customers expected the surf shop would be open.

3. A Kansas boy's parents read to him while he was still in his mother's womb. Now three years old, the boy can say his ABC's in Greek, can count in Spanish, and has already read over a thousand books.

   ____ a. In all likelihood, one of the boy's parents was Greek and one was Spanish.

   ____ b. The boy knows a lot for his age.

   ____ c. The boy will soon get tired of reading.

   ____ d. The boy's parents feel early childhood education is very important.

(Continues on next page)

4. Eating corn and beans together provides better protein to people than if they ate either one of those foods alone. Now there is a chip on the market made from a blend of corn and beans.

   ____ a. The new chip was recently introduced to the market.

   ____ b. The new chip tastes better to most people than plain old corn chips.

   ____ c. The new chip has higher quality protein than ordinary corn chips.

   ____ d. The new chip is probably too expensive for the average person's budget.

5. Not all plants are safe around children and animals, whose diets are often made up of whatever catches their eye. If you have children or pets and want houseplants, you should look for safe, non-poisonous ones. Safe plants include ficus, rubber plants, ferns, and jade plants.

   ____ a. Some houseplants are dangerous.

   ____ b. Adults would not be harmed by eating any type of plant.

   ____ c. Violet plants are not safe for children and pets.

   ____ d. Children and pets have been known to eat the leaves of house plants.

INFERENCES: Test 2

After reading each passage, put a check by the **two** inferences that are most firmly based on the given information, logic, and your experience.

A. The National Association for the Self-Employed has compiled statistics on people who own their own business. Their figures include these:

- Three times as many men own a business as women.
- The average age at which someone starts a business is 28.
- Small business owners work an average of 52 hours per week, compared with 43.5 hours per week for non-owners.
- 39 percent of small business owners use personal computers.
- 63 percent said the main reason for starting their business was the opportunity to be their own boss.

____ 1. Male-owned businesses tend to succeed more than female-owned businesses.

____ 2. If they want to succeed, most small business owners must work long hours.

____ 3. If you are over 30, it's too late to start your own business.

____ 4. Most business owners prefer making their own decisions to following other people's orders.

____ 5. Self-employment is the best way to gain financial security.

(Continues on next page)

B.   Brumby rocking chairs are perhaps the most famous American rocking chairs ever made. The sturdy, comfortable rockers have been purchased by thousands of people. Even Jimmy Carter ordered five when he was in the White House. Brumby, which started production in 1875, is no longer in business. The chairs are still in demand, but the oak wood needed to make the chair is being exported to other countries. Also, the equipment needed to make the chairs was old and could not be replaced. So, unhappily, the Brumby factory has closed. With it has gone a little piece of America.

___ 6. There are probably only a handful of Brumby rocking chairs being used today.

___ 7. Brumby rocking chairs are still being made outside of America.

___ 8. Existing Brumby rocking chairs are likely to increase in value.

___ 9. If the oak wood were still available, the Brumby company would still be in business.

___ 10. People are sorry that Brumby has gone out of business.

INFERENCES: Test 3

After reading each passage, circle the letter of the answer to each question that is most firmly based on the information given, logic, and your experience.

A.   The job of vice president of the United States is largely ceremonial. The only constitutional duty of a vice president is to preside over the Senate. If the Senate votes on a matter and the outcome is a tie, the vice president casts the deciding vote. Some vice presidents, including Dan Quayle, never cast a vote. John Adams, the first vice president, cast a record twenty-nine votes.

1. We can conclude that
   a. a vice president of the U.S. has relatively little power.
   b. no one wants the job of vice president.
   c. the only thing a vice president does is preside over the Senate.

2. We can also conclude that
   a. the Senate did not want Dan Quayle to vote.
   b. the vice president also can break ties in the House of Representatives.
   c. John Adams was vice president when George Washington was president.

B.   President Calvin Coolidge was known to be a very quiet individual—his nickname was "Silent Cal." His refusal to say more than a few words at a time frustrated more than a few people. One victim of Coolidge's few words was a lady who sat beside him at a dinner party. After chatting gaily with the other people around her, she turned to Coolidge and smiled. "Mr. President," she confided, laughing, "I've made a bet with a friend of mine that I can get you to say more than three words tonight!" Coolidge barely glanced at her. "You lose," he responded.

3. Calvin Coolidge
   a. did not approve of betting.
   b. did not mind being thought of as a man of few words.
   c. had a speech problem.

(Continues on next page)

C. Three friends left a party to drive home. All three of them had been drinking quite a bit, but one swore that he could drive them home slowly and carefully. About halfway home, he realized that a police car had its red light on behind them, and he pulled over. The police officer walked up to him and asked him how fast he thought he was driving. "Uh, fifty-five, maybe sixty?" he answered. The officer shook his head. "You were going an amazing five miles an hour."

4. We can conclude that
   a. the three friends were not at all concerned about the dangers of drinking and driving.
   b. the driver intended to drive slowly and carefully.
   c. the driver had been stopped by police before in his life.

5. We can also conclude that
   a. the police officer had no idea that the driver had been drinking.
   b. the friends will certainly never drink and drive again.
   c. a person's view of reality can be greatly influenced by alcohol.

INFERENCES: Test 4

After reading each passage, circle the letter of the answer to each question that is most firmly based on the information given, logic, and your experience.

A.   In 1865, the state of Nevada issued $1,000 bonds in order to raise revenue. To attract investors, the state offered a very high interest rate of 24 percent. Recently, a couple found an uncashed bond and tried to cash it in. The state declined to pay the amount. In the 100-plus years since the bond was issued, the face value and interest would have amounted to a total of $657 trillion. When the state refused, the couple requested a reduction to $50 million. This was also refused, so the couple took the state to court where a judge ruled that they had waited too long to cash the bond.

1. We can infer that
   a. the couple knew all along that they would never get a cent from the state.
   b. the state of Nevada felt the bond was no longer in effect.
   c. the federal government will have to become involved in this case.

2. We can also infer that
   a. the bond was originally purchased by a relative of one of the couple.
   b. the judge sided with the state for fear of losing his job.
   c. most people who bought the bonds cashed them in years ago.

B.   The majority of advertisements are directed toward the age group with the most money. Marketing in recent years has been aimed at the so-called "yuppies," aged 18–49. Older generations have been ignored. Recent research has some companies rethinking this strategy. Research shows that people are living and working longer than ever before. They have more money than in the past, as well. The U.S. Social Security Administration statistics show that the 50–54 age group had almost the highest median income in the country, second only to the 45–49 age group. In third place was the 55–59 age group.

3. The paragraph implies that
   a. more advertising is likely to be directed at older generations.
   b. advertisers will soon aim very few ads at yuppies.
   c. older generations spend very little of their money.

4. We can conclude that
   a. advertising will become less influential in the future.
   b. government can be a valuable source of information for advertisers.
   c. the income of yuppies is going down.

(Continues on next page)

5. We can conclude from the passage that
    a. advertisers have not benefited from appealing to yuppies.
    b. yuppies are less influenced by ads than older people.
    c. some yuppies are about to become part of the older generation.

INFERENCES: Test 5

After reading each passage, circle the letter of the answer to each question that is most firmly based on the information given, logic, and your experience.

A. In years past, high schools from New York to Oregon had their own newspapers. Papers with nicknames like "The Facts," "The View," and "The Inquirer" were written by students for the student body. Students would read with interest about how their school did in the weekend football game, who was running for homecoming queen, and when various clubs were meeting. Now, however, high school newspapers across the country are quietly going out of existence. There are many reasons. Not enough students are interested in reading the paper. Good writers are getting harder to find. And budget cutbacks at schools have hurt, as well.

1. We can infer that "good writers are getting harder to find" because
    a. school newspapers today have higher writing standards.
    b. no one is looking for good writers.
    c. writing skills have probably declined.

2. We can conclude that budget cutbacks
    a. have hit all areas of school operations equally.
    b. show that school newspapers are not a high priority.
    c. are the most important reason for the high school paper's disappearance.

B. A tropical plant named kenaf (which rhymes with *giraffe*) has been found to be a good raw material for various paper products, including newsprint, paper boxes, and tissues. Similar in appearance to bamboo and sugar cane, kenaf grows to full maturity in five months. (A pine tree requires sixty years to become fully grown.) In addition, kenaf has a tough outer fiber that is almost insect-proof. Thus pesticides are unnecessary. Another plus for kenaf is that it yields two to four times as much paper pulp per acre as southern pine.

3. We can conclude from the passage that
    a. kenaf makes better quality paper than pine trees do.
    b. recycling paper products is not the only way to save trees.
    c. sugar cane has also been used to make paper.

(Continues on next page)

C. Sleep disorder clinics have discovered that some people have to be taught how to sleep. If you are having trouble sleeping, there are several things you can do. First, make your bedroom an inviting, restful place. Colors and fabrics should be soft, and the room should be free of clutter. Second, don't work up until the time you go to bed. Gradually relax. Third, don't exercise before going to bed. Exercise is stimulating, and activities before going to bed should be restful ones. Fourth, don't eat a large meal before bedtime. A small bowl of ice cream or a glass of milk is okay, but a large meal will disrupt sleep.

4. The passage suggests that if you are having trouble sleeping, it would be helpful just before you go to sleep to
   a. listen to quiet classical music.
   b. play a video game.
   c. take a long walk.

5. The passage suggests that if you want to sleep better, your bedroom
   a. should contain nothing more than a bed.
   b. should be painted pink.
   c. should not be the busiest room in your house.

INFERENCES: Test 6

After reading each passage, circle the letter of the best answer to each question, based on the information given, logic, and your experience.

A. The past decade has seen a decline in the number of Americans earning advanced college degrees. Their places have been taken by foreign students. Non-Americans now account for more than 25 percent of the doctorates granted by American universities. In some cases, there are more foreigners than Americans. For instance, at the University of Texas at Austin, there are approximately 350 graduate students in civil engineering. Of these, over 200 come from other countries. Most are sponsored by their governments.

1. The number of foreign students attending American universities suggests that
   a. there are no universities in most foreign countries.
   b. the quality of education in American universities is high.
   c. many foreign students will not graduate because of great language problems.

2. We can infer that the number of doctorates given by American universities to foreigners
   a. is greater in civil engineering than in other fields.
   b. has increased in recent years.
   c. will soon be more than the number given to Americans.

B. The world has many different kinds of forests. There are oak forests in Europe, teakwood forests in Asia, and pine forests in North America. But a United Nations report predicts that in the twenty-first century, the forest of choice will be one of eucalyptus (pronounced yoo'kə-lip'təs) trees. In 1955, approximately 1.4 million acres of eucalyptus were planted around the world. This increased to 10 million acres by 1980 and has increased by 450,000 acres a year since then. In places where the tree can be grown, there are many advantages. Eucalyptus trees are fast-growing. Also, they are excellent sources for timber, firewood, and wood pulp used for paper. Fewer worker-hours are needed for management of eucalyptus than for almost any other tree. In addition, they serve as excellent windbreaks. Finally, a variety of wildlife thrives among eucalyptus.

3. We can infer that eucalyptus trees
   a. are going to replace most other trees in Europe, Asia, and North America.
   b. can be planted anywhere.
   c. have benefits which other trees do not.

(Continues on next page)

353

4. We can infer that eucalyptus trees
   a. are easy to grow in desert regions.
   b. are more resistant to disease than other trees.
   c. require less care than many other trees.

5. We can conclude that
   a. eucalyptus trees are rarely cut down.
   b. many other kinds of trees grow more slowly than eucalyptus trees do.
   c. keeping wildlife away from eucalyptus trees is a problem.

COMBINED SKILLS: Test 1

Read each passage below and then answer the questions that follow.

A. [1]In 1991, a total eclipse of the sun occurred over Mexico, providing scientists with a rare opportunity. [2]The duration of the event was over six minutes. [3]Birds stopped singing. [4]Bees stopped flying. [5]Further, flowers began to close their petals. [6]Grazing animals began to head home. [7]Scientists were able to gather data that they will be studying for years. [8]The next total eclipse in North America will not occur until 2017.

1. In sentence 2, the word *duration* means
    a. fear.
    b. location.
    c. memory.
    d. length of time.

2. The relationship of sentence 5 to sentence 4 is one of
    a. time order.
    b. addition.
    c. illustration.
    d. contrast.

3. We can infer that because of the eclipse,
    a. scientists were frightened.
    b. flowers died.
    c. animals behaved as though it were evening.
    d. birds didn't sing again for days.

4. _____ TRUE OR FALSE? We can infer that there is still much for scientists to learn about eclipses.

5. The main idea of this paragraph is expressed in sentence
    a. 1.
    b. 2.
    c. 6.
    d. 8.

(Continues on next page)

355

B. ¹Fire-walking involves taking five steps over hot coals. ²The traditional belief is that in order to walk over the hot coals, you must condition your mind. ³The theory is that with proper mental fitness, the pain will not be felt. ⁴Yet science has come up with another explanation. ⁵The coals that are used are made of wood. ⁶Though they look hot, they do not conduct heat well. ⁷Thus taking five short steps over the coals is not enough time to get singed toes or blisters on the bottom of the feet.

6. In sentence 2, the word *condition* means
   a. close.
   b. search.
   c. prepare.
   d. notice.

7. According to tradition, the act of fire-walking is
   a. unhealthy.
   b. lengthy.
   c. a religious experience.
   d. a mental challenge.

8. The relationship of sentence 4 to sentence 3 is one of
   a. time.
   b. addition.
   c. comparison.
   d. contrast.

9. We can infer from the passage that
   a. scientists are opposed to fire-walking.
   b. many scientists have tried fire-walking.
   c. walking very slowly over hot coals would probably be painful.
   d. scientists have never really measured the heat on the surface of hot coals.

10. Which of the following statements best expresses the main idea of the paragraph?
    a. Fire-walking is dangerous.
    b. Tradition and science have differing explanations for fire-walking.
    c. Difficult activities can be accomplished with proper mental conditioning.
    d. Traditional beliefs are usually contradicted by science.

COMBINED SKILLS: Test 2

Read each passage below and then answer the questions that follow.

A. [1]The Worm Concern is an unusual recycling business that is benefiting the environment in various ways. [2]The business takes in refuse such as lawn clippings, tree trimmings, table scraps, and manure. [3]All of this is then fed to six acres of common earthworms. [4]The worms convert the garbage into an inexpensive rich fertilizer. [5]This organic recycling has cut down on the amount of trash dumped into landfills. [6]Also, it has provided a first-class soil for lawns and gardens.

1. In sentence 4, the word *convert* means
   a. change.
   b. put.
   c. carry.
   d. permit.

2. According to the paragraph, organic recycling
   a. is expensive.
   b. results in more room in landfills.
   c. requires chemicals.
   d. is a nonprofit activity.

3. The relationship between sentences 2 and 3 is one of
   a. time.
   b. addition.
   c. comparison.
   d. contrast.

4. We might conclude from the paragraph that the Worm Concern
   a. is the best organic recycling company.
   b. is making its owners very rich.
   c. produces the world's healthiest worms.
   d. is supported by environmental groups.

5. The main idea of this paragraph is best expressed in sentence
   a. 1.
   b. 2.
   c. 5.
   d. 6.

(Continues on next page)

B. ¹The odor of food draws bears. ²As a result, bears are often found around campsites. ³Fish and Game officials have suggestions on what to do and not to do if you see a bear. ⁴First of all, they suggest that if the bear has not sensed your presence, back away downwind. ⁵Do not run, as the bear is likely to give chase. ⁶If the bear sees you, stand up and raise your arms, so that you look as large as you can. ⁷Don't crouch down thinking the bear will avoid you if you appear small. ⁸If the bear charges, try yelling and throwing rocks at the bear. ⁹Don't run away even then—the bear is faster than you. ¹⁰If the animal attacks you, cover your head and neck and bring your legs up into your chest. ¹¹Don't lie flat on the ground looking as if you are dead. ¹²The bear is not likely to fall for this.

6. According to the paragraph, if a bear sees you, you should
    a. run as fast as you can.
    b. make yourself look as large as possible.
    c. play dead.
    d. try to get downwind of the animal.

7. The relationship between sentences 1 and 2 is one of
    a. time.
    b. comparison.
    c. illustration.
    d. cause and effect.

8. The main pattern of organization of this paragraph is
    a. list of items.
    b. comparison.
    c. contrast.
    d. definition and example.

9. We can conclude from this paragraph that
    a. the population of bears is rising.
    b. you are always safe when downwind from a bear.
    c. yelling and throwing rocks has scared bears away in the past.
    d. people meet bears only around campsites.

10. The main idea of this paragraph is expressed in sentence
    a. 1.
    b. 2.
    c. 3.
    d. 10.

COMBINED SKILLS: Test 3

Read each passage below and then answer the questions that follow.

A.   [1]A drought can be disastrous to farmers. [2]If the crops don't get enough water, then the plants fail to grow properly, leading to little or no income for the farmers. [3]Some farmers have found crops that are drought-resistant. [4]One is canola, a plant whose oil is being touted as a healthy cooking oil. [5]Another plant requiring much less water than most plants is buffalo gourd. [6]It needs to be planted only once and continues to produce plants yearly. [7]Lubricating oil and fuel can be made from buffalo gourd. [8]Kenaf, another hearty grower, can be used in the production of newspapers. [9]It prevents newsprint from coming off on readers' hands. [10]Several drought-resistant plants, then, hold special promise for farmers.

1. In sentence 4, the word *touted* means
   a. promoted.
   b. replaced.
   c. grown.
   d. rejected.

2. Buffalo gourd is a source of
   a. a healthy cooking oil.
   b. lubricating oil.
   c. a special kind of newsprint.
   d. water.

3. Sentence 2 expresses relationships of
   a. time.
   b. comparison and/or contrast.
   c. illustration.
   d. cause and effect.

4. The main pattern of organization of this paragraph is
   a. time order.
   b. list of items.
   c. contrast.
   d. definition and example.

5. The main idea of this paragraph is expressed in sentence
   a. 1.
   b. 2.
   c. 7.
   d. 10.

(Continues on next page)

B.   ¹In ice hockey, skaters using special sticks try to knock a hard rubber disk called a "puck" into a net that is guarded by a player called a goalie. ²Goalies wear helmets and masks to protect them from being hurt if they are hit by a puck. ³They began to wear such protective gear after Bobby Hull started playing in the National Hockey League. ⁴Hull had a shot that put fear into goalies. ⁵It was clocked at a hundred miles per hour. ⁶While the shot terrorized everyone around Hull, he said that once he made a shot that scared even him. ⁷That time, Hull wound up and slapped the puck, which took off toward the goalie and then rose. ⁸The goalie tried to get out of the way, but could not. ⁹As he tried to move, the puck hit him on the side of the face and then ripped into his ear. ¹⁰The ear was severed and so had to be sewn back on. ¹¹From then on, that goalie began wearing a facemask whenever his team played against Hull. ¹²Other goalies followed, and eventually all goalies were wearing helmets and masks.

6. In sentence 10, the word *severed* means
   a. bleeding.
   b. struck hard.
   c. missed.
   d. cut off.

7. According to the paragraph, goalies did not wear helmets and masks
   a. until after Bobby Hull came into the league.
   b. until the league required it.
   c. unless Bobby Hull was playing.
   d. because they were not allowed to.

8. The relationship of sentence 11 to sentence 10 is one of
   a. time.
   b. contrast.
   c. comparison.
   d. illustration.

9. We can infer from this paragraph that
   a. hockey is the most dangerous sport.
   b. Bobby Hull had a permanent effect on the game of ice hockey.
   c. today's players shoot faster and harder than Bobby Hull did.
   d. goalies let in fewer goals once they began wearing protective gear.

10. Which statement best expresses the main idea of this paragraph?
   a. A National Hockey League goalie once had his ear cut off by a puck.
   b. Unusual events often change the way a game is played.
   c. One of Bobby Hull's shots led to goalies wearing helmets and masks.
   d. Bobby Hull's shots put terror into the hearts of National Hockey League goalies.

COMBINED SKILLS: Test 4

Read each passage below and then answer the questions that follow.

A. [1]A Bowling Green University poll surveyed young men and women to find out what they considered romantic. [2]The survey, which listed the top ten activities for men and women, found some similarities and some differences. [3]Kissing, cuddling, hugging, and taking walks were favored by both men and women. [4]Both also chose sending or receiving flowers, candle-lit dinners, and sending or receiving cards or love letters. [5]Saying "I love you," getting surprise gifts, and slow dancing rounded out the women's list, but were not on the men's list. [6]On the other hand, sitting by the fireplace, holding hands, and making love were found on the men's list but not on the women's.

1. According to the paragraph,
   a. hugging was on the women's list, but not the men's.
   b. making love was on both lists.
   c. slow dancing was on the women's list, but not the men's.
   d. taking walks was on the women's list, but not the men's.

2. The relationship between sentences 5 and 6 is one of
   a. time.
   b. comparison.
   c. cause and effect.
   d. contrast.

3. The main pattern of organization of this paragraph is
   a. time order.
   b. comparison and/or contrast.
   c. cause and effect.
   d. definition and example.

4. We might infer from this paragraph that
   a. pleasing a man is expensive.
   b. men have a lot to learn if they want to please women.
   c. men and women like many of the same romantic activities.
   d. there are really no differences in men's and women's views of romance.

5. Which statement best expresses the main idea of this paragraph?
   a. A survey found that there are more similarities than differences in what men and women find romantic.
   b. One survey shows how differently men and women think about romance.
   c. Young men and women agree and disagree about a variety of things, including romance.
   d. Women have a better understanding of what is romantic than men.

(Continues on next page)

B. ¹How can you tell if someone is lying? ²The polygraph test is designed to be a simple way to prove if someone is lying or telling the truth. ³The test involves a machine that is hooked up to a person with the use of wires and straps. ⁴Questions are asked, and bodily responses are recorded. ⁵Usually, no more than ten questions are asked. ⁶Two or three of the questions are pointed, as in "Did you steal the picture?" ⁷The remaining questions may not seem important, but they help the questioner to determine the veracity of the subject. ⁸Supporters of polygraph tests claim that they have a 95 percent accuracy rating. ⁹However, opponents of polygraph tests dispute this. ¹⁰They say that a good liar and anyone accustomed to taking the test can beat one, thus making the tests useless.

6. In sentence 8, the word *veracity* means
   a. confusion.
   b. age.
   c. honesty.
   d. interests.

7. According to the paragraph, during a polygraph test
   a. no more than ten questions are ever asked.
   b. wires and straps are moved around on the subject's body.
   c. a person used to taking polygraph tests will finish more quickly than someone unaccustomed to the tests.
   d. some physical responses of the person taking the test are recorded.

8. The relationship between sentences 8 and 9 is one of
   a. time.
   b. contrast.
   c. comparison.
   d. illustration.

9. We might conclude from this paragraph that
   a. polygraph tests cannot be improved.
   b. often as few as two questions are asked on polygraph tests.
   c. some people can "fool" polygraph tests regularly.
   d. there are more supporters of polygraph tests than opponents.

10. Which sentence best expresses the main idea of this paragraph?
    a. The polygraph is a machine used as a lie detector.
    b. People who operate polygraph tests must be very skilled in the operation of the machine and in asking questions.
    c. An important part of a polygraph test is a series of questions intended to help the questioner discover dishonesty.
    d. There is disagreement over the accuracy of the polygraph test, which is designed to sense when people are lying.

COMBINED SKILLS: Test 5

Read each passage below and then answer the questions that follow.

A. [1]The Food and Drug Administration recently opened a new division called the Office of Criminal Investigations. [2]The office was set up to investigate consumer hoaxes. [3]The first task for the office was to investigate claims by people who said they found syringes in cans of Pepsi-Cola. [4]One hundred investigators were used to try to substantiate the truth about hundreds of reports nationwide. [5]The investigators, being experienced, used techniques that would get fast results. [6]In most cases, people admitted within two days that their claims were untrue. [7]Not one of the claims about cans of Pepsi has been proven true. [8]Moreover, over forty of those who made claims have been arrested for trying to cheat the company.

1. In sentence 4, the word *substantiate* means
    a. hide.
    b. prove.
    c. delay.
    d. read about.

2. The Office of Criminal Investigations
    a. found that few claims in the Pepsi-Cola fraud case were true.
    b. has been paid for by the Pepsi-Cola company.
    c. had as its first case a Pepsi-Cola investigation.
    d. was recently transferred to the Food and Drug Administration.

3. The relationship of sentence 8 to the two sentences before it is one of
    a. time.
    b. addition.
    c. contrast.
    d. illustration.

4. The Pepsi case suggests that
    a. there will be no consumer cheating in the future in this country.
    b. the Pepsi-Cola company itself should be investigated.
    c. the Office of Criminal Investigations will be a highly effective agency.
    d. most government agencies are highly effective.

5. Which statement best expresses the main idea of this paragraph?
    a. A new federal division demonstrated great skill in its very first case.
    b. There are many divisions within the Food and Drug Administration.
    c. In the Pepsi-Cola investigation, no consumers told the truth.
    d. It took the most experienced investigators in the government to solve a difficult case.

(Continues on next page)

B.   [1]Two of America's most beloved presidents were assassinated—Abraham Lincoln and John F. Kennedy. [2]There are a number of striking coincidences in President Lincoln's and President Kennedy's lives. [3]Lincoln was elected president in 1860, one hundred years before Kennedy was elected president. [4]Both had vice presidents named Johnson: Andrew Johnson was Lincoln's vice president, and Lyndon Johnson was Kennedy's. [5]Both Johnsons were Southern Democrats who had served in the U.S. Senate. [6]Andrew Johnson was born in 1808, and Lyndon Johnson was born in 1908. [7]Furthermore, Lincoln and Kennedy were both advocates of civil rights and racial equality. [8]Both were shot in the head, both on a Friday and in the presence of their wives. [9]John Wilkes Booth, Lincoln's killer, was born in 1839, a hundred years before Kennedy's killer, Lee Harvey Oswald, was born. [10]Both assassins were themselves killed before they could be brought to justice.

6. In sentence 7, the word *advocates* means
   a. victims.
   b. critics.
   c. supporters.
   d. historians.

7. According to the paragraph, Lincoln and Kennedy
   a. were both born in Illinois.
   b. had the same birthday.
   c. had vice presidents who had served in the Senate.
   d. were both Southerners.

8. The main pattern of organization of this paragraph is
   a. time order.
   b. comparison.
   c. contrast.
   d. cause and effect.

9. We can conclude from this paragraph that
   a. both Lincoln and Kennedy were killed because of their interest in civil rights.
   b. Andrew Johnson and Lyndon Johnson came from the same Southern state.
   c. John Kennedy was elected President in 1960.
   d. Booth and Oswald were both killed by police officers.

10. The main idea of this paragraph is expressed in sentence
    a. 1.
    b. 2.
    c. 3.
    d. 10.

COMBINED SKILLS: Test 6

Read each passage below and then answer the questions that follow.

A. ¹San Francisco Bay isn't what it used to be. ²Sailing ships from around the world have brought with them diverse sea animals. ³These different organisms have changed the population of the bay. ⁴For instance, New Zealand slugs with no natural enemies have eliminated the oysters once plentiful in the bay. ⁵Russian jellyfish are eating microscopic organisms that native fish eat. ⁶Green crabs from the Atlantic Ocean were brought in by a company that had packaged lobsters in seaweed. ⁷The crabs hid in the seaweed and began multiplying when the seaweed was thrown into the bay. ⁸Scientists report that very few original inhabitants remain in the bay.

1. In sentence 2, the word *diverse* means
   a. varied.
   b. local.
   c. single.
   d. dead.

2. New Zealand slugs
   a. are eaten by fish.
   b. hide in seaweed.
   c. have no natural enemies.
   d. are original inhabitants of the bay.

3. The relationship of sentence 4 to sentence 3 is one of
   a. addition.
   b. time.
   c. contrast.
   d. illustration.

4. The author implies that
   a. the changes in San Francisco Bay are all beneficial to humans.
   b. people do not eat green crabs.
   c. nobody will miss the oysters once found in the bay.
   d. Russian jellyfish compete with native fish for some food.

5. Which of the following best expresses the main idea of this paragraph?
   a. San Francisco Bay has an unusual mixture of sea animals.
   b. Organisms from around the world have changed the population of San Francisco Bay.
   c. The original inhabitants of San Francisco Bay have chosen to leave it.
   d. Creatures with no natural enemies have taken over San Francisco Bay and will soon spread to other locations.

(Continues on next page)

B.   [1]Air travel today is made possible by a powerful and efficient engine developed over fifty years ago. [2]In 1939, the jet engine was developed simultaneously by two inventors who had never met or spoken to each other. [3]Hans von Ohain was a German inventor. [4]His counterpart was a British citizen named Frank Whittle. [5]Though each had thought up the same invention, the lives of these men took different routes. [6]In Germany, Hans von Ohain was able to continue his work with government support. [7]He convinced Adolf Hitler that World War II would be won if he could perfect a quiet turbine engine that would make planes fly faster. [8]Von Ohain's progress was slowed as Germany began to lose the war, and Germany never used the jet engine. [9]In contrast, Frank Whittle's government responded less positively. [10]Whittle was unable to convince the British government that the jet engine he developed would revolutionize flying. [11]Nevertheless, he continued to work on the engine throughout the war. [12]Once the war ended, Whittle found buyers for his invention.

6. In sentence 2, the word *simultaneously* means
    a. in partnership.
    b. in different years.
    c. at the same time.
    d. with no success.

7. In sentence 4, the word *counterpart* means
    a. someone with a similar role.
    b. a friend.
    c. coworker.
    d. an enemy.

8. According to the paragraph, Frank Whittle
    a. knew of the work being done by Hans von Ohain.
    b. was not liked by the British government.
    c. kept working on the jet engine throughout World War II.
    d. was tempted to move from Britain to Germany.

9. We can infer from this paragraph that
    a. the jet engine is the first invention created at the same time by two people.
    b. Adolf Hitler wanted to have Frank Whittle work with Hans von Ohain in developing the jet engine.
    c. Germany may have had a major advantage in the war had von Ohain been able to perfect the jet engine.
    d. neither von Ohain nor Whittle ever made much money from his invention.

10. Which statement best expresses the main idea of this paragraph?
    a. Due to its inability to develop a jet engine, Germany lost World War II.
    b. The two inventors of the jet engine had different career paths.
    c. The jet engine is an invention that has changed the world.
    d. It usually takes many years for inventions to become accepted by the world.

Part III

TEN READING SELECTIONS

1

Life Over Death
Bill Broderick

Preview

When the author saw a cat lying in the middle of the road, he stopped his car. All he expected to do was to move a dead animal off the road. When he found that the cat was still alive, his day became a complicated one. But the trouble he went through was worth it. The chance to save a life doesn't come along every day.

Words to Watch

grimaced (2): made a twisted face
immobile (2): not moving
ligament (5): a band of tissue which connects bones or supports organs
tendon (5): a tissue which connects muscles to bones and other parts of the body
good Samaritan (6): someone who helps others unselfishly
resignation (9): acceptance without resistance
dejected (11): depressed
pathetic (11): pitiful

My reaction was as it always is when I see an animal lying in the roadway. My heart sank. And a lump formed in my throat at the thought of a life unfulfilled. I then resolved to move him off the road, to ensure that one of God's creations does not become a permanent part of the pavement. Some might ask what difference it makes. If it's already dead, why not just leave it there? My answer is that I believe in death with dignity, for people and for animals alike. 1

So I pulled my car over to the side of the road and walked back to
where the cat lay motionless. Two cars passed over him, managing to
avoid running him over. With no other cars in sight, I made my way to
the lifeless form just as a jogger went by. The jogger grimaced° at the
sight of the immobile° cat, blood dripping from his mouth. "How'd it
happen?" he asked. I replied that I didn't know; he probably got hit by
some careless driver. I just wanted to get him off the road. I reached
down for the cat and got the surprise of my life. The little creature
lifted his head ever so slightly and uttered a pitiful, unforgettable little
"meow." He was still alive.

What was I going to do now? I was already late for work. All I
had intended to do was move the cat off the road. I didn't need this. But
I knew I had no choice. I sighed deeply, then reached down and
carefully cradled the cat in my hands. I asked the jogger to open my car
trunk and remove the things from a small box. Then I gently placed the
cat in the box. He was in shock, so he probably could not feel the pain
from his obvious injuries. "Kinda funny lookin', isn't he?" asked the
jogger. I was annoyed by his question, but I had to admit that he was
right. This cat looked peculiar. Not ugly, mind you. But he seemed to
have a comical look on his face, even at such a dreadful time.

"What are you gonna do with him?" the jogger asked. I told him I
would take the cat to the local vet and let him decide what to do.

The vet was only five minutes away. My wife and I had been
bringing our animals to him for several years, and I knew I could rely
on him to do what was best for the cat. I brought the cat into the
reception room and placed it on the counter. As this was an emergency,
the vet was summoned right away. He examined the cat thoroughly,
listing the injuries for his assistant to write down. "Broken jaw, that'll
have to be set. Two teeth broken. A couple more loose. Possible
internal injuries, but they don't look too bad. Uh-oh. This doesn't look
good. He doesn't appear to have any movement in his right front leg.
Possible break, definite ligament° and tendon° damage."

The vet completed his examination, then looked at me and asked
what I wanted to do. I knew what he meant. Did I want to have the cat
"put to sleep"? I became uneasy. I clumsily explained that I was hoping
to get advice from him on what to do. Fair enough. The jaw would have
to be wired shut for six weeks, and the cat would have to wear a cast on
its leg for three months. There was no way of knowing if the damage to
the leg was permanent. He could have the cast removed and still not be
able to use the leg. The cost of all the surgery would be high, but I would
get a 50 percent "good Samaritan°" discount if I went ahead with it.

Now I was really at a loss. If I went ahead with the surgery, I'd be
paying for a cat which wasn't mine, whose owner I'd probably never

find, and who might end up with the use of only three legs. And on top of it, this was one of the funniest-looking cats ever born. Black and white, spotted where it shouldn't be, kinked tail, and a silly half-smile on its face. I chuckled at that and the entire situation.

"What do you want to do, Bill?" asked the vet.   8

I shrugged my shoulders in resignation°. "Dan, I'll choose life   9
over death every time. Let's give it our best shot."

I called back later in the day and learned that the surgery had been   10
successful. "You can pick up your cat tomorrow morning," I was told.
My cat. I started to say that he was not my cat, but I knew otherwise.

The next morning, my wife and I drove to the vet and picked up   11
the cat. He looked ghastly. His jaw was now bandaged, and a cast
covered one leg entirely and wrapped around his midsection. We were
dejected°. But, as we drove him home, we began thinking that perhaps
this cat was not as pathetic° as he looked. As frightened as he must have
been, as much pain as he must have felt, he sat calmly in my wife's lap.
He purred and stared out the window with his curious half-smile.

When we got home, we introduced him to our two Siamese cats,   12
who stared in disbelief at this strange creature. They sensed it might be
a cat, but they had never seen one like this. It took him very little time
to get used to his new surroundings. It took him longer to get used to
the cast, which made even walking a chore. Surely he must have been
embarrassed. After all, an animal normally able to glide around quietly
should not make a resounding thump every time he moves.

In due time, the cast came off. To our relief, Pokey, as we now   13
called him, had about 90 percent mobility in the leg. He got around okay,
but he limped whenever he tried to move any faster than a slow walk.

All this occurred four years ago. Pokey is still with us today. In   14
fact, he has become our most beloved cat. Because of his injury, he is
strictly an indoor cat. This does not seem to bother him at all. It is hard
to believe that any cat has ever enjoyed himself more. Maybe it's
because he had been slowed after being hit by a car, or perhaps he just
has a special individuality. He is never bored. At times he will race
around the house like he is leading the Indy 500. Or he'll leap into the
air at an imaginary foe. Or he'll purr loudly at the foot of our bed,
staring into space with that silly grin on his face. And he couldn't care
less that he still looks funny.

It would have been easy to let Pokey lie in the middle of the road.   15
And it would have been just as simple to have the vet put him to sleep.
But when I think of all the pleasure this cat has given us, and of how
much fun he has living with us, I know the right decision was made.
And I'd do it again in a second. I'll take life over death every time.

VOCABULARY QUESTIONS

A. Use context clues to help you decide on the best definition for each italicized word. Then circle the letter of each choice.

1. The word *resolved* in "I then resolved to move him off the road, to ensure that one of God's creations does not become a permanent part of the pavement" (paragraph 1) means
   a. forgot.
   b. hid.
   c. decided.
   d. drove.

2. The word *summoned* in "As this was an emergency, the vet was summoned right away. He examined the cat thoroughly" (paragraph 5) means
   a. informed.
   b. called for.
   c. telephoned.
   d. thought of.

3. The word *ghastly* in "He looked ghastly. His jaw was now bandaged, and a cast covered one leg entirely" (paragraph 11) means
   a. clever.
   b. appealing.
   c. terrible.
   d. marvelous.

4. The word *disbelief* in "our two Siamese cats . . . stared in disbelief at this strange creature. They sensed it might be a cat, but they had never seen one like this" (paragraph 12) means
   a. uncertainty.
   b. time.
   c. pleasure.
   d. hatred.

5. The word *resounding* in "After all, an animal normally able to glide around quietly should not make a resounding thump every time he moves" (paragraph 12) means
   a. soft.
   b. brave.
   c. relaxed.
   d. loud.

B. Below are words, or forms of words, from "Words to Watch." Write in the one that best completes each sentence.

dejected	good Samaritan	grimace
immobile	tendon	

6. TV wrestling may be fake, but when the wrestlers are thrown, they appear to _____ because of real pain.

7. Veronica was _____ for days when she learned she hadn't been accepted at the college her best friend was attending.

8. A sore _____ in the leg can keep a runner from finishing a race.

9. When the doctor stopped his car to help an accident victim, he was just being a _____, so everyone was surprised when the victim sued him.

10. The woman wearing a gown in the department store window was so _____ that people thought she was a display dummy.

READING COMPREHENSION QUESTIONS

Central Point and Main Ideas

1. Which sentence best expresses the central point of the selection?
   a. People and animals should be allowed to die with dignity.
   b. Every life is valuable.
   c. Cats make great pets.
   d. Pokey is strictly an indoor cat because of his injury.

2. Which sentence best expresses the main idea of paragraphs 3 and 4?
   a. The author didn't know what to do.
   b. The author was willing to take responsibility for the cat.
   c. The author was annoyed at the jogger's questions.
   d. The cat was funny-looking.

3. Which sentence best expresses the main idea of paragraph 14?
   a. Pokey enjoys life a great deal now.
   b. Pokey sometimes leaps into the air at imaginary enemies.
   c. Pokey must spend the rest of his life indoors.
   d. Pokey was injured four years ago.

Supporting Details

4. The author
   a. saw a car hit the cat.
   b. was very surprised that the cat was still alive.
   c. was surprised that the jogger came by.
   d. thought that the cat was ugly.

5. The author
   a. had heard about the vet.
   b looked for the nearest vet.
   c. knew and trusted the vet.
   d. drove for hours till he found a vet.

Transitions

6. The transition word *then* in the sentence below signals
   a. an example.
   b. time.
   c. comparison.
   d. contrast.

   I sighed deeply, then reached down and carefully cradled the cat in my hands. (Paragraph 3)

7. The second sentence below begins with a transition that shows
   a. addition.
   b. contrast.
   c. an example.
   d. cause and effect.

   He looked ghastly. . . . But, as we drove him home, we began thinking that perhaps this cat was not as pathetic as he looked. (Paragraph 11)

Patterns of Organization

8. The pattern of organization of paragraph 2 is
   a. time order.
   b. list of items.
   c. comparison and/or contrast.
   d. definition and example.

Inferences

9. The author implies that he
   a. tried very hard to find the cat's owner.
   b. often removes cats and dogs from roadways.
   c. has always had pets at home.
   d. has a great respect for all living things.

10. From the selection, we can conclude that
    a. Pokey is less friendly than many other cats.
    b. Pokey was probably named for his slow walk after the surgery.
    c. Pokey was very young when he was hurt.
    d. all vets give discounts to "good Samaritans."

MAPPING ACTIVITY

This selection is organized by time: first one thing happened; then another; after that, another; and so on. The major events are scrambled in the list below. Write the letters of the events in their correct order in the diagram below.

A. The author chooses surgery for the cat.
B. The cat is taken to the author's home to recover.
C. The cat is taken to the vet, who offers the choice of putting the animal to sleep or doing expensive surgery.
D. The cat recovers and stays on as a happy and welcome household pet.
E. A very badly injured cat is found.

Central point: A decision in favor of life is always best, as Pokey's recovery and rich life make clear.

DISCUSSION QUESTIONS

1. In the first paragraph, the author uses the expression "death with dignity." What does he mean?

2. Can and should something be done to make the world a better place for hurt and homeless creatures like Pokey? Explain your answer.

WRITING ACTIVITIES

1. Write a paragraph about an animal that has played a role in your life. First introduce the animal, and then explain what it was like or what it meant to you. Include examples to make clear any qualities you mention. For instance, if you write that the animal was clever, describe one or two events which are good examples of that cleverness.

2. The author felt he had to help the injured cat because he "had no choice." Write a letter to Broderick describing a time you also did something because you felt it was the only right thing to do. Describe the situation and explain your decision. An example of a topic sentence for this assignment is: "When my sister lost her job, I had no choice—I had to invite her and her children to live with me for a while."

Check Your Performance   **LIFE OVER DEATH**

Skill	Number Right	Points	Total
VOCABULARY			
Vocabulary in Context (5 items)	_____	x 10 =	_____
Words to Watch (5 items)	_____	x 10 =	_____
		SCORE =	_____%
COMPREHENSION			
Central Point and Main Ideas (3 items)	_____	x 7 =	_____
Supporting Details (2 items)	_____	x 7 =	_____
Transitions (2 items)	_____	x 7 =	_____
Patterns of Organization (1 item)	_____	x 7 =	_____
Inferences (2 items)	_____	x 7 =	_____
Mapping (5 items)	_____	x 6 =	_____
		SCORE =	_____%

FINAL SCORES: Vocabulary _____%   **Comprehension** _____%

Enter your final scores into the reading performance chart on the inside back cover.

2

Cipher in the Snow
Jean Mizer Todhunter

Preview

In every school, there are some students whom nobody really knows. We may be aware of their names but little else about them. No one seems to really care about who they are. This selection looks at one such student, who led a short, unhappy life. The question raised is whether the people around him could have made his life a better one.

Words to Watch

cipher (title): a person or thing of no importance
lurched (1): staggered
blurted out (11): said suddenly
bleakly (14): gloomily
peaked (17): thin and tired
veiled (17): hidden
resolve (20): determination

> On most snowy mornings on my way to the high school where I 1 teach, I drive behind the school bus. I was trailing the bus on one biting cold February morning when it veered and stopped short at the town hotel. It had no business doing this, and I was annoyed as I had to bring my car to an unexpected stop. A boy lurched° out of the bus, reeled, stumbled, and collapsed on the snowbank at the curb. The bus driver and I reached him at the same moment. His thin, hollow face was white even against the snow.
>
> "He's dead," the driver whispered. 2

It didn't register for a minute. I glanced quickly at the scared 3
young faces staring down at us from the school bus. "A doctor! Quick!
I'll phone from the hotel . . ."

"No use. I tell you he's dead." The driver looked down at the 4
boy's still form. "He never even said he felt bad," he muttered, "just
tapped me on the shoulder and said, real quiet, 'I'm sorry. I have to get
off at the hotel.' That's all. Polite and apologizing like."

At school the giggling, shuffling morning noise quieted as the 5
news went down the halls. I passed a huddle of girls. "Who was it? Who
dropped dead on the way to school?" I heard one of them half whisper.

"Don't know his name; some kid from Milford Corners," was the 6
reply.

It was like that in the faculty room and the principal's office. "I'd 7
appreciate your going out to tell the parents," the principal told me.
"They haven't a phone, and anyway, somebody from school should go
there in person. I'll cover your classes."

"Why me?" I asked. "Wouldn't it be better if you did it?" 8

"I didn't know the boy," the principal admitted levelly. "And in 9
last year's sophomore personalities column I noted that you were listed
as his favorite teacher."

I drove through the snow and cold down the bad canyon road to 10
the Evans place and thought about the boy, Cliff Evans. His favorite
teacher! Why, he hasn't spoken two words to me in two years! I could
see him in my mind's eye all right, sitting back there in the last seat in
my afternoon literature class. He came in the room by himself and left
by himself. "Cliff Evans," I muttered to myself, "a boy who never
talked." I thought a minute. "A boy who never smiled. I never saw him
smile once."

The big ranch kitchen was clean and warm. I blurted out° my 11
news somehow. Mrs. Evans reached blindly for a chair. "He never
said anything about bein' ailing."

His stepfather snorted. "He ain't said nothin' about anything 12
since I moved in here."

Mrs. Evans got up, pushed a pan to the back of the stove, and 13
began to untie her apron. "Now hold on," her husband snapped. "I got
to have breakfast before I go to town. Nothin' we can do now anyway.
If Cliff hadn't been so dumb, he'd have told us he didn't feel good."

After school I sat in the office and stared bleakly° at the records 14
spread out before me. I was to close the boy's file and write his
obituary for the school paper. The almost bare sheets mocked the effort.
"Cliff Evans, white, never legally adopted by stepfather, five half
brothers and sisters." These meager strands of information and the list
of D grades were about all the records had to offer.

Cliff Evans had silently come in the school door in the mornings 15
and gone out of the school door in the evenings, and that was all. He
had never belonged to a club. He had never played on a team. He had
never held an office. As far as I could tell, he had never done one
happy, noisy kid thing. He had never been anybody at all.

How do you go about making a boy into a zero? The grade school 16
records showed me much of the answer. The first and second grade
teachers' annotations read "sweet, shy child"; "timid but eager." Then
the third grade note had opened the attack. Some teacher had written in
a good, firm hand, "Cliff won't talk. Uncooperative. Slow learner." The
other academic sheet had followed with "dull"; "slow-witted"; "low
IQ." They became correct. The boy's IQ score in the ninth grade was
listed at 83. But his IQ in the third grade had been 106. The score
didn't go under 100 until the seventh grade. Even timid, sweet children
have resilience. It takes time to break them.

I stomped to the typewriter and wrote a savage report pointing out 17
what education had done to Cliff Evans. I slapped a copy on the
principal's desk and another in the sad, dog-eared file; slammed the
file; and crashed the office door shut as I left for home. But I didn't feel
much better. A little boy kept walking after me, a boy with a peaked°
face, a skinny body in faded jeans, and big eyes that had searched for a
long time and then had become veiled°.

I could guess how many times he'd been chosen last to be on a 18
team, how many whispered child conversations had excluded him. I
could see the faces and hear the voices that said over and over, "You're
dumb. You're dumb. You're just a nothing, Cliff Evans."

A child is a believing creature. Cliff undoubtedly believed them. 19
Suddenly it seemed clear to me: When finally there was nothing left at
all for Cliff Evans, he collapsed on a snowbank and went away. The
doctor might list "heart failure" as the cause of death, but that wouldn't
change my mind.

We couldn't find ten students in the school who had known Cliff 20
well enough to attend the funeral as his friends. So the student body
officers and a committee from the junior class went as a group to the
church, looking politely sad. I attended the service with them and sat
through it with a lump of cold lead in my chest and a big resolve°
growing in me.

I've never forgotten Cliff Evans or that resolve. He has been my 21
challenge year after year, class after class. Each September, I look up
and down the rows carefully at the unfamiliar faces. I look for veiled
eyes or bodies scrunched into a seat in an alien world. "Look, kids," I
say silently, "I may not do anything else for you this year, but not one
of you is going out of here a nobody. I'll work or fight to the bitter end

doing battle with society and the school board, but I won't have one of
you leaving here thinking yourself into a zero."

Most of the time—not always, but most of the time—I've 22
succeeded.

VOCABULARY QUESTIONS

A. Use context clues to help you decide on the best definition for each italicized
word. Then circle the letter of each choice.

1. The word *veered* in "the bus . . . veered and stopped short at the town hotel"
   (paragraph 1) means
   a. went in reverse.
   b. turned suddenly.
   c. sped up.
   d. closed its doors.

2. The word *reeled* in "a boy lurched out of the bus, reeled, stumbled, and
   collapsed on the snowbank at the curb" (paragraph 1) means
   a. jumped.
   b. laughed.
   c. moved unsteadily.
   d. pushed.

3. The word *meager* in "these meager strands of information and the list of D
   grades were about all the records had to offer" (paragraph 14) means
   a. impressive.
   b. injured.
   c. few.
   d. proud.

4. The word *annotations* in "the . . . teachers' annotations read 'sweet, shy
   child'; 'timid but eager'" (paragraph 16) means
   a. written comments.
   b. lies.
   c. excuses.
   d. criticisms.

5. The word *resilience* in "even timid, sweet children have resilience. It takes
   time to break them" (paragraph 16) means
   a. pleasant voices.
   b. illnesses.
   c. ability to recover.
   d. secrets.

B. Below are words from "Words to Watch." Write in the one that best completes each sentence.

blurted out	cipher	lurched
peaked	resolve	

6. It takes great _____ to quit smoking.

7. Kara explained that her _____ appearance was due to a bad case of the flu.

8. My boss is really mean to his secretary. He treats her as if she doesn't count at all, as if she's nothing but a _____.

9. When her ankle twisted, Mom _____ forward, but Dad caught her in time to prevent her from falling down the steps.

10. James was so anxious to show he had studied the chapter that he _____ answers even before the teacher finished her questions.

READING COMPREHENSION QUESTIONS

Central Point and Main Ideas

1. Which sentence best expresses the central point of the selection?
   a. A boy nobody knew died on the way to school.
   b. Children need to believe that they are valued and important.
   c. One teacher has found a way to help influence students.
   d. Children believe everything they are told.

2. Which sentence best expresses the main idea of paragraph 17?
   a. The author was angered and upset by what the school had done to Cliff.
   b. The author didn't feel well.
   c. The school never helped Cliff.
   d. The author disliked doing paperwork.

3. Which sentence best expresses the main idea of paragraph 19?
   a. Cliff died of heart failure.
   b. Children are innocent.
   c. Cliff's heart failed because others convinced him he was nothing.
   d. The doctor listed Cliff's cause of death as "heart failure."

Supporting Details

4. Cliff had
   a. never been adopted by his stepfather.
   b. been one of the author's favorite students.
   c. a small group of close friends.
   d. been very sick for a long time.

5. At the funeral,
   a. everyone was sad and cried.
   b. the author saw many of Cliff's teachers.
   c. the author became determined to help other students like Cliff.
   d. ten of Cliff's friends showed up.

Transitions

6. The transitional word *but* in the sentence below signals
   a. addition.
   b. comparison.
   c. contrast.
   d. cause and effect.

   The doctor might list "heart failure" as the cause of death, but that wouldn't change my mind. (Paragraph 19)

7. The second sentence below begins with a transition that shows
   a. addition.
   b. time.
   c. cause and effect.
   d. illustration.

   We couldn't find ten students in the school who had known Cliff well enough to attend the funeral as his friends. So the student body officers and a committee from the junior class went as a group to the church, looking politely sad. (Paragraph 20)

Patterns of Organization

8. The pattern of organization of paragraph 1 is
   a. time order.
   b. list of items.
   c. comparison and/or contrast.
   d. cause and effect.

Inferences

9. The author implies that Cliff
   a. wanted to run away from home.
   b. and his stepfather did not have a good relationship.

c. was a troublemaker at home.

d. had no chance of finishing high school.

10. From the selection, we can conclude that

a. no one cared that Cliff had died.

b. the school system helped convince Cliff that he was a zero.

c. Cliff was on drugs when he got off the bus.

d. the author is the most popular teacher at the school.

MAPPING ACTIVITY

This selection is organized by time: first one thing happened, then another, then another, and so on. Major events of the selection are scrambled in the list below. Write them in their correct order in the diagram based on the reading.

- Visit to Cliff's home
- What the records revealed
- Teacher's decision (to keep other students from becoming like Cliff)
- Funeral
- Unexpected bus stop
- Search in school records

Central point: People had so convinced Cliff that he was a zero that he gave up and died.

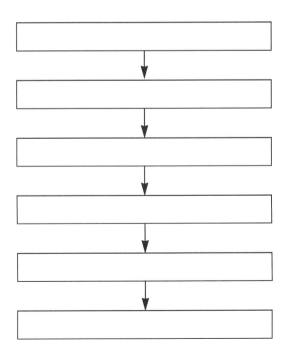

DISCUSSION QUESTIONS

1. From the article, what information do you learn and infer about Cliff's home life? How do you think he was treated by his mother? His stepfather?

2. Todhunter states that Cliff "had never been anybody at all." What does she mean? What is needed for a person to be "somebody"— either in school or out of school?

WRITING ACTIVITIES

1. The author asks, "How do you go about making a boy into a zero?" How did Cliff become a zero? Write a paragraph explaining why he thought so little of himself. You might begin with this topic sentence: "The attitudes and behavior of people around Cliff Evans convinced him that he was a zero." Then you could go on to explain briefly how teachers, students, and family influenced Cliff's poor self-image.

2. What would you say to Cliff's mother or stepfather if you had the chance? Write a letter to either, or both, explaining how you think each might have influenced Cliff. Use whatever tone you wish—angry, sad, questioning, or sympathetic.

Check Your Performance   **CIPHER IN THE SNOW**

Skill	Number Right	Points	Total
VOCABULARY			
Vocabulary in Context (5 items)	_____	x 10 =	_____
Words to Watch (5 items)	_____	x 10 =	_____
		SCORE =	_____ %
COMPREHENSION			
Central Point and Main Ideas (3 items)	_____	x 7 =	_____
Supporting Details (2 items)	_____	x 7 =	_____
Transitions (2 items)	_____	x 7 =	_____
Patterns of Organization (1 item)	_____	x 7 =	_____
Inferences (2 items)	_____	x 7 =	_____
Mapping (6 items)	_____	x 5 =	_____
		SCORE =	_____ %

FINAL SCORES: **Vocabulary** _____ %   **Comprehension** _____ %

Enter your final scores into the reading performance chart on the inside back cover.

3

Rosa: A Success Story
Edward Patrick

Preview

This selection tells of a woman who meets and conquers more obstacles than many of us have experienced. She does not spend a lot of time asking why these things are happening to her. She does what she must to make her life and her family's life better. We can all learn from Rosa.

Words to Watch

plantation (1): large estate where crops are grown
to no avail (3): without success
trek (3): journey
conveyed (5): communicated
sentiment (5): attitude; thought
halting (6): hesitant
prodded (7): urged
deported (17): forced to leave a country
attained (17): gained
collect myself (20): gain control of myself
immigrants (21): people who come to another country to live
oppressive (21): harsh and cruel

> Up until six months before I met her, life for Rosa Perez had been   1
> easy. Her father was a wealthy plantation° owner in Nicaragua. Her
> family owned a large house with all the comforts of the rich. Then
> came the same type of violent civil war that has torn apart so many
> Latin American countries.

Rosa's father was identified as a supporter of the rebel cause, and the family's plantation was seized. During the government takeover, her father was shot and killed. Her mother gathered as much money as she could and fled with Rosa and her two younger brothers, Adolpho and Roberto. Their destination was the United States. Rosa's mother knew a man who knew another man who could get them through Mexico and across the U.S. border into Texas or California. There was nothing to worry about, they were told. Rosa believed it. 2

At first, things went smoothly. Twelve others joined Rosa and her family. The group had no trouble getting into and across Mexico. But just before they were to cross into California, the guide said he could go no further. Another man would take them the rest of the way. Rosa's mother protested, but to no avail°. They were led across by a man they did not know. He told them to follow his every command. They must move quickly and silently or risk detection by the Border Patrol. It was a difficult trek°. It was dark. It was cold. Coyotes howled in what all hoped was the distance. Everyone was tired and frightened. 3

And then came the bright lights. Just as they were about to cross into the United States, the U.S. Border Patrol sighted the group and turned on the searchlights on their jeeps to track them down. People scattered. Rosa held on to Adolpho and Roberto. She looked back, but could not see her mother. "Aqui. Ahora," commanded their guide, appropriately called a "coyote." Rosa blindly followed him and watched as the lights of the jeeps sped after the others. They waited quietly for what seemed like hours. Only when he was convinced that it was safe did their guide take the five who had managed to follow him the rest of the way. Eleven were not with them, including Rosa's mother. 4

I first saw Rosa three months after this nightmare. I arrived at my office early, wanting only to unwind from the freeway drive before my first class. I was annoyed that someone was standing outside my office so early in the morning. But I spoke with her, and soon realized that there was something special about this slender, dark-skinned young woman with large, expressive brown eyes. I didn't know then what it was I saw in her. Now I know she projected an inner strength, conveyed° an unspoken sentiment° that "You don't know me, but you can believe in me." It was magnetic. I knew that I would help in any way I could. 5

Rosa wanted to learn English. She wanted to do more than just get by. Her halting° English told me she could manage that already. She wanted to be able to read and write the language so that she could provide for her brothers. My basic reading class had been recommended to her. She asked what materials she could get to work on even before the semester started. 6

Eager students are always easy to work with, and Rosa proved to be one of my most ardent students. She kept me on my toes and constantly challenged me. She prodded° me to provide more information, additional examples, better explanations. If I used a word she didn't understand, she would stop me. She would make me explain it so that she and her classmates could grasp its meaning. If we looked for the main idea in a paragraph and her answer was different from mine, she insisted on giving the reasons why she felt she was right and I was wrong. I could not always convince her that my answer was better. But I always encouraged her to ask questions whenever she was confused or unconvinced. While I looked forward to the class she had enrolled in, I was always exhausted at its conclusion.

Rosa advanced from our basic reading classes to the more difficult study-skills class. Then she moved through the writing classes offered in the department. She enrolled in the Early Childhood Program at the college. This is a program which can lead to certification as a child-care worker. Her progress in her classes was reflected in a steady stream of A's and B's.

It took Rosa three years to complete the coursework that she needed to graduate. I made plans to attend the graduation ceremonies where she would receive her associate's degree. She insisted that I attend the graduation party her friend Alberto was giving. I said I would be honored to go.

The ceremony was typical, with boring speeches made for proud accomplishments. The party was something special. Rosa had come a long way in the three years I had known her. She had made some wonderful friends, had secured a decent job at a nearby day-care center, and had provided a good home for her two brothers.

Rosa greeted me when I arrived. She wanted for me to meet everyone there, and she hinted at a surprise she had for me.

"Dr. P, may I present to you my brothers, Adolpho and Roberto."

"Mucho gusto," I began.

"Right," said the smaller brother. "Call me Bobby. Nice to meet you, Doc. Say, you don't mind if me and Al 'mingle,' if you know what I mean?"

I knew, and encouraged them to meet and greet the others—especially the young ladies—in attendance.

I commented on how quickly her brothers had adjusted to life in the States. But Rosa seemed preoccupied. I was puzzled until I saw that we were walking toward an older woman who had the same brown expressive eyes as Rosa. It was her mother.

Rosa's mother had been captured by the Border Patrol and

deported° to Nicaragua. There, she was jailed. Rosa had been despondent over her mother's lack of the freedom she and her brothers enjoyed. She had located her mother and worked for close to three years to get her released. I don't know all the details of how she did it. Perhaps it is best that I don't. At the moment I met her, I did not care at all about how she had attained° freedom. I was just overjoyed that she was here with her children.

Rosa entered San Diego State University, some ninety miles 18 away. As often happens with students who move on, I saw very little of her. She was working hard toward a degree in early childhood education, I was on leave for a year, and our paths rarely crossed. Sometimes she would come by right before Christmas or at the end of a school year. She stopped by the office again yesterday, with a purpose. She carried two babies in her arms. The six-month-old twins were hers. Their huge, expressive brown eyes told me that before she did.

Rosa proudly recounted what had happened in the five years since 19 her graduation. I listened enthusiastically as she described her completion of a Bachelor of Arts degree, her marriage to Alberto, their jointly opening a child-care center, and the birth of their twin sons. "And now," she said, "I want to tell you their names. This is Alberto," she said, nodding toward the larger twin. Then she looked toward the smaller one. Her eyes smiled as much as her mouth. "He is smaller, yes, but obviously more intellectual. That is why we have chosen to name him Eduardo."

I gasped, tried to collect myself°, but did not succeed. Rosa came 20 to the rescue. She calmly explained that Alberto and she decided to name the baby after me because of all the help I had provided when she needed it most. I babbled something about how proud I felt. It was true.

Some people, I know, object to the flow of immigrants° entering 21 our country. They forget that almost all of us came to America from somewhere else. We need every so often to be reminded of success stories like Rosa's. Like many of our ancestors, she fled an oppressive° government and poor economic conditions. She then worked hard to create a new life for herself. Hers is not an uncommon story. Many others like her have come to enrich their lives, and they have enriched our country as well.

VOCABULARY QUESTIONS

A. Use context clues to help you decide on the best definition for each italicized word. Then circle the letter of each choice.

1. The word *detection* in "They must move quickly and silently or risk detection by the Border Patrol" (paragraph 3) means
   a. assistance.
   b. trust.
   c. discovery.
   d. noise.

2. The word *ardent* in "Eager students are always easy to work with, and Rosa proved to be one of my most ardent students" (paragraph 7) means
   a. difficult.
   b. enthusiastic.
   c. healthy.
   d. slow.

3. The word *secured* in "She had made some wonderful friends, had secured a decent job at a nearby day-care center" (paragraph 10) means
   a. gotten.
   b. hired.
   c. paid.
   d. quit.

4. The word *despondent* in "Rosa had been despondent over her mother's lack of the freedom she and her brothers enjoyed" (paragraph 17) means
   a. joyful.
   b. comfortable.
   c. depressed.
   d. cruel.

5. The word *recounted* in "Rosa proudly recounted what had happened . . . she described her completion of a Bachelor of Arts degree, her marriage to Alberto, their jointly opening a child care center, and the birth of their twin sons" (paragraph 19) means
   a. ignored.
   b. complained about.
   c. told.
   d. forgot.

B. Below are words, or forms of words, from "Words to Watch." Write in the one that best completes each sentence.

deported	oppressive	prodded
sentiments	treks	

6. The earliest _____ across America were difficult, since few roads or bridges existed.

7. Are you an energetic riser, or do you have to be _____ to get out of bed?

8. The _____ ruler tortured anyone who dared to oppose him.

9. I agreed so strongly with what the speaker said that I stood up and shouted, "My _____ exactly!"

10. People from other countries who commit crimes here are sometimes _____ back to the places they came from.

READING COMPREHENSION QUESTIONS

Central Point and Main Ideas

1. Which sentence best expresses the central point of the selection?
   a. Civil wars have destroyed many countries.
   b. Like many immigrants fleeing oppression, Rosa came to America and made a successful life for herself.
   c. Rosa finally brought her mother to the United States.
   d. Rosa married and gave birth to twins, one of whom she named after the author.

2. Which sentence best expresses the main idea of paragraph 4?
   a. The Border Patrol turned on bright searchlights.
   b. Rosa held on to her brothers but couldn't see her mother.
   c. Rosa and her brothers successfully crossed the border, but her mother was among those who did not.
   d. The guide was very cautious and waited for what seemed like hours until it seemed safe to continue crossing the border.

3. Which sentence best expresses the main idea of paragraphs 6–7?
   a. Rosa's English was not very good.
   b. Rosa always asked questions in class.
   c. Rosa kept the author on his toes.
   d. Rosa was a very eager student.

Supporting Details

4. _____ TRUE OR FALSE? According to the author, Rosa's success story is unusual.

5. According to the article, Rosa's
   a. brothers had trouble adjusting to life in the United States.
   b. mother spent about three years in a Nicaraguan jail.
   c. graduation party was boring.
   d. husband has never met the author.

Transitions

6. *Fill in the blank:* In the sentence below, the transition that signals a comparison is _____.

   . . . Rosa seemed preoccupied. I was puzzled until I saw that we were walking toward an older woman who had the same brown expressive eyes as Rosa. (Paragraph 16)

7. *Fill in the blank:* In the sentence below, the transition word *but* *(compares, contrasts, gives an example of)* _____ the author's effort to gain control over himself with his failure to do so.

   I gasped, tried to collect myself, but did not succeed. (Paragraph 20)

Patterns of Organization

8. The pattern of organization of paragraph 18 is
   a. time order.
   b. list of items.
   c. comparison and/or contrast.
   d. definition and example.

Inferences

9. The author implies that Rosa and her brothers
   a. received very little education in Nicaragua.
   b. had friends waiting for them in the United States.
   c. entered the country illegally.
   d. are very rich again.

10. From the selection, we can conclude that Rosa
    a. never wanted to leave Nicaragua.
    b. will be a benefit to our country.
    c. will have a large family of her own.
    d. will move back to Nicaragua when the situation there improves.

MAPPING ACTIVITY

This selection is organized by time: first one thing happened; then another; after that, another; and so on. Major events of the selection are scrambled in the list below. Write them in their correct order in the diagram based on the reading.

- Rosa's education toward a bachelor's degree
- Rosa's escape to the U.S.
- Rosa's education toward an associate's degree
- Rosa's visit with the twins
- Rosa's graduation and party

Central point: Many immigrants, like Rosa, come to America to escape oppression and then work hard to become productive citizens.

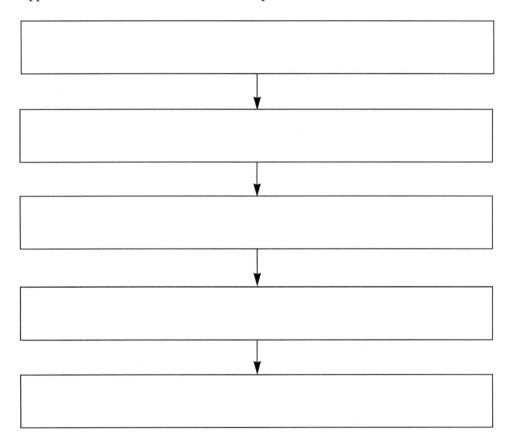

DISCUSSION QUESTIONS

1. As Rosa reached the border of the United States, she realized that her mother was not with her. Should she have looked for her mother, or was she right to cross into the U.S. when she did?

2.   The author writes that "we need . . . to be reminded of success stories like Rosa's." What are the values of hearing such a story?

WRITING ACTIVITIES

1.   Patrick writes, "Almost all of us came to America from somewhere else." Where did your family come from, and when? Write a paragraph on the members of your family who first came to America. Include information such as the following: 1) where they came from, 2) the reason they came to America, and 3) what life was like for them at first in America.

2.   Rosa's education prepared her for a career. If you want your education to lead to a career, write a paragraph on which one and why you've picked it. Be specific about the types of positions you'd like to hold and why they appeal to you. If you're not sure about the type of career you want, write about one or two that you're considering. Here are two sample topic sentences for this paragraph: 1) "I'm aiming for a career in _____ for two main reasons"; 2) "I'm in the process of weighing the values and drawbacks of a career in _____."

Check Your Performance		**ROSA: A SUCCESS STORY**	
Skill	*Number Right*	*Points*	*Total*
VOCABULARY			
Vocabulary in Context (5 items)	_____	x 10 =	_____
Words to Watch (5 items)	_____	x 10 =	_____
		SCORE =	_____ %
COMPREHENSION			
Central Point and Main Ideas (3 items)	_____	x 7 =	_____
Supporting Details (2 items)	_____	x 7 =	_____
Transitions (2 items)	_____	x 7 =	_____
Patterns of Organization (1 item)	_____	x 7 =	_____
Inferences (2 items)	_____	x 7 =	_____
Mapping (5 items)	_____	x 6 =	_____
		SCORE =	_____ %

FINAL SCORES: **Vocabulary** _____ %   **Comprehension** _____ %

Enter your final scores into the reading performance chart on the inside back cover.

4

Classroom Notetaking
Clarissa White

Preview

What do you do during a classroom lecture? Do you sit and stare at the instructor, wondering if he or she will ever stop? Do you look at the person next to you, trying to figure out what he could possibly be writing when you haven't heard anything interesting? Do you try to write down everything that is said, but can't keep up? Knowing what to do and how to do it during a lecture is a skill. Mastering this skill will make you a better student. Keep that in mind as you read the next selection, which gives you tips on how to make the best use of class time.

Words to Watch

deaden (3): dull
glazed (3): glassy
launching pad (7): starting point
groping (8): reaching
cement (14): fix firmly

How would you feel if you were forced to spend 1800 hours—the equivalent of 75 days in a row—sitting in a hard-backed chair, eyes wide open, listening to the sound of someone else's voice? You wouldn't be allowed to sleep, eat, or smoke. You couldn't leave the room. To make matters worse, you'd be expected to remember every important point the speaker made, and you'd be punished for forgetting. And, to top it off, you'd have to pay thousands of dollars for the experience.

Sound like the torture scene from the latest spy thriller? Actually, it's nothing of the kind. It's what all college students do who take a full load of five courses for four years. Those 1800 hours are the time they'll spend in the lecture room.

Unfortunately, many students do regard these hours as torture, and they do all sorts of things to deaden° the pain. Some of them sit through class with glazed° eyes, minds wandering to the athletic field or the movie theater. Others hide in the back of the room, sneaking glances at the newspaper or the book they're being tested on in their next class. Still others reduce the pain to zero: they simply don't come to class. These students do not realize that if they don't listen in class—and take notes—they're missing out on one of the most important aspects of their education.

WHY TAKE LECTURE NOTES?

One reason you should take lecture notes is that lectures add to what you read in textbooks. Lecturers combine the material and approaches of many texts, saving you the trouble of researching an entire field. They keep up to date with their subjects and can include the latest studies or discoveries in their presentations; they needn't wait for the next edition of the book to come out. They can provide additional examples or simplify difficult concepts, making it easier for you to master tricky material. And the best lecturers combine knowledge with expert showmanship. Both informative and entertaining speakers, they can make any subject, from ancient civilizations to computers, leap vividly to life.

True, you say, but isn't it good enough just to listen to these wonderful people without writing down what they say? Actually, it isn't, which leads us to another reason for taking lecture notes. Studies have shown that after two weeks, you'll forget 80 percent of it. And you didn't come to the lecture room just to be entertained. You came to learn. The only way to keep the material in your head is to get it down in permanent form—in the form of lecture notes.

HOW TO TAKE LECTURE NOTES

There are three steps to mastering the art of taking good lecture notes: the preparation, the note-taking process itself, and the post-lecture review.

Preparation

First, mentally prepare yourself to take good notes. Examine your attitude. Remember, you're not going to the lecture room to be bored, tortured, or entertained; you're going there to learn. Also, examine the material the lecture will cover. Read the textbook chapter in advance. If your instructor's lecture usually follows the organization of the textbook, you'll be familiar with the material and won't have to spend half the lecture wondering what it's about or how to spell a key term. If, however, your instructor merely uses the textbook as a launching pad° and devotes most of the lecture to supplementary material, at least you'll have the background to follow what is being said.

Second, prepare yourself physically. Get a good night's sleep, and   8
get to class—on time. Even better, get to class early, so you can get a good seat near the front of the room. You'll hear better there and be less tempted to let your mind wander. You'll also have time to open your notebook to a new page, find your pen, and write the date, course, and topic of the lecture at the top. This way, you won't still be groping° under your chair or flipping through pages when the instructor begins to speak.

Process

When you take class notes, always use 8½ x 11″ paper, preferably   9
in a looseleaf notebook so you can insert handouts. Write on only one side of the paper. Later, you might want to spread all your notes out in front of you. Have a pen to write with rather than a pencil, which moves more slowly across a page and is not as legible.

Be prepared to do a good deal of writing in class. A good rule of   10
thumb for taking notes is "When in doubt, write it down." After class, you will have time to go over your notes and make decisions about what is important enough to study and what is not. But in the midst of a lecture, you don't always have time to decide what is really important and what is quite secondary. You don't want to miss getting down a valuable idea that the instructor does not repeat later.

Be sure to always write down what the instructor puts on the   11
board. If he or she takes the time to write something on the board, it is generally safe to assume that such material is important. And don't fall into the trap that some students fall into. They write down what is on the board but nothing more. They just sit and listen while the instructor explains all the connections between those words that have been chalked on the board. Everything may be perfectly clear to a student then, but several days later, chances are that all the connecting material will be forgotten. If you write down the explanations in class, it will be much easier for you to make sense of the material and to study it later.

As much as possible, organize your notes by starting main points   12
at the margin. Indent secondary points under the main points and indent

examples even further. Skip lines between main sections. Wherever possible, number the points. If the instructor explains three reasons for poverty, or four results of the greenhouse effect, make sure you number each of those reasons or results. The numbers help organize the material and make it easier for you to study and remember it.

Here are some other hints for taking good classroom notes: 13

- If you miss something, don't panic. Leave space for it in your notes and keep going. Later, get the missing information from a classmate or your textbook.

- Be alert for signals that something is an important point ("A major cause of anxiety is . . ."), a new topic ("Another problem of urban living is . . ."), the beginning of an enumeration ("There are seven warning signals . . ."), or a summary ("In conclusion . . ."). These signals will help you organize your note-taking. If your instructor says, "The point I am trying to make is . . . ," be sure you *get the point*—in your notes.

- Use abbreviations in order to save time. Put a key for abbreviated words in the top margin of your notes. For instance, in a business class, *com* could stand for *communication; info* for *information.* In a psychology class, *beh* could stand for *behavior; mot* for *motivation.* You can also abbreviate certain common words, using a "+" for *and,* a "*w/*" for *with,* and an "*ex*" for *example.*

- Finally, don't ignore the very beginning and end of class. Often, instructors devote the first five minutes of their lectures to a review of material already covered or a preview of the next day's lecture. The last five minutes of a lecture can contain a clear summary of the class—or ten more major points the instructor simply *has* to make before the bell rings. Don't spend the first five minutes of class getting your materials out and the last five minutes putting them away. If you do, you'll probably miss something important.

Post-Lecture Review

Taking good notes lets you bring the lecture home with you. The   14
real learning takes place after class. As soon as you have time, sit down and reread your notes. Fill in anything unclear or missing while it's still fresh in your mind. Then, in the left-hand column of each page, write a few key words and phrases that summarize the points of the lecture. Cover your notes, and, using only these key words, try to reconstruct as

much of the lecture as you can. This review will cement° the major
points in your memory—and will save significant time when you study
for the exam.

To sum all this up, be prepared to go into class and be not just an   15
active listener but an active notetaker as well. Being in class and taking
good notes while you are there are the most valuable steps you can take
to succeed in college.

VOCABULARY QUESTIONS

A. Use context clues to help you decide on the best definition for each italicized
word. Then circle the letter of your choice.

1. The word *equivalent* in "1800 hours—the equivalent of 75 days in a row"
   (paragraph 1) means
   a. rest.
   b. equal.
   c. difference.
   d. first.

2. The word *showmanship* in "And the best lecturers combine knowledge with
   expert showmanship. . . . they can make any subject, from ancient
   civilizations to computers, leap vividly to life" (paragraph 4) means
   a. dramatic skill.
   b. handwriting.
   c. research ability.
   d. popularity.

3. The word *vividly* in "entertaining speakers, they can make any subject, from
   ancient civilizations to computers, leap vividly to life" (paragraph 4) means
   a. in a quiet way.
   b. in a lively way.
   c. in a civilized way.
   d. in a confusing way.

4. The word *supplementary* in "If, however, your instructor merely uses the
   textbook as a launching pad and devotes most of the lecture to
   supplementary material, at least you'll have the background to follow what
   is being said" (paragraph 7) means
   a. textbook.
   b. unimportant.
   c. additional.
   d. boring.

5. The word *enumeration* in "Be alert for signals that something is . . . the beginning of an enumeration ('There are seven warning signals . . . ')" (paragraph 13) means
   a. a new topic.
   b. a signal.
   c. a list.
   d. a beginning.

B. Below are words from "Words to Watch." Write in the one that best completes each sentence.

cement	deaden	glazed
groping	launching pad	

6. Victor was not convinced that working in the mail room would be a good

   _____ for his new career.

7. A muffler is used to _____ the sound of a jackhammer, which is otherwise unbearably loud.

8. When called on for the answer, Marlene got a _____ look in her eyes—she had no idea of what the answer was.

9. Certain memory techniques can help _____ in our minds facts which are otherwise hard to remember.

10. As I was _____ under my desk to find the pencil I had dropped, I noticed the teacher had taken off her shoes.

READING COMPREHENSION QUESTIONS

Central Point and Main Ideas

1. Which sentence best expresses the central point of the selection?
   a. Students can learn more from lectures than from reading textbooks.
   b. Taking lecture notes is an important skill involving three main steps.
   c. College lectures are more than just entertainment.
   d. Use lecture notes to learn after class.

2. The main idea of paragraph 4 can be found in its
   a. first sentence.
   b. second sentence.
   c. third sentence.
   d. last sentence.

3. Which sentence best expresses the main idea of paragraph 14?
   a. Notetaking allows you to bring a copy of the lecture home with you.
   b. Always fill in the blanks in your notes as soon as class ends.
   c. Completing and reviewing lecture notes soon after class will help you remember the material.
   d. Reread your notes soon after class, filling in any missing information and making unclear information clear.

Supporting Details

4. _____ TRUE OR FALSE? Students need to prepare for class both physically and mentally.

5. When taking classroom notes, students should always
   a. write on both sides of the notebook page.
   b. write in ink.
   c. write on index cards.
   d. write words out fully.

6. Numbering lecture points
   a. helps organize material.
   b. makes it easier for you to study the material.
   c. makes it easier for you to remember the points.
   d. all of the above.

Transitions

7. Paragraphs 7 and 8 both begin with transitions that show
   a. addition.
   b. contrast.
   c. illustration.
   d. cause and effect.

8. The transition beginning the second sentence below signals
   a. an addition.
   b. a comparison.
   c. an illustration.
   d. a cause and effect.

   Put a key for abbreviated words in the top margin of your notes. For instance, in a business class, *com* could stand for *communication.* . . . (Paragraph 13)

Patterns of Organization

9. The pattern of organization of paragraphs 4 and 5 is
   a. time order.
   b. comparison and/or contrast.
   c. cause and effect.
   d. definition and example.

Inferences

10. From the selection, we can conclude that
    a. classroom notetaking is very easy.
    b. classroom notetaking is a detailed but rewarding skill.
    c. there is only one good reason to take classroom notes.
    d. most colleges now teach notetaking procedures to incoming students.

MAPPING ACTIVITY

This selection is organized into lists—a list of reasons for taking lecture notes and a list of steps for lecture notetaking. Complete the diagram by filling in the five missing points.

Central point: Students should take lecture notes, a skill that involves three main steps.

A. Reasons for Taking Classroom Notes

1. Lectures add to what you read in textbooks.

2. _____
   _____
   _____
   _____

B. _____
   _____

1. Prepare yourself mentally and physically.

2. Follow a careful notetaking process.

   a. Write in ink on one side of looseleaf notebook paper.

   b. When in doubt, write it down in your notes.

   c. Always write what the instructor puts on the board and the explanations of that material.

   d. _____
      _____

   e. If you miss something, just leave space for it.

   f. _____
      _____

   g. Use abbreviations.

   h. _____
      _____

3. Complete and review notes after class.

DISCUSSION QUESTIONS

1. Of all the advice in this article, what three points will be the most helpful for you to remember and practice?

2. Besides knowing how to take lecture notes, what other study skills do you think are important for students to know and practice? For example, what skills are useful when reading, studying material, or taking a test?

WRITING ACTIVITIES

1. Draw a line down the middle of a notebook page. On the top left hand side, write the words "Things I do." On the top right hand side, write the words "Things I don't do." In the "Things I do" column, list tips the author gives which you already do while taking notes. In the "Things I don't do" column, list those things you don't do now but, according to the article, might help you take better notes. Then write a paragraph on the tips you hope will help you take better notes.

2. White says that the best lecturers "combine knowledge with expert showmanship" and are "informative and entertaining speakers" who "can make any subject . . . leap vividly to life." If you're lucky, you've known at least one teacher who is both well-informed and entertaining. Write about this teacher, listing and illustrating two or three of his or her ways of keeping students interested. As an alternative, describe a teacher you've known who was not effective.

Check Your Performance   CLASSROOM NOTETAKING

Skill	Number Right	Points	Total

VOCABULARY

Vocabulary in Context (5 items)   _____   x   10 =   _____

Words to Watch (5 items)   _____   x   10 =   _____

             SCORE =   _____%

COMPREHENSION

Central Point and Main Ideas (3 items)   _____   x   7 =   _____

Supporting Details (3 items)   _____   x   7 =   _____

Transitions (2 items)   _____   x   7 =   _____

Patterns of Organization (1 item)   _____   x   7 =   _____

Inferences (1 item)   _____   x   7 =   _____

Mapping (5 items)   _____   x   6 =   _____

             SCORE =   _____%

FINAL SCORES: **Vocabulary** _____%   **Comprehension** _____%

Enter your final scores into the reading performance chart on the inside back cover.

5

Looking Back on Our Youth
Darrell Sifford

Preview

A common complaint of the not-so-young is "I wish I'd known years ago the things I know today." Life would be so much easier if we all didn't have to make the same mistakes to gain the wisdom of experience. In this selection, columnist Darrell Sifford tries to save young readers from some of these mistakes. He passes along some of what he's learned through the years.

Words to Watch

midlife (1): middle age
prosper (6): succeed
adversity (6): misfortune
reciprocating (7): paying back
mentors (8): guides
nurture (10): nourish
adequate (11): enough
moderation (11): avoidance of extremes
modify (11): change
excessive (12): too much
blue funk (14): bad mood
solely (15): only

Well, here you are—in midlife° or wherever—and, as you look back, do you realize how little you knew in the bloom of youth, even though you thought you knew it all?

Do you ever wish that you could go back to those early years and   2 do it all over again—knowing what you now know?

That's not possible, of course. But what may be possible—and what I had the opportunity to do not long ago—is to appear before an audience of high school juniors and seniors and talk to them about "what I wish somebody had told me when I was 17 or 18." ₃

What would you say to students? In forty-five minutes, what would you single out as the most important things for them to take away from the meeting? ₄

Let me share with you some of what I talked about: ₅

The world is not always fair. As adults, some of us know this, but, as adolescents, most of us didn't. We had the sense that good input always resulted in good outcome, that if we did our part, the result would be in line with what we expected. It would be nice if things worked this way, but they don't. The world can be—and often is—a friendly place in which we can prosper°, but, at times, it can be hostile and unfair. People who expect this and who aren't disabled when adversity° strikes them for no reason are way ahead of everybody else. Bad things do happen to good people, and, occasionally, nothing makes sense. ₆

Parenting is a tough job—maybe the toughest—and it's helpful to realize sooner than later that parents, for all their flaws, probably are doing the best they can. Try to share with your parents, even if they don't share back with you. *Tell* them you love them and *show* them you love them, even if they aren't comfortable reciprocating°. Question your parents. When it's appropriate, challenge them. But don't grind them down. Don't polish their guilt. Most parents, I'm convinced, feel guilty to some extent about not doing more or doing better for their children. ₇

It's important to find mentors° at various stages throughout life. Latch onto somebody who is older and wiser, and let that person guide you around the potholes. What's in it for the mentor? A feeling of satisfaction in helping somebody. Remember that the mentor gets something out of it, too—so don't be afraid of trying to recruit a mentor. ₈

We need goals throughout life and plans for pursuing our goals. Goals never stop changing, if we're lucky. We accomplish one goal, and then we move on to the next. Don't ever be without goals, short-range and long-range. They are the fuel that keeps us going. ₉

We need relationships. Barbra Streisand says it all in the song: "People who need people are the luckiest people in the world." In the final analysis, the relationships that we nurture° with the few core people in our lives are the most precious things we have. Don't ever get too busy to take time to care for and feed relationships with people who matter. ₁₀

Our bodies are marvelous works of nature, but it's our 11 responsibility to care for them. It's important to get adequate° rest, to eat reasonably, to act in moderation°. The patterns we set in childhood often are the patterns we carry into adulthood, so take a look at what you're doing now—and modify° it if that's called for.

It's a serious world much of the time, but don't be afraid to have 12 fun—and don't ever feel guilty about having fun. The psychologist Arnold Lazarus, on hearing of the death of a friend, always says the same thing: "I hope he had enough fun." He doesn't say that he hopes the person had enough money, a big-enough title, an office with enough windows. But enough *fun*. How much is enough? Only you can decide how much is enough for you. Fun doesn't come at the expense of reasonable responsibility. It comes at the expense of excessive° seriousness.

What you think about yourself is far more important than what 13 others think about you. If you remember this, you'll never feel the need to live your life in ways that you *think* will win approval from others. You can live your life in a way that makes sense to you, that meets your needs and goals. It's said that life is not for amateurs, and I believe that. Amateurs are those of us who let others tell us how to run our lives.

People will disappoint you at times and fall short of your 14 expectations. If you always expect perfection or even reasonable behavior, you're going to find yourself in a blue funk° much of the time. But if you accept that others, just like you, sometimes shoot themselves in the foot, you'll consume less Maalox and sleep more soundly.

You can't control anybody else, but you can control how you react 15 to other people. It's a waste of time and energy to try to change another person. Use that same time and energy to work on yourself—and you'll find that life is a lot sweeter for everybody. This is true now and forevermore.You alone can define what success means to you. Don't let anybody else try to define success for you. This was what John Ehrlichman told me was the most important thing he learned from his Watergate experience. His sin, he said, was letting others sell him their value systems. How do I now define success? The achievement of a life that contains a balance of love, work and play. That's a far different definition than I might have offered twenty years ago, when the focus solely° was on work.

There's no need to be in any hurry to get married. It's wise to get 16 your life somewhat in place before you complicate it by incorporating with another person. Marriages that come later seem to prosper more than marriages that come sooner.

People are more alike than they are different. You're probably 17 more typical than you think you are—so when you feel like an outsider who is staring in through the window, remember that a lot of other people feel that way, too. You're probably not odd or weird, just typical.

If you need help, don't be afraid to ask for it. It's a tremendous 18 burden to go through life with the feeling that you have to do it all by yourself. There's some virtue, as Frank Sinatra sings, in doing it your way, but doing it your way doesn't mean that you can't find a firm shoulder to lean on at times. The strongest people, in my opinion, are those who know when to ask for help.

Well, that's what I said to the students. How about you?   19

VOCABULARY QUESTIONS

A. Use context clues to help you decide on the best definition for each italicized word. Then circle the letter of each choice.

1. The word *hostile* in "the world can be . . . a friendly place . . . , but, at times, it can be hostile and unfair" (paragraph 6) means
   a. generous.
   b. holy.
   c. active.
   d. unfriendly.

2. The word *flaws* in "Parenting is a tough job . . . and it's helpful to realize . . . that parents, for all their flaws, probably are doing the best they can" (paragraph 7) means
   a. nagging.
   b. talents.
   c. controls.
   d. faults.

3. The word *recruit* in "Latch onto somebody who is older and wiser . . . don't be afraid of trying to recruit a mentor" (paragraph 8) means
   a. take on.
   b. fire.
   c. teach.
   d. bribe.

4. The word *core* in "the relationships that we nurture with the few core people in our lives are the most precious things we have" (paragraph 10) means
   a. hard-working.
   b. educated.
   c. central.
   d. young.

5. The word *incorporating* in "There's no need to be in any hurry to get married. It's wise to get your life somewhat in place before you complicate it by incorporating with another person" (paragraph 16) means
   a. buying.
   b. joining.
   c. meeting.
   d. arguing.

B. Below are words from "Words to Watch." Write in the one that best completes each sentence.

adequate	adversity	midlife
moderation	prosper	

6. We all face _____ in our lives. We can often make life better by somehow turning these tough times to our advantage.

7. You should have _____ savings before even beginning to think of buying a home.

8. Nutritionists advise us not to eat and drink too much or too little, but to consume in _____.

9. It can take years of hard work before a small business really begins to _____.

10. When you reach _____ yourself, you may decide that life really does begin at forty.

READING COMPREHENSION QUESTIONS

Central Point and Main Ideas

1. Which sentence best expresses the central point of the selection?
   a. The author's experience has taught him what advice to give the young.
   b. Young people need to be told what to do.
   c. Young people think they know everything.
   d. Most people would like a second chance in life.

2. Which sentence best expresses the main idea of paragraph 6?
   a. Young people expect life to be fair.
   b. It would be nice if life were fair.
   c. It's best to realize life is not always fair.
   d. The real world is sometimes a friendly place.

3. The main idea of paragraph 12 can be found in its
   a. first sentence.
   b. second sentence.
   c. next-to-the-last sentence.
   d. last sentence.

Supporting Details

4. The author tells us that all people have
   a. the same definition of success.
   b. the same goals throughout life.
   c. very little control over the way other people behave.
   d. very little control over the way they react to others.

5. It's a poor idea to
   a. find mentors.
   b. nurture important relationships.
   c. expect perfection in others.
   d. ask for help when you need it.

Transitions

6. The transition *even though* in the sentence below signals
   a. addition.
   b. contrast.
   c. an example.
   d. cause and effect.

   Well, here you are . . . and, as you look back, do you realize how little you knew in the bloom of youth, even though you thought you knew it all? (Paragraph 1)

7. The sentence below contains
   a. a time signal.
   b. a contrast signal.
   c. an example signal.
   d. a cause-and-effect signal.

   We had the sense . . . that if we did our part, the result would be in line with what we expected. (Paragraph 6)

Patterns of Organization

8. Just as paragraphs are organized according to patterns, so are entire selections. The main pattern of organization of this selection is
   a. time order.
   b. list of items.
   c. cause and effect.
   d. definition and example.

Inferences

9. The author implies that
   a. many of his ideas have changed over the years.
   b. people would do better if they married at a young age.
   c. many parents do too much for their kids.
   d. people aren't as serious as they used to be.

10. The author implies that
    a. once you become an adult, you don't need to have goals.
    b. he is a parent.
    c. even an eighty-year-old should have goals.
    d. it is important to seek the approval of others.

MAPPING ACTIVITY

The ideas in this selection are mainly organized in a list. Five points in that list are missing in the diagram on the next page. Complete the diagram by writing in a brief summary of the missing points.

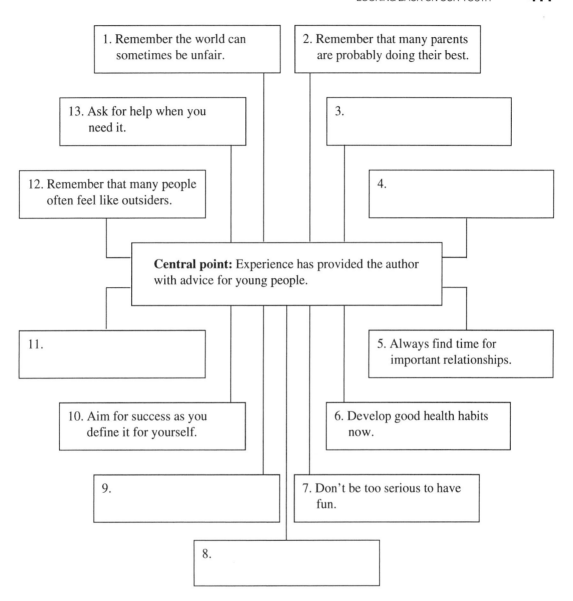

1. Remember the world can sometimes be unfair.

2. Remember that many parents are probably doing their best.

13. Ask for help when you need it.

3.

12. Remember that many people often feel like outsiders.

4.

Central point: Experience has provided the author with advice for young people.

11.

5. Always find time for important relationships.

10. Aim for success as you define it for yourself.

6. Develop good health habits now.

9.

7. Don't be too serious to have fun.

8.

DISCUSSION QUESTIONS

1. Sifford says that "the world is not always fair" and that "bad things do happen to good people." Do you agree? When, in your experience, has the world seemed unfair to you?

2. Of all the things Sifford says, which piece of advice do you think would be hardest for a high school audience to accept? Why did you choose this one?

WRITING ACTIVITIES

1. As the author says, it is not possible to go back in life and change things. But what if we could? Write about one thing you have done which you would change if you could. Possible topics include: deciding to marry (or not to marry) a certain person at a certain age, deciding to stay at home or to leave home and move into your own place, taking (or not taking) a particular job when it was offered to you, and deciding on a particular career direction.

2. Choose one of Sifford's points and write about an experience that proved its truth to you. For example, you could tell about a time in your life that showed that the world can be unfair, that it's difficult to be a parent, or that people need important relationships. Your topic sentence will be the point you choose from the reading. Your support will be a narrative of the experience that proves the point.

Check Your Performance   **LOOKING BACK ON OUR YOUTH**

Skill	Number Right	Points	Total
VOCABULARY			
Vocabulary in Context (5 items)	_____	x 10 =	_____
Words to Watch (5 items)	_____	x 10 =	_____
		SCORE =	_____%
COMPREHENSION			
Central Point and Main Ideas (3 items)	_____	x 7 =	_____
Supporting Details (2 items)	_____	x 7 =	_____
Transitions (2 items)	_____	x 7 =	_____
Patterns of Organization (1 item)	_____	x 7 =	_____
Inferences (2 items)	_____	x 7 =	_____
Mapping (5 items)	_____	x 6 =	_____
		SCORE =	_____%

FINAL SCORES: Vocabulary _____%   **Comprehension** _____%

Enter your final scores into the reading performance chart on the inside back cover.

6

Knowledge Is Power
Anna-Maria Petricic

Preview

When Anna-Maria Petricic read the words "Knowledge is real power" as a student in Croatia, she was intrigued by the phrase. She wasn't sure of its meaning, but she knew that its message was an important one. This is the story of the author's struggle to unlock the secret of that phrase.

Words to Watch

proclaimed (1): announced
essence (1): central point
dismayed (4): discouraged
objective (5): unaffected by personal feelings
certified (8): guaranteed as authentic
terse (9): short and direct
pretentious (10): flashy and egotistical; inclined to show off
imprinted (10): fixed
formidable (13): difficult
shrouded (16): covered
resolved (16): firmly decided
earnestly (17): seriously
steadfast (17): firm; unbending
quest (21): pursuit
ascended (22): climbed

"Knowledge is real power," proclaimed° the bold letters on a   1
bookmark showing Superman soaring upward from between two
blocks of books. As I read this, a wave of energy swept over me. I

studied the bookmark, trying to comprehend its exact meaning. It seemed like the essence° of life was revealed on that small piece of red and blue paper. But, as a teenager in high school, I had no idea what it meant. I only knew that this great excitement I was experiencing had something to do with knowledge. I wanted the power that knowledge brought. For that to happen, I knew I had to attend college. I also knew that this would not be easy.

As a high school student in Sisak, a town near Zagreb, Croatia, all 2 I heard were horror stories about college. "First you sweat preparing for the entrance exams. If you survive that and are lucky enough to be accepted into college, you must deal with your teachers. They will be your enemies for the next four years. The first lesson they teach is that they will do everything they can to crush your confidence, to break your spirit, to make you quit." Such tales were commonly whispered in the high school hallways by students aspiring to go to college.

I was shocked. Surely these stories could not be true. College was 3 supposed to build my confidence in the process of attaining knowledge. Teachers were supposed to encourage me with their wisdom and compassion. They should prepare me for all challenges, not turn me against learning. The more I heard the whispers, the more convinced I became that I must not attend college in my homeland. If I wanted knowledge, I must attend a university in America.

I read all I could about colleges in the U.S. I was dismayed°. The 4 costs were staggering. Then I read about a small, private university in Iowa that was offering work-study scholarships for international students. The school would cover tuition, room, and board in exchange for a twenty-hour-per-week work commitment. In return, students had to show the university that they had sufficient funds in the bank for health insurance and personal expenses. Including airfare from Croatia to America, I calculated that I would need $2,000 per year.

I could hardly contain myself. I dashed into the kitchen that cold 5 winter evening to proudly announce the news to my mother. "I am going to school in America!" My mother looked up at me while still working in the foamy sink full of dirty dishes. "Yes? And who is going to pay for that?" My mother's voice was heavy yet coolly objective°. In my excitement, I overlooked the fact that my mother hardly made enough money to provide for our immediate needs. I brushed that thought aside, not willing to let it spoil my enthusiasm. I wanted my mother's support. Everything else would work out somehow.

I eagerly wrote a letter of inquiry to the American university. 6 Within a couple of weeks, I received a thick envelope. My mother stood beside me while I ripped it open and spread the contents on the table. I picked up the letter on top. It was from the dean of the College of Arts and Sciences. I was blinded with tears as I read the words of encouragement and warm invitation to attend the college. I felt that at this school, my desire for education would be sacredly cherished and respected. My educational heaven was waiting in America. To get there, I knew that I had to be prepared to wage a long, hard battle. And I had to start now.

When she saw how understanding the university was, my mother   7
took a strong stand of support. She vowed to do all she could to help make my dream become reality. She pointed to a row of dictionaries on the bookshelf. I reached for the Croatian-English dictionary and began the first of many long, difficult, and sometimes discouraging steps.

Although my English was quite good, the application forms sent   8
by the college included many words I didn't understand. After a few hours of trying to interpret meanings and of translating, my head was spinning. I needed to take the Test of English as a Foreign Language (TOEFL) and the Scholastic Aptitude Test (SAT). I also needed to send a certified° translation of my high school transcripts. The application deadline was in April. I was not even going to get my high school diploma until June. Suddenly, everything was moving so fast. I couldn't keep up. "Maybe I should postpone this until next year," I thought. We had little money, and I wasn't even sure I could get accepted. I could attend the University of Zagreb for a year, and then transfer the units. My mother suggested that I send a letter to the admissions officer explaining the situation.

After sending the letter, I went to a branch of the University of   9
Zagreb to get information about the entrance exams. I waited for an hour in a small, crowded room thick with cigarette smoke. Two ladies behind the admissions desk provided meager answers to students' questions. The women were apparently upset that all these students were wasting their precious gossip time. Their sharp, terse° responses offered no help. Instead, they managed to make the students feel guilty for even asking. I gave up in my attempt to find out about the entrance exams.

As I walked toward the exit, I stopped to observe the college   10
students who were in the hallway. They wore torn jeans, and they spoke in pretentious° sentences. Their eyes were dull and they had lifeless smiles imprinted° on pale faces. Burning cigarette butts between their fingers were their only well-defined feature. I did not know whether to feel pity for them or for myself. As I left the building, I was both disappointed and humiliated. I had only been there for an hour, and I wondered how I would feel after four years of classes here. My dream had spoiled me. I wanted the luxury of being treated like a human being, and I knew just the place where that would happen.

Shortly, I received a new letter from my admissions officer in 11 Iowa that provided encouragement. He asked me to continue my application process and said that I should not worry about my high school transcripts. They could be mailed as soon as I graduated. What was needed at this time were my test results.

A month later, I took the TOEFL and SAT at the American school 12 in Zagreb. I had studied hard and was satisfied with my performance. The results of both tests were sent directly to the university in America. When the admissions officer received them, he called me to offer congratulations. I had done well. My application was almost complete. Besides my transcripts, which I knew would not be a problem, I needed only one more thing: the money.

My mother joined forces with me in this last, but most 13 formidable°, obstacle. She borrowed money from a friend and deposited it in my account so that I could obtain the bank's confirmation that I had the funds required by the university. However, at the last minute, my mother's friend decided that he needed his money back. I was forced to withdraw the money.

When I returned home from the bank, I found my mother 14 unwrapping our old paintings, works of art by Vladimir Kirin, a famous Croatian artist who was now deceased. Mother had collected his work for as long as I can remember and had planned to open an art gallery in the artist's memory. As I walked across the room, my mother's words stopped me in my tracks. "You have to write an ad for the weekend paper," she said. These paintings meant more than anything to my mother. Yet she was prepared to sell them so that I could live my dream.

The ad was placed. All we had to do was wait for the phone calls. 15 But none came. After two weeks, we ran the ad again, but nothing happened.

I suddenly felt afraid. Even though I could see myself walking 16 around the campus of my new college, even though I could visualize my new classrooms and teachers, it was all still just a dream. I felt like I was looking at slowly dissolving fog. The dream world was fading away, leaving the old, gray reality. I was trapped in truth that I could not accept. I became paralyzed as I imagined myself slowly sinking into ignorance and despair. I would become one of those lifeless, gray faces that walked daily to the bus station through the smog-shrouded° streets. I would work with people who can only afford to think about survival, people who see no values beyond the crispness of bills in their wallets. The ignorant world threatened to swallow me. Though scared to death, I resolved° not to yield. I was not just fighting for money; I was fighting for principle. I would not live a life of deliberate humiliation. I refused to expect from life only as much as others thought I should expect. I alone was responsible to make the best of my life. I had to continue my fight.

For the first time in my life, I earnestly° prayed for myself. I went 17 to church in the early afternoon when I knew nobody would be there. My wooden-soled shoes echoed on the cold floor that led to the main altar. I knelt down and prayed. I prayed for *money*. That humiliated me because I have always thought it was selfish to pray for myself. My prayers had always been devoted to my friends, family, and to those who suffered. I never prayed for anything for myself because I believed that if God took care of the world, I would be taken care of. Now, I prayed for the most selfish thing of all, and I hated myself for it. Full of shame, I prayed, my eyes steadfast° on the ground. Finally, I gained enough strength to look up at the crucifix. I surrendered completely. I forgot all of my thoughts, and my mind began to flow toward some new space. The pressure dissolved. I felt as if I'd been let out of prison. I was free. My guilt and shame were gone, and my heart was beating with a new force. Everything was going to be fine.

In the meantime, my mother continued to search for funds. She 18 called an old friend who owned a jewelry store. He had known me since I was a little girl and bragged that he would do anything for me. He fell silent when he heard my mother's request. He was sorry, but he had just invested all of his money in a new project. He tried to comfort my mother. "I would teach her myself if she were my daughter," he boasted. "School in America. Who does she think she is? She doesn't need college. A woman shouldn't be too smart. She can marry either of my two sons. I promise she will have the freedom to go to church whenever she wants. What more could she need?" Struggling to remain civil, my mother thanked him sarcastically and walked away.

Time was slipping by. I had already obtained a U.S. visa, and I 19 had made my air reservation. The travel agent found a cheap student rate. Despite strict regulations, she was willing to sell me a one-way ticket. My hopes were raised, but even the low-cost ticket had to be paid for. And there was precious little time.

That evening, my mother, brother, grandmother, and I gathered in 20 the living room of our small apartment. I stared at the wall. My brother leaned against the doorway cursing fate. My grandmother tightly held her prayer book, her lips moving slowly. Gloomy silence threatened to break down the walls. Then, as if by magic, words I did not think about came from my lips. "Mother, what about a credit card?" Unlike

America, it was not easy to obtain a credit card in Croatia. Yet my mother knew an influential officer of a local bank. Could he help us? My mother sighed and acknowledged that it was worth a try. Once again my hopes were raised.

21   I returned home from school the next day to find a sense of calm that our household had not known for weeks. Before I had a chance to ask, my mother smiled and nodded her head. My prayers had been answered. My quest° for knowledge was to become a reality.

22   Later that summer, I was on a flight to America. As the plane ascended° into the clouds, my thoughts turned from the quickly disappearing city I was leaving to the destination I knew so little about. I suddenly realized that I was all alone. I was on my own. Everything that happened from that moment on would be the result of my own actions. I was not afraid. My dream had come true, and I was about to begin living a different reality.

23   That reality turned out to be all that I wanted: loving teachers, a real chance to pursue knowledge, and wonderful friends from all over the world. My life as a college student is better than I ever dreamed. It has not been easy. In my job with the University Food Service, I have had to work very hard. I have also had to deal with some irresponsible and disinterested students who refuse to carry out their assignments or pretend they don't understand simple instructions. I must remind myself that this is the only way to keep my scholarship. But my work has many rewards. I have become assistant director of Food Services. I have also received the first Outstanding Student-Employee Award presented by the university, and my work has been recognized by the Board of Trustees.

24   And I have begun the study of literature. This has opened up a new world for me. Every reading assignment, each class discussion has deepened my understanding of life. I am getting to know myself. I can feel the power growing inside me as I complete each assignment. I am beginning to live the magic of knowledge. In everything I learn, I find the same lesson: I can never know everything, but with what I know, I can accomplish anything. The old Superman bookmark is pasted on my door: "Knowledge is real power." Now I know what it means.

VOCABULARY QUESTIONS

A. Use context clues to help you decide on the best definition for each italicized word. Then circle the letter of your choice.

1. The word *comprehend* in "I studied the bookmark, trying to comprehend its exact meaning" (paragraph 1) means
   a. remember.
   b. write down.
   c. understand.
   d. pass by.

2. The word *aspiring* in "Such tales were commonly whispered in the high school hallways by students aspiring to go to college" (paragraph 2) means
   a. paying.
   b. hoping.
   c. remembering.
   d. forgetting.

3. The word *attaining* in "College was supposed to build my confidence in the process of attaining knowledge" (paragraph 3) means
   a. recognizing.
   b. creating.
   c. pleasing.
   d. gaining.

4. The word *meager* in "Two ladies behind the admissions desk provided meager answers to students' questions. The women were apparently upset that all these students were wasting their precious gossip time" (paragraph 9) means
   a. complicated and difficult.
   b. complete.
   c. careful.
   d. brief and inadequate.

5. The word *civil* in "Struggling to remain civil, my mother thanked him sarcastically and walked away" (paragraph 18) means
   a. outraged.
   b. feminine.
   c. pleasant.
   d. superior.

B. Below are words from "Words to Watch." Write in the one that best completes each sentence.

certified	dismayed	ascended
steadfast	terse	

6. Barbie was _____ in her desire to become a model, even though it meant many sacrifices.

7. The balloon _____ to the ceiling, hit a warm light, and exploded.

8. Carla was _____ when the company announced that 10 percent of the work force was going to be laid off.

9. When Juanita accused Alfredo of being unfaithful, his response was _____. "No way!" was all he had to say.

10. Francis studied hard for the auto repair test because he knew he would make more money as a _____ mechanic.

READING COMPREHENSION QUESTIONS

Central Point and Main Ideas

1. Which sentence best expresses the central point of the selection?
   a. There are big differences between Croatia and America.
   b. Education is better in the United States than in Croatia.
   c. By not giving up, the author has achieved the college experience she dreamt of.
   d. Colleges and universities should provide more low-cost opportunities for foreign students.

2. Which sentence best expresses the main idea of paragraph 23?
   a. Even though she has become a successful college student, Petricic is disappointed with life in America.
   b. Despite challenges, Petricic is happy with how things have turned out in America.
   c. Petricic's hard work in Food Services has paid off with an award and official recognition.
   d. Petricic must work hard to keep her scholarship.

Supporting Details

3. _____ TRUE OR FALSE? According to the author, in order to be accepted to the university, all she needed to show was that she had enough money.

4. According to the author,
   a. one of her mother's friends was able to help her go to college in the United States.
   b. selling precious paintings helped her raise the money she needed.
   c. the University of Zagreb was willing to offer her a scholarship.
   d. she was able to raise the money to begin college in the United States through a credit card.

Transitions

5. The relationship between the second part of the sentence below and the first part is one of
   a. cause and effect.
   b. comparison.
   c. contrast.
   d. time.

   After sending the letter, I went to a branch of the University of Zagreb to get information about the entrance exams. (Paragraph 9)

6. The sentence below expresses a relationship of
   a. time.
   b. comparison.
   c. contrast.
   d. cause and effect.

   I never prayed for anything for myself because I believed that if God took care of the world, I would be taken care of. (Paragraph 17)

Patterns of Organization

7. The main pattern of organization of paragraph 14 is
   a. time order.
   b. list of items.
   c. comparison.
   d. definition and example.

8. The main pattern of organization of paragraph 23 is
   a. time order.
   b. list of items.
   c. comparison.
   d. definition and example.

Inferences

9. The author implies that
    a. life is constantly changing in Croatia.
    b. credit cards have just been introduced to Croatia.
    c. what Croatian high school students whisper about college in that country is true, at least at the University of Zagreb.
    d. the university in America was one of many that she applied to.

10. From the selection, we can infer that
    a. the author has a loving, supportive family.
    b. because of her job, the author's grades have been only average.
    c. the author's family has moved to America.
    d. there are no luxuries in Croatia.

MAPPING ACTIVITY

This selection was written according to a time order. Complete the map on the next page by filling in the following statements that divide the reading into a few parts.

- Petricic decides to go to college.
- She decides that going to a special college in the U.S. would be better than attending the University of Zagreb.
- Finally in the U.S., Petricic has found her new life to be all that she had hoped for.
- As a high school student, Petricic is inspired by the phrase "Knowledge is real power."
- After much struggle, Petricic and her family find the money needed to get to the U.S.

Central point: With persistence and support, Petricic has achieved the education she wished for.

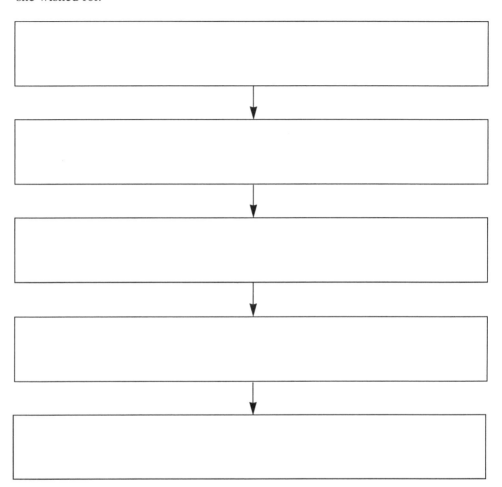

DISCUSSION QUESTIONS

1. The author writes that when she went to high school, students told horror stories about college. When you were in high school, what was your perception of college? Now that you are in college, has your perception changed? If so, in what ways?

2. At the conclusion of the selection, Petricic writes that she now knows the meaning of the phrase "Knowledge is real power." What does this phrase mean to you?

WRITING ACTIVITIES

1.   The author knew that coming to America would not be easy. There were times when she was afraid her dream would not be realized. Write a paragraph telling of something you wanted very badly, but were afraid you would not be able to attain. Tell of the struggles you had to overcome to get to your goal. How did you finally reach it?

2.   Petricic would not have been able to come to America without the support of her mother. Who has helped you the most in your quest for education? Write a paper explaining who this person is and how he or she has helped you. Use the kind of specific detail Petricic has used in her essay to dramatize your story for your readers.

Check Your Performance   **KNOWLEDGE IS POWER**

Skill	*Number Right*	*Points*	*Total*
VOCABULARY			
Vocabulary in Context (5 items)	_____	x 10 =	_____
Words to Watch (5 items)	_____	x 10 =	_____
		SCORE =	_____ %
COMPREHENSION			
Central Point and Main Ideas (2 items)	_____	x 7 =	_____
Supporting Details (2 items)	_____	x 7 =	_____
Transitions (2 items)	_____	x 7 =	_____
Patterns of Organization (2 items)	_____	x 7 =	_____
Inferences (2 items)	_____	x 7 =	_____
Mapping (5 items)	_____	x 6 =	_____
		SCORE =	_____ %

FINAL SCORES: **Vocabulary** _____ %   **Comprehension** _____ %

Enter your final scores into the reading performance chart on the inside back cover.

7

How to Write Clearly
Edward T. Thompson

Preview

Do you like to write? Or is writing, in your opinion, pure torture? If you answered "torture," cheer up: you're about to receive some valuable help. Certain tricks of the trade can make writing easier and more effective for everyone. In this selection, the editor-in-chief of *Reader's Digest* shares with you his ideas on how to write what you mean— clearly and briefly.

Words to Watch

objective (10): unbiased
detract (10): take away from
clarity (10): clearness
ironically (14): contrary to what is expected
delete (17): remove
mentality (19): mind
biota (21): living things
mortality (21): death
endeavoring (22): trying
artistry (28): the work of an artist
excess (28): extra
anecdotes (28): brief stories
belabor (28): to explain in too much detail
invariably (28): always

> If you are afraid to write, don't be.   1
> If you think you've got to string together big fancy words and   2
> high-flying phrases, forget it.

To write well, unless you aspire to be a professional poet or novelist, you only need to get your ideas across simply and clearly. 3

It's not easy. But it is easier than you might imagine. 4

There are only three basic requirements: 5

First, you must *want* to write clearly. And I believe you really do, if you've stayed this far with me. 6

Second, you must be willing to *work hard*. Thinking means work—and that's what it takes to do anything well. 7

Third, you must know and follow some *basic guidelines*. 8

If, while you're writing for clarity, some lovely, dramatic or inspired phrases or sentences come to you, fine. Put them in. 9

But then with cold, objective° eyes and mind ask yourself: "Do they detract° from clarity°?" If they do, grit your teeth and cut the frills. 10

FOLLOW SOME BASIC GUIDELINES

I can't give you a complete list of "do's and don'ts" for every writing problem you'll ever face. 11

But I can give you some fundamental guidelines that cover the most common problems. 12

1. Outline what you want to say.

I know that sounds grade-schoolish. But you can't write clearly until, *before you start*, you know where you will stop. 13

Ironically°, that's even a problem in writing an outline (i.e., knowing the ending before you begin). 14

So try this method: 15

- On 3″ x 5″ cards, write—one point to a card—all the points you need to make.

- Divide the cards into piles—one pile for each group of points *closely related* to each other. (If you were describing an automobile, you'd put all the points about mileage in one pile, all the points about safety in another, and so on.)

- Arrange your piles of points in a sequence. Which are most important and should be given first or saved for last? Which must you present before others in order to make the others understandable?

- Now, *within* each pile, do the same thing—arrange the *points* in logical, understandable order.

There you have your outline, needing only an introduction and conclusion. 16

This is a practical way to outline. It's also flexible. You can add, 17
delete° or change the location of points easily.

2. Start where your readers are.

How much do they know about the subject? Don't write to a level 18
higher than your readers' knowledge of it.

CAUTION: Forget that old—and wrong—advice about writing to 19
a twelve-year-old mentality°. That's insulting. But do remember that
your prime purpose is to *explain* something, not prove that you're
smarter than your readers.

3. Avoid jargon.

Don't use words, expressions, phrases known only to people with 20
specific knowledge or interests.

Example: A scientist, using scientific jargon, wrote, "The biota° 21
exhibited a one hundred percent mortality° response." He could have
written: "All the fish died."

4. Use familiar combinations of words.

A speech writer for President Franklin D. Roosevelt wrote, "We 22
are endeavoring° to construct a more inclusive society." F.D.R. changed
it to, "We're going to make a country in which no one is left out."

CAUTION: By familiar combinations of words, I do *not* mean 23
incorrect grammar. *That* can be unclear. Example: John's father says he
can't go out Friday. (Who can't go out? John or his father?)

5. Use "first-degree" words.

These words immediately bring an image to your mind. Other 24
words must be "translated" through the first-degree word before you
see the image. Those are second/third-degree words.

First-degree words	Second/third-degree words
face	visage, countenance
stay	abide, remain, residue
book	volume, tome, publication

First-degree words are usually the most precise words, too. 25

6. Stick to the point.

Your outline—which was more work in the beginning—now 26
saves you work. Because now you can ask about any sentence you
write: "Does it relate to a point in the outline? If it doesn't, should I add
it to the outline? If not, I'm getting off the track." Then, full steam
ahead—on the main line.

7. Be as brief as possible.

Whatever you write, shortening—*condensing*—almost always 27
makes it tighter, straighter, easier to read and understand.

Condensing, as *Reader's Digest* does it, is in large part artistry°. 28
But it involves techniques that anyone can learn and use.

- *Present your points in logical ABC order:* Here again, your
  outline should save you work because, if you did it right, your
  points already stand in logical ABC order—A makes B understandable, B makes C understandable and so on. To write in a
  straight line is to say something clearly in the fewest possible
  words.

- *Don't waste words telling people what they already know:*
  Notice how we edited this: "Have you ever wondered how
  banks rate you as a credit risk? ~~You know, of course, that it's
  some combination of facts about your income, your job, and so
  on. But actually,~~ Many banks have a scoring system. . . ."

- *Cut out excess° evidence and unnecessary anecdotes°:* Usually,
  one fact or example (at most, two) will support a point. More
  just belabor° it. And while writing about something may remind
  you of a good story, ask yourself: "Does it really help to tell the
  story, or does it slow me down?"

  (Many people think *Reader's Digest* articles are filled with
  anecdotes. Actually, we use them sparingly and usually for one
  or two reasons: either the subject is so dry it needs some
  "humanity" to give it life; or the subject is so hard to grasp, it
  needs anecdotes to help readers understand. If the subject is
  both lively and easy to grasp, we move right along.)

- *Look for the most common word wasters:* windy phrases.

Windy phrases	Cut to . . .
at the present time..now	
in the event of ....if	
in the majority of instances............................usually	

- *Look for passive verbs you can make active:* Invariably°, this produces a shorter sentence. "The cherry tree was chopped down by George Washington." (Passive verb and nine words.) "George Washington chopped down the cherry tree." (Active verb and seven words.)

- *Look for positive/negative sections from which you can cut the negative:* See how we did it here: "The answer ~~does not rest with carelessness or incompetence. It lies largely in~~ is having enough people to do the job."

- Finally, to write more clearly by saying it in fewer words: *when you've finished, stop.*

VOCABULARY QUESTIONS

A. Use context clues to help you decide on the best definition for each italicized word. Then circle the letter of each choice.

1. The word *aspire* in "To write well, unless you aspire to be a professional poet or novelist, you only need to get your ideas across simply and clearly" (paragraph 3) means
   a. pretend.
   b. wish.
   c. neglect.
   d. sweat.

2. The word *fundamental* in "I can't give you a complete list of 'do's and don'ts'. . . . But I can give you some fundamental guidelines that cover the most common problems" (paragraphs 11–12) means
   a. unusual.
   b. extra.
   c. boring.
   d. basic.

3. The word *sequence* in "Arrange your piles of points in a sequence. Which are most important and should be given first or saved for last? Which must you present before others . . . ?" (paragraph 15) means
   a. circle.
   b. time.
   c. order.
   d. space.

4. The word *prime* in "do remember that your prime purpose is to *explain* something, not prove that you're smarter than your readers" (paragraph 19) means
   a. main.
   b. old.
   c. easy.
   d. not required.

5. The word *sparingly* in "*Cut out excess evidence and unnecessary anecdotes . . .* Many people think *Reader's Digest* articles are filled with anecdotes. Actually, we use them sparingly" (paragraph 28) means
   a. at the beginning.
   b. in a limited way.
   c. pleasantly.
   d. frequently.

B. Below are words, or forms of words, from "Words to Watch." Write in the one that best completes each sentence.

| anecdote | artistry | delete |
| mortality | objective | |

6. Public speakers often begin with a funny _____ to warm up the audience.

7. The _____ of Van Gogh appeals to people of all ages, who delight in the energy and beauty of his paintings.

8. My English teacher suggested that I _____ all the "you knows" from my essay.

9. Because our weapons are now so powerful, the _____ rate of even a short war can be very high.

10. Totally _____ reporting is hard to find, as reporters usually have feelings toward their subjects.

READING COMPREHENSION QUESTIONS

Central Point and Main Ideas

1. Which sentence best expresses the central point of the selection?
   a. Many people are afraid to write.
   b. Clear writing has three basic requirements.
   c. Good writers know when to stop writing.
   d. Everyone wants to write clearly.

2. Which sentence best expresses the main idea of paragraph 15?
   a. Try an outlining method that uses 3″ x 5″ cards.
   b. Write one point to a card.
   c. Put the cards into piles, with each pile containing closely related points.
   d. Arrange the piles in an order.

3. Which sentence best expresses the main idea of paragraph 28?
   a. Present your points in a logical order.
   b. Don't tell people what they already know.
   c. There are a few techniques to writing briefly.
   d. Look for and eliminate common word wasters.

Supporting Details

4. The author states that writing well requires
   a. hard work.
   b. getting your ideas across simply and clearly.
   c. learning some basic guidelines for writing.
   d. all of the above.

5. A clear writer
   a. tells people what they already know.
   b. prefers passive verbs.
   c. makes every sentence relate to the point.
   d. uses big words and fancy phrases.

Transitions

6. Paragraphs 6, 7, and 8 all begin with
   a. addition signals.
   b. comparison signals.
   c. example signals.
   d. cause and effect signals.

7. The relationship of the second sentence below to the first sentence is one of
   a. addition.
   b. time.
   c. comparison.
   d. contrast.

   This is a practical way to outline. It's also flexible. (Paragraph 17)

Patterns of Organization

8. Just as paragraphs are organized according to patterns, so are entire selections. The main pattern of organization of this selection is
   a. time order.
   b. list of items.
   c. comparison and/or contrast.
   d. definition and example.

Inferences

9. The author implies that, in writing, a single word
   a. is always more clear than two.
   b. should never be scientific.
   c. should never be negative.
   d. is better than two that mean the same thing.

10. The author implies that a good writer
    a. never has trouble writing anything.
    b. has to make many decisions.
    c. is a wealthy writer.
    d. doesn't need a dictionary.

MAPPING ACTIVITY

The suggestions in this selection are organized into lists of requirements and guidelines. Complete the diagram of the selection below by filling in the missing points—one requirement and four guidelines.

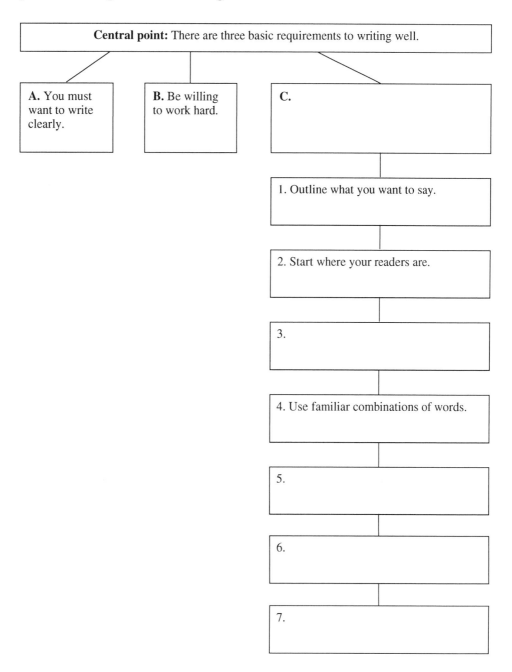

Central point: There are three basic requirements to writing well.

A. You must want to write clearly.

B. Be willing to work hard.

C.

1. Outline what you want to say.

2. Start where your readers are.

3.

4. Use familiar combinations of words.

5.

6.

7.

DISCUSSION QUESTIONS

1. Of the guidelines for writing that Thompson gives in his article, which three are the most valuable for you—and why?

2. Do you think that the author's advice can also apply to speaking clearly? Which suggestions in particular could help make you a better speaker?

WRITING ACTIVITIES

1. Write a letter to Edward Thompson telling him what you think of his suggestions and why. Try to follow his suggestions for clear writing in your letter.

2. Thompson recommends that before people write, they should make an outline—a plan for what they are going to put on paper. In what other activities is planning ahead a good idea? Think of one and write about how to plan such a project. You might, for example, write about one of the following: giving a large party, such as a wedding reception or a graduation party; moving into a new home or apartment; taking a family vacation; going on a special date; writing a term paper. Be sure to describe the steps that must be taken in order for the event to succeed. Your topic sentence will be similar to: "There are a few steps one should follow when giving a large party."

Check Your Performance			**HOW TO WRITE CLEARLY**
Skill	*Number Right*	*Points*	*Total*
VOCABULARY			
Vocabulary in Context (5 items)	_____	x 10 =	_____
Words to Watch (5 items)	_____	x 10 =	_____
		SCORE =	_____ %
COMPREHENSION			
Central Point and Main Ideas (3 items)	_____	x 7 =	_____
Supporting Details (2 items)	_____	x 7 =	_____
Transitions (2 items)	_____	x 7 =	_____
Patterns of Organization (1 item)	_____	x 7 =	_____
Inferences (2 items)	_____	x 7 =	_____
Mapping (5 items)	_____	x 6 =	_____
		SCORE =	_____ %

FINAL SCORES: Vocabulary _____ %   Comprehension _____ %

Enter your final scores into the reading performance chart on the inside back cover.

8

Friendship and Living Longer
Vicky Chan

Preview

Maybe the old saying should be changed from "An apple a day . . ." to "Friendship each day keeps the doctor away." As this selection explains, strong social ties appear to be good preventive medicine. How do we know that family and friends keep us healthier? And why would a strong social life make for a strong body? Vicky Chan offers some interesting evidence.

Words to Watch

subjects (2): people being studied in an experiment
confirms (4): supports
tend (5): are likely
responsive (5): reacting easily
abrupt (9): sudden
literally (11): actually

Do you want to be healthier and live longer? Spend time with 1
your friends. That is the prescription given by several medical studies.
These surveys show that people with strong social ties—to friends,
family and loved ones, even pets—live longer and enjoy better health
than lonely people.

One study in California, for example, followed 7,000 people over a period of nine years. The subjects° were asked to describe their social ties. Some said that they were isolated from others. These subjects had death rates two or three times higher than people with families and friends.   2

The stronger the social ties to others, the study found, the lower the death rate. This pattern held true for men and women, young and old, rich and poor. The race of the subject did not change the result. It also applied to people with different lifestyles. Cigarette smokers who had friends lived longer than friendless smokers. Joggers involved with other people lived longer than joggers who lived isolated lives.   3

Another study confirms° this result. The University of Michigan looked at 2,754 adults in Tecumseh, Michigan. The researchers carefully measured their subjects' health at the beginning of the study. The lonely, isolated people started out as healthy as the others. But over ten years, they were two to four times as likely to die.   4

Other findings also show the health value of personal ties. Married men and women tend° to live longer than single, divorced, or widowed people of the same age. In nursing homes, patients became more aware and responsive° when they played with cats and dogs. Pet owners are more likely to survive heart attacks than people without pets.   5

Another kind of proof that social ties support good health comes from Japan. Most Japanese people live hectic lives in cities as crowded, noisy, and polluted as ours. Such a way of life seems unhealthy. Yet the Japanese are among the healthiest and longest-lived people in the world. One reason may be their diet. Another reason, though, is their way of life. Japanese have strong ties to family and coworkers. These ties are rarely broken. For example, companies tend to move coworkers as a group, rather than one at a time. Thus the work groups remain the same.   6

Studies of Japanese-Americans support the importance of the role of Japanese social life in preserving their health. Japanese-Americans who live in strongly Japanese neighborhoods and have mainly Japanese friends tend to live longer than those who do not. Both groups eat mostly American-style food, and many in both groups smoke and drink. Thus it appears to be the strong social ties of Japanese communities that keep their members healthy.   7

Why is it more healthy to have friends and loved ones? We don't know, exactly. But it is probably a combination of several explanations. In part, people with strong social ties may simply have more to live for. They have loved ones or family who share their lives. They have friends who call them and ask them how they're doing. They have get-togethers to look forward to.   8

Social contacts also provide us with a buffer against the shocks of 9
life. At some point, each of us moves, changes a job, or loses a loved
one. Such abrupt° changes tend to cause increases in the rates of many
diseases. These include heart disease, cancer, strokes, and mental
illnesses. Accidents are also more likely to happen to people whose
lives have suddenly changed. Friends, loved ones, even a loyal dog can
help us to get through the otherwise very rough changes that we must
deal with in life.

Finally, friends and loved ones can affect our health in still 10
another way. If we are smokers, they may help us to quit. If we overeat,
they may urge us to cut back. They can remind us to go for medical
checkups. And if we have fears or sadnesses bottled up inside us,
friends can help us face and overcome them. By caring for us, in other
words, friends and family help us to care for ourselves.

Close human ties make life not only fuller, but also longer. Caring 11
for others, and being cared for by them, is literally° a more healthy way
to live.

VOCABULARY QUESTIONS

A. Use context clues to help you decide on the best definition for each italicized
word. Then circle the letter of each choice.

1. The word *surveys* in "Spend time with your friends. That is the prescription
given by several medical studies. These surveys show that people with
strong social ties . . . live longer" (paragraph 1) means
a. prescriptions.
b. friends.
c. studies.
d. ties.

2. The word *isolated* in "Some said that they were isolated from others. These
subjects had death rates two or three times higher than people with families
and friends" (paragraph 2) means
a. joined.
b. coming.
c. separated.
d. taking.

3. The word *hectic* in "Most Japanese people live hectic lives in cities as crowded, noisy, and polluted as ours" (paragraph 6) means
   a. boring and empty.
   b. busy and rushed.
   c. brief and happy.
   d. long and peaceful.

4. The word *buffer* in "Social contacts also provide us with a buffer against the shocks of life" (paragraph 9) means
   a. protection.
   b. bad attitude.
   c. honesty.
   d. problem.

5. The words *bottled up* in "if we have fears or sadnesses bottled up inside us, friends can help us face and overcome them" (paragraph 10) mean
   a. fully repaired.
   b. balanced.
   c. welcomed.
   d. held in.

B. Below are words, or forms of words, from "Words to Watch." Write in the one that best completes each sentence.

abrupt	confirm	literally
responsive	tend	

6. The _____ ending of the movie surprised the moviegoers, who expected a more gradual conclusion.

7. Scientists have learned that there are _____ dozens of viruses that can cause colds.

8. Without proper guidance, students _____ to enroll in only those classes which interest them.

9. The sick child just lay motionless in her hospital bed, but when her father arrived, she became more _____.

10. One research study isn't enough to prove a point. Other studies must _____ an idea before it's accepted as true.

READING COMPREHENSION QUESTIONS

Central Point and Main Ideas

1. Which sentence best expresses the central point of the selection?
   a. Everyone wants to be healthy and live a long life.
   b. People live longer when they have strong social relationships.
   c. The Japanese are among the healthiest people in the world.
   d. Friends and loved ones help get us through hard times.

2. Which is the topic sentence of paragraph 5?
   a. The first sentence
   b. The second sentence
   c. The third sentence
   d. The fourth sentence

3. Which sentence best expresses the main idea of paragraph 10?
   a. The second sentence
   b. The third sentence
   c. The next-to-the-last sentence
   d. The last sentence

Supporting Details

4. According to the reading, a married man is more likely to live longer than a
   a. married woman.
   b. smoker.
   c. divorced man.
   d. friend.

5. _____ TRUE OR FALSE? Japanese-Americans who live in Japanese communities and have mainly Japanese friends are likely to live longer than Japanese-Americans who do not.

6. According to Chan, people whose lives suddenly change are more likely than others to
   a. have friends.
   b. have accidents.
   c. quit smoking.
   d. smoke.

Transitions

7. The transitions which introduce paragraphs 4, 5, and 6 signal
   a. addition.
   b. time.
   c. cause and effect.
   d. illustration.

8. The relationship of the second sentence below to the first is one of
   a. addition.
   b. comparison.
   c. contrast.
   d. cause and effect.

> Such a way of life seems unhealthy. Yet the Japanese are among the healthiest and longest-lived people in the world. (Paragraph 6)

Patterns of Organization

9. Just as paragraphs are organized according to patterns, so are entire selections. The main pattern of organization of this selection is
   a. time order.
   b. list of items.
   c. definition and example.

Inferences

10. _____ TRUE OR FALSE? The author implies that lonely people are more likely to get sick.

MAPPING ACTIVITY

This selection is made up of a central point along with evidence and possible explanations for that point. Complete the diagram on the next page by filling in the scrambled items that follow.

- According to a University of Michigan study, lonely people tend to die sooner.
- Friendship leads to better health and longer lives.
- Strong ties may give people more to live for.
- Social contacts buffer us against life's shocks.

Central point: _____

**Evidence
for the Point**

1. According to a California study, the stronger the social ties, the lower the death rate.

2. _____
   _____
   _____

3. Studies show that married people tend to live longer and that relationships with pets make people stronger.

4. Studies show that Japanese-Americans with strong social ties are healthier than other Americans.

**Possible Explanations
for the Point**

1. _____
   _____
   _____
   _____

2. _____
   _____
   _____
   _____

3. By caring for us, friends often help us care for ourselves.

DISCUSSION QUESTIONS

1. Do you agree that "social contacts . . . provide us with a buffer against the shocks of life"? What are some of the ways that these contacts keep us from feeling pain? Give an example.

2. How can people who have trouble making friends cope with crisis? In what ways could they form more social ties?

WRITING ACTIVITIES

1.   "Friendship and Living Longer" states that we need friends and relatives when we face major changes in our lives. Think back to when you lost a loved one, moved to a new town, began a new job, changed schools, started college, or experienced any other difficult change. Whom did you rely on to soften the shock? Write about what happened and how this person helped you adjust. One example of a topic sentence for this paper is: "Without the help of my best friend, Andy, I would never have been able to deal with the death of my father."

2.   While we need friends and family, we also require privacy at times. How do you find privacy? Walk around a park alone? Meditate in your bedroom? Write a paper in which you list and explain ways you find privacy. Or instead list and explain the benefits that private time gives you.

Check Your Performance	**FRIENDSHIP AND LIVING LONGER**		
Skill	*Number Right*	*Points*	*Total*
VOCABULARY			
Vocabulary in Context (5 items)	_____	x 10 =	_____
Words to Watch (5 items)	_____	x 10 =	_____
		SCORE =	_____ %
COMPREHENSION			
Central Point and Main Ideas (3 items)	_____	x 7 =	_____
Supporting Details (3 items)	_____	x 7 =	_____
Transitions (2 items)	_____	x 7 =	_____
Patterns of Organization (1 item)	_____	x 7 =	_____
Inferences (1 item)	_____	x 7 =	_____
Mapping (4 items)	_____	x 7.5 =	_____
		SCORE =	_____ %

FINAL SCORES: **Vocabulary** _____ %   **Comprehension** _____ %

Enter your final scores into the reading performance chart on the inside back cover.

9

Room with a New View
Steve Lopez

Preview

Nameless, almost faceless, homeless people camp on the streets of every American city. Here's the story of one such man who came to have a name and a face for the people who saw him daily on one Philadelphia street. By responding to him as a real person, the people on his street changed his life and their own.

Words to Watch

inspiration (6): encouragement
oblivious to (6): unaware of
distribution (10): supply
barrier (11): something that separates
apparently (14): seeming to be
alcove (15): small space off to the side
maintaining (16): keeping in good condition
fragments (21): pieces
displaced (24): away from home

Three years ago, architect Peter Fox is fresh out of college and catches a bus for his first day on the job. The bus pulls up to 20th and Chestnut, the door opens, and there's some guy camped out on the sidewalk like he owns the property.

Next day, same thing. And the next day, and the next.

"I had to step over him every morning," Fox says.

Fox would continue on to work, where he sat against a window 4 one flight above 20th Street. Sometimes he'd design a new swimming pool for someone who was unhappy with their old swimming pool. And when his work didn't seem to reflect reality, there was always the window.

Three years later, the man is still out there. Peter Fox is still 5 looking.

They don't know each other. But Fox has found comfort and 6 inspiration° in just looking. And the man—oblivious to° his starring role in the drama Fox sees through his window—is comfortable with his own invisibility.

The man outside says he is John Madison, Vietnam veteran. 7

"Shortly after I started," Fox wrote in a letter, "a Korean fruit stand 8 opened. At first the street guy would bum them for food and money."

It looked like only a matter of time before one of them drove out 9 the other. But that didn't happen.

"Pretty soon they had him helping unload their truck in the 10 morning when it arrived from the food distribution° center."

This despite a language barrier°. On some level, maybe because 11 both Madison and the Koreans were on the edge of things, they made a connection.

"Next, he was sweeping the sidewalk, then driving the truck for 12 them, all the time his appearance improving."

Partly because he was getting paid by the Korean fruit vendors. A 13 couple bucks here, a couple bucks there. What was emerging, gradually, was the new John Madison.

"Better clothes, haircut, apparently° now off the street. And the 14 wild look disappearing from his eyes."

What Fox didn't know—nobody knew—was that Madison had 15 taken to camping in a quiet alcove° near the Boy Scouts of America office several blocks away. Though it was still the street, to him it was a fancier address, fit for a man of his upward mobility.

"As the fortunes of the vendors improved, they, along with their 16 relatives, bought several shops on the block, and the street guy became responsible for maintaining° all the shops, as well as the street and sidewalk along the entire block."

Fox watched as the John Madison Corporation conquered new 17 territory. With a household broom, he had staked out the west side of 20th Street from Market to Chestnut. He had the sidewalk so clean you had to look twice to figure out what was wrong with the picture. He even dug cigarette butts out of cracks.

And he was diversifying.   18

"He is now holding down two jobs—collecting trash for a private   19
hauler in the early morning and then arriving (usually hanging off the
side of the trash truck) to work for the Koreans and other merchants."

Madison's abilities did not escape the notice of the management   20
of Nuts to You, one of the few remaining non-Korean businesses on the
block. Manny Radbill, the owner, occasionally had Madison clean his
van. One time Madison found money in it and immediately gave it to
Radbill. Debbie Alexander, Radbill's manager, remembers the time she
handed Madison a Christmas bonus. He refused.

To John Madison, words and possessions are confusing   21
fragments° of a complicated world. His luxury is to need so little.

His only vice, Radbill says, is a beer or two on a warm afternoon,   22
a habit the Koreans do not seem to appreciate. Most of them, however,
see in Madison a little bit of themselves. He works hard, says Hyun Jin.
What else is there?

There is Peter Fox, watching the whole thing out the window.   23
And there's Madison, the man he used to step over.

"It has been very inspiring to watch all of this happen. It's a great   24
reflection of the Korean merchants, refugees themselves, who in
establishing themselves and their families in this country have found
room in their plan to reach down to someone more displaced° than
themselves and pull him up with them."

Madison says he's off the streets now and rents space in a North   25
Philadelphia house for $3 a night. He liked hearing that people have
seen the change in him and appreciate what he's done for the block.

As Madison smiled at the thought, broom in hand, Peter Fox   26
watched through the window.

VOCABULARY QUESTIONS

A. Use context clues to help you decide on the best definition for each italicized
word. Then circle the letter of each choice.

1. The word *vendors* in "a Korean fruit stand opened. . . . Pretty soon they had
   him helping unload their truck . . . he was getting paid by the Korean fruit
   vendors" (paragraphs 8–13) means
   a. pickers.
   b. sellers.
   c. machines.
   d. tasters.

2. The word *emerging* in "all the time his appearance improving. . . . What was emerging, gradually, was the new John Madison" (paragraphs 12–13) means
   a. appearing.
   b. hurting.
   c. ending.
   d. playing.

3. The phrase *upward mobility* in "it was a fancier address, fit for a man of his upward mobility" (paragraph 15) means
   a. expensive tastes.
   b. great needs.
   c. improving position.
   d. extreme poverty.

4. The word *diversifying* in "And he was diversifying. 'He is now holding down two jobs'" (paragraphs 18–19) means
   a. doing more.
   b. earning less.
   c. becoming harder to manage.
   d. collecting trash.

5. The word *vice* in "His only vice . . . is a beer or two on a warm afternoon, a habit the Koreans do not seem to appreciate" (paragraph 22) means
   a. fear.
   b. change.
   c. fault.
   d. strength.

B. Below are words, or forms of words, from "Words to Watch." Write in the one that best completes each sentence.

alcoves	distribution	inspiration
maintaining	oblivious to	

6. As Kevin stepped up to the free throw line, he was _____ the crowd's booing.

7. Companies usually set up large _____ centers in areas where they make many sales.

8. One key to _____ a car's appearance is frequent waxing.

9. Libraries usually provide good places for study by putting reading tables in quiet _____.

10. Ryan White was a schoolboy who died of AIDS. His brave struggle to live was an _____ to all who knew him.

READING COMPREHENSION QUESTIONS

Central Point and Main Ideas

1. Which sentence best expresses the central point of the selection?
   a. Peter Fox enjoys looking out his window at John Madison and others.
   b. Homeless men should be put to work.
   c. Some Korean merchants helped John Madison begin a new life.
   d. Everyone needs to earn a living.

2. Which sentence best expresses the main idea of paragraphs 8–10?
   a. Some Koreans opened a fruit stand.
   b. Madison asked the Koreans for money and food.
   c. Fox expected trouble between Madison and the Koreans.
   d. New Korean businessmen got Madison to work for them.

3. Which sentence best expresses the main idea of paragraphs 10–17?
   a. At first, Madison helped the Korean businessmen unload their truck.
   b. Madison was getting paid by the Korean fruit vendors.
   c. As Madison worked more and more for the Koreans, his personal life improved.
   d. Madison cleaned the sidewalks so well that they looked strange.

Supporting Details

4. According to the author, the Koreans
   a. were afraid of Madison.
   b. kept asking Madison to move.
   c. taught Madison to drive a truck.
   d. did well in their businesses.

5. As a result of his efforts, Madison
   a. has convinced Peter Fox to give money to the homeless.
   b. now works for the Boy Scouts of America.
   c. is now living in a house in North Philadelphia.
   d. is finding jobs for other homeless men.

Transitions

6. The transition *after* in the sentence below signals
   a. addition.
   b. contrast.
   c. time.
   d. cause and effect.

   > "Shortly after I started," Fox wrote in a letter, "a Korean fruit stand opened." (Paragraph 8)

7. The transition *however* in the sentence below signals
   a. time.
   b. contrast.
   c. an example.
   d. cause and effect.

   > His only vice . . . is a beer or two on a warm afternoon, a habit the Koreans do not seem to appreciate. Most of them, however, see in Madison a little bit of themselves. (Paragraph 22)

Patterns of Organization

8. The main pattern of organization of the entire reading selection is
   a. time order.
   b. list of items.
   c. comparison and/or contrast.
   d. definition and example.

Inferences

9. The author implies that
   a. Madison was wounded in Vietnam.
   b. Fox wants to meet Madison.
   c. Madison wants to return to his family.
   d. Fox has avoided any direct personal involvement with Madison.

10. We can conclude that the author wrote the selection
    a. to complain about the poor treatment Vietnam veterans receive.
    b. after reading Fox's letter and interviewing people on the block.
    c. to help Madison find a home.
    d. to give hope to all homeless people everywhere.

MAPPING ACTIVITY

This selection is organized by time: first one thing happened; then another; after that, another; and so on. Four major events are scrambled in the list below. Write them in the diagram in their correct order.

- Madison then takes on more jobs and improves his appearance.
- Madison camps on the street.
- Madison moves off the street.
- Korean businessmen pay him for odd jobs.

Central point: By offering work to John Madison, a homeless man, Korean businessmen start a new life for him.

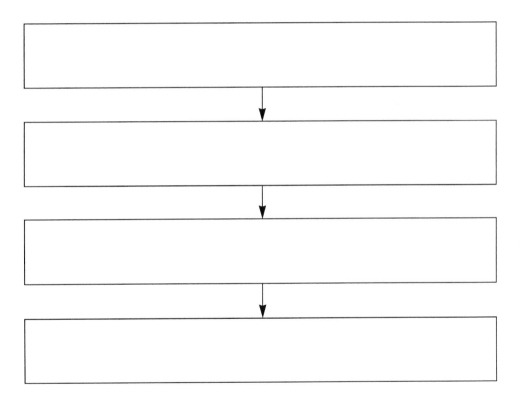

DISCUSSION QUESTIONS

1. John Madison found money in a van and returned it. He also refused to accept a Christmas bonus. What do these facts tell us about him? Would you have done the same? Why or why not?

2. The author states that John Madison's "luxury is to need so little." What does this mean? How much—or how little—do you need to make you happy?

WRITING ACTIVITIES

1. Write a paragraph in which you list and explain the reasons why you think that many are homeless. Begin the paragraph with your topic sentence.

2. Write about someone who, like the Korean businessmen, went to some trouble to help someone else overcome a problem. Like Lopez, first describe the problem, and then go on to explain how the situation got better.

Check Your Performance			ROOM WITH A NEW VIEW
Skill	*Number Right*	*Points*	*Total*
VOCABULARY			
Vocabulary in Context (5 items)	_____	x 10 =	_____
Words to Watch (5 items)	_____	x 10 =	_____
		SCORE =	_____ %
COMPREHENSION			
Central Point and Main Ideas (3 items)	_____	x 7 =	_____
Supporting Details (2 items)	_____	x 7 =	_____
Transitions (2 items)	_____	x 7 =	_____
Patterns of Organization (1 item)	_____	x 7 =	_____
Inferences (2 items)	_____	x 7 =	_____
Mapping (4 items)	_____	x 7.5 =	_____
		SCORE =	_____ %

FINAL SCORES: **Vocabulary** _____%   **Comprehension** _____%

Enter your final scores into the reading performance chart on the inside back cover.

10

Why Johnny Can't Think
Peter Kugel

Preview

"I don't know if you ever noticed, but it's a lot harder for teachers to fall asleep in class than it is for students," writes Peter Kugel. The reason, he suggests, is that teachers are doing something which the students are not. What is that activity? Could a change in the American curriculum encourage students to do it as well? See what you think after reading this selection.

Words to Watch

occurred (1): came to mind
campaign (1): activities aimed at winning an election
evidence: (1): proof
seldom (5): rarely
sound (5): reasonable
sound bite (6): brief bit of TV news
curriculum (7): the courses of study offered at a school

It occurred° to me the other day that this year's rather mindless 1 presidential campaign° might be further evidence° of the decline of American education. Maybe the candidates are giving us such a thin diet because our schools never taught us how to deal with anything more substantial.

Look at how we teach people to think. We have teachers stand in 2 front of classrooms and think out loud, while the students listen.

It seems to me that expecting students to learn from such 3 instruction is like expecting people to learn to play football by lying on a couch and watching it on TV. Schools don't teach football that way; they teach their students to play football by having them play football.

How come schools don't teach their students how to think by having them think?   4

Of course, that's what the students are supposed to be doing while the teacher is thinking out loud in front of them, but they seldom° do. And, even when they do, they can seldom tell whether what they are thinking is sound°.   5

All they can evaluate is how it makes them feel. That's perfect preparation for the sound bite° on the evening news: you evaluate the candidate by how he makes you feel.   6

Can we do any better? We might consider an idea from an educational movement that started in Great Britain called "writing across the curriculum°." It suggests that one way to make students think about something is to make them write about it.   7

Writing can help you learn. For example, suppose you're learning about the tides. There's five minutes of class time left that the teacher might use to give you more facts.   8

But, instead, the teacher asks you to write a short letter to a ten-year-old explaining what causes tides. You might wonder what you would learn from doing that.   9

Would five more minutes of lecturing by the teacher, who knows the material, be more useful than five minutes of writing by a student who doesn't?   10

Not necessarily. For one thing, listening is passive, while writing is active. It's a lot easier to pay attention when you're being active. I don't know if you ever noticed, but it's a lot harder for teachers to fall asleep in class than it is for students.   11

When students are writing, they're doing something. It not only keeps them awake, but, while they're writing, they're doing a very active form of thinking.   12

We learn to ride a bicycle through the activity of riding a bicycle, and we never forget how to do it. Maybe if we learned to think by writing, we'd forget less of what we had learned.   13

Sure, I know students already do a lot of writing in school. They write essays and term papers. But those who advocate "writing across the curriculum" are suggesting a different kind of writing: writing to learn; writing to develop ideas; writing in all your classes (that's why it's called "writing across the curriculum"); the kind of writing you do when you write notes to yourself on the backs of envelopes; writing to help you think.   14

Suppose that when we were in school we had spent more time 15
writing about what we were thinking and less listening to what others
thought? We might have learned to consider whether what the
candidates are saying makes sense and whether their ideas fit together.

If we were ready to do that, don't you think that the candidates 16
would give us a different kind of campaign? Can you imagine what
campaign speeches would be like if, at the end of each one, the entire
audience sat down and tried to write a letter to a ten-year-old,
explaining what the candidates had just said?

VOCABULARY QUESTIONS

A. Use context clues to help you decide on the best definition for each italicized
word. Then circle the letter of each choice.

1. The word *decline* in "this year's rather mindless presidential campaign might
be further evidence of the decline of American education" (paragraph 1)
means
   a. birth.
   b. great worth.
   c. lowered quality.
   d. strong tradition.

2. The word *substantial* in "Maybe the candidates are giving us such a thin diet
because our schools never taught us how to deal with anything more
substantial" (paragraph 1) means
   a. noisy.
   b. solid.
   c. lean.
   d. wrong.

3. The word *evaluate* in "they can seldom tell whether what they are thinking is
sound. All they can evaluate is how it makes them feel" (paragraphs 5–6)
means
   a. judge.
   b. write about.
   c. ignore.
   d. plan.

4. The word *passive* in "listening is passive, while writing is active" (paragraph 11) means
   a. lively.
   b. boring.
   c. out-of-date.
   d. inactive.

5. The word *advocate* in "those who advocate 'writing across the curriculum' are suggesting a different kind of writing" (paragraph 14) means
   a. notice.
   b. strongly criticize.
   c. learn about.
   d. speak in favor of.

B. Below are words, or forms of words, from "Words to Watch." Write in the one that best completes each sentence.

campaign	curriculum	evidence
occurs	sound	

6. The last presidential _____ left many voters dissatisfied with both candidates.

7. Researchers keep finding more and more _____ that a diet low in fat can protect us against disease.

8. If your doctor's thinking doesn't seem to be _____, find a new doctor.

9. The science _____ in many schools has come under attack for preparing students poorly for today's highly technical life.

10. Marian is such a good student because it never _____ to her that there may be others who are smarter.

READING COMPREHENSION QUESTIONS

Central Point and Main Ideas

1. Which sentence best expresses the central point of the selection?
   a. Great Britain is doing a wonderful job of educating its students.
   b. If American students wrote more, they'd learn how to think better.
   c. Teachers in American schools talk too much.
   d. The American public deserves a better presidential campaign.

2. Which sentence best expresses the main idea of paragraphs 2–4?
   a. We're not helping students learn how to think.
   b. All of our thinking should be done out loud.
   c. You can't learn to play football by watching it.
   d. All students are expected to do is to listen.

3. Which sentence best expresses the main idea of paragraph 14?
   a. Students already write a lot of essays and term papers.
   b. Unlike other writing,"writing across the curriculum" teaches thinking.
   c. "Writing across the curriculum" involves writing in all school classes.
   d. Writing notes on the backs of envelopes can help you think.

Supporting Details

4. "Writing across the curriculum"
   a. takes too much time away from the students' need to ask questions.
   b. reduces valuable lecture time.
   c. should replace listening in the classroom.
   d. takes place in all classes.

5. Writing helps us
   a. learn.
   b. think.
   c. develop ideas.
   d. all of the above.

Transitions

6. The transition *while* in the sentence below signals
   a. addition.
   b. time.
   c. comparison.
   d. an example.

   We have teachers stand in front of classrooms and think out loud, while the students listen. (Paragraph 2)

7. The transition word *like* in the sentence below signals
   a. time.
   b. comparison.
   c. an example.
   d. cause and effect.

   It seems to me that expecting students to learn from such instruction is like expecting people to learn to play football by lying on a couch and watching it on TV. (Paragraph 3)

Patterns of Organization

8. The pattern of organization of paragraph 3 is
    a. time order.
    b. list of items.
    c. comparison and/or contrast.
    d. cause and effect.

Inferences

9. The author implies that
    a. our present system of education needs improvement.
    b. campaign speeches are too long.
    c. our educational system has made both teachers and students lazy.
    d. teachers don't assign enough essays and term papers.

10. The author implies that as our thinking skills improve,
    a. more people will vote.
    b. more people will write letters to the president.
    c. there will be less need for campaign speeches.
    d. campaign speeches will also improve.

MAPPING ACTIVITY

This selection is about a problem and a suggested solution. Both are shown in the list below. Write them in the diagram where they belong.

- Students don't learn to think in school.
- Schools should have students write to think in all their classes.

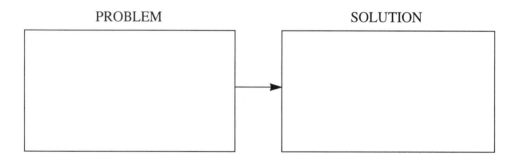

PROBLEM   SOLUTION

DISCUSSION QUESTIONS

1. Kugel says that teachers "stand in front of classrooms and think out loud, while the students listen." What does he mean? Is this what happened in your high school classes?

2. Not all writing is assigned. There is also the type of "writing you do when you write notes to yourself on the backs of envelopes." How much *non-required* writing do you do in a week, both in and out of school? Does it help you think and, if so, how?

WRITING ACTIVITIES

1. Use writing to help you make a decision by describing the advantages and disadvantages of a matter. Here is an example of a topic sentence: "There are advantages and disadvantages to working twenty-five hours a week, rather than fifteen" (or to "exercising for a half hour every day," or to "getting another car," or to "dropping one of my courses," or to "continuing to see the person I am seeing rather than ending the relationship," or to "leaving home and getting an apartment").

2. Kugel contrasts feeling and thinking. What is the difference between making a decision according to how you feel and making a decision according to how you think? Write a paragraph contrasting the two methods in some way. If you like, use one of these topic sentences: "When it comes to the foods I eat, my feelings and thinking differ"; "The way I feel about doing homework often contrasts with what I think about doing it."

Check Your Performance   WHY JOHNNY CAN'T THINK

Skill	*Number Right*	*Points*	*Total*
VOCABULARY			
Vocabulary in Context (5 items)	_____	x 10 =	_____
Words to Watch (5 items)	_____	x 10 =	_____
		SCORE =	_____ %
COMPREHENSION			
Central Point and Main Ideas (3 items)	_____	x 7 =	_____
Supporting Details (2 items)	_____	x 7 =	_____
Transitions (2 items)	_____	x 7 =	_____
Patterns of Organization (1 item)	_____	x 7 =	_____
Inferences (2 items)	_____	x 7 =	_____
Mapping (2 items)	_____	x 15 =	_____
		SCORE =	_____ %

FINAL SCORES: **Vocabulary** _____%   **Comprehension** _____%

Enter your final scores into the reading performance chart on the inside back cover.

Limited Answer Key

An Important Note: To strengthen your reading skills, you must do more than simply find out which of your answers are right and which are wrong. You also need to figure out (with the help of this book, the teacher, or other students) *why* you missed the questions you did. By using each of your wrong answers as a learning opportunity, you will strengthen your understanding of the skills. You will also prepare yourself for the review and mastery tests in Parts I and II and the reading comprehension questions in Part III, for which answers are not given here.

1   Dictionary Use

Practice 1

1. cheetah, chemist
2. gnaw, glorify
3. industry, inertia
4. misfortune, misspell
5. notable, notch

Practice 2

1. revise
2. kidnap
3. carry
4. giant
5. really
6. schoolteacher
7. please
8. coming
9. relief
10. tunnel

Practice 3

1. hic•cup, 2
2. min•i•mal, 3
3. dis•pos•al, 3
4. in•sen•si•tive, 4
5. com•mu•ni•ca•tion, 5

Practice 4

A. 1. a
   2. a
   3. a
   4. a
   5. b
   6. a
   7. b
   8. b
   9. b
   10. b

B. 11. continue, 1
   12. freckle, 1
   13. prisoner, 2
   14. committee, 1
   15. miscellaneous, 2

C. 16. brŭth′ər-hŏod′
   17. dē-hī′drāt′
   18. frăk′chər
   19. ō′vər-kăst′
   20. tĕm′pər-ə-mənt *or* tĕm′prə-mənt

Practice 5

1. 3; first
2. 4; third
3. 4; second
4. 4; third
5. 3; second

Practice 6

1. verb, noun
2. noun, adverb, preposition
3. adjective, adverb
4. preposition, adjective, noun
5. adjective, noun, verb

Practice 7

1. hid, hidden, hiding
2. older *or* elder; oldest *or* eldest
3. denied
4. wrote, written, writing
5. identities

Practice 8

1. Definition 3
2. Definition 3
3. Definition 2
4. Definition 1
5. Definition 1

Practice 9

1. Latin, "greater"
2. Perhaps Old French, "to bang into"
3. Arabic, "storehouse"
4. Hindi, "loose-fitting trousers"
5. Perhaps Spanish, "slice"

Practice 10

1. peaceful, placid, quiet, serene, still, tranquil
2. chill, chilly, cool, nippy
3. betray, delude, double-cross, mislead

2   Vocabulary in Context

Practice 1

1. Examples: *a length of 100', a width of 15', a depth of 10'*; c
2. Examples: *actor Tom Cruise, tennis star Steffi Graf, film critics Siskel and Ebert*; b
3. Examples: *lowland gorillas, snow leopards, koala bears*; a
4. Examples: *Columbo, Jessica Fletcher*; c
5. Examples: *she felt half-interested in going on to college, she was a little worried that a sister who had married early was now divorced*; c

Practice 2

1. *steady customer*
2. *job*
3. *famous*
4. *ridiculous*
5. *came between*

Practice 3

1. *simple*; c
2. *famous*; a
3. *did not apply*; b
4. *out of order*; b
5. *serious*; c

Practice 4

1. a
2. b
3. b
4. a
5. c

3   Main Ideas

Practice 1

A.
1. pet	6. bedding
2. shape	7. greetings
3. direction	8. noise
4. beverage	9. command
5. taxi	10. punishment

B.
11. sparrow	16. Venus
12. chair	17. polka
13. car	18. grasshopper
14. cloudy	19. eye shadow
15. potato chips	20. waiter

(Note: Other answers for Part B are possible.)

Practice 2

1. 1, 3, 2	6. 2, 1, 3
2. 2, 1, 3	7. 1, 3, 2
3. 2, 1, 3	8. 2, 1, 3
4. 3, 1, 2	9. 3, 2, 1
5. 3, 2, 1	10. 3, 1, 2

Practice 3

1. B	2. T	3. T
T	B	N
N	N	B
addicts	headaches	seat belts
cover	include	surveys

Practice 4

1. N	2. T	3. B
B	B	T
T	N	N

Practice 5

1. MI	2. SD	3. SD
SD	T	MI
SD	MI	T
T	SD	SD
sex		
specific		

Practice 6

A.
1. b
   broad, narrow, work-sharing
2. a
   benefits, employees, employers

B. 3. c
   4. c

C. 5. b
   6. a

4   Supporting Details

Practice 1
1. c
2. a
3. a
4. c
5. b

Practice 2
1. 5
2. 4
3. 3
4. 2
5. 4

Practice 3
A. 1. T
   2. b
   3. c
   4. a
   5. b

B. 6. T
   7. b
   8. c
   9. c
  10. c

5   Locations of Main Ideas

Practice, pp. 94–96
1. 2
2. 1
3. 4
4. 1, 6
5. 2

Practice: Level 1
1. 3
2. 1
3. 5
4. 1
5. 2

Practice: Level 2
1. 3
2. 1
3. 1, 6
4. 2
5. 1

Practice: Level 3
1. 2
2. 1
3. 6
4. 4
5. 1, 7

Practice: Level 4
1. 1, 9
2. 3
3. 4
4. 4
5. 3

6   Implied Main Ideas

Practice 1
1. a
2. b
3. b
4. b
5. c
6. c
7. c
8. c
9. c
10. c

Practice 2
1. ways of cooking eggs
2. vegetables
3. sharp objects
4. weapons
5. red items
6. minor injuries
7. ways to succeed in school
8. tall items
9. countries
10. luxury automobiles

Practice 3
Group 1. b
Group 2. b
Group 3. c

Practice 4
1. c
2. a
3. d

Practice 5
1. You can get out of quicksand by following these steps.
   Hint: get out of
2. Different shoes are best suited to different walking surfaces.
   Hint: shoes; surfaces
3. A cat's body language shows how it is feeling.
   Hint: show

7   More About Supporting Details

Practice 1

List 1
1. a. Snakes
   c. Rats
2. Traditional pets
   a. Dogs
   b. Cats

List 2
1. Junk food
   a. Potato chips
   c. Candy
2. Healthy food
   a. Apples
   b. Strawberries

List 3
1. a. California's beaches attract people year-round.
   c. Las Vegas, Nevada, has gambling and shows featuring famous stars.
2. The South has much to offer.
   a. New Orleans is especially popular during Mardi Gras.
   c. Florida has beautiful beaches and many theme parks.
3. The East has a wealth of historical sites.
   b. Boston has sites that date back to the Revolutionary War.
   c. Philadelphia has attractions such as the Liberty Bell.

Practice 2

A. *Heading:* Three Subcultures *in Any High School*
1. The delinquent group
2. The academic subculture
3. The fun subculture

B. *Heading:* Various Type*s of Remedies for Snoring*
1. Remedies that keep people from sleeping on their backs
2. Anti-snoring chin straps
3. Surgery

Practice 3

A. *Heading:* Three Way*s to Reduce the Risks of Smoking*
1. Switch to a low-tar, low-nicotine brand.
2. Allow less smoke to enter your lungs.
3. Put out the cigarette when it's half gone.

B. *Heading:* A Few Simple Suggestion*s for Doing Better on Tests*
1. Prepare slowly and steadily.
2. Arrive early for a test.
3. Answer the easier questions first.
2. Make a brief outline before beginning to write essay questions.

Practice 4

A. 1. c
  2. b
  3. a
    4. floating on air
    5. air-conditioned domes

B. 6. c
  7. c
  8. medicine should always be stored in its own labeled bottle.
    9. c
    10. other drugs the patient is using.

8   Transitions

Note: Answers to these practices will vary.

Practice 1
1. In addition
2. Furthermore
3. Moreover
4. also
5. Additionally

Practice 2
1. first
2. often
3. After
4. While
5. during

Practice 3
1. Although
2. but
3. Even though
4. Despite
5. In contrast

Practice 4
1. like
2. similar
3. in the same way
4. like
5. identical

Practice 5
1. including
2. To illustrate
3. For example
4. such as
5. For instance

Practice 6
1. on account of
2. cause
3. Therefore
4. because
5. Thus

Practice 7
1. so
2. but
3. and
4. On the other hand
5. Yet
6. Consequently
7. Therefore
8. Moreover
9. Yet
10. On the other hand

Practice 8
1. First of all
2. Second
3. Instead
4. Last
5. but
6. Consequently
7. Furthermore
8. since
9. However
10. Finally

9   Patterns of Organization

Note: Wording of answers to these practices will vary.

Practice 1a
2. California's population was at 80,000.
3. By 1860, it had grown to 380,000.

Practice 1b

3, 5, 2, 6, 4, 1

Practice 2

A. 3; Signs of stress in children
B. 3; Healthful ingredients in pizza

Practice 3

A. Both; stepfamilies and "natural" families
B. Comparing; bad men drivers and bad women drivers

Practice 4

A. 2. *Cause:* The contract did not satisfy the players.
Effect: They decided to go on strike.
3. *Cause:* Cindy and Tomas argue constantly.
Effect: They are going to a marriage counselor.
4. *Cause:* Mashed banana fights certain germs that spoil food.
Effect: The bananas refused to spoil.
5. *Cause:* The amount of waste produced by plastic food containers worries people.
Effect: An effort is being made to produce edible packaging.

B. 6. E   7. C   8. C
C   E   E
E   E
E   E

Practice 5

A. *Definition:* 1; *Example 1:* 2; *Example 2:* 3
B. *Definition:* 1; *Example:* 3
C. *Definition:* 1; *Example 1:* 4; *Example 2:* 6

Practice 6

1. c   4. c
2. b   5. a
3. c

10 Inferences

Practice 1   *Practice 2*

1. a, c   A. 1. b   B. 4. a
2. b, c   2. b   5. b
3. b, c   3. a   6. b
4. c, d
5. b, c

Practice 3

A. 1. c   B. 3. b
   2. b   4. b
               5. c

Acknowledgments

The American Heritage Dictionary, Second College Paperback Edition. Pronunciation key and entries on pages 10, 12, 14, 17–22, 27, 28, 236, 238, 239, and 242. Copyright © 1983 by Houghton Mifflin Company. Reprinted by permission from *The American Heritage Dictionary*, Second College Paperback Edition.

Broderick, Bill. "Life Over Death." Reprinted by permission.

Chan, Vicky. "Friendship and Living Longer." Reprinted by permission.

Fisher, Ed. Drawing on page 213. Copyright © 1993 by The New Yorker Magazine, Inc. Reprinted by permission.

Greene, Bob. "Handled with Care," from *American Beat.* Copyright © 1983 by Bob Greene. Reprinted by permission of Sterling Lord Literistic, Inc.

Isaacs, Maggie. "Dinner Was Reserved for the Family." Reprinted by permission of Maggie Isaacs and *The Philadelphia Inquirer.*

Kellmayer, John. "The Voyage of Tri Lee." Reprinted by permission.

Kugel, Peter. "Why Johnny Can't Think." Copyright © 1988 by The New York Times Company. Reprinted by permission.

Lam, Andrew. "They Shut My Grandmother's Room Door." Reprinted by permission.

Lopez, Steve. "Room with a New View." From *The Philadelphia Inquirer*, April 9, 1989. Reprinted by permission.

Malcolm X with Alex Haley, "Discovering Words," from *The Autobiography of Malcolm X* by Malcolm X, with the assistance of Alex Haley. Copyright © 1964 by Alex Haley and Malcolm X and copyright © 1965 by Alex Haley and Betty Shabazz. Reprinted by permission of Random House, Inc.

Marjan, Irina. "My Own Two Feet." Reprinted by permission.

Norris, Ruth. "The Dream Inside." Reprinted by permission.

Patrick, Edward. "Rosa: A Success Story." Reprinted by permission.

Petricic, Anna-Maria. "Knowledge Is Power." Reprinted by permission.

Piassa, Bernadete. "A Love Affair with Books." Reprinted by permission.

Rayder, Regina Lynn. "Determined to Succeed." Reprinted by permission.

Sanchez, Peter. "The Amazing Monarch Butterfly." Reprinted by permission.

Sifford, Darrell. "Looking Back on Our Youth." From *The Philadelphia Inquirer*, January 25, 1987. Reprinted by permission.

Thompson, Edward T. "How to Write Clearly." Reprinted by permission of the International Paper Company.

Todhunter, Jean Mizer. "Cipher in the Snow." From *Today's Education,* March-April 1975. Reprinted by permission.

White, Clarissa. "Classroom Notetaking." Reprinted by permission.

Index